McGraw-Hill Reading
Wonders

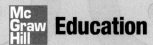

Education

Bothell, WA • Chicago, IL • Columbus, OH • New York, NY

(ETS) *TextEvaluator.*

ETS and the ETS logo are registered trademarks of Educational Testing Service (ETS).
TextEvaluator is a trademark of Educational Testing Service.

Cover and Title Pages: **Nathan Love**

www.mheonline.com/readingwonders

C

The McGraw·Hill Companies

 Education

Send all inquiries to:
McGraw-Hill Education
Two Penn Plaza
New York, New York 10121

Printed in the United States of America.

9 RMN 17 16 15 14

McGraw-Hill Reading Wonders

CCSS Reading/Language Arts Program

Program Authors

Dr. Diane August
Managing Director,
American Institutes
for Research
Washington, D.C.

Dr. Donald Bear
Iowa State University
Ames, Iowa

Dr. Janice A. Dole
University of Utah
Salt Lake City, Utah

Dr. Jana Echevarria
California State University, Long Beach
Long Beach, California

Dr. Douglas Fisher
San Diego State University
San Diego, California

Dr. David J. Francis
University of Houston
Houston, Texas

Dr. Vicki Gibson
Educational Consultant
Gibson Hasbrouck and Associates
Wellesley, Massachusetts

Dr. Jan Hasbrouck
Educational Consultant
and Researcher
J.H. Consulting
Vancouver, Washington
Gibson Hasbrouck and Associates
Wellesley, Massachusetts

Margaret Kilgo
Educational Consultant
Kilgo Consulting, Inc.
Austin, Texas

Dr. Jay McTighe
Educational Consultant
Jay McTighe and Associates
Columbia, Maryland

Dr. Scott G. Paris
Vice President, Research
Educational Testing Service
Princeton, New Jersey

Dr. Timothy Shanahan
University of Illinois at Chicago
Chicago, Illinois

Dr. Josefina V. Tinajero
University of Texas at El Paso
El Paso, Texas

Mc Graw Hill Education

Bothell, WA • Chicago, IL • Columbus, OH • New York, NY

PROGRAM AUTHORS

Dr. Diane August

American Institutes for Research, Washington, D.C.

Managing Director focused on literacy and science for ELLs for the Education, Human Development and the Workforce Division

Dr. Donald R. Bear

Iowa State University

Professor, Iowa State University

Author of *Words Their Way, Words Their Way with English Learners, Vocabulary Their Way,* and *Words Their Way with Struggling Readers, 4–12*

Dr. Janice A. Dole

University of Utah

Professor, University of Utah

Director, Utah Center for Reading and Literacy

Content Facilitator, National Assessment of Educational Progress (NAEP)

CCSS Consultant to Literacy Coaches, Salt Lake City School District, Utah

Dr. Jana Echevarria

California State University, Long Beach

Professor Emerita of Education, California State University

Author of *Making Content Comprehensible for English Learners: The SIOP Model*

Dr. Douglas Fisher

San Diego State University

Co-Director, Center for the Advancement of Reading, California State University

Author of *Language Arts Workshop: Purposeful Reading and Writing Instruction* and *Reading for Information in Elementary School*

Dr. David J. Francis

University of Houston

Director of the Center for Research on Educational Achievement and Teaching of English Language Learners (CREATE)

Dr. Vicki Gibson

Educational Consultant
Gibson Hasbrouck and Associates

Author of *Differentiated Instruction: Grouping for Success, Differentiated Instruction: Guidelines for Implementation,* and *Managing Behaviors to Support Differentiated Instruction*

Dr. Jan Hasbrouck

J.H. Consulting
Gibson Hasbrouck and Associates

Developed Oral Reading Fluency Norms for Grades 1–8

Author of *The Reading Coach: A How-to Manual for Success* and *Educators as Physicians: Using RTI Assessments for Effective Decision-Making*

Margaret Kilgo

Educational Consultant
Kilgo Consulting, Inc., Austin, TX

Developed Data-Driven Decisions process for evaluating student performance by standard

Member of Common Core State Standards Anchor Standards Committee for Reading and Writing

Dr. Scott G. Paris

Educational Testing Service, Vice President, Research

Professor, Nanyang Technological University, Singapore, 2008–2011

Professor of Education and Psychology, University of Michigan, 1978–2008

Dr. Timothy Shanahan

University of Illinois at Chicago

Distinguished Professor, Urban Education

Director, UIC Center for Literacy

Chair, Department of Curriculum & Instruction

Member, English Language Arts Work Team and Writer of the Common Core State Standards

President, International Reading Association, 2006

Dr. Josefina V. Tinajero

University of Texas at El Paso

Dean of College of Education

President of TABE

Board of Directors for the American Association of Colleges for Teacher Education (AACTE)

Governing Board of the National Network for Educational Renewal (NNER)

Consulting Authors

Kathy R. Bumgardner

National Literacy Consultant

Strategies Unlimited, Inc. Gastonia, NC

Jay McTighe

Jay McTighe and Associates

Author of *The Understanding by Design Guide to Creating High Quality Units* with G. Wiggins; *Schooling by Design: Mission, Action, Achievement* with G. Wiggins; and *Differentiated Instruction and Understanding By Design* with C. Tomlinson

Dr. Doris Walker-Dalhouse

Marquette University

Associate Professor, Department of Educational Policy & Leadership

Author of articles on multicultural literature, struggling readers, and reading instruction in urban schools

Dinah Zike

Educational Consultant

Dinah-Might Activities, Inc. San Antonio, TX

Program Reviewers

Kelly Aeppli-Campbell
Escambia County School District
Pensacola, FL

Marjorie J. Archer
Broward County Public Schools
Davie, FL

Whitney Augustine
Brevard Public Schools
Melbourne, FL

Antonio C. Campbell
Washington County School District
Saint George, UT

Helen Dunne
Gilbert Public School District
Gilbert, AZ

David P. Frydman
Clark County School District
Las Vegas, NV

Fran Gregory
Metropolitan Nashville Public Schools
Nashville, TN

Veronica Allen Hunt
Clark County School District
Las Vegas, NV

Michele Jacobs
Dee-Mack CUSD #701
Mackinaw, IL

LaVita Johnson Spears
Broward County Public Schools
Pembroke Pines, FL

Randall B. Kincaid
Sevier County Schools
Sevierville, TN

Matt Melamed
Community Consolidated School District 46
Grayslake, IL

Angela L. Reese,
Bay District Schools
Panama City, FL

Eddie Thompson
Fairfield City School District
Fairfield Township, OH

Patricia Vasseur Sosa
Miami-Dade County Public Schools
Miami, FL

Dr. Elizabeth Watson
Hazelwood School District
Hazelwood, MO

TEACHING WITH

McGraw-Hill Reading
Wonders

INTRODUCE

Weekly Concept
Grade Appropriate
Topics, including Science
and Social Studies

- **Videos**
- **Photographs**

Reading/Writing Workshop Big Book

TEACH AND APPLY

**Listening
Comprehension**
Complex Text

**Shared Reading
Minilessons**

Comprehension
Skills and Strategies,
Genre, Phonics,
High-Frequency
Words, Writing,
Grammar

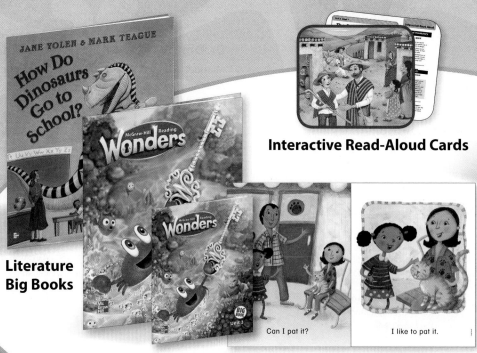

Interactive Read-Aloud Cards

- **Visual Glossary**
- **eBooks**
- **Interactive Texts**
- **Listening Library**
- **English/Spanish
  Summaries**

**Literature
Big Books**

**Reading/Writing Workshop
Big Book and Little Book**

Master the Common Core State Standards!

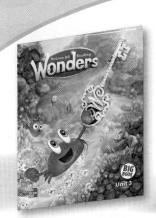

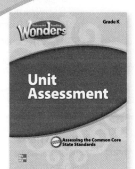

Leveled Readers

- eBooks
- Interactive Texts
- Leveled Reader Search
- Listening Library
- Interactive Activities

Collection of Texts

- Online Research
- Interactive Group Projects

Unit Assessment   **Benchmark Assessment**

- Online Assessment
- Test Generator
- Reports

DIFFERENTIATE

Leveled Readers
Small Group Instruction with Differentiated Texts

INTEGRATE

Research and Inquiry
Research Projects

Text Connections
Reading Across Texts

Talk About Reading
Analytical Discussion

ASSESS

Unit Assessment

Benchmark Assessment

PROGRAM COMPONENTS

Big Book and Little Book of Reading/Writing Workshop

Literature Big Books

Interactive Read-Aloud Cards

Teacher Editions

Teaching Posters

Puppet

Leveled Readers

Your Turn Practice Book

Visual Vocabulary Cards

Leveled Workstation Activity Cards

 **Assessing the Common Core State Standards**

Retelling Cards

Photo Cards

High-Frequency Word Cards

Sound-Spelling Cards

Response Board

Unit Assessment

Benchmark Assessment

 **Go Digital**

  For the Teacher

 For the Students

For the Teacher

 Plan
Customizable Lesson Plans

 Assess
Online Assessments
Reports and Scoring

 Professional Development
Lesson and CCSS Videos

 Teach
Classroom Presentation Tools
Instructional Lessons

 **Collaborate**
Online Class Conversations
Interactive Group Projects

Additional Online Resources
ELL Activities
Tier 2 Intervention
Interactive Games and Activities
Word-Building Cards
Sound-Spelling Songs
Sound Pronunciation Audio

 Manage and Assign
Student Grouping and Assignments

 School to Home
Digital Open House Activities and Messages

For the Students

My To Do List
Assignments
Assessment

Words to Know
Build Vocabulary

Read
eBooks
Interactive Texts

Play
Interactive Games

Write
Interactive Writing

School to Home
Activities for Home
Messages from the Teacher
Class Wall of Student Work

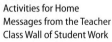 www.connected.mcgraw-hill.com

UNIT 2 CONTENTS

Unit Planning

Weekly Lessons

Program Information

Nathan Love

UNIT 2 OVERVIEW

Week 1

TOOLS WE USE

READING

Oral Language
ESSENTIAL QUESTION
How do tools help us to explore?

Build Background
CCSS **Oral Vocabulary Words**
L.K.5c *tool, discover, defeated, fetch, rumble*
CCSS Category Words: Colors
L.K.5a

Comprehension
Genre: Informational Text
Strategy: Ask and Answer Questions
CCSS **Skill**
RL.K.7 Key Details

Word Work
CCSS **Phonemic Awareness**
RF.K.2d Phoneme Isolation
Phoneme Blending
Phoneme Categorization
CCSS **Phonics** /p/p ♪
RF.K.3a **Handwriting:** Pp
CCSS **High-Frequency Words:** *a*
RF.K.3c
Fluency
Letter and Word Automaticity
Model Fluency

LANGUAGE ARTS

Writing
Trait: Ideas
Gather Information
CCSS Shared Writing
W.K.2 Explanatory Sentence
Interactive Writing
Explanatory Sentence
Independent Writing
Explanatory Sentence
CCSS **Grammar**
L.K.1b Verbs

Week 2

SHAPES ALL AROUND US

Oral Language
ESSENTIAL QUESTION
What shapes do you see around you?

Build Background
CCSS **Oral Vocabulary Words**
L.K.4a *materials, nature, decoration, games, world*
CCSS Category Words: Shapes
L.K.5a

Comprehension
Genre: Informational Text
Strategy: Ask and Answer Questions
CCSS **Skill**
RL.K.7 Key Details

Word Work
CCSS **Phonemic Awareness**
RF.K.2d Phoneme Isolation
Phoneme Blending
Phoneme Identity
CCSS **Phonics** /t/t ♪
RF.K.3a **Handwriting:** Tt
CCSS **High-Frequency Words:** *like*
RF.K.3c
Fluency
Letter and Word Automaticity
Model Fluency

Writing
Trait: Ideas
Make Observations
CCSS Shared Writing
W.K.2 Shape Poster
Interactive Writing
Shape Poster
Independent Writing
Shape Poster
CCSS **Grammar**
L.K.1b Verbs

Judy Barranco/Vetta/Getty Images; Jeff Sarpa/Stockfood Creative/Getty Images; PKG Photography/Flickr/Getty Images

UNIT 2

Week 3

WORLD OF BUGS

Oral Language
ESSENTIAL QUESTION
What kind of bugs do you know about?

Build Background

CCSS **Oral Vocabulary Words**
L.K.4.a *curious, observe, attaches, process, slender*

CCSS Category Words: Movement Words
L.K.1b

Comprehension
Genre: Fiction

Strategy: Ask and Answer Questions

CCSS **Skill**
RL.K.7 Key Details

Word Work
CCSS **Phonemic Awareness**
RF.K.2d Phoneme Segmentation
Phoneme Blending

CCSS **Phonics** Review /m/m, /a/a, /s/s, /p/p, /t/t ♪
RF.K.3a

CCSS **Handwriting:** Mm, Aa, Ss, Pp, Tt

CCSS **High-Frequency Words:** *the, a,*
RF.K.3c *see, we, like*

Fluency
Letter and Word Automaticity
Model Fluency

Unit 2 Assessment
Unit Assessment Book
pages 15–28

Writing
Trait: Ideas
Generate Ideas

CCSS Shared Writing
W.K.3 Story Sentence

Interactive Writing
Story Sentence

Independent Writing
Story Sentence

CCSS **Grammar**
L.K.1b Verbs

Half Day Kindergarten

Use the chart below to help you plan your kindergarten schedule to focus on key instructional objectives for the week. Choose Small Group and Workstation Activities as your time allows during the day.

Oral Language

- **Essential Questions**
- **Build Background**
- **Oral Vocabulary**
- **Category Words**

Word Work

- **Phonemic Awareness**
- **Phonics** /p/p, /t/t ♪
- **High-Frequency Words** *a, like*
- **Letter and Word Automaticity**

Reading/Comprehension

- **Reading/Writing Workshop**
  Pam Can See; We Can See!; We Like Tam!; I Like Sam; Pat; Tap! Tap! Tap!
- **Big Books:**
  The Handiest Things in the World; Shapes All Around; I Love Bugs!
- **Interactive Read-Aloud Cards**
  "Timimoto;" "Kites in Flight;" "From Caterpillar to Butterfly"

Language Arts

- **Shared Writing**
- **Interactive Writing**
- **Independent Writing**

Independent Practice

- **Practice Book pages**
- **Workstation Activity Cards**

www.connected.mcgraw-hill.com
Interactive Games and Activities

Reading/Writing Workshop Big Book

Unit
2

Let's Explore

The Big Idea
What can you find out when you explore?

Caballito Blanco
(Little White Pony)

Caballito blanco,
Take me far away.
Take me to my birthplace,
where I want to stay.

READING/WRITING WORKSHOP, pp. 4–5

The Big Idea *What can you find out when you explore?*

 Talk About It

Have children think about how they can learn about places by exploring. Ask children to close their eyes and think about a particular familiar place at home or at school. Who are the people that they see? What are some of the objects that children notice in those places? As children relate their observations, encourage them to include details that describe the people and things that they observe. Then have them share a new place they would like to explore. Acknowledge their responses, and ask additional questions to help children recognize what they can learn from careful observation.

 Sing the Song

Introduce the unit song: *Caballito Blanco* (*Little White Pony*). Read the lyrics of the song. Ask children:

→ *If you were going to explore a far-away place, where would you like to go?*

→ *What would you expect to find there?*

→ *Would you want to explore that place for a short visit or for a long time?*

Play the song "Caballito Blanco." After listening to the song a few times, ask children to join in. Audio files of the song can be found in the Teacher Resources on www.connected.mcgraw-hill.com.

Research and Inquiry

Weekly Projects Each week children will be asked to find out more about the topic they are reading about. Children will be asked to work in pairs or small groups to complete their work. Children use what they learn from their reading and discussions as well as other sources to find additional information.

Shared Research Board You may wish to set up a Shared Research Board in the classroom. You can post illustrations and other information that children gather as they do their research.

> **WEEKLY PROJECTS**
> Students work in pairs or small groups.
> **Week 1** Tool Belt
> **Week 2** Shape Chart
> **Week 3** Bug Bulletin Board

Writing

Write about Reading Throughout the unit children will write in a variety of ways. Each week, writing is focused on a specific writing trait. Scaffolded instruction is provided through Shared Writing and Interactive Writing. Children review a student writing sample together and then write independently, practicing the trait.

> **WEEKLY WRITING**
> **Week 1** Gather Information
> **Week 2** Make Observations
> **Week 3** Generate Ideas

Music Links

www.connected.mcgraw-hill.com Integrate music into your classroom using the downloadable audio files in the Teacher's Resources online. Songs for this unit include:

> **WEEKLY SONGS**
> → Eency Weency Spider
> → Polly and Paul Play the Piano
> → My Two-Ton Turtle
> **HOLIDAY SONGS**
> → Buenos Dias, Amigo (Good Day, Friend)
> → Boo!
> → I Caught a Rabbit
> → Five Fat Turkeys (speech piece)
> → A Mince Pie and Pudding

Celebration Posters

Celebrate Display the Fall Celebrations poster. Use it to remind students of important holidays during the season. Commemorate the holidays by selecting from the activity suggestions provided in the Teacher Resources found at www.connected.mcgraw-hill.com.

Teaching Posters are available for Fall, Winter, Spring, and Summer.

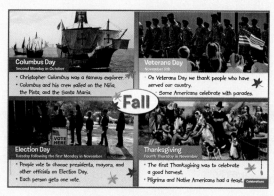

Teaching Posters, pp. 1–4

WEEKLY OVERVIEW

Listening Comprehension

The Handiest Things in the World, 4–35
Genre Informational Text

"Discover with Tools," 36–40
Genre Informational Text

Interactive Read-Aloud Cards

"Timimoto"
Genre Tale

Oral Vocabulary

defeated	**rumble**
discover	**tool**
fetch	

Minilessons ✔ TESTED SKILLS CCSS

✔ **Comprehension Strategy** .... Ask and Answer Questions, T13

✔ **Comprehension Skill** .... Key Details, T22

☞ **Go Digital**

www.connected.mcgraw-hill.com

Nathan Love

Essential Question
How do tools help us to explore?

WEEK 1

Big Book and Little Book
Reading/Writing Workshop

Shared Reading

"Pam Can See," 8–13
Genre Fiction

"We Can See!" 14–19
Genre Nonfiction

High-Frequency Word   a, T17

Minilessons   ✔TESTED SKILLS CCSS

✔ **Phonics** . . . . /p/*p*, T15
Writing Trait . . . . Ideas, T18
Grammar . . . . Verbs, T19

Differentiated Text

Approaching   On Level   Beyond   **ELL**

TEACH AND MANAGE

INTRODUCE

Weekly Concept
Tools We Use

**Reading/Writing Workshop
Big Book, 6–7**

TEACH AND APPLY

Listening Comprehension

Big Book
The Handiest Things in the World
Paired Read "Discover with Tools"
Genre Informational Text

Minilessons
Strategy: Ask and Answer Questions
Skill: Key Details

Shared Reading

Reading/Writing Workshop
"Pam Can See"
"We Can See!"

Minilessons
/p/p, High-Frequency Word: *a*
Writing, Grammar

 Interactive Whiteboard

 Interactive Whiteboard

 Mobile

Go Digital

What Your Students Do

WEEKLY CONTRACT

PDF Online

PRACTICE AND ONLINE ACTIVITIES

Your Turn Practice Book, pp. 51–58

Leveled Readers

Go Digital

 **Online To-Do List**

Online Activities

Mobile

Go Digital! www.connected.mcgraw-hill.com

DIFFERENTIATE

Small Group Instruction
Leveled Readers

 **Mobile**

INTEGRATE

Research and Inquiry
Tool Belt, pp. T52–T53

Text Connections
Compare Tools, p. T54

Talk About Reading
Becoming Readers, p. T55

 Online Research

WORKSTATION CARDS

4

Tool Talk
Tools help us do many things.

SCIENCE

1. Get tools.   2. Draw a tool.

4

Begin and End with *Pp*
Say and write *Pp* words.

Pam
pat
map
tap
sap

PHONICS/WORD STUDY

1. Make a list.   2. Draw pictures.

Pam   map

3. Label *Pp* pictures.

18

Sentences That Explain
Some sentences can explain things.

WRITING

1. Read about trees.   2. Draw a tree.

A tre

Write a

More Activities on back of cards

4

Story Illustrations
Pictures help to tell a story.

READING

1. Pick a story book.   2. Look at each picture.

3. Tell where the story takes place.

Go Digital! www.connected.mcgraw-hill.com • Interactive Games and Activities • Grade K   4

Go Digital! www.connected.mcgraw-hill.com • Interactive Games and Activities • Grade K   4

Nathan Love

DEVELOPING READERS AND WRITERS

Write to Sources and Research

Respond to Reading, T13, T61, T69, T75, T79

Connect to Essential Question, T13, T45

Key Details, 22

Research and Inquiry, T52

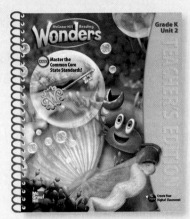

Teacher's Edition

Literature Big Book
The Handiest Things in the World
Paired Read: *"Discover with Tools"*

Interactive Whiteboard

Leveled Readers
Responding to Texts

Writing Process • **Independent Writing**

Informational Text
Explanatory Sentences, T40–T41, T50, T58

Conferencing Routines
Peer Conferences, T50

Interactive Whiteboard

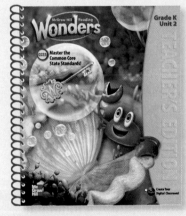

Teacher's Edition

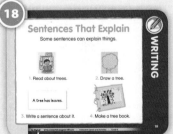

Leveled Workstation Card
Sentences That Explain, Card 18

Writing Traits • Shared and Interactive Writing

Writing Trait:
Ideas
Explanatory Sentences, T18, 32

Teacher's Edition

Ideas, pp. 22–23

Reading/Writing Workshop

Interactive Whiteboard

Leveled Workstation Card
Sentences That Explain, Card 18

Grammar and Spelling/Dictation

Grammar
Verbs, T19

Spelling/Dictation
Words with *p* and *m*, *a*, *s*, T47, T57

Interactive Whiteboard

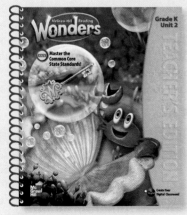

Teacher's Edition

Online Grammar Games

Handwriting

SUGGESTED LESSON PLAN

✔ TESTED SKILLS CCSS	DAY 1	DAY 2

READING

Whole Group

Teach and Model

Literature Big Book

Reading/ Writing Workshop

DAY 1

Build Background Tools We Use, T10
Oral Vocabulary Words tools, discover, T10
✔ **Listening Comprehension**
• Genre: Informational Text
• Strategy: Ask and Answer Questions, T13
Big Book *The Handiest Things in the World*
✔ **Word Work**
Phonemic Awareness
• Phoneme Isolation, T14
Phonics
• Introduce /p/p, T15
Handwriting Pp, T16
High-Frequency Word a, T17

Practice *Your Turn* 51–52

DAY 2

Oral Language Tools We Use, T20
✔ **Category Words** Colors, T21
✔ **Listening Comprehension**
• Genre: Informational Text
• Strategy: Ask and Answer Questions, T22
• Skill: Key Details
• Guided Retelling
• Model Fluency, T27
Big Book *The Handiest Things in the World*
✔ **Word Work**
Phonemic Awareness
• Phoneme Blending, T28
Phonics
• Blend Words with /p/p, T29
High-Frequency Word a, T29
Shared Reading "Pam Can See," T30–T31

Practice *Your Turn* 53

DIFFERENTIATED INSTRUCTION Choose across the week to meet your student's needs.

Small Group

Approaching Level

Leveled Reader *We Need Tools,* T60–T61
Phonological Awareness
Recognize Alliteration, T62 **TIER 2**
Phonics Sound-Spelling Review, T64 **TIER 2**
High-Frequency Words Reteach Words, T66 **TIER 2**

Leveled Reader *We Need Tools,* T60–T61
Phonemic Awareness
Phonemic Isolation, T62 **TIER 2**
Phonics Connect *p* to /p/, T64 **TIER 2**
High-Frequency Words
Reread for Fluency, T66 **TIER 2**

On Level

Leveled Reader *A Trip,* T68–T69
Phonemic Awareness Phoneme Isolation, T70

Leveled Reader *A Trip,* T68–T69
Phoneme Awareness Phoneme Blending, T70
Phonics Review Phonics, T71
High-Frequency Words Review Words, T72

Beyond Level

Leveled Reader *What Can You See?* T74–T75
Phonics Review, T76

Leveled Reader *What Can You See?* T74–T75
High-Frequency Words Review, T76

English Language Learners

Leveled Reader *A Trip,* T78–T79
Phonological Awareness
Recognize Alliteration, T62 **TIER 2**
Phonics Sound-Spelling Review, T64 **TIER 2**
Vocabulary Preteach Oral Vocabulary, T80
Writing Shared Writing, T82

Leveled Reader *A Trip,* T78–T79
Phonemic Awareness
Phonemic Isolation, T62 **TIER 2**
Phonics Connect *p* to /p/, T64 **TIER 2**
Vocabulary Preteach ELL Vocabulary, T80

LANGUAGE ARTS

Whole Group

Writing and Grammar

Shared Writing
Writing Trait: Ideas, T18
Write an Explanatory Sentence, T18
Grammar Verbs, T19

Interactive Writing
Writing Trait: Ideas, T32
Write an Explanatory Sentence, T32
Grammar Verbs, T33

Nathan Love

Go Digital

CUSTOMIZE YOUR OWN LESSON PLAN

www.connected.mcgraw-hill.com

WEEK 1 →

DAY 3	DAY 4	DAY 5 Review and Assess

Oral Language Tools We Use, T34

Oral Vocabulary defeated, fetch, rumble, T34

✓**Listening Comprehension**
• Genre: Tale
• Strategy: Ask and Answer Questions, T35
• Make Connections, T35

Interactive Read Aloud "Timimoto," T35

✓**Word Work**

Phonemic Awareness
• Phonemic Isolation, T36

Phonics
• Blend words with *p* and *m, s, a,* T37

High-Frequency Word a, T39

Practice *Your Turn* 54–56

Oral Language Tools We Use, T42

✓**Category Words** Colors, T43

✓**Listening Comprehension**
• Genre: Informational Text
• Strategy: Ask and Answer Questions, T44
• Text Feature: Headings
• Make Connections, T45

Big Book Paired Read: "Discover with Tools," T44

✓**Word Work**

Phonemic Awareness
• Phoneme Blending, T46

Phonics
• Blend Words with *p* and *m, a, s,* T46

High-Frequency Word a, T47

Shared Reading "We Can See!" T48–T49

Integrate Ideas Research and Inquiry, T52–T53

Practice *Your Turn* 57

Integrate Ideas
• Text Connections, T54
• Talk About Reading, T55
• Research and Inquiry, T55

✓**Word Work**

Phonemic Awareness
• Phoneme Categorization, T56

Phonics
• Blend Words with *p* and *m, a, s,* T56

High-Frequency Word a, T57

Practice *Your Turn* 58

Leveled Reader *We Need Tools,* T60–T61

Phonemic Awareness Phonemic Categorization, T63

Phonics Reteach, T64

High-Frequency Words Reteach Words, T66

Leveled Reader *We Need Tools,* T60–T61

Phonemic Awareness Phonemic Blending, T63

Phonics Blend Words with /p/p, T65

Oral Vocabulary Review Words, T67

Leveled Reader Literacy Activities, T61

Phonemic Awareness Phoneme Blending, T63

Phonics Build Words with /p/p, T65

Build Fluency with Phonics, T65

Comprehension Self-Selected Reading, T67

Leveled Reader *A Trip,* T68–T69

Phonemic Awareness Phoneme Categorization, T70

Phonics Picture Sort, T71

Leveled Reader *A Trip,* T68–T69

Phonics Blend Words with *p,* T72

High-Frequency Words Reread for Fluency, T73

Leveled Reader Literacy Activities, T69

Comprehension Self-Selected Reading, T73

Leveled Reader *What Can You See?* T74–T75

Vocabulary Oral Vocabulary: Synonyms, T77

Gifted and Talented

Leveled Reader *What Can You See?* T74–T75

Leveled Reader Literacy Activities, T75

Comprehension Self-Selected Reading, T77

Gifted and Talented

Leveled Reader *A Trip,* T78–T79

Phonemic Awareness Phonemic Categorization, T63

Phonics Reteach, T64

High-Frequency Words Review Words, T81

Writing Writing Trait: Ideas, T82

Leveled Reader *A Trip,* T78–T79

Phonemic Awareness Phonemic Blending, T63

Phonics Blend Words with /p/p, T65

High-Frequency Words Review Category Words, T81

Grammar Verbs, T83

Leveled Reader Literacy Activities, T79

Phonemic Awareness Phoneme Blending, T63

Phonics Build Words with /p/p, T65

Build Fluency with Phonics, T65

Independent Writing

Writing Trait: Ideas, T40

Write an Explanatory Sentence

Prewrite/Draft, T41

Grammar Verbs, T41

Independent Writing

Writing Trait: Ideas, T50

Write an Explanatory Sentence

Revise/Final Draft, T50

Grammar Verbs, T51

Independent Writing

Write an Explanatory Sentence

Prepare/Present/Evaluate/Publish, T58

Grammar Verbs, T59

DIFFERENTIATE TO ACCELERATE

 Scaffold to Access Complex Text

IF the text complexity of a particular section is too difficult for children

THEN see the references noted in the chart below for scaffolded instruction to help children Access Complex Text.

Qualitative | Quantitative
Reader and Task
TEXT COMPLEXITY

	Literature Big Book	**Reading/Writing Workshop**	**Leveled Readers**	

	Literature Big Book	**Reading/Writing Workshop**	**Leveled Readers**	
Quantitative	*The Handiest Things in the World* **Lexile** 390	*"Pam Can See"* **Lexile** BR	**Approaching Level** **Lexile** BR	**On Level** **Lexile** BR
	Paired Selection: "Discover with Tools" **Lexile** 430	Paired Selection: "We Can See!" **Lexile** BR	**Beyond Level** **Lexile** 90	**ELL** **Lexile** BR
Qualitative	**What Makes the Text Complex?** • **Connection of Ideas** Connections Between Pages, T22 *See Scaffolded Instruction in Teacher's Edition, T22.*	**What Makes the Text Complex?** **Foundational Skills** • Decoding with *p*, T28–T29 • Identifying high-frequency words, T29	**What Makes the Text Complex?** **Foundational Skills** • Decoding with *p* • Identifying high-frequency words *a* *See Level Up lessons online for Leveled Readers.*	
Reader and Task	The Introduce the Concept lesson on pages T10–T11 will help determine the reader's knowledge and engagement in the weekly concept. See pages T12–T13, T23–T27, T44–T45 and T52–T55 for questions and tasks for this text.	The Introduce the Concept lesson on pages T10–T11 will help determine the reader's knowledge and engagement in the weekly concept. See pages T30–T31, T48–T49, and T52–T55 for questions and tasks for this text.	The Introduce the Concept lesson on pages T10–T11 will help determine the reader's knowledge and engagement in the weekly concept. See pages T60–T61, T68–T69, T74–T75, T78–T79 and T52–T55 for questions and tasks for this text.	

Nathan Love

BR = Epitome of a beginning reader

Go Digital! www.connected.mcgraw-hill.com

Monitor and *Differentiate*

IF you need to differentiate instruction

THEN use the Quick Checks to assess children's needs and select the appropriate small group instruction focus.

✓ Quick Check

Comprehension Strategy Ask and Answer Questions, T35

Phonemic Awareness/Phonics /p/*p* (initial, final), T17, T29, T39, T47, T57

High-Frequency Words *a*, T17, T29, T39, T47, T57

If No → | **Approaching** | **Reteach,** pp. T60–T67
| **ELL** | **Develop,** pp. T78–T83

If Yes → | **On Level** | **Review,** pp. T68–T73
| **Beyond Level** | **Extend,** pp. T74–T77

Level Up with Leveled Readers

IF children can read their leveled text fluently and answer comprehension questions

THEN work with the next level up to accelerate children's reading with more complex text.

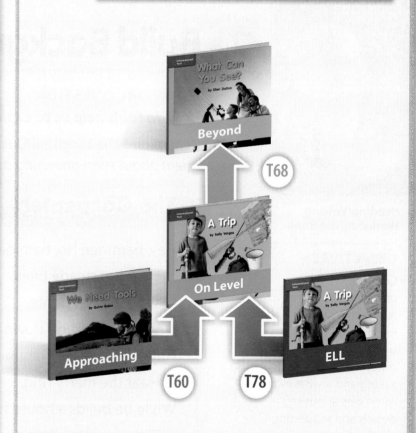

ENGLISH LANGUAGE LEARNERS

ELL SCAFFOLD

IF ELL students need additional support **THEN** scaffold instruction using the small group suggestions.

| Reading-Writing Workshop T11 "Come and Explore" Integrate Ideas T53 | Leveled Reader T78–T79 *A Trip* | Phonological Awareness Recognize Alliteration, T62 Phoneme Isolation, T62 Phoneme Categorization, T63 Phoneme Blending, T63 | Phonics, /p/*p* (initial, final), T64–T65 | Oral Vocabulary, T80 tool, discover, fetch, rumble, defeated High-Frequency Words, T81 *a* | Writing Shared Writing, T82 Writing Trait: Ideas, T82 | Grammar T83 Verbs |

Note: Include ELL Students in all small groups based on their needs.

Materials

Reading/Writing Workshop Big Book
UNIT 2

Literature Big Book
The Handiest Things in the World

Visual Vocabulary Cards
discover
tools

Photo Cards
dog   pen
kitten   piano
mouse   pie
peach   pig

High-Frequency Word Cards
a
I
see

Sound-Spelling Cards
Piano

Response Board

Think Aloud Clouds

♪ **"Polly and Paul Play the Piano"**

Reading/Writing Workshop Big Book

OBJECTIVES

CCSS Confirm understanding of a text read aloud or information presented orally or through other media by asking and answering questions about key details and requesting clarification if something is not understood. **SL.K.2**

CCSS Identify real-life connections between words and their use. **L.K.5c**

→ # Introduce the Concept

MINILESSON 10 Mins

Build Background

ESSENTIAL QUESTION

How do tools help us to explore?

Read aloud the Essential Question. Then say: *We are going to read a poem about someone using a tool.*

The Carpenter

Hey, hammer! Ho, hammer!
   Hear the steady blow.
'Tis the jolly carpenter
   Who's pounding down below.
Hey, hammer! Ho, hammer!
   Hear the merry ring,
While he builds a house for us,
   The carpenter doth sing.

Read the poem "The Carpenter" with children. Ask children what tool the carpenter used in the poem. Tell them that this week they will read to learn about tools. They will also learn how we use tools to make our work easier and to explore the world around us.

Oral Vocabulary Words

Use the **Define/Example/Ask** routine to introduce the oral vocabulary words **tools** and **discover**.

Discuss the theme "Tools We Use" and explain that children can use tools to learn more about the world around them. Have children name some tools they use in the classroom and at home.

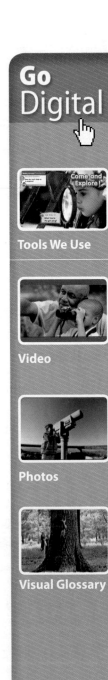

Go Digital

Tools We Use

Video

Photos

Visual Glossary

Visual Vocabulary Cards

Oral Vocabulary Routine

<u>Define:</u> **Tools** are things that help people do work or help people learn.

<u>Example:</u> Pencils are tools that you use to write.

<u>Ask:</u> What tools can you use to make art?

<u>Define:</u> When you **discover**, you learn something new.

<u>Example:</u> I watched a squirrel to discover where it hid acorns.

<u>Ask:</u> What could you discover in the park?

Talk About It: Tools We Use

Guide children to discuss tools. *Which tools help you discover more about the world around you? Which tools help you do your work?* Display pages 6–7 of the **Reading/Writing Workshop Big Book** and have children do the **Talk About It** activity with a partner.

READING/WRITING WORKSHOP BIG BOOK, pp. 6–7

Collaborative Conversations

Ask and Answer Questions As children engage in partner, small group, and whole group discussions, encourage them to:

→ Ask questions to clarify ideas they do not understand.

→ Ask for help getting information.

→ Wait after asking a question to give others a chance to think.

→ Answer questions with complete ideas, not one-word answers.

ELL

ENGLISH LANGUAGE LEARNERS SCAFFOLD

Beginning

Use Visuals Display scissors. Say: *This pair of scissors is a tool. I can use them to cut paper.* (Demonstrate) Display a ruler and use it to measure an object, such as a pencil. Say: *This ruler is another tool. I can use it to find out how long something is.*

Intermediate

Use Prompts Display scissors. Ask: *Are these scissors a tool?* (yes) *How can the scissors help you?* (They can cut paper.)

Advanced/Advanced High

Make a List Ask students to list tools that could help them do work at school. (pencils, scissors, pens, markers, computer)

→ Listening Comprehension

Literature Big Book

The Handiest Things in the World

Think Aloud Cloud

Go Digital

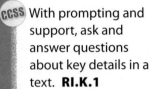

OBJECTIVES

CCSS With prompting and support, ask and answer questions about key details in a text. **RI.K.1**

CCSS Actively engage in group reading activities with purpose and understanding. **RI.K.10**

- Recognize characteristics of informational text
- Connect Big Book to Weekly Concept

ACADEMIC LANGUAGE

- *cover, photographs, title*
- Cognates: *fotografías, título*

MINILESSON
10 Mins

Read the Literature Big Book

Connect to Concept: Tools We Use

Tell children that you will now read about how we can use our hands as tools and to use other tools. Ask: *What kinds of tools do you see in the video?*

Concepts of Print

Book Handling and Directionality Display the **Big Book**. Open the cover and model how to turn the pages of the book. Point to the first sentence on page 4. Track the print from left to right, word for word, as you read the sentence aloud. Tell children that this is a sentence and point out that each word in the sentence is separated by a space.

Genre: Informational Text

Model *The Handiest Things in the World* is an informational text. Share these characteristics of informational text with children:

→ Informational text gives information about real people, places, or things.

→ Informational text often has photographs that give information about the topic.

> **Selection Words** Preview these words before reading:
>
> **handiest:** easiest or most useful
> **scooping:** digging
> **enormously:** in a big way

Set a Purpose for Reading

→ Read aloud the title, the author's name, and the photographer's name.

→ Remind children that the author wrote the words in the story and the photographer took the pictures.

→ Ask children to listen as you read aloud the Big Book. Tell them they will find out how they can use their hands or tools to do many useful things.

Strategy: Ask and Answer Questions

Explain Tell children that they can ask and answer questions as they read about what is happening in the selection. Good readers ask questions before, during, or after reading to help them better understand what they read.

Think Aloud When I look at the cover, I see a boy holding a butterfly. He is using his hands. I wonder what else he can use his hands for. I will pay attention as I read to try and answer my questions.

Model As you read, use the **Think Aloud Cloud** to model the strategy.

Think Aloud On page 4, I read "Which things are handiest for you? Depends on what you need to do." I am at school today, so I wonder how my hands can help me at school? What tools can help me at school? I will keep reading to find out.

Respond to Reading

After reading, prompt children to share what they learned about the things we can do with our hands. Discuss what questions they had as they listened to the selection, and if they found the answers in the book. Have children draw a picture of the tool from the selection that they think is the handiest.

Make Connections

Use *The Handiest Things in the World* to discuss how tools can help us learn more about the world around us. Revisit the concept behind the Essential Question: *How do tools help us to explore?* by paging through the **Big Book** and having children name ways to use tools to explore.

Write About It Have children write about one of the ways hands are used as tools in the story. Discuss some of the ways they use their hands as tools every day.

→ # Word Work

MINILESSON 5 Mins
Phonemic Awareness

OBJECTIVES

CCSS Isolate and pronounce the initial, medial vowel, and final sounds in three-phoneme words. **RF.K.2d**

CCSS Demonstrate basic knowledge of one-to-one letter-sound correspondences by producing the primary or many of the most frequent sounds for each consonant. **RF.K.3a**

Phoneme Isolation

Photo Card

1 Model Introduce initial /p/. Display the **Photo Card** for *piano. Listen for the /p/ sound at the beginning of this word:* piano. Piano *has the /p/ sound at the beginning. Say the sound with me: /p/ /p/ /p/. Say each of the following words and have children repeat. Emphasize /p/:* pan, pear, pick.

♪ *Let's play a song. Listen for words with /p/ at the beginning.* Play "Polly and Paul Play the Piano," and have children listen for /p/. *Let's listen to the song again and pat your head when you hear words that begin with /p/.* Play or sing the letter song again, encouraging children to join in. Have children pat their head when they hear words that begin with /p/.

2 Guided Practice/Practice Display and name the *Pen, Pie, Pig, Peach* Photo Cards. *Say each picture name. Tell me the sound at the beginning of the word.* Guide practice with the first word.

Photo Cards

ELL

ENGLISH LANGUAGE LEARNERS

Pronunciation
Display and have children name Photo Cards from this lesson to reinforce phonemic awareness and word meanings. Point to a card. *What do you see?* (a pie) *What is the sound at the beginning of the word* pen? (/p/) Repeat using Photo Cards with words that begin with /p/.

ARTICULATION SUPPORT

Demonstrate the way to say /p/. Press your lips together. Keep your tongue in the bottom of the mouth. Don't use your voice. Force a little air against the back of your lips. Let the air build up until it pushes out between your lips. Say *pet, pan, pen, paint* and have children repeat. Emphasize initial /p/.

Phonics

10 Mins MINILESSON

Pp piano

Sound-Spelling Card

Introduce /p/p

① Model Display the *Piano* **Sound-Spelling Card**. *This is the* Piano *card. The sound is /p/. The /p/ sound is spelled with the letter* p. *Say it with me: /p/. This is the sound at the beginning of the word* piano. *Listen: /p/, /p/, /p/,* piano. *What is the name of this letter?* (p) *What sound does this letter stand for?* (/p/)

Display the song "Polly and Paul Play the Piano" (see **Teacher's Resource Book** online). Read or sing the song with children. Reread the title and point out that the word *piano* begins with the letter *p*. Model placing a self-stick note below the *p* in *piano*.

② Guided Practice/Practice Read the song lyrics. Stop after each line and ask children to place self-stick notes below words that begin with *P* or *p* and say the letter name.

Polly and Paul Play the Piano

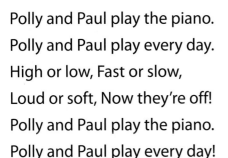

Polly and Paul play the piano.

Polly and Paul play every day.

High or low, Fast or slow,

Loud or soft, Now they're off!

Polly and Paul play the piano.

Polly and Paul play every day!

Corrective Feedback

Sound Error Model the sound /p/ in the initial position, then have children repeat the sound. Say: *My turn. Pie. /p/. Pie. /p/. Now it's your turn.* Have children say the word and isolate the initial sound in *pan* and *pile*.

YOUR TURN PRACTICE BOOK pp. 51–52

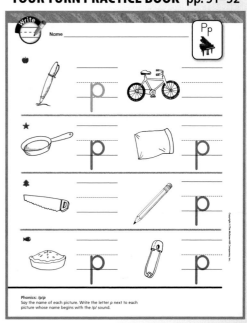

→ # Word Work

 **MINILESSON 5 Mins**

Handwriting: Write *Pp*

1 **Model** Say the handwriting cues below as you write and identify the uppercase and lowercase forms of *Pp*. Then trace the letters on the board and in the air as you say /p/.

Straight down. Go back to the top. Around and in at the dotted line.

Straight down, past the bottom line. Circle around all the way.

2 **Guided Practice/Practice**

→ Say the cues together as children trace both forms of the letter with their index finger. Have children identify the uppercase and lowercase forms of the letter.

→ Have children write *P* and *p* in the air as they say /p/ multiple times.

→ Distribute **Response Boards**. Observe children's pencil grip and paper position, and correct as necessary. Have children say /p/ every time they write the letter *Pp*.

 Daily Handwriting

Throughout the week teach uppercase and lowercase letters *Pp* using the Handwriting models. At the end of the week, have children use **Your Turn Practice Book** page 58 to practice handwriting.

Go Digital

Handwriting

the	is
you	do

High-Frequency Word Routine

MINILESSON 5 Mins

High-Frequency Words

a

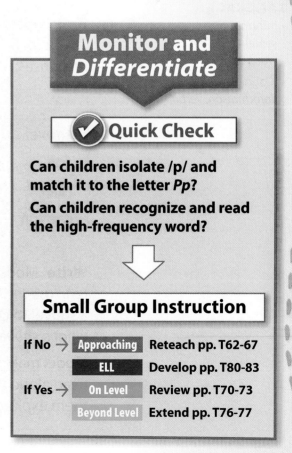

High-Frequency Word Card

a

① Model Display page 22 of the **Big Book** *The Handiest Things in the World*. Read the sentence "Flap *a* hand to make *a* breeze." Point out the high-frequency word *a*. Then use the **High-Frequency Word Card** *a* with the **Read/Spell/Write** routine to teach the word.

→ **Read** Point to the word *a* and say the word. *This is the word* a. *Say it with me:* a. *I see* a *rainbow.*

→ **Spell** The word *a* is spelled *a*. *A* is a word with just one letter. Let's read and spell it together.

→ **Write** *Let's write the word in the air. Let's spell the word as we write it*: a.

→ Point out to children that the word *a* has a different sound from the /a/ sound in the word *am*.

COLLABORATE

→ Have partners create sentences using the word.

② Guided Practice/Practice Build sentences using the High-Frequency Word Cards, **Photo Cards**, and teacher-made punctuation cards. Have children point to the high-frequency word *a*. Use these sentences.

Also online

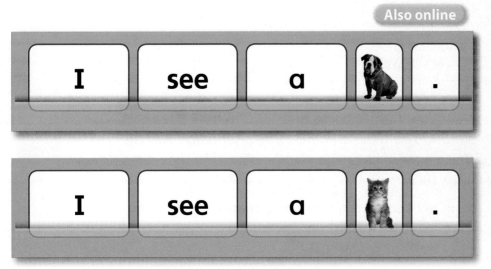

| I | see | a | 🐕 | . |

| I | see | a | 🐱 | . |

High-Frequency Words Practice

Monitor and *Differentiate*

✓ **Quick Check**

Can children isolate /p/ and match it to the letter *Pp*?

Can children recognize and read the high-frequency word?

⬇

Small Group Instruction

If No →	Approaching	Reteach pp. T62-67
	ELL	Develop pp. T80-83
If Yes →	On Level	Review pp. T70-73
	Beyond Level	Extend pp. T76-77

→ Language Arts

MINILESSON 10 Mins

Shared Writing

OBJECTIVES

CCSS Use a combination of drawing, dictating, and writing to compose informative/ explanatory texts in which they name what they are writing about and supply some information about the topic.
W.K.2

CCSS Use frequently occurring nouns and verbs. **L.K.1b**

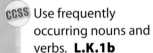

ACADEMIC LANGUAGE

• *information, sentence, action word, verb*

• Cognates: *información, verbo*

Writing Trait: Ideas

❶ **Model** Tell children that writers gather information before they start writing. *Writers often write information in sentences. A sentence is a group of words that tells a complete idea.*

→ Write and read aloud: *We use our hands to clap. This sentence gives information about hands. It tells what hands are used for.*

❷ **Guided Practice/Practice** Write this sentence: *We use our hands to wave.* Read aloud the sentence and help children tell what information it gives about hands.

Write an Explanatory Sentence

Focus and Plan Tell children that this week they will learn how to write a sentence that gives information about a tool.

Brainstorm Have children name each tool they see in *The Handiest Things in the World*. Ask what each tool is used to do. Record children's responses.

Tool	What We Use It to Do
shovel	dig
fan	stay cool
ruler	measure
crayon	write

Write Model writing a sentence using information from the chart. *I can use the information from this chart to make a sentence.* We use a shovel to dig. *This sentence gives information about the shovel. It tells what a shovel is used to do.*

Model making sentences using the other information in the chart. Read aloud the sentences with children. Ask how each tool helps them explore or learn about something.

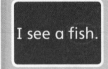

MINILESSON
5 Mins

Grammar

Verbs

❶ Model As you clap your hands, ask children what you can do with your hands. Write the word *clap* and read it aloud. Clap *is an action word. An action word tells what I do. An action word is also called a* verb.

→ Write and read aloud the words: *throw , wave,* and *point.* Explain to children that these are all action words that tell what you can do with your hands.

→ Ask children to demonstrate each action. As they are doing each action, have them say the action: *I throw a ball. I wave to my friends. I point to the sign.*

❷ Guided Practice/Practice Use *The Handiest Things in the World* to point out other action words or *verbs.* Have children name some actions that they see. Write the words they name. Then point to and read aloud each word. Have children show each action. Remind children that these action words are called *verbs.*

Track the print as you read aloud sentences from the **Big Book**. Have children say "verb" when they hear an action word.

Talk About It

COLLABORATE

Have partners work together to orally generate sentences with verbs. Encourage them to create sentences about things they do when they play ball, such as *I throw the ball.*

Daily Wrap Up

● Review the Essential Question and encourage children to discuss it, using the new oral vocabulary words. *What tools did we learn about today? How do tools help us explore our world?*

● Prompt children to share the skills they learned. How might they use those skills?

Materials

Reading/Writing Workshop Big Book
UNIT 2

Literature Big Book
The Handiest Things in the World

Visual Vocabulary Cards
discover
tools

Response Board

a b c
Word-Building Cards

Photo Cards

apple	egg	ladder
balloon	feather	mouse
bike	hay	nut
bird	hippo	snow
boots	horse	star
bowl	jacket	top
corn	jet	vest
dog	kitten	

Pp
piano
Sound-Spelling Cards
Piano

a
High-Frequency Word Cards
a
can
I
see
the
we

Puppet

Retelling Cards

→ Build the Concept

Oral Language

OBJECTIVES

CCSS Demonstrate understanding of spoken words, syllables, and sounds (phonemes). **RF.K.2**

CCSS Use words and phrases aquired through conversations, reading and being read to, and responding to texts. **L.K.6**

CCSS Sort common objects into categories (e.g., shapes, foods) to gain a sense of the concepts the categories represent. **L.K.5a**

Recognize alliteration

ACADEMIC LANGUAGE
facts, events

ESSENTIAL QUESTION

How do tools help us to explore?

Remind children that this week they are learning how different tools can help them learn more about the world around them. Invite them to point out tools in the classroom, such as scissors, a measuring tape, or a computer.

Draw a hammer and a nail on the board. Read aloud the poem "The Carpenter" and have students echo the lines as they pretend to hammer a nail.

Phonological Awareness

Recognize Alliteration

Say the first line of the poem: *Hey hammer, Ho hammer.* Ask children what they notice about the beginning sound of each word. Point out that each word in the line begins with the same sound, /h/. Tell children that when two or more words in a sentence begin with the same sound, it is called *alliteration*. Say another alliterative sentence, such as *Summer sun is simply super.* Ask what sound children hear at the beginning of the words. (/s/) Have children come up with their own alliterative phrases.

Review Oral Vocabulary

Use the **Define/Example/Ask** routine to review the oral vocabulary words **tools** and **discover**. Prompt children to use the words in sentences.

Visual Vocabulary Cards

Visual Glossary

Category Words

Go Digital

Category Words: Colors

❶ Model Use the **Big Book** *The Handiest Things in the World* to point out colors: blue handprints, pages 4–5; yellow calculator, page 9; blue umbrella, page 12. Explain that we use color words to tell the colors of different objects. Point out the different objects in the photographs and ask children to say what color each one is. *What color is the watering can?* (green)

Recite the following poem:

Roses are red,
Violets are blue,
I know my colors,
How about you?

→ Repeat the first line of the poem and tell children that *red* is a color word. *What things in the classroom are red?* Repeat with the second line of the poem. Then ask children to name other color words that describe classroom objects.

❷ Guided Practice/Practice Distribute the following **Photo Cards**: *apple, balloon, bike, bird, boots, bowl, corn, egg, feather, hay, hippo, horse, jacket, jet, ladder, mouse, nut, snow, star and vest.* Have children sort themselves by the color of the object on the Photo Card. *Each of you has a picture of something that is the color* red, brown, white *or* yellow. *Find other children holding a picture of something that has the same color as you.* Guide children to form a group for red, (apple, balloon, bird, bowl, jacket) brown, (hay, hippo, horse, ladder, nut) white (feather, egg, jet, mouse, snow) and yellow (bike, boots, corn, star, vest).

LET'S MOVE!

Give children simple directions that include color words: *Do a jumping jack if you are wearing yellow. Jump up and down if you are wearing green. Touch your toes if you are wearing red.*

ENGLISH LANGUAGE LEARNERS

Understand Help children understand that we use color words to describe objects. Look around the classroom and point to different objects. Use color words to describe them. Provide a sentence frame for them to repeat after you. *My shoes are _____. My shirt is _____.*

→ # Listening Comprehension

CLOSE READING

Literature Big Book

OBJECTIVES

CCSS With prompting and support, ask and answer questions about key details in a text. **RI.K.1**

CCSS With prompting and support, describe the relationship between illustrations and the text in which they appear (e.g., what person, place, thing, or idea in the text an illustration depicts). **RI.K.7**

- Strategy: Ask and Answer Questions
- Skill: Key Details
- Retell story

MINILESSON 15 Mins

Reread Literature Big Book

Genre: Informational Text

Display *The Handiest Things in the World*. Remind children that informational text gives information, or tells facts, about real people, places, or things. *How do you know that* The Handiest Things in the World *is informational text?* Have children point to evidence in the text and the photographs to show that this is an informational text. (It's about real tools and it has photographs.)

Strategy: Ask and Answer Questions

Remind children that good readers ask and answer questions before and during reading. *As we reread, you can ask questions and look for the answers in the text.*

Skill: Key Details

Tell children that they can learn more information about what is happening in a selection by looking for information in the text and the photographs. Point out that photographs sometimes include information that is not in the author's words. *Details from the text and the photographs can help you when you are looking for answers to your questions.* As you read, have children listen for evidence in the text to find details.

Access Complex Text

Connections of Ideas The connection between the two pages on each spread is not explicitly stated. Children may need help making connections.

→ Point out that the text and photograph on the left page directly relate to the text and photograph on the right page. On page 6, the boy is eating with his hands and it is messy. On page 7, the boy is using chopsticks to eat and stay clean.

→ Page through the book and give other examples of the connections between pages on each spread.

Go Digital

The Handiest Things in the World

Retelling Cards

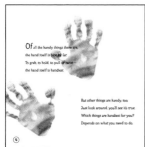

PAGES 4–5

ASK AND ANSWER QUESTIONS

Think Aloud I read that hands help us do many things. I also read that other things can help me, too. What kinds of things are more useful than hands? I will keep reading to find out the answer.

pp. 4–5

handy: Reread the first sentence on page 4, substituting *useful* for *handy*. Point out that *handiest* means *most useful*.

PAGES 6–7

KEY DETAILS

The text tells us to keep our fingers clean "this way." What do you see in the photograph that could help keep your fingers clean while you eat? (chopsticks)

pp. 6–7

mealtime: Mealtime is when people eat meals, or food. Meals can also be called breakfast, lunch, supper, or dinner. Which mealtime is your favorite?

PAGES 8–9

KEY DETAILS

The boy in the picture is holding up his hands. What is he using them to do? How do you know? (count to ten. The words on the page are numbers.)

PAGES 10–11

HIGH-FREQUENCY WORDS

Have children identify and read the high-frequency word *a* on page 11.

pp. 10–11

a whole lot: Tell children that if a tool will help "a whole lot" more, it will help much more. Say: *A watering can holds much more water than someone's hands.*

Listening Comprehension

PAGES 12–13

CONCEPTS OF PRINT

Remind children of how we turn pages. Track the print from left to right as you reread the sentence on page 13. Remind children that a sentence is made of a group of words.

PAGES 14–15

ASK AND ANSWER QUESTIONS

Think Aloud When I started reading, I asked: What kinds of things can be more useful than hands? As I read these pages, I see two things that can be more useful than hands: a broom and a dustpan. I will ask and answer more questions as I continue to read.

pp. 14–15

wish I might: Tell children that *wish I might* is another way of saying that you wish you could do something. Say: *I wish I might get a new bike.* Ask children to tell something they wish for.

PAGES 16–17

KEY DETAILS

What things in the picture help to stop the sunlight from going in the boys' eyes? (a hand, a hat)

pp. 16–17

squinty: Show children your eyes when you are squinting. Have children practice squinting their eyes as if they are looking into a bright sun.

PAGES 18–19

ASK AND ANSWER QUESTIONS

Think Aloud I read the words *digging* and *scooping* on page 18. I wonder: What can we dig and scoop? I find the answer on page 19. We can dig and scoop dirt.

PAGES 20–21

KEY DETAILS

What does the girl do to make her hair tidy? How do you know? (She combs it. She is using a comb in the photograph.)

pp. 20–21

tidy: Show children the difference between *messy* and *tidy* by tossing a pile of papers on a desk and messing them up. Say: *Messy.* Then stack the papers neatly, and say: *Tidy.* Repeat the process if necessary.

PAGES 22–23

PHONICS

Reread the page and have students identify the word that has the initial /p/ sound. (push) *What letter makes the /p/ sound?* (p)

PAGES 24–25

KEY DETAILS

Point out the hands and the pots that are being used as tools on page 24. Have children study the photograph on page 25. Ask: *What is the girl using to make more music?* (drumsticks, drum set)

pp. 24–25

make some heat: Tell children that the phrase *make some heat* means to make louder, better music. Ask children to list their favorite musical instruments.

PAGES 26–27

ASK AND ANSWER QUESTIONS

Think Aloud On this page I see a boy trying to measure blocks. I wonder what he could use to help him? On the next page I see that his friend has a ruler. He can use the ruler to measure.

pp. 26–27

width, length, height: Use gestures to indicate the measurements in the text: width, length, height. Explain that your height is how tall you are.

Listening Comprehension

CLOSE READING
ELL

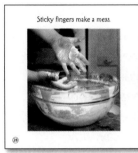

PAGES 28–29

HIGH-FREQUENCY WORDS

Have children identify and read the high-frequency word *a* on page 28.

pp. 28–29

mixer: Guide children to make the connection between the word *mixer* and the photograph. Explain that we sometimes use mixers to help us cook. Pantomime using a mixer and have children mimic.

PAGES 30–31

KEY DETAILS

Children may have difficulty reading some of the words on the sand and notebook paper. Write them clearly on the board. Read them aloud and have children echo: *away, stay.*

PAGES 32–33

ASK AND ANSWER QUESTIONS

Think Aloud I read that there is one fact about sharing love and tenderness that remains forever true. What is this fact? I will look for the answer as I continue to read.

pp. 32–33

unfold: Tell children that on this page, *unfold* means "to happen." Ask children to tell you some things that might happen at school as this year unfolds.

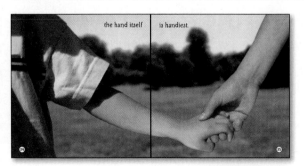

PAGES 34–35

AUTHOR'S PURPOSE

Why do you think the author wrote this story? (Possible answer: He wanted us to think about all the things our hands can help us do, and all the ways we can use tools to help us too!)

Guided Retelling

Tell children that now they will use the **Retelling Cards** to retell the selection.

→ Display Retelling Card 1. Based on children's needs, use either the Modeled, Guided or ELL retelling prompts. The ELL prompts contain support for English language learners based on levels of language acquisition. Repeat with the rest of the cards, using the prompts as a guide.

→ Discuss the informational text. Flip through the pages with children, and have them raise their hands when they see a tool they have used. Have children explain why or how they used these tools.

→ Have children tell something new they learned about tools.

Model Fluency

Reread pages 8–9 of *The Handiest Things in the World*. Point to the commas and tell children that commas mean to stop, or pause, for a very short time while reading. Read the pages and skip the commas to show what happens when readers run all of the words together. Then read again, pausing as appropriate. Have children echo and mimic your phrasing. Continue, having children locate other pages with commas for you to read aloud.

Text Evidence

Explain Remind children that when they answer a question, they need to show where in the text (both words and photographs) they found the answer.

Discuss *How do you know that using mixers will make less mess when you are baking?* (The person using the mixer in the photo on page 29 has clean hands. The author writes: "Mixers make the mess much less.")

Retelling Cards

YOUR TURN PRACTICE BOOK p. 53

Word Work

Quick Review

Build Fluency: Sound-Spellings: Show the following **Word-Building Cards:** *a, m, p, s*. Have children chorally say each sound. Repeat and vary the pace.

MINILESSON 5 Mins

Phonemic Awareness

Puppet

Phoneme Blending

OBJECTIVES

CCSS Demonstrate basic knowledge of one-to-one letter-sound correspondences by producing the primary or many of the most frequent sounds for each consonant. **RF.K.3a**

CCSS Read common high-frequency words by sight. **RF.K.3c**

Blend phonemes to make a word

❶ **Model** Use the puppet to demonstrate how to blend phonemes to make words. *The puppet is going to say sounds in a word, /p/ /a/ /t/. It can blend those sounds to make a word: /paaat/ pat. When the puppet blends the sounds, it makes the word* pat. *Listen as it blends more sounds to make words.* Model phoneme blending with the following:

/p/ /i/ /k/ pick   /p/ /a/ /n/ pan   /p/ /e/ /t/ pet

❷ **Guided Practice/Practice** *Listen to the puppet say the sounds in a different word: /p/ /i/ /g/. Say the sounds with the puppet: /p/ /i/ /g/. Let's blend the sounds and say the word with the puppet: /piiig/, pig.* Tell children to listen as the puppet says the sounds in words. Tell them to repeat the sounds, and then blend them to say the word.

/p/ /i/ /t/ pit   /p/ /a/ /k/ pack   /p/ /o/ /t/ pot

MINILESSON 5 Mins

Phonics

Pp
piano
Sound-Spelling Card

Review /p/*p*

ENGLISH LANGUAGE LEARNERS

High-Frequency Words: Build Meaning To reinforce the singular context of the word *a*, display common classroom objects and say the following sentences:

• This is *a* book.
• This is *a* pencil.
• This is *a* bookcase.
• This is *a* marker.

❶ **Model** Display the *Piano* **Sound-Spelling Card**. *This is the letter* p. *The letter* p *can stand for the sound /p/ as in the word* piano. *What is the letter?* (p) *What sound does the letter* p *stand for?* (/p/)

❷ **Guided Practice/Practice** Have children listen as you say some words. Ask them to write the letter *p* on their **Response Boards** if the word begins with /p/. Do the first two words with children.

push   mix   pinch   pour
sock   pencil   pile   sad

Go Digital

Phonemic Awareness

c a t
Phonics

| the | is |
| you | do |

High-Frequency Word Routine

A A
a a
Handwriting

Blend Words with /p/*p*

❶ Model Place **Word-Building Cards** *P, a,* and *m* in a pocket chart. Point to the letter *P*. *This is a capital or uppercase letter* P. *The letter* p *stands for /p/. Say /p/. This is the letter* a. *The letter* a *stands for /a/. Say /a/. This is the letter* m. *The letter* m *stands for /m/. Say /m/. Listen as I blend the sounds together: /paaammm/. Now blend the sounds with me to read the word.*

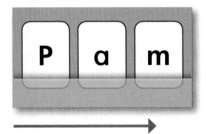

❷ Guided Practice/Practice Use Word-Building Cards or write the word *map*. Point to the letter *m* and have children say the sound. Point to the letter *a* and have children say the sound. Point to the letter *p* and have children say the sound. Move your hand from left to right under the word and have children blend and read *map*.

MINILESSON
5 Mins

High-Frequency Words

a

❶ Guided Practice Display the **High-Frequency Word Card** *a*. Use the **Read/Spell/Write** routine to teach the word. Ask children to close their eyes, picture the word in their minds, and then write it the way they see it. Have children self-correct by checking the High-Frequency Word Card.

a

High-Frequency Word Card

❷ Practice Add the high-frequency word *a* to the word bank.

→ Have partners create sentences using the word.

→ Have children count the number of letters in the word and then write the word again.

Cumulative Review Review words: *I, can, the, we, see.*

→ Repeat the **Read/Spell/Write** routine. Then mix the words and have children chorally say each one.

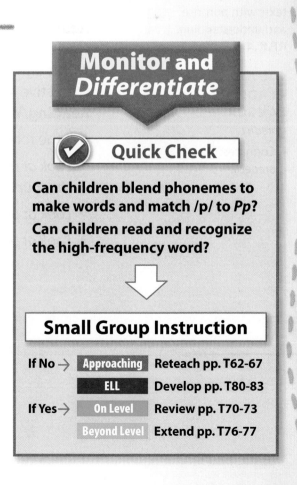

Monitor and *Differentiate*

✔ **Quick Check**

Can children blend phonemes to make words and match /p/ to *Pp*?

Can children read and recognize the high-frequency word?

Small Group Instruction

If No →	Approaching	Reteach pp. T62-67
	ELL	Develop pp. T80-83
If Yes →	On Level	Review pp. T70-73
	Beyond Level	Extend pp. T76-77

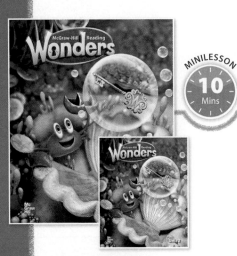

→ # Shared Read

MINILESSON 10 Mins

Read "Pam Can See"

Reading/Writing Workshop Big Book and Reading/Writing Workshop

OBJECTIVES

CCSS Read common high-frequency words by sight. **RF.K.3c**

CCSS Read emergent-reader texts with purpose and understanding. **RF.K.4**

ACADEMIC LANGUAGE

• *predict*

• Cognates: *predecir*

Model Skills and Strategies

Model Book Handling Demonstrate book handling. *This is how I hold a book. This is the front cover. I make sure that the book is not upside down so that I can read the words. This is how I turn the pages of the book. When I turn to each page, I stop to read the words on it.*

Model Concepts About Print Read the title of the story on page 8, and then point to the sentence on page 9. *This is a sentence. A sentence is made up of a group of words.* Point to the first word in the sentence. *This is a word. I will read the words from left to right, like this.* Read the sentence aloud, and track the print with your finger.

Predict Read the title together, and look at the illustration. Ask children to predict who they think the story will be about and where the story will take place.

Read Have children chorally read the story with you. Point to each word as you read it together. Help children sound out the decodable words and say the sight words. If children have difficulty, provide corrective feedback and guide them page by page using the student **Reading/Writing Workshop**.

Ask the following:

→ *Look at page 9. Which items do you see on the page that begin with the sound /p/?* (Possible answers: panda bear, pink top, pot, pans)

→ *Look at page 10. What does Pam see?* (a purple pen)

→ *Look at page 13. What do Pam and her mother buy?* (a pot, a pen, a pad, and a pillow)

Go Digital

"Pam Can See"

"Pam Can See"

READING/WRITING WORKSHOP, pp. 8–13

Rereading

Have small groups use the **Reading/Writing Workshop** to reread "Pam Can See." Then review the skills and strategies using the *Phonics* and *Words to Know* pages that come before the selection.

→ Tell children that as they reread, they can ask themselves questions. Explain that they can find the answers in the words. Remind them that they can also look for details in the illustrations to help them answer questions.

→ Have children use page 7 to review high-frequency word *a*.

→ Have children use page 6 to review that the letter *p* can stand for the sound /p/. Guide them to blend the sounds to read the words.

→ # Language Arts

MINILESSON 10 Mins

Interactive Writing

Writing Trait: Ideas

Review Remind children that writers often write sentences to give information. *I can give information about a tool in a sentence:* The umbrella keeps me dry. *The sentence tells what I use the umbrella for.*

Write an Explanatory Sentence

Discuss Display the chart of tools from Day 1. Read aloud each tool and its use. Guide children to choose one tool to write about, such as the ruler.

Model/Apply Grammar Tell children that you will work together to write a sentence that gives information about a ruler. Remind them to use an action word to tell what the tool does.

What do we use a ruler to do? Record children's responses. Read the responses aloud.

Then, write the following sentence frame: *We _____ with a ruler.* (measure)

Read aloud the sentence with the verbs that children suggested.

Model another sentence by choosing the name of a tool from the left column of the chart and an action word, or phrase, from the right column. Read the sentence together, tracking the print. Point to the capital letter that starts the sentence and the period at the end.

Write Have children help you write sentences about other tools not on the chart, such as a fork.

Provide the sentence frame: *We _____ with a fork.* (eat)

Guide children to complete the sentence frame. Write the words. Share the pen with children and have them write the letters they know.

Go Digital

Writing

I see a fish.

Grammar

Grammar

MINILESSON 5 Mins

Verbs

1 Review Remind children that verbs are action words that tell what someone or something does. Write and read aloud this sentence: *We work. What is the action word in this sentence?* (work) *The word* work *tells about something we can do.*

Write the following sentences:

We work in school.
We go home.

Read the sentences aloud. Have children tell the action word in each sentence.

2 Guided Practice Show the **Photo Card** for *top.* Write and read aloud: *A top _____.* Have children tell what a top can do. *What does a top do?* (spin) *Complete the sentence frame with: A top spins.* Have children identify the verb in the sentence.

Ask children to tell other actions that a top can do, such as *falls* and *stops.* Write their responses on the board. Guide children in writing a sentence, such as: *A top falls.*

3 Practice Have children work in small groups. Provide each group with a Photo Card of an object or animal. Have groups think of actions the object or animal on the Photo Card can do. Provide chart paper with the name of the object or animal in a sentence frame, such as: *The fish _____.* Help children record their action words on the chart paper. Have groups share their information about each item by reading the sentences aloud.

Talk About It

Have partners work together to orally generate sentences with action words. Encourage them to create sentences about things they do at school, such as *I read a book.*

ENGLISH LANGUAGE LEARNERS

Use Visuals Display the Photo Cards for *dog* and *kitten.* Ask children to draw one of the animals doing an action, such as playing, eating, or sleeping. Guide children in pronouncing the verb in each drawing. Model correct pronunciation as needed.

Daily Wrap Up

- Discuss the Essential Question and encourage children to use the oral vocabulary words. *What did you discover about tools? What do tools help us do?*

- Prompt children to share the skills they learned. How might they use those skills?

Materials

Reading/Writing Workshop Big Book
UNIT 2

Visual Vocabulary Cards
fetch
rumble
defeated

Response Board

Word-Building Cards

Interactive Read-Aloud Cards

Photo Cards

bat	penguin
doll	piano
jump	pie
map	pizza
mop	sheep
nut	soap
paint	soup
peach	top

High-Frequency Word Cards
a
can
I
see
the
we

"Polly and Paul Play the Piano"

→ Build the Concept

MINILESSON 10 Mins Oral Language

OBJECTIVES

CCSS Actively engage in group reading activities with purpose and understanding. **RL.K.10**

CCSS Identify real-life connections between words and their use. **L.K.5c**

Develop oral vocabulary

ACADEMIC LANGUAGE
• *tale, fable*
• Cognates: *fábula*

ESSENTIAL QUESTION

Remind children that this week they are talking and learning about how tools help us explore. Guide children to discuss the Essential Question using information from the **Big Book** and the weekly rhyme.

Remind children about the hammer the carpenter used in "The Carpenter." *A hammer is a tool.* Say the rhyme and have children join in.

Oral Vocabulary

Review last week's oral vocabulary words, as well as *tool* and *discover* from Day 1. Then use the **Define/Example/Ask** routine to introduce *fetch, rumble,* and *defeated.*

> **Oral Vocabulary Routine**
>
> **Define:** When you **fetch** something, you go after it and then bring it back.
>
> **Example:** My dog goes to fetch the newspaper in the morning.
>
> **Ask:** What would you fetch at the store to make pizza?
>
> **Define:** A **rumble** is a long, low sound like thunder.
>
> **Example:** I heard the car tires rumble down the rocky road.
>
> **Ask:** What usually happens during a storm after you hear the rumble of thunder?
>
> **Define:** When you have **defeated** someone in a game, you have won the game.
>
> **Example:** Our basketball team defeated the other team, so we cheered!
>
> **Ask:** When have you watched one team that defeated another?

Vocab...
Define...
Exampl...
Ask:

Visual Vocabulary Cards

Go Digital

Visual Glossary

Timimoto

I wonder...

Think Aloud Cloud

Listening Comprehension

 MINILESSON 10 Mins

Read the Interactive Read Aloud

Genre: Tale

Tell children that you will be reading a tale. A *tale,* like a *fable,* is a fiction story that often teaches a lesson. Display the **Interactive Read-Aloud Cards**.

Read the title. Point out that Timimoto is a character in the tale and that this is a tale from the country of Japan.

Interactive Read-Aloud Cards

Strategy: Ask and Answer Questions

Guide children in recalling that good readers ask themselves questions about what is happening in a story to help them understand as they read. Remind them that they can use the **Think Aloud Cloud** as they ask and answer questions before and during reading.

Think Aloud I read that Timimoto's mother and father gave him many tools. They gave him a needle to use as a sword. I wonder what he will need to protect himself from. How will he use the other tools that his parents gave him? I will keep reading to find out.

Read the story. Pause to model asking and answering questions. Encourage children to share questions that they have.

Make Connections

 Guide partners to connect "Timimoto" with *The Handiest Things in the World.* Discuss the ways both stories show how tools can help us explore. *What tools from these stories have you used?*

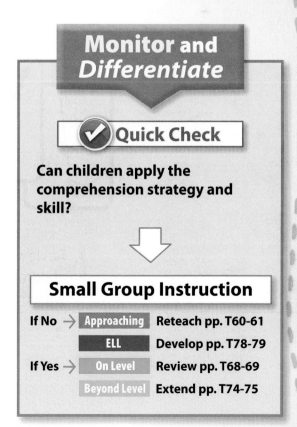

ELL

ENGLISH LANGUAGE LEARNERS

Reinforce Meaning As you read "Timimoto," make meaning clear by pointing to specific characters, places, or objects in the illustrations, demonstrating word meanings, paraphrasing text, and asking children questions. For example, on Card 4, point to Timimoto. Say: *This character is Timimoto.* Then say: *This character is the giant.* Point to Timimoto's mother. Ask: *Who is this character?*

Monitor and *Differentiate*

✔ Quick Check

Can children apply the comprehension strategy and skill?

⬇

Small Group Instruction

If No →	**Approaching**	Reteach pp. T60-61
	ELL	Develop pp. T78-79
If Yes →	**On Level**	Review pp. T68-69
	Beyond Level	Extend pp. T74-75

→ # Word Work

Quick Review

Build Fluency: Sound-Spellings: Show the following **Word-Building Cards:** *a, m, p, s*. Have children chorally say each sound. Repeat and vary the pace.

OBJECTIVES

CCSS Isolate and pronounce the initial, medial vowel, and final sounds in three-phoneme words. **RF.K.2d**

CCSS Demonstrate basic knowledge of one-to-one letter-sound correspondences by producing the primary or many of the most frequent sounds for each consonant. **RF.K.3a**

MINILESSON 5 Mins

Phonemic Awareness

Phoneme Isolation

1 Model Display the *Piano* **Photo Card** and say the word. Piano *has the /p/ sound at the beginning: /p/, /p/,* piano. *Say the sound with me: /p/.* Tell children that now they will listen for the /p/ sound at the end of words. Display the Photo Card for *map.* Have children say the word *map* with you. Map *has the /p/ sound at the end. Listen: /m/ /a/ /p/,* map. Emphasize final /p/. *Let's say /p/ because we hear /p/ at the end of* map: /p/.

Photo Card

2 Guided Practice/Practice Say each of the following words and have children repeat. Have them say /p/ if they hear /p/ at the end of the word. Guide children with the first word.

rip   nut   mop   tap   cat   sip   cup   man   lip

Then show Photo Cards for *bat, doll, mop, nut, sheep, soap, top.* Have children say the name of each picture with you. Ask them to say /p/ if they hear /p/ at the end of the word. Guide children with the first word.

Photo Cards

♪ Review initial /p/. Play "Polly and Paul Play the Piano." Have children clap when they hear initial /p/. Demonstrate as you sing with them.

Go Digital

Phonemic Awareness

Phonics

Handwriting

Phonics

MINILESSON 5 Mins

Word-Building Card

Review /p/p

❶ **Model** Display **Word-Building Card** p. *This is the letter* p. *The letter* p *stands for /p/, the sound you hear at the end of* map. *Say the sound with me: /p/. I will write the letter* p *because* map *has the /p/ sound at the end.*

❷ **Guided Practice/Practice** Tell children that you will say some words that have /p/ at the end and some words that do not. Have children say /p/ and write the letter *p* on their **Response Boards** when they hear /p/ at the end of a word. Guide practice with the first word.

lap   sip   fin   keep   not   tap   ten   slip   bit   step

Blend Words with *p* and *m, s, a*

❶ **Model** Display Word-Building Cards *m, a, p. This is the letter* m. *It stands for /m/. This is the letter* a. *It stands for /a/. This is the letter* p. *It stands for /p/. Let's blend the three sounds together: /mmmaaap/. The word is* map. *Repeat with* am, Pam, *and* sap.

❷ **Guided Practice/Practice** Write the following words and sentences. Have children read each word, blending the sounds. Guide practice with the first word.

Pam   sap   am   Sam   map

Write these sentences and prompt children to read the connected text, sounding out the decodable words: *I am Pam. I see the map.*

YOUR TURN PRACTICE BOOK p. 54

Corrective Feedback

Blending: Sound Error Model the sound that children missed, then have them repeat. For example, for the word *map*, say: *My turn.* Tap under the letter *p* and ask: *What's the sound?* Return to the beginning of the word. Say: *Let's start over.* Blend the word with children again.

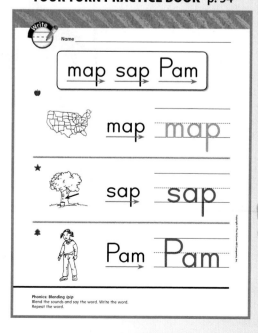

→ # Word Work

Photo Cards

MINILESSON
5 Mins

Phonics

Phonics

Picture Sort

1 Model Remind children that the letter *p* stands for /p/. Place the **Word-Building Card** *p* at the top of a pocket chart. Hold up the **Photo Card** for *pie*. Pie *has /p/ at the beginning of the word. Listen /p/ /p/ pie.* Place the Photo Card for *pie* on the left side of the pocket chart. Repeat with final /p/ using the *Top* Photo Card and place it on the right side of the pocket chart.

Hold up the Photo Card for *paint. Here is the picture for* paint. Paint *has the /p/ sound at the beginning. I will place* paint *under the* pie *because both words begin with /p/.* Place the *Paint* Photo Card under the *Pie* Photo Card. Repeat for final /p/ using the *Sheep* Photo Card.

2 Guided Practice/Practice Display and name the following Photo Cards in random order: *map, mop, peach, penguin, piano, pizza, soap, soup.* Have children sort Photo Cards by initial and final *p* /p/. Have them tell if the card should be placed under the *Pie* Photo Card for initial /p/p or the *Sheep* Photo Card for final /p/p.

Photo Cards

High-Frequency Word Cards

High-Frequency Words

a

❶ Guided Practice Display the **High-Frequency Word Card** *a*. Review the word using the **Read/Spell/Write** routine.

❷ Practice Point to the High-Frequency Word Card *a* and have children read it. Repeat with the previous weeks' words *I, can, the, we, see*.

Build Fluency

Word Automaticity Build sentences in the pocket chart using the High-Frequency Word Cards, **Photo Cards**, and teacher-made punctuation cards. Read each sentence aloud, then have children chorally read as you track the print with your finger. Use the following sentences

> I see a pumpkin.
> We can see a penny.
> I see a map.
> We can see the sky.

Read for Fluency Distribute pages 55–56 of the **Your Turn Practice Book** and help children assemble their Take-Home Books. Chorally read the Take-Home Book with children. Then have children reread the book to review high-frequency words and build fluency.

YOUR TURN PRACTICE BOOK pp. 55–56

Monitor and *Differentiate*

✓ **Quick Check**

Can children sort names of objects by initial and final /p/p?

Can children read and recognize the high-frequency word?

⬇

Small Group Instruction

If No →	**Approaching**	Reteach pp. T62-67
	ELL	Develop pp. T80-83
If Yes →	**On Level**	Review pp. T70-73
	Beyond Level	Extend pp. T76-77

→ # Language Arts

Reading/Writing Workshop Big Book

OBJECTIVES

CCSS Use a combination of drawing, dictating, and writing to compose informative/ explanatory texts in which they name what they are writing about and supply some information about the topic. **W.K.2**

CCSS Use frequently occurring nouns and verbs. **L.K.1b**

ACADEMIC LANGUAGE

- *sentence, information, action word, verb*

- Cognates: *información, verbo*

MINILESSON
10 Mins

Independent Writing

Writing Trait: Ideas

❶ Practice Tell children that they will write a sentence that will give information about a tool. Write this sentence: *I draw with a crayon.* Have children name the word in the sentence that tells what the crayon is used to do.

❷ Guided Practice Share the Readers to Writers page in the **Reading/ Writing Workshop Big Book**. Read the model sentences aloud. Guide children in identifying the action word in each sentence.

READING/WRITING WORKSHOP BIG BOOK, pp. 22–23

Write an Explanatory Sentence

Model Write the following sentence frame: *We _____ with a _____.* Point to the second blank. *I need to write what tool I'm telling about.* Draw a picture of a pencil. Write a label for the pencil below the picture. Then point to the first blank. *I need to write what the tool does.* Write the word *write. This sentence gives information about what a pencil can do.* Read the sentence aloud, tracking the print.

Go Digital

Present the Lesson

Writing

I see a fish.

Grammar

Prewrite

Tell children that before they can begin writing their sentences, they must choose a tool to write about.

Brainstorm Have children work with a partner to choose the tool they would like most to use. *What can you do with the tool?*

Draft

Ask children to draw and label a picture of a tool. Guide them in choosing a verb that tells what the tool is used to do. Help them write the verb as a label. Then help children to copy the sentence frame: *I _____ with a _____.*

Apply Writing Trait As children complete their sentences, have them tell you what information they are communicating about their tools.

Apply Grammar Tell children to point to and tell you the verbs in the sentences.

Grammar

MINILESSON
5 Mins

Verbs

❶ **Review** Display the **Photo Card** for *jump*. Remind children that verbs are action words. Write and read aloud: *I jump rope. What do I do with the rope?* (jump) *What is the verb?* (jump)

❷ **Guided Practice/Practice** Ask children about actions they do in the classroom or in the school. Have children dictate sentences telling actions that they do, such as eat lunch, read a book, and draw pictures. Write some dictated sentences.

Read aloud the sentences. Guide children in circling the action words.

Write and read aloud: *The door _____. The teacher _____. The children _____.* Have children help you fill in the blanks with various action words. Then read a sentence and have children carry out the action.

Talk About It

Have partners work together to orally generate sentences with verbs. Encourage them to create sentences about things they do with their parents, such as *We buy food.*

Daily Wrap Up

- Review the Essential Question and encourage children to discuss using the oral vocabulary words *tool* and *discover*. *How can we use tools to discover things around us?*

- Prompt children to review and discuss the skills they used today. Guide them to give examples of how they used each skill.

Materials

Reading/Writing Workshop Big Book
UNIT 2

Literature Big Book
The Handiest Things in the World

Visual Vocabulary Cards
a

Puppet

Word-Building Cards

Interactive Read-Aloud Cards

High-Frequency Word Cards
a
can
I
see
the

Photo Cards
bear	jump
blue	mix
brown	purple
deer	sing
green	tiger
horse	yellow
juggle	

(→) Extend the Concept

 MINILESSON
10 Mins

Oral Language

OBJECTIVES

CCSS Use words and phrases acquired through conversations, reading and being read to, and responding to texts. **L.K.6**

CCSS Demonstrate understanding of spoken words, syllables, and sounds (phonemes). **RF.K.2**

Develop oral vocabulary

ESSENTIAL QUESTION

Remind children that this week they have been talking and reading about how tools help us explore. Have them recite "The Carpenter" and think about how the hammer helps the carpenter. Then ask which tool the child in *The Handiest Things in the World* uses to sweep dust.

Phonological Awareness

Recognize Alliteration

Have children say: *Hey, hammer! Ho, hammer!* Then say: *I hear the same sound at the beginning of each word: /h/.* Emphasize /h/ as you say it again. Then say: *We can say other words that have the same beginning sound. Listen:* bat, ball, bit, bite. Have children repeat: *bat, ball, bit, bite.* Tell children you will say groups of words. Ask them to raise their hands if all the words begin with the same sound: *road/sewed/go; tie/take/tell; dad/date/do; leaf/lake/let; pat/sat/dot.*

Review Oral Vocabulary

Reread the Interactive Read Aloud Use the **Define/Example/Ask** routine to review the oral vocabulary words *tool, discover, fetch, rumble,* and *defeated.* Have children listen as you reread "Timimoto." Then ask:

→ *Why did the ground start to rumble when Timimoto returned to the dock?* (The giant was walking toward him.)

→ *How did the people in the town feel after Timimoto defeated the giant?* (They were happy and they cheered.)

Category Words: Colors

1 Explain/Model Read the following story. *Raise your hand when I say a color word.*

We gave Mom flowers for her birthday. I bought red *roses. Dad bought* yellow *and* white *daisies. My brother Max liked* pink *tulips. The man at the flower shop gave us* green *leaves. We put the flowers and leaves together and gave them to Mom. She said, "I love my rainbow flowers."*

Demonstrate how to sort by color using crayons or math manipulatives. Use five colors with four or five crayons or math manipulatives for each color. Demonstrate for children how to sort colors to make five groups.

2 Guided Practice Distribute sets of crayons or math manipulatives to small groups or partners. Each set should contain five different colors with at least four crayons or manipulatives for each color. Have children sort crayons or manipulatives by color. Guide practice as needed.

LET'S MOVE!

Display the **Photo Cards** for *brown, blue, green, purple,* and *yellow* in different areas of the classroom. Call out each color and have children walk to the Photo Card that matches the color.

ENGLISH LANGUAGE LEARNERS

Reinforce Meaning Point to different objects in the classroom. Name each object and its color. Then point to another object that is the same color and ask children to identify its color. Correct children's responses as needed by providing vocabulary.

YOUR TURN PRACTICE BOOK p. 57

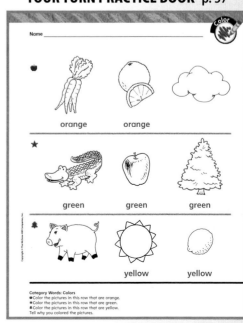

→ # Listening Comprehension

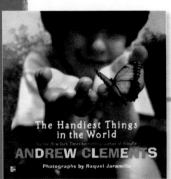

Literature Big Book

Read "Discover with Tools"

Genre: Informational Text

Display "Discover with Tools" on pages 36–40 of the **Big Book** and read aloud the title. Explain to children that this informational text gives true information about tools.

Set a Purpose for Reading

Read aloud the first sentence on page 36. Tell children to listen as you continue reading to learn how tools are used to explore new things.

Strategy: Ask and Answer Questions

Remind children that good readers ask and answer questions as they read. Have children look at page 36. *We can ask: What tool is the boy using to observe a leaf? We can answer: a magnifying glass.*

Text Feature: Headings

Explain Point out and read aloud the heading on page 36. *Headings tell us what kind of information we will find on the page.*

Apply Turn to page 37. Have children identify which part of the text is the heading. (Discover Far Away)

OBJECTIVES

CCSS With prompting and support, ask and answer questions about key details in a text. **RI.K.1**

- Understand the characteristics of informational text
- Use the text feature headings to gather information
- Apply the comprehension strategy: Ask and Answer Questions
- Make connections across texts

ACADEMIC LANGUAGE

- *title, heading*
- Cognates: *título*

Go Digital

"The Handiest Things in the World"

LITERATURE BIG BOOK   PAGES 36–37

ASK AND ANSWER QUESTIONS

What do people use a telescope to explore? (objects in space like the moon and the stars)

LITERATURE BIG BOOK   PAGES 38–39

KEY DETAILS

In the smaller photograph on page 38, what is the scientist using to clean away dirt? (a brush)

LITERATURE BIG BOOK PAGE 40

ASK AND ANSWER QUESTIONS

What tool are the children in the picture using? (a magnifying glass) *What are they using the tool to observe?* (pinecones and rocks)

ENGLISH LANGUAGE LEARNERS

Reinforce Meaning As you read aloud the text, make the meaning clear by pointing to the tools in the photographs. Ask children questions and elicit language.

Retell and Respond

Have children discuss the selection by asking the following questions:

→ *What can a telescope help you see?* (things far away)

→ *What tool does a scientist use to find new medicines?* (a microscope)

Make Connections

Have children recall the selections they have read this week.

→ *What are two tools we can use with our hands?* (broom, comb)

Write About It Write about the tool Timimoto used to fight off the frog. Draw a picture.

CONNECT TO CONTENT

Tools to Observe Review with children some of the tools that people use to make careful observations. (magnifying glass, telescope, microscope) Have partners think of things they would like to observe. Ask them to identify the tool that they would use to make their observations.

STEM

→ # Word Work

Quick Review

Build Fluency: Sound-Spellings: Show the following **Word-Building Cards:** *a, m, p, s.* Have children chorally say each sound. Repeat and vary the pace.

MINILESSON 5 Mins
Phonemic Awareness

Puppet

Phoneme Blending

❶ **Model** *The puppet is going to say the sounds in a word. Listen: /t/ /a/ /p/. It can blend these sounds together: /taaap/,* tap. *Now say the word with the puppet:* tap. Repeat with *top.*

❷ **Guided Practice/Practice** Have children blend sounds to form words. *The puppet is going to say the sounds in a word. Listen as it says each sound. Repeat the sounds, then blend them to say the word.* Guide practice with the first word.

/m/ /a/ /p/	/s/ /i/ /p/	/m/ /o/ /p/	/t/ /i/ /p/	/l/ /a/ /p/
/p/ /a/ /n/	/p/ /a/ /k/	/p/ /i/ /n/	/p/ /e/ /t/	/p/ /ī/

MINILESSON 5 Mins
Phonics

Blend Words with *p* and *m, a, s*

❶ **Guided Practice** Display **Word-Building Cards** *P, a, m.* Point to the letter P. *This is the uppercase or capital letter* P. *The letter* p *stands for /p/. Say /p/. This is the letter* a. *The letter* a *stands for /a/. Listen as I blend the two sounds together /paaa/. Say /paaa/. This is the letter* m. *The letter* m *stands for /m/. Listen as I blend the three sounds: /paaammm/,* Pam. *Now you say it. Let's change* P *to* S. *Use the same routine to blend* Sam.

❷ **Practice** Write *map* and *sap.* Have children blend and read the words. Have children say both words and tell which sounds are different. (/m/, /s/) Ask children to tell which letters are different. (*m, s*) Discuss the sounds each letter stands for and how it changes the word. Repeat with *Pam* and *Sam.*

OBJECTIVES

CCSS Distinguish between similarly spelled words by identifying the sounds of the letters that differ. **RF.K.3d**

CCSS Read common high-frequency words by sight. **RF.K.3c**

Blend phonemes to make words

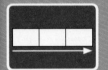

Phonics

5 Mins MINILESSON

Dictation

Review Dictate the following sounds for children to spell. Have them repeat the sound and then write the letter that stands for the sound.

/m/   /a/   /s/   /p/

Dictate the following words for children to spell: *map, am, Sam, Pam*. Model for children how to segment each word to scaffold the spelling.

When I say the word map, *I hear three sounds: /m/ /a/ /p/. I know the letter* m *stands for /m/, the letter* a *stands for /a/, and the letter* p *stands for /p/. I will write the letters* m, a, p *to spell the word* map.

When children are finished, write the letters and words for them to self-correct.

High-Frequency Words

5 Mins MINILESSON

Practice Say the word *a* and have children write it. Then display the **Visual Vocabulary Card** *a*. Follow the Teacher Talk routine on the back of the card.

Visual Vocabulary Card

Build Fluency Build sentences in a pocket chart using **High-Frequency Word Cards**, **Photo Cards**, and teacher-made punctuation cards. Have children chorally read the sentences as you track the print. Then have them identify the word *a*.

I can see *a* deer.

I can see *a* bear.

I can see *a* tiger.

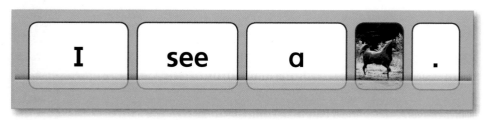

High-Frequency Words Practice

Have partners create sentences using the word *a*.

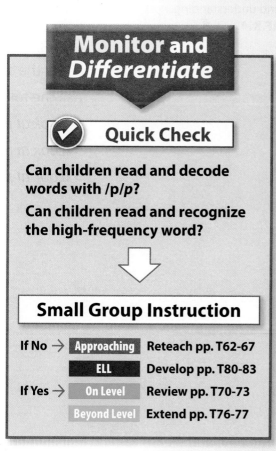

Monitor and Differentiate

✓ **Quick Check**

Can children read and decode words with /p/p?

Can children read and recognize the high-frequency word?

⬇

Small Group Instruction

If No →	**Approaching**	Reteach pp. T62-67
	ELL	Develop pp. T80-83
If Yes →	**On Level**	Review pp. T70-73
	Beyond Level	Extend pp. T76-77

→ Shared Read

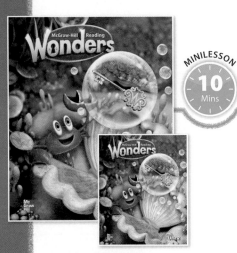

Reading/Writing Workshop Big Book and Reading/Writing Workshop

---

OBJECTIVES

CCSS Read common high-frequency words by sight. **RF.K.3c**

CCSS Read emergent-reader texts with purpose and understanding. **RF.K.4**

MINILESSON
10 Mins

Read "We Can See!"

Model Skills and Strategies

Model Book Handling Demonstrate book handling. *This is how I hold a book. This is the front cover. I make sure that the book is not upside down so that I can see the words. This is how I turn the pages of the book. When I turn to each page, I stop to read the words on it.*

Model Concepts About Print Before you read the story, remind children that a sentence is made up of a group of words. *When I read each sentence, my eyes read the words from left to right, like this.* Model reading a sentence from the story, tracking the print from left to right using your finger or a pointer.

Predict Read the title, and ask children to repeat it. Encourage them to describe the photograph. *What do you think the selection will be about?*

Read Point out each rebus, and discuss what it stands for. Then have children chorally read the story. Children should sound out the decodable words and say the sight words. Offer support as needed using the student **Reading/Writing Workshop**.

Ask the following:

→ *Look at page 15. What do you see?* (a map of a zoo)

→ *Look at page 17. What are the children looking at?* (a seal)

→ *Look at page 19. What is the panda looking at?* (a parrot)

Go
Digital

"We Can See!"

"We Can See!"

READING/WRITING WORKSHOP, pp. 14–19

Rereading

Have small groups use the **Reading/Writing Workshop** to reread "We Can See!" Then review the skills and strategies using the *Phonics* and *Words to Know* pages that come before the selection.

→ As children reread the story, encourage them to ask themselves questions and find the answers in the words and photographs.

→ Have children use page 7 to review the high-frequency word *a*.

→ Have children use page 6 to review that the letter *p* can stand for the sound /p/. Guide them to blend the sounds to read the words.

ELL

ENGLISH LANGUAGE LEARNERS

Reinforce Vocabulary Display the **High-Frequency Word Cards** *I, can, see, the, a.* Point to classroom objects and groups of children as you use the high-frequency words in sentences such as the following: *I can see a box of crayons. Can you see a box of crayons?* (Yes, I can see a box of crayons.) *I can see a map of the United States. Can you see a map of the United States?* (Yes, I can see a map of the United States.)

→ # Language Arts

MINILESSON
10
Mins

Independent Writing

Writing Trait: Ideas

Revise

Distribute the children's draft drawings and sentences from Day 3.

Apply Writing Trait Ideas Explain that as writers revise, they can add more information to their writing. Write this sentence: *We draw with a marker.* Read the sentence aloud. *Let's work together to make sure this sentence tells what we can do with the tool. What is the name of the tool?* (marker) *What is the action word?* (draw) Then have children reread the sentences they wrote on Day 3 and check for the following:

→ What is the tool?

→ What does the sentence tell about the tool?

→ Is there another action word I can use?

→ Did I write the correct label for my tool and what it does?

Apply Grammar Explain that writers can add more action words to give more information. Write: *We write and draw with a marker.* Point out that the action word *write* gives more information about what a marker is used for.

 Peer Edit Have children work with a partner to do a peer edit. Children should read aloud their own draft while the partner looks at the draft. Ask partners to check that the sentences tell what the tools do. Provide time for children to make revisions to their sentences.

Final Draft

After children have edited their own papers and finished their peer edits, have them write their final draft. Explain that they should try to write letters carefully and leave spaces between words so that readers can read their writing. As children work, conference with them to provide guidance.

Grammar

MINILESSON
5 Mins

Verbs

1 Review Remind children that verbs are action words that tell what someone or something does. Have children tell about actions they do.

2 Guided Practice Display a sentence strip with a sentence in which the action word can be replaced easily with another action word, such as *The cat sleeps.* Read the sentence aloud, tracking the print.

Cut the sentence strip into two pieces: *The cat* and *sleeps.* Write other action words. Ask children to choose a new action word for the sentence. Work with children to read each new sentence aloud.

3 Practice Make sentence strips for the sentence: *My hands touch.* Read the sentence aloud. Then cut off the action word *touch.* Provide pairs of children with strips of the sentence stem and strips with other words that tell what hands do, such as *hold, grab, pull, push,* and *feel.* Have partners work together to complete the sentence with a new action word. Ask partners to read aloud the sentence. Provide support as needed. *What can your hands do?* Tell children that their hands can do a lot of actions.

Talk About It

Have partners work together to orally generate sentences with verbs. Encourage them to create sentences about actions they have seen an animal do, such as *The cat licks its paws.*

ENGLISH LANGUAGE LEARNERS

Picture Cards and Sentences Provide sentences with action words that go with images on the **Photo Cards** for *juggle, jump, mix,* and *sing.* As you say a sentence aloud, hold up a Photo Card as you say the action, such as *He can juggle.*

Daily Wrap Up

- Review the Essential Question and encourage children to discuss it, using the oral vocabulary words.

- Prompt children to discuss the skills that they practiced and learned today. Guide them to share examples of each skill.

☞ **Go** Digital

www.connected.mcgraw-hill.com
RESOURCES
Research and Inquiry

→ ## Wrap Up the Week
Integrate Ideas

RESEARCH AND INQUIRY

Tools We Use

OBJECTIVES

 Participate in shared research and writing projects (e.g., explore a number of books by a favorite author and express opinions about them). **W.K.7**

 With guidance and support from adults, recall information from experiences or gather information from provided sources to answer a question. **W.K.8**

ACADEMIC LANGUAGE
resources, research

Make a Tool Belt

Tell children that today they will do a research project with a partner to learn about tools and how they help us explore. Explain that they will make a page about a tool to add to a class tool belt that will be posted on the bulletin board. Review the steps in the research process below.

STEP 1 Choose a Topic

Prompt a discussion about the different kinds of tools people use. Guide pairs to select a tool to research.

STEP 2 Find Resources

Talk about locating and using resources. Guide children in finding information online. Direct children to use the selections from the week. Point out that children can also use their own experiences as resources. Ask children to use the Research Process Checklist online.

STEP 3 Keep Track of Ideas

Have children note their ideas by drawing pictures or writing words. Help them print out information from online sites.

Collaborative Conversations

Ask and Answer Questions Review with children that as they engage in partner, small-group, and whole-class discussions, they should:

→ ask questions to clarify ideas they do not understand.

→ ask for help in getting information.

→ give others a chance to think before they respond.

→ answer questions with complete ideas, not one-word answers.

STEM

We use a trowel to dig.

STEP 4 **Create the Project: Tool Belt**

Explain the characteristics of the project:

→ **Information** The class tool belt will give information about tools and how we use them.

→ **Text** Each drawing in the tool belt will have a sentence that tells what people do with the tool. Provide this sentence frame:

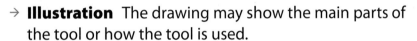
We use a _____ to _____.

→ **Illustration** The drawing may show the main parts of the tool or how the tool is used.

Explain that each pair will create one tool for the tool belt. Direct partners to work together to create their drawing for the tool belt.

→ Guide them to write the name of the tool and a verb to complete the sentence frame.

→ Encourage children who can generate more writing to do so.

→ Have children include details in their illustration that show where the tool is being used.

ELL ENGLISH LANGUAGE LEARNERS SCAFFOLD

Beginning	Intermediate	Advanced/Advanced High
Use Sentence Frames Pair children with more fluent speakers. Provide additional sentence frames to help children talk about their chosen tool. For example: *We _____. We use a _____.*	**Discuss** Ask children what they can learn or want to learn from using their chosen tool. Tell them to share this information when they show their page to the class.	**Describe** Tell partners to include details in their pictures that show where and when people might use the chosen tool. When children share their page with the class, direct them to point to and name the details in their illustrations.

Materials

**Reading/Writing
Workshop Big Book**
UNIT 2

Literature Big Book
*The Handiest Things in
the World*

**Interactive Read-Aloud
Cards**

**Word-Building
Cards**

**Visual
Vocabulary
Cards**
a

**High-Frequency
Word Cards**

a   see
can   the
I   we

**Photo
Cards**
box
boy
feet
goat
juice
leaf
lock

moon
mop
paint
peach
pear
penny
pie
pig
pizza
plate
purple
saw
seal
soap

Response Board

"Polly and
Paul Play
the Piano"

→ Integrate Ideas

TEXT CONNECTIONS

Connect to Essential Question

OBJECTIVES

 With prompting and support, identify basic similarities in and differences between two texts on the same topic (e.g., in illustrations, descriptions, or procedures). **RI.K.9**

 Participate in collaborative conversations with diverse partners about *kindergarten topics and texts* with peers and adults in small and larger groups. **SL.K.1**

• Make connections among texts

• Make connections to the world

Text to Text

Remind children that, all week, they have been reading selections about tools. Tell them that now they will connect the texts, or think about how they are alike and different. Model comparing *The Handiest Things in the World* with another selection from the week.

 Think Aloud In *The Handiest Things in the World,* I learned about so many tools. The photos showed children using many different tools, and I use many of them as well. In "Discover With Tools," I also saw many tools used for looking at things very closely. I could not use my hands to do any of the things in this selection!

Guide children to compare the tools they have seen in other selections throughout the week, including Leveled Readers.

Text to Self

Have children name tools from the selections that they have seen at school or at home. Ask each child to name one tool they have used and how they used it.

Text to World

Talk about tools children have seen grown-ups using in the community. Lead children to understand that workers all have different kinds of tools that help them do their jobs.

TALK ABOUT READING

OBJECTIVES

 CCSS Confirm understanding of a text read aloud or information presented orally or through other media by asking and answering questions about key details and requesting clarification if something is not understood. **SL.K.2**

Becoming Readers

Talk with children about the genre, strategy, and skill they have learned about this week. Prompt them to discuss how this knowledge helps them to read and understand selections.

→ Remind children that they learned about informational texts. Have children recall some characteristics of informational texts.

→ Talk about the strategy of asking and answering questions. *How did stopping to ask and answer questions help you learn about the tools we read about?*

→ Point out that children learned to look for key details in the words and photos to help them understand a text. Have students think back to one of the informational texts. *What kinds of details did you notice in photos? How did those details help you understand the text?*

RESEARCH AND INQUIRY STEM

OBJECTIVES

 CCSS Participate in shared research and writing projects (e.g., explore a number of books by a favorite author and express opinions about them). **W.K.7**

Wrap Up the Project

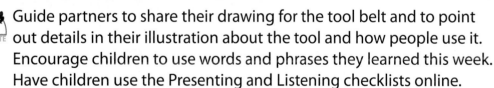 Guide partners to share their drawing for the tool belt and to point out details in their illustration about the tool and how people use it. Encourage children to use words and phrases they learned this week. Have children use the Presenting and Listening checklists online.

→ # Word Work

Quick Review

Build Fluency: Sound-Spellings: Show the following **Word-Building Cards:** *a, m, p, s.* Have children chorally say each sound. Repeat and vary the pace.

MINILESSON
5 Mins

Phonemic Awareness

Phoneme Categorization

OBJECTIVES

CCSS Isolate and pronounce the initial, medial vowel, and final sounds (phonemes) in three-phoneme words. **RF.K.2d**

CCSS Spell simple words phonetically, drawing on knowledge of sound-letter relationships. **L.K.2d**

CCSS Read common high-frequency words by sight. **RF.K.3c**

Blend sounds to read words with /p/p

1 Model Display **Photo Cards** for *pie, seal, penny. I will say three picture names. Listen for the names that begin with the same sound. Say the picture names. Pie and penny both begin with /p/. Seal does not begin with /p/. Seal does not belong.*

2 Guided Practice/Practice Show children sets of Photo Cards. Name the pictures with children and have them identify the initial sounds. Have them tell which picture does not begin with the same sound. Guide children with the first set of words.

pear, paint, mop	saw, pig, soap	lock, juice, leaf
pizza, peach, moon	feet, purple, plate	box, goat, boy

MINILESSON
5 Mins

Phonics

Read Words with *p* and *m, a, s*

1 Guided Practice Remind children that the letter *p* can stand for the sound /p/. Display **Word-Building Cards** *m, a, p.* Point to the letter *m. The letter* m *stands for the sound /m/. Say /mmm/. The letter* a *stands for /a/. Say /aaa/. The letter* p *stands for /p/. Say /p/. Let's blend the sounds to read the word: /mmmaaap/* map. *Now let's change the* m *to* s. Blend and read *sap* with children.

2 Practice Write the words and sentences for children to read:

Pam   map   sap   Sam

We see Pam.
I can see Sam.
We see a map.

Remove words from view before dictation.

♪ Review /p/p. Play and sing "Polly and Paul Play the Piano." Have children point to the letter *p* in the pocket chart when they hear initial /p/. Demonstrate as you sing with children.

Go Digital

Phonemic Awareness

Phonics

Handwriting

High-Frequency Words

Dictation

1 **Review** Dictate the following sounds for children to spell. As you say each sound, have children repeat it and then write the letter on their **Response Boards** that stands for the sound.

/p/   /s/   /m/   /a/

2 **Dictate** the following words for children to spell. Model for children how to use sound boxes to segment each word to scaffold the spelling. *I will say a word. You will repeat the word, then think about how many sounds are in the word. Use your sound boxes to count the sounds. Then write one letter for each sound you hear.*

map   Pam   am   Sam   sap

Write the letters and words for children to self-correct.

MINILESSON 5 Mins High-Frequency Words

a

1 **Review** Display **Visual Vocabulary Card** *a*. Choose a Partner Talk activity on the back of the card. Have children **Read/Spell/Write** the word.

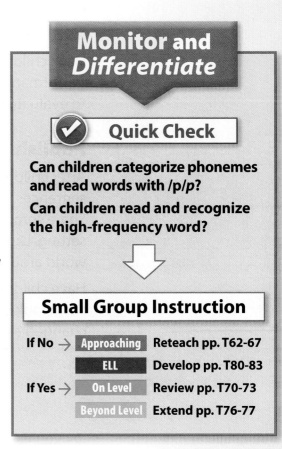

Visual Vocabulary Card

Distribute one of the following **High-Frequency Word Cards** to children: *I, can, the, we, see, a.* Tell children that you will say some sentences. Say: *When you hear the word that is on your card, stand and hold up your word card.*

Mike uses *a* shovel to plant vegetables.
Rita and *I can see* planets with *a* telescope.
We can use *a* magnifying glass to look closely at leaves.
I measured *the* table with *a* ruler.
We see birds in *the* trees with our binoculars.

2 **Build Fluency: Word Automaticity** Display High-Frequency Word Cards *I, can, the, we, see* and *a.* Point to each card, at random, and have children read the word as quickly as they can.

Monitor and Differentiate

✔ **Quick Check**

Can children categorize phonemes and read words with /p/*p*?

Can children read and recognize the high-frequency word?

⬇

Small Group Instruction

If No → | Approaching | Reteach pp. T62–67
| ELL | Develop pp. T80–83
If Yes → | On Level | Review pp. T70–73
| Beyond Level | Extend pp. T76–77

→ Language Arts

Independent Writing

OBJECTIVES

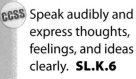 Speak audibly and express thoughts, feelings, and ideas clearly. **SL.K.6**

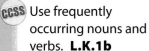 Use frequently occurring nouns and verbs. **L.K.1b**

ACADEMIC LANGUAGE

• *present, action words, verbs*

• Cognates: *presente, verbo*

Writing Trait: Ideas

Prepare

Tell children that they will present to the class their finished sentences with drawings from Day 4. Hold up an example from Day 4 and read it aloud, tracking the print. *I read my sentence loudly and clearly enough so that everyone could hear me. Then I held my picture up high so everyone could see.*

Present

Providing assistance as needed, ask children to take turns reading their sentences aloud. Remind children to speak clearly and to hold up their drawings so that everyone can see them. Encourage the rest of the class to listen quietly and to wait until the presenter has finished before asking any questions.

Evaluate

Have children discuss their own presentations and evaluate their performances, using the presentation rubric. Use the teacher's rubric to evaluate children's writing.

Publish

After children have finished presenting, collect their drawings and sentences. Create a binder with the title *Explore the World with Tools*. Share some sentences and drawings from the binder in a group setting. Discuss how each tool helps children find out more about the world around them.

Have children add their writing to their Writer's Portfolio. Then have them look back at their previous writing and discuss how they have changed as writers throughout the year.

Go Digital

Writing

I see a fish.

Grammar

Grammar

Verbs

1 **Review** Remind children that verbs are action words that tell what someone or something does. Write and read aloud the following sentence: *The rabbits hop across the field. What is the verb?* (hop)

2 **Review Practice** Write and read aloud this sentence:

I _____ across the field.

Ask children to name action words that can be used to complete the sentence. Write their responses on the board. Read aloud the sentences with the different actions together with children. Have children demonstrate some of the actions.

Have children work with a partner to think of action words that tell how they play a game. *What kinds of actions do you use when you play ball?* Ask volunteers to share their action words with the class, and, if appropriate, to pantomime them.

Wrap Up the Week

- Review blending words with initial and final /p/ *p*.
- Remind children that action words are called *verbs*.
- Use the **High-Frequency Word Cards** to review the **Words to Know**.
- Remind children that a sentence can give information to explain an idea.

→ Approaching Level

Leveled Reader

OBJECTIVES

 With prompting and support, ask and answer questions about key details in a text. **RI.K.1**

 With prompting and support, identify the main topic and retell key details of a text. **RI.K.2**

 With prompting and support, describe the relationship between illustrations and the text in which they appear (e.g., what person, place, thing, or idea in the text an illustration depicts). **RI.K.7**

 Read emergent-reader texts with purpose and understanding. **RF.K.4**

Leveled Reader:
We Need Tools

Before Reading

Preview and Predict

Read the title and the name of the author and illustrator. Discuss the photo on the cover. Ask: *When do people need tools? What kind of tools do you think you might read about in this book?* Preview the photos and identify the rebus pictures.

Review Genre: Informational Text

Explain to children that informational text is about real people, places, or events. Ask children to tell how they know this is informational text. (photos of real people doing real things)

Model Concepts of Print

Turn to page 2. Use your finger to point to where you begin reading on the left and then move to the right-hand page. Point to the text and explain that the words make a sentence and that we read the sentence from left to right across the line.

Review High-Frequency Words

Point out the word *a* on page 2, and read it with children. Have them locate *a* on all the other pages.

Essential Question

Set a purpose for reading: *As we read this book, think about the tools you and your family use. How do they help?*

During Reading

Guided Comprehension

As children read *We Need Tools,* provide guidance by correcting blending and modeling the skill and strategy.

Strategy: Ask and Answer Questions

Remind children that as they read they can ask questions about things they don't understand and look for answers in the text and pictures.

Skill: Key Details

Remind children that photos are important because they show what is happening. After reading, ask: *What details about the story did you learn from the pictures?*

Think Aloud The words on page 2 don't give me a lot of details, but the picture does. It shows a child using a pencil. I know that a pencil is a tool that people use to write. I'm going to use the pictures on each page to understand the tools in this book and how they help people.

As children read, guide them to identify key details in the pictures.

After Reading

Respond to Reading

→ *What is this book about?* (tools that people use) *How do you know that?* (Every page shows a person using a different tool.)

→ *Which tools shown in the book do we use most often at school?* (Possible answers: pencil, paintbrush)

→ *Why do people need tools?* (They help us get things done.)

Retell

Have children take turns retelling the story. Help them make personal connections by asking: *What kind of tools do you like to use?*

Model Fluency

Read the book aloud, pausing after each page to have children chorally repeat.

Apply

Have children practice reading with partners as you observe and provide assistance as needed.

LITERACY ACTIVITIES

Have children complete the activities on the inside back cover of the reader.

Level Up

IF Children read *We Need Tools* **Approaching Level** with fluency and correctly answer the Respond to Reading questions,

THEN Tell children that they will read another story about how people use tools.

• Have children page through *A Trip* **On Level** as you identify the tools in the book and how people use them to explore.

• Have children read the story, monitoring their comprehension and providing assistance as necessary.

Approaching Level

Phonological Awareness

RECOGNIZE ALLITERATION

 TIER 2

OBJECTIVES

 Demonstrate understanding of spoken words, syllables, and sounds (phonemes). **RF.K.2**

I Do Say the first line of "The Carpenter": *Hey hammer, Ho hammer*. Point out that each word in the line begins with the same sound, /h/. Tell children that when two or more words in a line begin with the same sound, it is called *alliteration*.

We Do Say an alliterative sentence, such as *Summer sun is simply super*. Ask children what sound they hear at the beginning of the words. (/s/) Say the following alliterative phrases. Have children identify and say the initial sound for each phrase: *ten tall trees, many merry mice, big blue buses*. (/t/, /m/, /b/)

You Do Have children create their own simple alliterative phrases. Then ask them to identify the initial sound for each phrase.

Phonemic Awareness

PHONEME ISOLATION

 TIER 2

OBJECTIVES

 Isolate and pronounce the initial, medial vowel, and final sounds (phonemes) in three-phoneme words. **RF.K.2d**

I Do Display the *Peach* **Photo Card**. *This is a peach. The first sound I hear in* peach *is* /p/. Repeat the word, emphasizing its initial sound. Repeat with the *Map* Photo Card, emphasizing /p/ in the final position.

We Do Display the *Penguin* Photo Card. Name the photo and have children say the initial sound: /p/. *What is the first sound in* penguin? (/p/) Say the sound together. Repeat with the *Soap* Photo Card, emphasizing final /p/.

You Do Display the *Pig* Photo Card. Have children name it and say the initial sound. Repeat with the *Pillow* Photo Card (initial position) and the *Top* Photo Card (final position).

You may wish to review Phonological Awareness and Phonemic Awareness with **ELL** using this section.

PHONEME CATEGORIZATION

OBJECTIVES

CCSS Isolate and pronounce the initial, medial vowel, and final sounds (phonemes) in three-phoneme words. **RF.K.2d**

 Display the *Penny, Pitcher,* and *Saw* **Photo Cards**. Say each picture name, emphasizing the initial sound. Penny *and* pitcher *begin with* /p/. *Say the sound with me:* /p/. Saw *does not begin with* /p/. Saw *does not belong.*

 Display the *Anchor, Moth,* and *Mule* Photo Cards. Have children say the name of each picture with you, emphasizing the beginning sound. *Which words begin with the same sound?* Repeat the routine with the *Pear, Sock,* and *Pea* Photo Cards.

 Display the *Moth, Mule,* and *Pitcher* Photo Cards. Have children name each picture and tell which words have the same beginning sound. Repeat the routine with the *Pea, Penny,* and *Sock* Photo Cards.

PHONEME BLENDING

OBJECTIVES

CCSS Isolate and pronounce the initial, medial vowel, and final sounds (phonemes) in three-phoneme words. **RF.K.2d**

 The puppet is going to say the sounds in a word. Listen: /p/ /aaa/ /mmm/. *The puppet can blend these sounds together:* /paaammm/, Pam. *Repeat with* pass.

 Now the puppet is going to say the sounds in another word. Say the sounds with the puppet: /sss/ /aaa/ /p/. *Let's blend the sounds together:* /sssaaap/, sap.

 Have children blend sounds to form words. Practice together: /p/ /aaa/ /lll/, /paaalll/, *pal*. Then have children practice blending the following sounds to say the words.

/p/ /a/ /t/ pat   /k/ /a/ /p/ cap   /p/ /a/ /d/ pad

ELL **ENGLISH LANGUAGE LEARNERS**

For the **ELLs** who need **phonics, decoding,** and **fluency** practice, use scaffolding methods as necessary to ensure children understand the meaning of the words. Refer to the Language Transfer Handbook for phonics elements that may not transfer in students' native languages.

→ # Approaching Level

Phonics

TIER 2

SOUND-SPELLING REVIEW

OBJECTIVES

 CCSS Demonstrate basic knowledge of one-to-one letter-sound correspondences by producing the primary or many of the most frequent sounds for each consonant. **RF.K.3a**

 I Do Display **Word-Building Card** *p*. Say the letter name and the sound it stands for: *p, /p/.* Repeat for *m, /m/, s, /s/,* and *a, /a/.*

 We Do Display the *Pea* **Photo Card** and together say the first letter in the word and the sound that it stands for. Repeat with the *Anchor, Mix,* and *Soil* Photo Cards. Repeat the routine with *map,* emphasizing the /p/.

 You Do Display the *Astronaut, Man, Pain,* and *Sun* Photo Cards one at a time. Have children say the first letter in the word and the sound that it stands for.

CONNECT *p* TO /p/

TIER 2

OBJECTIVES

CCSS Demonstrate basic knowledge of one-to-one letter-sound correspondences by producing the primary or many of the most frequent sounds for each consonant. **RF.K.3a**

 I Do Display the *Piano* **Sound-Spelling Card**. *The letter* p *can stand for /p/ at the beginning of* piano. *What is this letter? What sound does it stand for? I will write* p *when I hear /p/ in these words:* sad, page, push, mop, act, tap.

 We Do *The word* park *begins with /p/. Let's write* p. Guide children to write *p* when they hear a word that begins or ends with /p/: *pack, pilot, sail, map, add.*

 You Do Say the following words and have children write the letter *p* if a word begins or ends with /p/: *peck, talk, tap, pond, pit, sap, monkey, tip.*

RETEACH

OBJECTIVES

 CCSS Demonstrate basic knowledge of one-to-one letter-sound correspondences by producing the primary or many of the most frequent sounds for each consonant. **RF.K.3a**

 I Do Display **Reading/Writing Workshop**, p. 6. *The letter* p *stands for the /p/ sound you hear at the beginning of* piano. Say *piano,* emphasizing the /p/.

 We Do Have children say the name of each picture in the apple row. Repeat the name, emphasizing /p/. Repeat for the star row.

 You Do Say the name of the first picture in the tree row, emphasizing the final sound. Have children read the remaining words in that row. Offer assistance as needed.

BLEND WORDS WITH /p/ *p*

OBJECTIVES

 Isolate and pronounce the initial, medial vowel, and final sounds (phonemes) in three-phoneme words. **RF.K.2d**

 I Do Display **Word-Building Cards** P, a, m. *This is the letter* P. *It stands for* /p/. *This is the letter* a. *It stands for* /a/. *This is the letter* m. *It stands for* /m/. *Listen as I blend all three sounds:* /paaammm/. *The word is* Pam. Repeat for *map.*

 We Do *Now let's blend the sounds together to make the word:* /paaasss/, pass. Repeat for *sap.*

 You Do Distribute sets of Word-Building Cards for *a, m, p,* and *s.* Write: *map.* Have children form the words and then blend and read the words.

BUILD WORDS WITH /p/ *p*

OBJECTIVES

Demonstrate basic knowledge of one-to-one letter-sound correspondences by producing the primary or many of the most frequent sounds for each consonant. **RF.K.3a**

 I Do Display Word-Building Cards m, a, p. *These are letters* m, a, *and* p. *They stand for* /m/, /a/, *and* /p/. *I will blend* /mmm/, /aaa/, *and* /p/ *together:* /mmmaaap/, map. *The word is* map.

 We Do Distribute sets of Word-Building Cards for *m, a, p,* and *s.* Show how to make the word *sap* and have children do the same. *Let's blend* /sssaaap/, sap. *Now we have read a new word,* sap.

 You Do Have children change the *s* in *sap* to *m* and read the new word, *map.* Point out that by changing one letter we make a new word.

BUILD FLUENCY WITH PHONICS

Sound/Spelling Fluency

Display the following Word-Building Cards: *m, a, p,* and *s.* Have children chorally say each sound. Repeat and vary the pace.

Fluency in Connected Text

Write the following sentences. *We can see Pam. Sam can see a map.* Have children read the sentences and identify the words with /p/.

→ Approaching Level

High-Frequency Words

TIER 2

RETEACH WORDS

OBJECTIVES

CCSS Read common high-frequency words by sight. **RF.K.3c**

 I Do Use the **High-Frequency Word Card** *a* with the **Read/Spell/Write** routine to reteach the high-frequency word *a*.

 We Do Have children turn to p. 7 of **Reading/Writing Workshop** and discuss the first photo. Then read aloud the first sentence. Reread the sentence with children. Then distribute index cards with the word *a* written on them. Have children match their word card with the word *a* in the sentence. Use the same routine for the other sentence on the page.

 You Do Write the sentence frame *I can see a ___*. Have children copy the sentence frame on their **Response Boards**. Then have partners work together to read and orally complete the frame by talking about the different things that they can see in the classroom. Reteach previously introduced high-frequency words using the Read/Spell/Write routine.

TIER 2

REREAD FOR FLUENCY

OBJECTIVES

CCSS Read common high-frequency words by sight. **RF.K.3c**

 I Do Turn to p. 8 of Reading/Writing Workshop and read aloud the title. *Let's read the title together.* Page through the book. Ask children what they see in each picture. Ask children to find the word *a* on the pages.

 We Do Then have children open their books and chorally read the story. Have children point to each word as they read. Provide corrective feedback as needed. After reading, ask children to recall the things that Pam can see.

 You Do Have children reread "Pam Can See" with a partner for fluency.

Repeat for "We Can See!" on p. 14. Have children find the word *a*.

Oral Vocabulary

REVIEW WORDS

OBJECTIVES

Identify real-life connections between words and their use. **L.K.5c**

Develop oral vocabulary: *tool, discover, fetch, rumble, defeated*

I Do Use the **Define/Example/Ask** routine to review words. Use the following definitions and provide examples:

tool	A **tool** is a thing that helps people do work or helps people to learn.
discover	To **discover** something means to see or find out for the first time.
fetch	When you **fetch**, you go after something and then bring it back.
rumble	A **rumble** is a long, low sound like thunder.
defeated	When you have **defeated** someone in a game, you have won the game.

We Do Ask questions to build understanding. *How does a tool help you measure? Where can you discover facts about your town? What is something that a dog likes to fetch? What do you usually see after you hear the rumble of thunder? How does a person on a defeated team probably feel?*

You Do Have children complete these sentence frames: *I use tools like crayons and pencils to ___. I discover new facts when I ___. I taught my dog to fetch a ___. I heard the rumble of a ___. I was on a defeated team when ___.*

Comprehension

SELF-SELECTED READING

OBJECTIVES

With prompting and support, ask and answer questions about key details in a text. **RL.K.1**

Apply the strategy and skill to reread the text.

Read Independently

Help children select a nonfiction text with photographs for sustained silent reading. Tell them to look for information in the photographs to understand key details, such as information about tools. Guide them to ask and answer questions to help them understand what they read.

Read Purposefully

Before reading, guide children in identifying an interesting photograph. After reading, have children recall the photograph they identified earlier. Have them explain how the photograph helped them understand something in the text.

→ # On Level

Leveled Reader

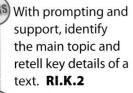

OBJECTIVES

CCSS With prompting and support, ask and answer questions about key details in a text. **RI.K.1**

CCSS With prompting and support, identify the main topic and retell key details of a text. **RI.K.2**

CCSS Demonstrate understanding of the organization and basic features of print. **RF.K.1**

CCSS Read emergent-reader texts with purpose and understanding. **RF.K.4**

Leveled Reader:
A Trip

Before Reading

Preview and Predict

Read aloud the title. Ask children to tell what they see in the cover photograph. Ask children if they have an idea about what kind of trip the book is about. Guide children through the book to preview the photos and identify the rebuses on each page.

Review Genre: Informational Text

Explain that informational text is about real people, places, or events. Ask: *How can you tell that this is informational text?* (there are photos; it is about real places)

Model Concepts of Print

Say: *I read each word from left to right.* Have children follow along with their books as you read the words on page 2 aloud, tracking the print.

Review High-Frequency Words

Point out the word *a* on page 2, and read it with children. Have them look at pages 3–7 and locate the word *a*.

Essential Question

Set a purpose for reading: *How would these tools help on a fishing trip?*

During Reading

Guided Comprehension

As children read *A Trip*, monitor and provide guidance by correcting blending and modeling the strategy and skill for children.

Go
Digital

Leveled Readers

Strategy: Ask and Answer Questions

Remind children that as they read they can ask questions about things they don't understand and look for answers in the text and pictures.

Skill: Key Details

Reinforce with children the importance of using both the pictures and the print when they read. After reading ask: *What details did you find in the pictures?*

Think Aloud I can get details from the picture on page 2. I see a backpack that people use to go for long walks. They use it to carry their water and other important things. I think that the backpack will be used for a walking trip. I'll keep reading to find out if I'm right.

As children read, guide them to identify details in the pictures that help confirm their word choice and support their thinking.

After Reading

Respond to Reading

→ *What is this book about?* (tools for a fishing trip)

→ *What things could a person do with the tools in this book?* (Possible answers: take walks/hikes, boat, fish)

→ *What is the pump used for?* (to put air in things; inflate the boat)

Retell

Have children retell the story details to a partner. Help them make personal connections by asking: *What kind of a trip would you like to take? What tools would you bring?*

Model Fluency

Read the book aloud, pausing after each page to have children chorally repeat.

Apply

Observe and provide assistance as needed as children practice reading with partners.

LITERACY ACTIVITIES

Have children complete the activities on the inside back cover of the reader.

Level Up

IF Children read *A Trip* On Level with fluency and correctly answer the Respond to Reading questions,

THEN Tell children that they will read another story about tools. The tools in this book help you explore and learn about the world.

• Have children page through *What Can You See?* Beyond Level as you help children identify the tools and how they help us learn.

• Have children read the story, monitoring their comprehension and providing assistance as necessary.

→ # On Level

Phonemic Awareness

PHONEME ISOLATION

OBJECTIVES

CCSS Isolate and pronounce the initial, medial vowel, and final sounds (phonemes) in three-phoneme words. **RF.K.2d**

 I Do Display the *Pear* **Photo Card**. *This is a pear. The first sound in* pear *is /p/. Say it with me.* Repeat with the *Jump* Photo Card and the final sound /p/.

 We Do Say *pear* and have children repeat it. *What is the first sound in* pear? Say the sound together. Repeat with *pat, mad, sat, cap,* and *nap.*

 You Do Say *pad, am, mad, pan, sack, ant, pal.* Have children tell the initial sound. Then say *Sam, map,* and *sap* and have children tell the ending sound.

PHONEME BLENDING

OBJECTIVES

CCSS Isolate and pronounce the initial, medial vowel, and final sounds (phonemes) in three-phoneme words. **RF.K.2d**

 I Do Place the *Map, Mop, Pen, Pig,* and *Pie* Photo Cards facedown. Choose a card. Do not show card to children. Say the sounds in the word. *These are the sounds in the word:* /m/ /o/ /p/. *I will blend the sounds:* /mmmooop/, mop. *The word is* mop. Show the picture.

 We Do Choose another picture and say the sounds in the word. Together say the sounds and blend them to say the word. Then show the picture.

 You Do Choose other Photo Cards. Say the sounds and have children blend the sounds and say the word.

PHONEME CATEGORIZATION

OBJECTIVES

CCSS Isolate and pronounce the initial, medial vowel, and final sounds (phonemes) in three-phoneme words. **RF.K.2d**

 I Do Display the *Penny, Pillow,* and *Moon* Photo Cards. *Listen:* penny, pillow, moon. Emphasize the initial sounds. Penny *and* pillow *begin with* /p/. Moon *does not begin with* /p/. Moon *does not belong.*

 We Do Display the *Paint, Pitcher,* and *Sing* Photo Cards. Have children name each picture with you. *Which word does not have the same beginning sound?*

 You Do Continue the activity with these Photo Card sets: *Pizza, Penguin, Man; Pea, Pie, Sandwich; Pumpkin, Pig, Apple.*

Phonics

REVIEW PHONICS

OBJECTIVES

 Demonstrate basic knowledge of one-to-one letter-sound correspondences by producing the primary or many of the most frequent sounds for each consonant. **RF.K.3a**

I Do Display **Reading/Writing Workshop**, p. 6. Point to the *Piano* **Sound-Spelling Card**. *What letter stands for the* /p/ *sound you hear at the beginning of* piano? *The letter is* p.

We Do Have children say the name of each picture. Then ask them to identify the words that begin and end with /p/.

You Do Have children read each word. Repeat, asking them to raise their hands if they hear /p/ in the beginning of the word. Ask them to clap their hands if they hear /p/ at the end of the word.

PICTURE SORT

OBJECTIVES

 Isolate and pronounce the initial, medial vowel, and final sounds (phonemes) in three-phoneme words. **RF.K.2d**

I Do Display **Word-Building Cards** *p* and *m* in a pocket chart. Then show the *Map* **Photo Card**. Say /m/ /a/ /p/, *map.* Tell children that the ending sound is /p/. *The letter* p *stands for* /p/. *I will put the* map *under the letter* p. Show the *Gem* Photo Card. Say /j/ /e/ /m/, gem. Tell children that the sound at the end of *gem* is /m/. The letter *m* stands for /m/. *I will put the* gem *Photo Card under the* m.

We Do Show the *Top* Photo Card and say *top.* Have children repeat. Then have them tell the sound they hear at the end of *top.* Ask them if they should place the photo under the *m* or the *p.* (*p*)

You Do Continue the activity using the *Farm, Mop, Inchworm, Soap,* and *Sheep* Photo Cards. Have children say the picture name and the sounds in the name. Then have them place the card under the *m* or *p.*

On Level

Phonics

BLEND WORDS WITH *p*

OBJECTIVES

 Isolate and pronounce the initial, medial vowel, and final sounds (phonemes) in three-phoneme words. **RF.K.2d**

I Do Write *s, a, p. This is the letter* s. *It stands for* /s/. *Say it with me:* /sss/. *This is the letter* a. *It stands for* /a/. *Say it with me:* /aaa/. *This is the letter* p. *It stands for* /p/. *Say it with me:* /p/. *I'll blend the sounds together to read the word:* /sssaaap/, sap.

We Do Write *map*. Guide children to blend the sounds in the word to read the word.

You Do Write *Pam, am*, and *sap* and have children blend the words sound by sound to read each word.

High-Frequency Words

REVIEW WORDS

OBJECTIVES

 Read common high-frequency words by sight. **RF.K.3c**

I Do Use High-Frequency Word Card *a* with the **Read/Spell/Write** routine to review *a*.

We Do Have children turn to p. 7 of **Reading/Writing Workshop 2**. Discuss the photographs and read aloud the sentences. Point to the word *a* and have children read it. Then chorally read the sentences. Have children frame the word *a* in the sentences and read the word.

You Do Say the word *a*. Ask children to close their eyes, picture the word, and write it as they see it. Have children self-correct.

Reteach previously introduced high-frequency words using the **Read/Spell/Write** routine.

Fluency Point to the **High-Frequency Word Cards** *I, can, the, we, see,* and *a* in random order. Have children chorally read. Repeat at a faster pace.

REREAD FOR FLUENCY

OBJECTIVES

CCSS Read emergent-reader texts with purpose and understanding. **RF.K.4**

 I Do

Point to the title "Pam Can See" on p. 8 of **Reading/Writing Workshop**. *When we read, we group words together rather than just read one word at a time. This makes our reading sound smoother and more natural.* Work with children to read for accuracy and expression. Model reading a page: *When I read, "Pam can see a pen," I read all the way to the end of the sentence before pausing. This makes my reading sound as if I am talking.*

 We Do

Reread p. 10. Then have children chorally read the page with you. Continue choral reading the remainder of the pages.

 You Do

Have children read "Pam Can See." Provide time to listen as children read the pages. Comment on their accuracy and expression and provide corrective feedback by modeling proper fluency.

Use the same routine for "We Can See!" on pp. 14–19.

Comprehension

SELF-SELECTED READING

OBJECTIVES

CCSS With prompting and support, ask and answer questions about key details in a text. **RL.K.1**

Apply the strategy and skill to reread the text.

Read Independently

Have children select a nonfiction text with photographs for sustained silent reading. Remind them to use the photographs to help them understand the information they are reading. Explain that details from the photographs can help them ask and answer questions before, during, and after reading.

Read Purposefully

Before reading, ask children to choose a photograph that shows an important detail in the text. After reading, invite children to explain how the photograph helped them answer a question they had while reading. Guide partners to explain how photographs help them understand the text.

→ Beyond Level

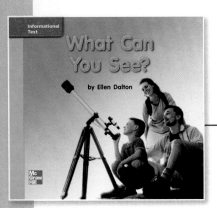

Leveled Reader

OBJECTIVES

 With prompting and support, ask and answer questions about key details in a text. **RI.K.1**

 With prompting and support, identify the main topic and retell key details of a text. **RI.K.2**

 With prompting and support, ask and answer questions about unknown words in a text. **RI.K.4**

 Read emergent-reader texts with purpose and understanding. **RF.K.4**

Leveled Reader:
What Can You See?

Leveled Readers

Before Reading

Preview and Predict

Read aloud the title and the author's name Ask: *What do you think this book will be about?* Turn to the title page and point out the title and the name of the author. Ask children to preview the photos. Did the photos confirm their predictions?

Review Genre: Informational Text

Explain that informational text is about real people, places, or events. Ask: *How can you tell that this is a informational text?* (There are photos. It is about real tools.)

Essential Question

Help children set a purpose for reading by asking: *Let's find out how tools help us learn about our world.*

During Reading

Guided Comprehension

Have children read the book. As they read, monitor and provide support by correcting blending and modeling the strategy and skill.

Strategy: Ask and Answer Questions

Remind children that good readers ask themselves questions as they read to help them understand the text. They can ask questions to help them read unfamiliar words and to help them understand what they are reading.

Skill: Key Details

Remind children that the words in the text don't always give all the key details. They can learn important information by looking at the pictures. After reading ask: *What details did you find in the pictures?*

Think Aloud As I read page 6, the words on the page don't tell me what tool the boy in the photograph is using. What I learn from the photograph is that a magnifying glass is one kind of tool that lets me see things up close.

Guide children to look at the photographs and tell what tool each child is using and what it does. Have them point to evidence in the text and photographs to support their statements.

After Reading

Respond to Reading

→ *How do the tools in this book help us see and learn about our world?* (Possible answers: They help us read about our world; look at tiny things; see things that are close and are far away; take pictures of things)

→ *Why do you think people need tools to learn?* (Possible answers: They help us see things better; they help us find out what other people have discovered.)

→ *What tools help us learn at school?* (Possible answers: books, pencils, the computer, magnifying glass)

Retell

Have children take turns retelling. Invite them to use the photographs, if needed, for support. Help children make a personal connection by asking: *Which one of the tools in the book would you like to use? Explain how it would help you learn more about your world.*

Gifted and Talented

EVALUATING Ask children why we need tools to help us learn more about our world. Challenge them to include examples of how specific tools make learning possible or to imagine new tools that would help us learn even more.

HAVE children share their ideas and decide which ones they like best and why.

LITERACY ACTIVITIES

Have children complete the activities on the inside back cover of the reader.

Beyond Level

Phonics

OBJECTIVES

 Demonstrate basic knowledge of one-to-one letter-sound correspondences by producing the primary or many of the most frequent sounds for each consonant. **RF.K.3a**

I Do Display **Reading/Writing Workshop**, p. 6. Point to the *Piano* **Sound-Spelling Card**. *What is the sound at the beginning of* piano? *What letter can stand for* /p/? *The letter is* p.

We Do Have children say the name of each picture. Then ask children to share other words they know that begin or end with /p/.

You Do Have partners read each word. Ask them to write the words on their **Response Boards**, underlining the letter in each word that stands for /p/.

High-Frequency Words

OBJECTIVES

 Read common high-frequency words by sight. **RF.K.3c**

I Do Create **High-Frequency Word Cards** for *boy* and *girl*. Introduce the words using the **Read/Spell/Write** routine.

We Do Display the High-Frequency Word Cards for *a, can, I, see, the,* and *we*. Have children help you complete the following sentence frames using the High-Frequency Word Cards: *The boy can see a* _____. *We see a girl* _____.

You Do Have partners write sentences using the High-Frequency Words *boy* and *girl* on their Response Boards. Have them read their sentences.

Fluency Have children turn to pp. 8–13 and 14–19 in Reading/Writing Workshop and reread the stories "Pam Can See" and "We Can See!" for fluency.

Innovate Have children create a new page for "Pam Can See," using the sentence frame *Pam can see* _____. For "We Can See!", have children complete the sentence frame *We can see a* _____. by adding other animals they might see in a zoo.

Vocabulary

ORAL VOCABULARY: SYNONYMS

OBJECTIVES

 With guidance and support from adults, explore word relationships and nuances in word meanings. **L.K.5**

Develop oral vocabulary: Synonyms

 I Do Review the meanings of the oral vocabulary words *discover* and *defeated*. Explain that a synonym is a word that means almost the same thing as another word. *A synonym for* discover *is* find. *When you* find *something, you see it and learn about it.* I want to find new plants in my backyard. *A synonym for* defeated *is* won. *If one team* won *it means they beat the other team.* Jill's soccer team won the game.

 We Do Think of a few sentences using the new words *find* and *won*. Say the sentences out loud.

 You Do Have partners orally complete and act out these sentence frames: I can *find* a _____. When my team *won* the game, we _____.

 Extend Remind children that antonyms are words that have opposite or nearly opposite meanings. Find and miss are antonyms. Won and lost are antonyms. Challenge partners to brainstorm a list of antonyms for find and won. Have them use their words in sentences.

Comprehension

SELF-SELECTED READING

OBJECTIVES

 With prompting and support, ask and answer questions about key details in a text. **RL.K.1**

Apply the strategy and skill to reread the text.

Read Independently

Have children pick a nonfiction text with photographs for sustained silent reading. Remind children that asking and answering questions as they read can help them understand key details in the text. The photographs often provide answers to their questions.

Read Purposefully

Before reading, ask children to choose a photograph that shows an important detail. After reading, invite children to share the photograph and explain how the details in it helped them answer a question they had while reading. Tell children to explain why photographs are often helpful in answering questions about nonfiction texts.

 Independent Study Have children write a few sentences describing what they found surprising or interesting about a nonfiction text they read this week. Ask them to create a book cover illustrating what they wrote about.

→ English Language Learners

Leveled Reader

OBJECTIVES

 With prompting and support, ask and answer questions about key details in a text. **RI.K.1**

 With prompting and support, ask and answer questions about unknown words in a text. **RI.K.4**

(CCSS) Actively engage in group reading activities with purpose and understanding. **RI.K.10**

Shared Read:
A Trip

Before Reading

Preview and Predict

Look at the cover photograph with children and ask them to name things they see. Make sure children understand the English words *fishing* and *trip* and the concept of a fishing trip. Read aloud the title and author as you point to them. Turn to the title page. Tell children that the photos show things that people might use on a fishing trip. Point to and name each item, using the pattern sentence: *I see a _____.* Guide children through the book to preview the photos and identify the rebuses on each page.

Essential Question

Set a purpose for reading: *What would these things be used for on a trip?* Encourage them to ask for help as needed. Remind children to look at the photos to help them read the words and answer the question.

During Reading

Interactive Question Response

Pages 2–3 Point to the photo on page 2. *What do we see on this page?* (a backpack) Point to the label next to the backpack and read it aloud with children. Say: *Let's read the words on this page.* Point to the photo on page 3 and ask children: *Now what can you see?* (a map) *Read this page with me.* Model and encourage children to point under each word as they read.

Pages 4–5 Point to the photo on page 4. Ask: *What do you see now?* (a pole) Point to the label next to the pole and read aloud the word. You may want to act out how you would use a fishing pole to provide context for children. Ask children to read page 4 with you. Have children look at page 5. Ask: *What do you see on this page?* (a pail)

Go
Digital

Leveled Readers

Pages 6–7 Ask children to look at the photo on page 6 and tell you what they see. (a paddle) Ask children to show how they would use a paddle. Have them point to the label on the page. Have children read the page with you. Continue to point under each word to reinforce basic print concepts. Point to the pump on page 7. Ask: *What do you see on this page?* (a pump) *What does a pump do?* Act out using a pump to provide context.

Page 8 Help children name the items in the photograph. Write the names of the items on self-stick notes and ask children where to place each label in your book.

After Reading

Respond to Reading

→ *What is this book about?* (things people use on a fishing trip)

→ *What are some things people bring on a fishing trip?* (a fishing pole, a map, a pail)

→ *What do you think is the most important thing to bring?* (a pole)

Retell

Ask children to look back through the book and take turns retelling. Prompt and support their retelling by modeling simple sentence structures they can use for their responses.

Model Fluency

Read the sentences one at a time as you track beneath the print, pointing to each word. Reread the sentences and have children echo-read with you.

Apply

Have children work with a partner to first name the tool on each page and then choral read the sentence together.

LITERACY ACTIVITIES

Have children complete the activities on the inside back cover of the reader.

Level Up

IF Children read *A Trip* **ELL Level** with fluency and correctly answer the Respond to Reading questions,

THEN Tell children that they will read another story about how people use tools.

• Have children page through *A Trip* **On Level** and conduct a picture walk to describe each picture in simple language.

• Have children read the story, monitoring their comprehension and providing assistance as necessary.

English Language Learners
Vocabulary

PRETEACH ORAL VOCABULARY

OBJECTIVES

Speak audibly and express thoughts, feelings, and ideas clearly. **SL.K.6**

LANGUAGE OBJECTIVE

Preview vocabulary

 I Do Display images from the **Visual Vocabulary Cards** and follow the routine to preteach the oral vocabulary words.

 We Do Display each image again and explain how it illustrates the word. Model using sentences to describe the image.

You Do Display the words again and have partners talk about how the picture demonstrates the word.

Beginning	Intermediate	Advanced/High
Have partners repeat each word. Then have them pantomime the meanings of *discover*, *defeated*, and *fetch*.	Provide sentence starters for the words. Have partners repeat and complete each sentence.	Ask partners to use one of the words in a sentence of their own.

PRETEACH ELL VOCABULARY

OBJECTIVES

Speak audibly and express thoughts, feelings, and ideas clearly. **SL.K.6**

LANGUAGE OBJECTIVE

Preview ELL vocabulary

 I Do Display the images from the **Visual Vocabulary Cards** one at a time to preteach the ELL vocabulary words *investigate* and *outdoors* and follow the routine. Say the word. Have children repeat it. Define the word in English.

 We Do Display each image again and incorporate the word in a short discussion about the image. Model using sentences to describe the image.

 You Do Display the image for *investigate* again and have children say the word. Provide children opportunities to use the word in a sentence by providing this sentence starter: *I investigate _____.*

Beginning	Intermediate	Advanced/High
Have children draw a picture of a person investigating something outdoors. Ask questions about the drawing to elicit language.	Ask pairs of children to work together to talk about the various things they might investigate.	Ask children to give additional examples of ways to complete the sentence frame *I investigate ____.*

High-Frequency Words

REVIEW WORDS

OBJECTIVES

Read common high-frequency words by sight (e.g., *the, of, to, you, she, my, is, are, do, does*). **RF.K.3c**

LANGUAGE OBJECTIVE

Review high-frequency words

 Display the **High-Frequency Word Card** for *a*. Read the word. Use the **Read/Spell/Write** routine to teach the word. Have children write the word on their **Response Boards**.

 Write a sentence frame using *a: This is a _____*. Point to a book as you read the sentence aloud and complete it with the word *book*. Ask children to repeat. Then point to other objects and ask children to help you complete the sentence. If necessary, refer to the back of the **Visual Vocabulary Card** for support.

 Ask partners to look through familiar books to find the word *a*.

Beginning	Intermediate	Advanced/High
Help children locate the word *a* in sentences. Read the sentence and have children repeat.	Read a sentence with the word *a* in it. Have children clap and say *a* when they hear the word.	Ask children to write the word *a* and use it in a sentence.

REVIEW CATEGORY WORDS

OBJECTIVES

Identify real-life connections between words and their use (e.g., note places at school that are colorful). **L.K.5c**

LANGUAGE OBJECTIVE

Use category words

 Display the following **Photo Cards**: *apple, balloon, horse, nut, egg, snow, corn, vest*. Say each word and have children repeat. Define the word in English and then, if appropriate, in Spanish, identifying any cognates.

 Write the words *red, brown, white,* and *yellow* and say the words aloud. Ask children to repeat each word after you. Tell children that these words name colors. Guide children to identify which Photo Card goes with each color.

 Have children work in small groups to identify the colors used in the illustrations in the **Reading/Writing Workshop**.

Beginning	Intermediate	Advanced/High
Prompt children to point out something in the picture that is blue. Say a sentence using the color word and have children repeat.	Ask children to talk about the colors they see with a partner.	Have children use the category words in sentences.

→ English Language Learners
Writing

SHARED WRITING

OBJECTIVES

 Use a combination of drawing, dictating, and writing to narrate a single event or several loosely linked events, tell about the events in the order in which they occurred, and provide a reaction to what happened. **W.K.3**

LANGUAGE OBJECTIVE

Contribute to a shared writing project

 I Do Review the words *shovel, fan, ruler,* and *crayon* from the Whole Group Shared Writing project as possible ideas for tools. Review the words *dig, stay cool, measure,* and *write* to tell what the tools do. Model writing a sentence about tools: *I use a ruler to measure.*

We Do Choose one of the tools. Ask children what the tool does and why people use it. Ask them to help you write a shared sentence using the word, for example: *We use a crayon to draw.*

You Do Have children choose a tool and write a sentence about it. Provide them with a sentence frame to get started, for example: *We use a _____ to _____.*

Beginning	Intermediate	Advanced/High
Provide pictures of tools to help children complete the sentence frame.	Provide a more complex sentence frame, such as: *A shovel is a tool that ____.*	Ask children to write and read a sentence about a tool. Provide feedback in pronunciation.

WRITING TRAIT: IDEAS

OBJECTIVES

 Use a combination of drawing, dictating, and writing to narrate a single event or several loosely linked events, tell about the events in the order in which they occurred, and provide a reaction to what happened. **W.K.3**

LANGUAGE OBJECTIVE

Use ideas in writing

 I Do Explain that writers must have good ideas to write about. Tell them that we can get ideas from things we read about. Say: *When I read, I get ideas for my writing.*

 We Do Point to the **Big Book** selection *The Handiest Things in the World.* Ask: *How does the story tell how tools help us explore?* Point out ideas from the text that demonstrate the idea of exploration.

 You Do Have children write a sentence about how tools can help us explore. Provide them with a sentence frame: *This tool can help us explore _____.*

Beginning	Intermediate	Advanced/High
Show children a picture of a tool, such as a shovel. Ask: *What is this tool? What can this tool help us do?*	Ask children to copy and complete the sentence frame with a partner.	Ask children to complete the sentence frame on their own. Challenge them to write another sentence about the tool.

Grammar

VERBS

OBJECTIVES

 Use frequently occurring nouns and verbs. **L.K.1b**

LANGUAGE OBJECTIVE

Identify and use verbs

Language Transfers Handbook

Cantonese, Haitian Creole, Hmong, Korean, and Vietnamese speakers do not use subject-verb agreement in their native language. Guide children to add an -s to present-tense verbs in third-person usage, such as *He likes pizza* instead of *He like pizza*.

I Do Review that a verb is an action word. Say the following sentence: *I swing the hammer.* Repeat the sentence. Say: *The verb in this sentence is* swing. Swing *is a word that shows action.*

We Do Say the following sentences. Have children help you identify the verb in each. Have them say: *The action word is _____.*

I play with toys.

You run to the park.

We jump.

You Do Say the following sentence: *Tools can _____.*

Pair children and have them orally complete the sentence frame by providing details from this week's readings. Circulate, listen in, and take note of each child's language use and proficiency.

Beginning	Intermediate	Advanced/High
Using the pictures of tools in the selections, ask: *What does this tool do?*	Ask children to use the illustrations to complete the sentence frame by providing a verb.	Ask children to complete the sentence frame without help, only looking back to the selection if necessary.

Use your Quick Check observations and the assessment opportunities identified below to evaluate children's progress in key skill areas.

✓ TESTED SKILLS CCSS	Quick Check Observations	Pencil and Paper Assessment
PHONEMIC AWARENESS/ PHONICS **p** /p/ (initial/final) **RF.K.3a**	Can children isolate /p/ and match it to the letter *Pp*?	Practice Book, pp. 51–52, 54
HIGH-FREQUENCY WORDS *a* **α** **RF.K.3c**	Can children recognize and read the high-frequency word?	Practice Book, pp. 55–56
COMPREHENSION Key Details **RI.K.1, RI.K.7**	As you read *The Handiest Things in the World* with children, can they identify and discuss key details using the photos and the text?	Practice Book, p. 53

Quick Check Rubric

Skills	1	2	3
PHONEMIC AWARENESS/ PHONICS	Does not connect the sound /p/ with the letters *Pp*.	Usually connects the sound /p/ with the letters *Pp*.	Consistently connects the sound /p/ with the letters *Pp*.
HIGH-FREQUENCY WORDS	Does not identify the high-frequency word.	Usually recognizes the high-frequency word with accuracy, but not speed.	Consistently recognizes the high-frequency word with speed and accuracy.
COMPREHENSION	Does not identify key details using the photos and text.	Usually identifies key details using the photos and text.	Consistently identifies key details using the photos and text.

Go Digital! www.connected.mcgraw-hill.com

Using Assessment Results

✓ TESTED SKILLS	If ...	Then ...
PHONEMIC AWARENESS/ PHONICS	**Quick Check Rubric:** Children consistently score 1 or **Pencil and Paper Assessment:** Children get 0–2 items correct	... reteach tested Phonemic Awareness and Phonics skills using Lessons 16–17 and 27–29 in the *Tier 2 Phonemic Awareness Intervention Online PDFs* and Lesson 12 in the *Tier 2 Phonics/Word Study Intervention Online PDFs.*
HIGH-FREQUENCY WORDS	**Quick Check Rubric:** Children consistently score 1	... reteach tested skills by using the High-Frequency Word Cards and asking children to read and spell the word. Point out any irregularities in sound-spellings.
COMPREHENSION	**Quick Check Rubric:** Children consistently score 1 or **Pencil and Paper Assessment:** Children get 0–1 items correct	... reteach tested skill using Lessons 13–15 in the *Tier 2 Comprehension Intervention Online PDFs.*

Response to Intervention

Use the children's assessment results to assist you in identifying children who will benefit from focused intervention.

Use the appropriate sections of the *Placement and Diagnostic Assessment* to designate children requiring:

 Tier 2 Intervention Online PDFs

 WonderWorks Intervention Program

→ Phonemic Awareness

→ Phonics

→ Vocabulary

→ Comprehension

→ Fluency

WEEKLY OVERVIEW

Literature Big Book

Listening Comprehension

Shapes All Around, 4–23
Genre Informational Text

"Find the Shapes," 24–31
Genre Informational Text

Interactive Read-Aloud Cards

"Kites in Flight"
Genre Informational Text

Oral Vocabulary

decoration	nature
games	world
materials	

Minilessons ✔ TESTED SKILLS (CCSS)

✔ **Comprehension Strategy** .... Ask and Answer
Questions, T95

✔ **Comprehension Skill** .... Key Details, T104

☞ **Go Digital**

www.connected.mcgraw-hill.com

Nathan Love

WEEK 2 →

Big Book and Little Book
Reading/Writing Workshop

Shared Reading

Tam can see Pam.

Sam can pat the cap.

"We Like Tam!" 26–31
Genre Fiction

"I Like Sam," 32–37
Genre Fiction

High-Frequency Word like, T99

Minilessons   ✓ TESTED SKILLS CCSS

✓ **Phonics** .... /t/t, T97

Writing Trait .... Ideas, T100

Grammar .... Verbs, T101

Differentiated Text

Approaching   **On Level**   **Beyond**   **ELL**

TEACH AND MANAGE

What You Do

INTRODUCE

Weekly Concept

Shapes All Around Us

**Reading/Writing Workshop
Big Book, 24–25**

TEACH AND APPLY

Listening Comprehension

Big Book
Shapes All Around
Paired Read "Find the Shapes"
Genre Informational Text

Minilessons
Strategy: Ask and Answer Questions
Skill: Key Details

Shared Reading

Reading/Writing Workshop
"We Like Tam!"
"I Like Sam"

Minilessons
/t/t, High-Frequency Word: *like*
Writing, Grammar

Go
Digital

**Interactive
Whiteboard**

**Interactive
Whiteboard**

Mobile

What Your Students Do

WEEKLY CONTRACT

PDF Online

PRACTICE AND ONLINE ACTIVITIES

Your Turn Practice Book, pp. 59–66

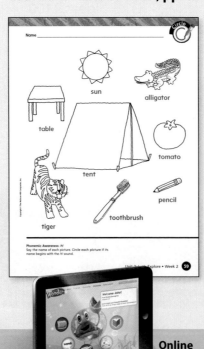

Leveled Readers

Go
Digital

**Online
To-Do List**

**Online
Activities**

Mobile

DIFFERENTIATE

Small Group Instruction
Leveled Readers

Mobile

INTEGRATE

Research and Inquiry
Shape Chart, pp. T134–T135

Text Connections
Compare Shapes, p. T136

Talk About Reading
Becoming Readers, p. T137

Online Research

WORKSTATION CARDS

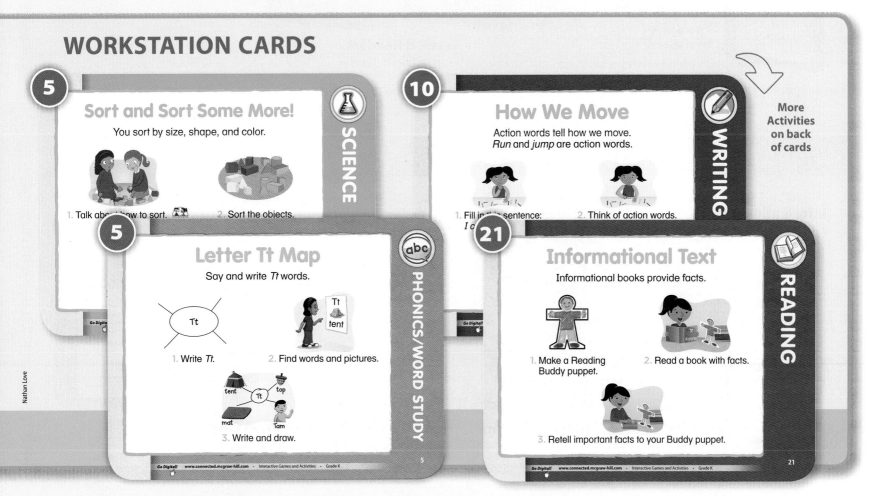

5 **Sort and Sort Some More!** *SCIENCE*
You sort by size, shape, and color.
1. Talk about how to sort. 2. Sort the objects.

10 **How We Move** *WRITING*
Action words tell how we move.
Run and *jump* are action words.
1. Fill in the sentence: *I c...* 2. Think of action words.

More Activities on back of cards

5 **Letter Tt Map** *PHONICS/WORD STUDY*
Say and write *Tt* words.
Tt
tent
1. Write *Tt*. 2. Find words and pictures.
tent — Tt — top
mat — Tam
3. Write and draw.

21 **Informational Text** *READING*
Informational books provide facts.
1. Make a Reading Buddy puppet. 2. Read a book with facts.
3. Retell important facts to your Buddy puppet.

Go Digital! www.connected.mcgraw-hill.com • Interactive Games and Activities • Grade K   5

Go Digital! www.connected.mcgraw-hill.com • Interactive Games and Activities • Grade K   21

Nathan Love

DEVELOPING READERS AND WRITERS

Write to Sources and Research

Respond to Reading, T95, T143, T151, T157, T161

Connect to Essential Question, T95, T127

Key Details, 104

Research and Inquiry, T134

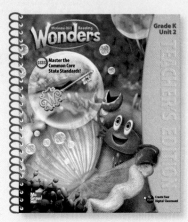

Teacher's Edition

Literature Big Book
Shapes All Around
Paired Read: *"Find the Shapes"*

Interactive Whiteboard

Leveled Readers
Responding to Texts

Informational Text
Observations, T122–T123, T132, T140

Conferencing Routines
Peer Conferences, T132

Interactive Whiteboard

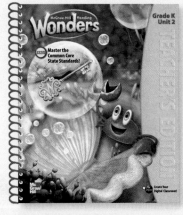

Teacher's Edition

Leveled Workstation Card
How We Move, Card 10

Writing Traits • Shared and Interactive Writing

Writing Trait:
Ideas
Observations, T100, T114

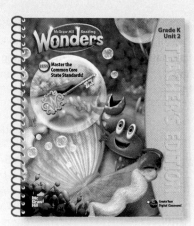

Teacher's Edition

Ideas,
pp. 38–39

Reading/Writing Workshop

Interactive Whiteboard

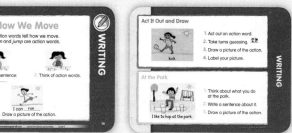

Leveled Workstation Card
How We Move, Card 10

Grammar and Spelling/Dictation

Grammar
Verbs, T101

Spelling/Dictation
Words with *t*, and *m, a, s, p,*
T129, T139

Interactive Whiteboard

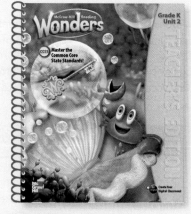

Teacher's Edition

Online Grammar Games

Handwriting

SUGGESTED LESSON PLAN

✓ TESTED SKILLS CCSS	**DAY 1**	**DAY 2**

READING — Whole Group

Teach and Model

Literature Big Book

Reading/ Writing Workshop

DAY 1

Build Background Shapes All Around Us, T92
Oral Vocabulary materials, nature, T92
✓ **Listening Comprehension**
• Genre: Informational Text
• Strategy: Ask and Answer Questions, T95
Big Book *Shapes All Around*
✓ **Word Work**
Phonemic Awareness
• Phoneme Isolation, T96
Phonics
• Introduce /t/t, T97
Handwriting Tt, T98
High-Frequency Word like, T99

Practice *Your Turn* 59–60

DAY 2

Oral Language Shapes All Around Us, T102
✓ **Category Words** Shape Words, T103
✓ **Listening Comprehension**
• Genre: Informational Text
• Strategy: Ask and Answer Questions, T104
• Skill: Key Details
• Guided Retelling
• Model Fluency, T109
Big Book *Shapes All Around*
✓ **Word Work**
Phonemic Awareness
• Phoneme Blending, T110
Phonics
• Blend Words with /t/t, T111
High-Frequency Words like, T111
Shared Reading "We Like Tam!" T112–T113

Practice *Your Turn* 61

DIFFERENTIATED INSTRUCTION — Small Group

Choose across the week to meet your student's needs.

Approaching Level

Day 1:
Leveled Reader *Shapes!* T142–T143
Phonological Awareness Onset and Rime Blending, T144 (TIER 2)
Phonics Sound-Spelling Review, T146 (TIER 2)
High-Frequency Words Reteach Words, T148 (TIER 2)

Day 2:
Leveled Reader *Shapes!* T142–T143
Phonemic Awareness Phoneme Isolation, T144 (TIER 2)
Phonics Connect *t* to /t/, T146 (TIER 2)
High-Frequency Words Reread for Fluency, T148 (TIER 2)

On Level

Day 1:
Leveled Reader *Play with Shapes!* T150–T151
Phonemic Awareness Phoneme Isolation, T152

Day 2:
Leveled Reader *Play with Shapes!* T150–T151
Phoneme Awareness Phoneme Blending, T152
Phonics Review Phonics, T153
High-Frequency Words Review Words, T154

Beyond Level

Day 1:
Leveled Reader *Use a Shape!* T156–T157
Phonics Review, T158

Day 2:
Leveled Reader *Use a Shape!*, T156–T157
High-Frequency Words Review, T158

English Language Learners

Day 1:
Leveled Reader *Play with Shapes!* T160–T161
Phonological Awareness Onset and Rime Blending, T144 (TIER 2)
Phonics Sound-Spelling Review, T146 (TIER 2)
Vocabulary Preteach Oral Vocabulary, T162
Writing Shared Writing, T164

Day 2:
Leveled Reader *Play with Shapes!* T160–T161
Phonemic Awareness Phoneme Isolation, T144 (TIER 2)
Phonics Connect *t* to /t/, T146 (TIER 2)
Vocabulary Preteach ELL Vocabulary, T162

LANGUAGE ARTS — Whole Group

Writing and Grammar

Day 1:
Shared Writing
Writing Trait: Ideas, T100
Make a Shape Poster, T100
Grammar Verbs, T101

Day 2:
Interactive Writing
Writing Trait: Ideas, T114
Make a Shape Poster, T114
Grammar Verbs, T115

DAY 3	DAY 4	DAY 5 Review and Assess

READING

Oral Language Shapes All Around Us, T116
Oral Vocabulary decoration, games, world, T116
✓**Listening Comprehension**
• Genre: Informational Text
• Strategy: Ask and Answer Questions, T117
• Make Connections, T117
Interactive Read Aloud "Kites in Flight,"T117
✓**Word Work**
Phonemic Awareness
• Phoneme Isolation, T118
Phonics
• Blend Words with *t*, and *m, s, a, p,* T119
High-Frequency Word like, T121

Practice *Your Turn* 62–64

Oral Language Shapes All Around Us, T124
✓**Category Words** Shapes, T125
✓**Listening Comprehension**
• Genre: Informational Text
• Strategy: Ask and Answer Questions, T126
• Text Feature: Bold Print
• Make Connections, T127
Big Book Paired Read: "Find the Shapes,"T126
✓**Word Work**
Phonemic Awareness
• Phoneme Blending, T128
Phonics
• Blend Words with *t*, and *m, a, s, p,* T128
High-Frequency Word like, T129
Shared Reading "I Like Sam,"T130–T131
Integrate Ideas Research and Inquiry, T134–T135

Practice *Your Turn* 65

Integrate Ideas
• Text Connections, T136
• Talk About Reading, T137
• Research and Inquiry, T137
✓**Word Work**
Phonemic Awareness
• Phoneme Identity, T138
Phonics
• Read Words with *t*, and *m, a, s, p,* T138
High-Frequency Word like, T139

Practice *Your Turn* 66

DIFFERENTIATED INSTRUCTION

Leveled Reader *Shapes!* T142–T143
Phonemic Awareness Phoneme Identity, T145
Phonics Reteach, T146
High-Frequency Words Reteach Words, T148

Leveled Reader *Shapes!* T142–T143
Phonemic Awareness Phoneme Blending, T145
Phonics Blend Words with /t/t, T147
Oral Vocabulary Review Words, T149

Leveled Reader Literacy Activities, T143
Phonemic Awareness Phoneme Blending, T145
Phonics Build Words with /t/t, T147
Build Fluency with Phonics, T147
Comprehension Self-Selected Reading, T149

Leveled Reader *Play with Shapes!* T150–T151
Phonemic Awareness Phoneme Identity, T152
Phonics Picture Sort, T153

Leveled Reader *Play with Shapes!* T150–T151
Phonics Blend Words with /t/t, T154
High-Frequency Words Reread for Fluency, T155

Leveled Reader Literacy Activities, T151
Comprehension Self-Selected Reading, T155

Leveled Reader *Use a Shape!* T156–T157
Vocabulary Oral Vocabulary: Synonyms, T159

Gifted and Talented

Leveled Reader *Use a Shape!* T156–T157
High-Frequency Words Innovate, T158

Leveled Reader Literacy Activities, T157
Comprehension Self-Selected Reading, T159

Gifted and Talented

Leveled Reader *Play with Shapes!* T160–T161
Phonemic Awareness Phoneme Identity, T145
Phonics Reteach, T146
High-Frequency Words Review Words, T163
Writing Writing Trait: Ideas, T164

Leveled Reader *Play with Shapes!* T160–T161
Phonemic Awareness Phoneme Blending, T145
Phonics Blend Words with /t/t, T147
High-Frequency Words
Review Category Words, T163
Grammar Verbs, T165

Leveled Reader Literacy Activities, T161
Phonemic Awareness Phoneme Blending, T145
Phonics Build Words with /t/t, T147
Build Fluency with Phonics, T147

LANGUAGE ARTS

Independent Writing
Writing Trait: Ideas, T122
Make a Shape Poster
Prewrite/Draft, T122–T123
Grammar Verbs, T123

Independent Writing
Writing Trait: Ideas, T132
Make a Shape Poster
Revise/Final Draft, T132
Grammar Verbs, T133

Independent Writing
Make a Shape Poster
Prepare/Present/Evaluate/Publish, T140
Grammar Verbs, T141

DIFFERENTIATE TO ACCELERATE

 A C T Scaffold to **A**ccess **C**omplex **T**ext

IF the text complexity of a particular section is too difficult for children

THEN see the references noted in the chart below for scaffolded instruction to help children Access Complex Text.

Qualitative / Quantitative
Reader and Task
TEXT COMPLEXITY

	Literature Big Book	Reading/Writing Workshop	Leveled Readers	

Quantitative	*Shapes All Around* **Lexile** 340	"We Like Tam!" **Lexile** BR	**Approaching Level** **Lexile** BR	**On Level** **Lexile** BR
	Paired Selection: "Find the Shapes" **Lexile** 70	"I Like Sam" **Lexile** BR	**Beyond Level** **Lexile** 140	**ELL** **Lexile** BR
Qualitative	**What Makes the Text Complex?** • **Connection of Ideas** Connect Text to Surroundings, T104 **A C T** *See Scaffolded Instruction in Teacher's Edition, T104.*	**What Makes the Text Complex?** **Foundational Skills** • Decoding with *t*, T110–T111 • Identifying high-frequency words, T111	**What Makes the Text Complex?** **Foundational Skills** • Decoding with *t* • Identifying high-frequency words *like* *See Level Up lessons online for Leveled Readers.*	
Reader and Task	The Introduce the Concept lesson on pages T92–T93 will help determine the reader's knowledge and engagement in the weekly concept. See pages T94–T95, T105–T109, T126–T127 and T134–T137 for questions and tasks for this text.	The Introduce the Concept lesson on pages T92–T93 will help determine the reader's knowledge and engagement in the weekly concept. See pages T112–T113, T130–T131 and T134–T137 for questions and tasks for this text.	The Introduce the Concept lesson on pages T92–T93 will help determine the reader's knowledge and engagement in the weekly concept. See pages T142–T143, T150–T151, T156–T157, T160–T161 and T134–T137 for questions and tasks for this text.	

Nathan Love

Monitor and *Differentiate*

IF	you need to differentiate instruction
THEN	use the Quick Checks to assess children's needs and select the appropriate small group instruction focus.

 **Quick Check**

Comprehension Strategy Ask and Answer Questions, T117

Phonemic Awareness/Phonics /t/*t* (initial, final), T99, T111, T121, T129, T139

High-Frequency Words *like*, T99, T111, T121, T129, T139

If No → | **Approaching** | **Reteach,** pp. T142–T149 |
|---|---|
| **ELL** | **Develop,** pp. T160–T165 |

If Yes → | **On Level** | **Review,** pp. T150–T155 |
|---|---|
| **Beyond Level** | **Extend,** pp. T156–T159 |

Level Up with Leveled Readers

IF	children can read their leveled text fluently and answer comprehension questions
THEN	work with the next level up to accelerate children's reading with more complex text.

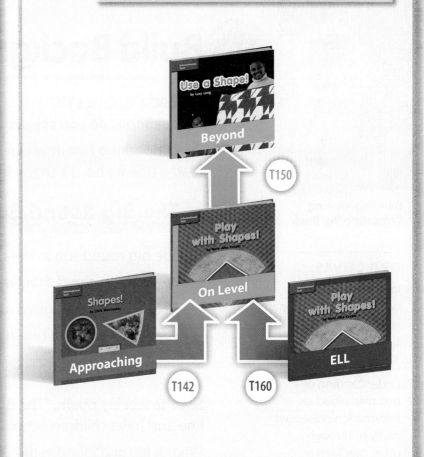

ENGLISH LANGUAGE LEARNERS
SCAFFOLD

| IF | ELL students need additional support | THEN | scaffold instruction using the small group suggestions. |

Reading-Writing Workshop T93	Leveled Reader T160–T161	Phonological Awareness	Phonics,	Oral Vocabulary, T162	Writing	Grammar
"Name That Shape""	*Play with Shapes!*	Onset and Rime Blending, T144	/t/*t* (initial, final), T146–T147	materials, nature, decoration, games, world	Shared Writing, T164	T165 Verbs
Integrate Ideas T135		Phoneme Isolation, T144		**High-Frequency Words,** T163	Writing Trait:	
		Phoneme Identity, T145		*like*	Ideas, T164	
		Phoneme Blending, T145				

Note: Include ELL Students in all small groups based on their needs.

Materials

Reading/Writing Workshop Big Book
UNIT 2

Literature Big Book
Shapes All Around

Visual Vocabulary Cards
materials
nature

Response Board

a b c

Word-Building Cards

Photo Cards
fork	sock
guitar	tie
jump	tiger
kite	toe
mix	top
pen	turtle
pie	
sing	

Sound-Spelling Cards
turtle

High-Frequency Word Cards
like

Think Aloud Cloud

"My Two-Ton Turtle"

Reading/Writing Workshop Big Book

OBJECTIVES

CCSS Identify real-life connections between words and their use. **L.K.5c**

CCSS Confirm understanding of a text read aloud or information presented orally or through other media by asking and answering questions about key details and requesting clarification if something is not understood. **SL.K.2**

→ Introduce the Concept

MINILESSON
10 Mins
Build Background

ESSENTIAL QUESTION

What shapes do you see around you?

Read aloud the Essential Question. Tell children that you are going to read a poem about a shape in the sky.

The Big Round Sun

The big round sun in the deep blue sky
Winked at a cloud that was passing by
The little cloud laughed as it scattered rain
Then out came the big round sun again.

Say the weekly poem, "The Big Round Sun," with children. Read each line and have children echo.

What is big and round in the sky? (the sun) Tell children that this week they will learn about shapes.

Oral Vocabulary Words

Use the **Define/Example/Ask** routine to introduce the oral vocabulary words **materials** and **nature**.

To introduce the theme "Shapes All Around Us," explain that we can find shapes in nature and in the things we use. Display an eraser. *What shape is this eraser?* (rectangle)

Go Digital

Shapes All Around Us

Video

Photos

Visual Glossary

Oral Vocabulary Routine

<u>Define:</u> **Materials** are things needed to make something or do an activity.

<u>Example:</u> I gathered the materials I need to make a birthday card.

<u>Ask:</u> What materials do you need to paint a picture?

<u>Define:</u> **Nature** is the animals, plants, and life around us.

<u>Example:</u> Two sounds I hear in nature are birds singing and leaves rustling.

<u>Ask:</u> What is your favorite way to spend time in nature?

Visual Vocabulary Cards

Talk About It: Shapes All Around Us

Discuss with children the shapes they see in nature each day. List their responses. Display pages 24–25 of the **Reading/Writing Workshop Big Book** and have children do the **Talk About It** activity with a partner.

READING/WRITING WORKSHOP BIG BOOK, pp. 24–25

Collaborative Conversations

Be Open to All Ideas As children engage in partner, small group, or whole group discussions, tell them:

→ That all ideas, questions, or comments are important.

→ To ask questions if something is unclear.

→ To respect the opinions of others.

→ To give their opinions, even if they are different from others'.

ENGLISH LANGUAGE LEARNERS SCAFFOLD

Beginning

Comprehend Point to one slice of pizza. *Is this a triangle shape?* (yes) Point to a pepperoni. *Is this a circle shape?* (yes) Repeat the answers as full sentences for the class.

Intermediate

Describe Ask children to describe the shapes they see in the photo. Encourage children to look for shapes inside other shapes. Elicit more details to support children's answers.

Advanced/Advanced High

Expand Have children use complete sentences to compare the shapes in the photograph. Provide the following prompts:

• The ____ has a ____ shape.

• The ____ and ____ have the same shape.

• The ____ and ____ have different shapes.

Correct the meaning of children's responses as needed.

→ # Listening Comprehension

Literature Big Book

OBJECTIVES

 CCSS With prompting and support, ask and answer questions about key details in a text. **RI.K.1**

CCSS Actively engage in group reading activities with purpose and understanding. **RI.K.10**

- Recognize characteristics of informational text
- Connect Big Book to Weekly Concept

ACADEMIC LANGUAGE

sentences, words

MINILESSON **10 Mins**

Read the Literature Big Book

Connect to Concept: Shapes All Around Us

Tell children that you will now read about the different shapes we see each day. *What shapes are in your room at home?*

Concepts of Print

Page Turning and Sentences Display the **Big Book**. Turn to pages 4–5. Remind children that sentences are made up of words. Point at each sentence as you count them with children. (three) Model how to turn the pages of the book from right to left. *When we turn a page, we begin reading on the left side.*

Genre: Informational Text

Model *Shapes All Around* is an informational text. Share these characteristics of informational text:

→ Informational texts give information about real things.

→ Many informational texts have photographs that show more information about the topic.

Selection Words Preview these words before reading:

rings: circle shapes
quilt: a blanket made from small squares of cloth
signs: pictures or words that tell directions

Set a Purpose for Reading

→ Read aloud the title and the name of the author.

→ Ask children to listen as you read the Big Book so they can find out about the shapes we see every day.

Go Digital

"Shapes All Around"

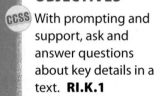

Think Aloud Cloud

Strategy: Ask and Answer Questions

Explain Remind children that they can ask questions before they read and as they read to help them better understand the story.

Think Aloud As I read this book, I will pause every few pages to ask questions. I will look for the answers as I continue reading. I can ask questions using words like *What?* or *Where?*

Model As you read, use the **Think Aloud Cloud** to model the strategy.

Think Aloud At the beginning of the book, I read that we are going to see many shapes. I ask: Which shapes will we see first? I find my answer on pages 6–7. We see circles first. There are many circles at the park. As I read, I will keep asking more questions.

Respond to Reading

After reading, prompt children to share the shapes they learned about and where they saw them. Discuss which questions they asked and how they found their answers. Then have children draw a picture of something from the book that is their favorite shape. Have children share what shape their picture is.

Make Connections

Use *Shapes All Around* to discuss how we can find shapes in the things we see each day. Revisit the concept behind the Essential Question *What shapes do you see all around you?* by paging through the Big Book.

Write About It Have children write about the different shapes they see as you flip the pages.

ENGLISH LANGUAGE LEARNERS SCAFFOLD

Beginning

Comprehend Point to the pictures on pages 6–7. Say: *We are looking for circles. Do you see circles?* (yes) *Do the rings have the same circle shape as the soccer ball?* (yes) Allow children ample time to respond.

Intermediate

Express Reread pages 6–7. Ask: *What is the same about the rings and the soccer ball?* (They are both round; both circles.) Have children point to the rings and circles on the pages. Model correct pronunciation as needed.

Advanced/Advanced High

Expand Reread pages 6–7. Remind children that they can find circles in other places, too. Ask: *Which items in our classroom have a circle shape?* (Possible responses: globe, clock) Repeat answers slowly and clearly to the class.

→ # Word Work

MINILESSON 5 Mins

Phonemic Awareness

OBJECTIVES

CCSS Isolate and pronounce the initial, medial vowel, and final sounds in three-phoneme words. **RF.K.2d**

CCSS Demonstrate basic knowledge of one-to-one letter-sound correspondences by producing the primary or many of the most frequent sounds for each consonant. **RF.K.3a**

Phoneme Isolation

1 Model Introduce initial /t/. Display the **Photo Card** for *turtle*. *Listen for the sound at the beginning of this word:* turtle. Turtle *has the /t/ sound at the beginning. Say the sound with me: /t/ /t/ /t/. Say each of the following words and have children repeat. Emphasize /t/: top, tank, ten.*

Photo Card

♪ *Let's play a song. Listen for words with /t/ at the beginning.* Play "My Two-Ton Turtle," and have children listen for /t/. *Let's listen to the song again and tap our heads when we hear words that begin with /t/.* Play or sing the letter song again, encouraging children to join in. Have children tap their heads when they hear a word that begins with /t/.

2 Guided Practice/Practice Display and name each Photo Card: *tiger, top, toe, tie. Say each picture name. Tell me the sound at the beginning of the word.* Guide practice with the first word.

Photo Cards

Phonemic Awareness

Phonics

Go Digital

ENGLISH LANGUAGE LEARNERS

Phonemic Awareness: Minimal Contrasts
Say /t/ and point out your mouth position. Have children repeat. Children may have difficulty distinguishing between final /t/ and /p/. Say the following word pairs emphasizing the final sounds and have children repeat: *lip/lit, hop/hot, cup/cut, deep/seat.*

ARTICULATION SUPPORT

Demonstrate the way to say /t/. Open your mouth a little. Put the tip of your tongue on the roof of your mouth. Don't use your voice. Flick the tongue forward and push out a little air. If you put your hand in front of your mouth, you should feel a quick puff of air. Say these words and have children repeat: *tip, tool, time, take, tale.* Emphasize initial /t/.

Phonics

10 Mins

turtle

Sound-Spelling Card

Introduce /t/ *t*

1 Model Display the *Turtle* **Sound-Spelling Card**. Say: *This is the Turtle card. The sound is /t/. The /t/ sound is spelled with the letter t. Say it with me: /t/. This is the sound at the beginning of the word turtle. Listen: /t/, /t/, /t/,* turtle. *What is the name of this letter?* (t) *What sound does this letter stand for?* (/t/)

Display "My Two-Ton Turtle" (see **Teacher's Resource Book** online). Read or sing the song with children. Reread the title and point out that the words *Two-Ton* and *Turtle* begins with the letter *t*. Model placing a self-stick note below the *t* in *Two-Ton* and *Turtle*.

2 Guided Practice/Practice Read each line of the song. Stop after each line and ask children to place self-stick notes below words that begin with *T* or *t* and say the letter name.

My Two-Ton Turtle

My two-ton turtle took a train to town.

My two-ton turtle tried to look around,

and then my two-ton turtle tried to trot,

but my two-ton turtle could not trot!

My two-ton turtle tried to climb a tree.

My two-ton turtle tried to see what he could see,

and then my two-ton turtle wondered why

he fell flat on his back when he tried to fly!

Oh, my two-ton turtle.

Oh, my two-ton turtle.

YOUR TURN PRACTICE BOOK pp. 59–60

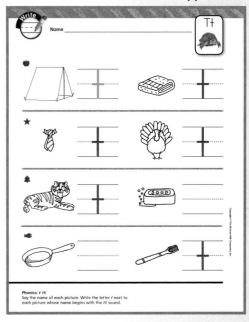

Corrective Feedback

Sound Error Model the sound /t/ in the initial position, then have children repeat the sound. *My turn.* Top. */t/.* Top. */t/. Now it's your turn.* Have children say the word and isolate the initial sound in *tie* and *ten*.

→ # Word Work

MINILESSON
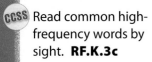
5 Mins

Handwriting: Write *Tt*

OBJECTIVES

CCSS Write a letter or letters for most consonant and short-vowel sounds. **L.K.2c**

CCSS Read common high-frequency words by sight. **RF.K.3c**

① Model Say the handwriting cues below as you write and then identify the upper and lowercase forms of *Tt*. Trace the letters on the board and in the air as you say /t/.

Straight down. Go back to the top. Straight across.

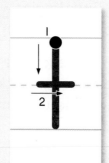
Start at the top line. Straight down. Go to the dotted line. Straight across.

② Guided Practice/Practice

→ Say the cues together as children trace both forms of the letter with their index finger. Have children identify the uppercase and lowercase forms of the letter.

→ Have children write *T* and *t* in the air as they say /t/ multiple times.

→ Distribute **Response Boards**. Observe children's pencil grip and paper position, and correct as necessary. Have children say /t/ every time they write the letter *Tt*.

 Daily Handwriting

Throughout the week teach uppercase and lowercase letters *Tt* using the Handwriting models. At the end of the week, have children use **Your Turn Practice Book** page 66 to practice handwriting.

Go Digital

Handwriting

| the | is |
| you | do |

High-Frequency Word Routine

MINILESSON
5 Mins

High-Frequency Words

like

like

High-Frequency Word Card

❶ Model Display the **Big Book** *Shapes All Around*. Point to the high-frequency word *like*. Then use the **High-Frequency Word Card** *like* with the **Read/Spell/Write** routine to teach the word.

→ **Read** Point to the word *like* and say the word. Say: *This is the word* like. *Say it with me:* like. *I like triangles*.

→ **Spell** *The word* like *is spelled* l-i-k-e. *Spell it with me*.

→ **Write** *Let's write the word in the air as we say each letter:* l-i-k-e.

→ Have partners create sentences using the word.

COLLABORATE
❷ Guided Practice/Practice Build sentences using the High-Frequency Word Cards, **Photo Cards**, and teacher-made punctuation cards. Have children point to the high-frequency word *like*. Use these sentences.

Also online

| I | like | the | 🐱 | . |

| I | like | the | ☕ | . |

| I | like | the | 📕 | . |

High-Frequency Words Practice

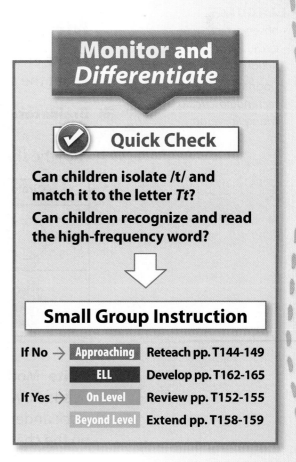

Monitor and *Differentiate*

✓ **Quick Check**

Can children isolate /t/ and match it to the letter *Tt*?

Can children recognize and read the high-frequency word?

⬇

Small Group Instruction

If No → | Approaching | Reteach pp. T144-149
| ELL | Develop pp. T162-165
If Yes → | On Level | Review pp. T152-155
| Beyond Level | Extend pp. T158-159

Language Arts

 Shared Writing
MINILESSON 10 Mins

OBJECTIVES

CCSS Use a combination of drawing, dictating, and writing to compose informative/explanatory texts in which they name what they are writing about and supply some information about the topic. **W.K.2**

CCSS Use frequently occurring nouns and verbs. **L.K.1b**

ACADEMIC LANGUAGE

• *observe, rectangle, circle, square, triangle, action word, verb*

• Cognates: *observar, rectángulo, círculo, triángulo, verbo*

Writing Trait: Ideas

1 Model Tell children that we can get ideas from observing our world. One way to observe is to look around and see things. Point out that *look* and *see* are action words.

→ Write and read aloud: *I look. I see a rectangle.* Draw a rectangle next to the sentence. Pick up a book. *This book has the shape of a rectangle.* Outline the shape, using your finger. *Look around the room. What do you see that has the shape of a rectangle?* Ask children to point to an object that is a rectangle, such as a table, and say *I see a rectangle.*

2 Guided Practice/Practice Write and read aloud: *I look. I see a circle.* Help children find objects in the room that are, or have, circle shapes, such as a clock.

Make a Shape Poster

Focus and Plan Tell children that this week they will make a poster about the shapes they see around them.

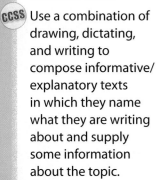 **Brainstorm** Have children name the shapes they are reading about. (circle, square, rectangle, triangle) Make a chart, labeling each column with the shape name and a picture of the shape.

Circle	Square	Rectangle	Triangle
○	□	▭	△

Write Model drawing a circular object, such as a clock, in the column headed *Circle. I see a circle. I see a clock. A clock has a circle shape.* Write *clock* under the drawing. Ask children to name other objects to draw on the chart. Draw each object on the chart and label it.

Go Digital

Writing

I see a fish.

Grammar

Grammar

5 Mins MINILESSON

Verbs

1 Model Remind children that a verb is an action word that tells what someone or something does. Display **Photo Cards** for *jump, mix,* and *sing.* Make sentences for each word.

→ Read aloud: *She jumps.* Ask children to name the action in the sentence. Ask a volunteer to demonstrate the action of jumping.

→ Read aloud: *He mixes.* Ask children to name the action in the sentence. Ask a volunteer to demonstrate the action of mixing.

→ Read aloud: *We sing.* Ask children to name the action in the sentence. Sing the weekly song together with children.

2 Guided Practice/Practice Display Photo Cards for *fork, guitar, kite,* and *pen.* Have children name an action that they can do with each object. Guide children in saying a sentence to describe the action, such as *I eat with a fork.*

Write children's sentences on the board. Read the sentences aloud. Have children raise their hands every time they hear an action word.

Talk About It

COLLABORATE

Have partners work together to orally generate sentences. Encourage children to create sentences with something they like to do, such as *I play tag.*

ENGLISH LANGUAGE LEARNERS SCAFFOLD

Beginning

Explain Demonstrate the action words *walk, jump,* and *clap.* Have children mirror the action. *I walk to school. Walk is an action word. I jump rope. Which word is the action word? I clap my hands. Which word is the action word?* Model correct pronunciation as needed.

Intermediate

Practice Write: *run, toy, jump, hop, book, play.* Read aloud the words slowly. Have children raise their hands when they hear an action word. Have children say the action words. Ask for volunteers to circle the action words. Repeat correct answers slowly and clearly to the class.

Advanced/Advanced High

Expand Direct children to do an action, such as *walk around a desk, jump three times,* and *clap your hands.* Encourage children to describe what they did in a sentence. Clarify children's responses as needed by providing vocabulary.

Daily Wrap Up

● Review the Essential Question and encourage children to discuss it, using the new oral vocabulary words. *What shapes do you see around you? What shapes can you see in nature?*

● Prompt children to share the skills they learned. How might they use those skills?

Materials

Reading/Writing Workshop Big Book
UNIT 2

Reading/Writing Workshop
UNIT 2

Literature Big Book
Shapes All Around

Visual Vocabulary Cards
materials
nature

Response Board

Retelling Cards

Puppet

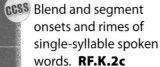
Word-Building Cards

Sound-Spelling Cards
turtle

High-Frequency Word Cards
a
can
I
like
see
the
we

Photo Cards
ball
cherry
game
ladder

⊙→ # Build the Concept

MINILESSON
10 Mins

Oral Language

OBJECTIVES

CCSS Use words and phrases acquired through conversations, reading and being read to, and responding to texts. **L.K.6**

CCSS Blend and segment onsets and rimes of single-syllable spoken words. **RF.K.2c**

CCSS Sort common objects into categories (e.g. shapes, foods) to gain a sense of the concepts the categories represent. **L.K.5a**

Develop oral vocabulary

ACADEMIC LANGUAGE
• poem
• Cognates: *poema*

ESSENTIAL QUESTION

What shapes do you see around you?

Remind children that this week they are learning about different shapes. Point out that they can see shapes in many places, such as the classroom or nature.

Read with children the weekly poem, "The Big Round Sun."

Phonological Awareness

Onset/Rime Blending

Remind children that the word *sun* is in today's poem. Say: *sun*. Have children tell you the first sound. (/s/) Tell them the ending sounds for this word are /un/. Show how to blend the beginning and ending sounds together to make a word. (/s/ /un/ *sun*) Have children repeat after you. Then tell them that you will say the first sound and the ending sound of a word. Have them put the sounds together and say the whole word: /r/ /un/ (run); /b/ /ig/ (big); /k/ /at/ (cat); /d/ /ôg/ (dog)

Review Visual Vocabulary

Use the **Define/Example/Ask** routine to review the oral vocabulary words **materials** and **nature**. Prompt children to use the words in sentences.

Visual Vocabulary Cards

Go Digital

Visual Glossary

Category Words

squares, rectangles and triangles. Tell children that we can sort things by their shape. Use blocks to demonstrate sorting by shapes. Use three blocks for each of the following shapes: *triangle, square, rectangle,* and *circle.* If needed, use a cylinder for a circle and point out the circular end.

Hold up a cube. *This is a square. I will make a square group.* Hold up a triangle. *This is a triangle. I will make a triangle group.* Continue demonstrating how to sort the blocks by shape.

❷ **Guided Practice/Practice** Distribute sets of blocks to small groups or partners. Each set should have three triangles, squares, rectangles and circles for a total of twelve blocks. Have children work together to sort by shape. Guide practice as needed.

LET'S MOVE!

Ask children to work together as one group, or in small groups, to stand in the shape of a triangle, circle, rectangle, and square. Challenge them to think of other ways to make shapes with their bodies.

Describe Point to objects in the classroom that are in the shapes of circles, squares, triangles, and rectangles. Say: *This table is in the shape of a rectangle.* Then move your hand around the edge of the table. Ask: *What other things are shaped like a rectangle?* Repeat with the shape words *circle, triangle,* and *square.*

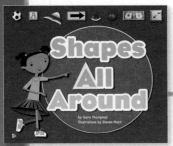

Literature Big Book

Reread Literature Big Book

Genre: Informational Text

Display *Shapes All Around*. Remind children that informational texts give facts about real life. The places and things in informational texts are real. *How do you know* Shapes All Around *is informational text?* (It tells about real things and real shapes.) Have children point to evidence in the text and photos that support their answers.

Strategy: Ask and Answer Questions

Remind children that good readers ask and answer questions before and during reading. *As we read, you can ask questions and look for the answers later in the story.*

Skill: Key Details

Tell children that they can learn important things from the text and the photographs in the story. Point out that sometimes photographs give information that is not in the author's words. *The photographs can help you find the answer to a question.* As you read, have children listen and look for evidence in the text and photographs to find details.

Access Complex Text

Connections of Ideas Children might be confused by the specificity of the text. For example, the windows in your classroom might be rectangles, not squares. Signs can be circles, but not all signs are circles. As the text later notes, signs can also be rectangles and triangles. Help children connect the information in the text to their environment, making adjustments.

→ Guide children to correctly name the shapes they see, such as your classroom windows.

OBJECTIVES

CCSS With prompting and support, ask and answer questions about key details in a text. **RI.K.1**

CCSS With prompting and support, describe the connection between two individuals, events, ideas, or pieces of information in a text. **RI.K.3**

• Strategy: Ask and Answer Questions
• Skill: Key Details
• Retell story

ACADEMIC LANGUAGE
before, after

Go Digital

"Shapes All Around"

Retelling Cards

PAGES 4–5

PHONICS

Reread the second sentence on page 5 and have children identify the word with the initial /t/ sound. (triangles)

KEY DETAILS

What shapes can you see in the picture? (circles, squares, rectangles, and triangles)

PAGES 6–7

CONCEPTS OF PRINT

Which page should I read first? (left) *Which page should I read next?* (right) *How should I turn the page to read more?* (from right to left)

PAGES 8–9

ASK AND ANSWER QUESTIONS

Think Aloud I know I can ask and answer questions as I read. This text asks me a question about the umbrellas on page 9. It asks: How many do you see? I count the umbrellas to answer the question. There are 23 umbrellas.

pp. 8–9

parade: Explain that *on parade* is another way of saying something is in a parade or on display. Have children pretend to hold umbrellas as they march in an imaginary parade. Encourage them to wave at the crowd.

Listening Comprehension

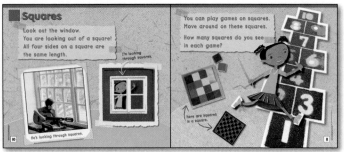

PAGES 10–11

KEY DETAILS

Point to the hopscotch game on page 11. *Look at the picture. What does this hopscotch game have besides squares?* (numbers)

PAGES 12–13

CONCEPTS OF PRINT

Remind children that sentences are made up of words. Trace the sentences with your finger as you count them aloud. Repeat the activity while children count with you.

pp. 12–13

quilt: Explain that a *quilt* is a kind of warm blanket. *Many quilts are made of many different pieces of cloth.* Point to the quilt in the picture to guide understanding.

PAGES 14–15

KEY DETAILS

What shapes do these pages tell about? (rectangles) *What other shapes do you see on these pages?* (a circle on the soccer field; triangles on the houses)

PAGES 16–17

ASK AND ANSWER QUESTIONS

Think Aloud I have read about circles, squares and rectangles. I wonder what other shapes the book will tell about. I will keep reading to find the answer.

pp. 16–17

find our way: When people say "find our way," they are talking about how to get somewhere. Do you know the way to the playground? How do we get there?

PAGES 18–19

KEY DETAILS

What does the text mean when it says, "Cut a square and make triangles?" How do you know? (It means cut up a sandwich. The photo shows a sandwich cut into triangles.)

pp. 18–19

runs off: Flutter your fingers in a downward motion to show what water looks like when it runs off a roof. Say the phrase aloud and have children echo.

PAGES 20–21

ASK AND ANSWER QUESTIONS

We have read about rectangle signs and triangle signs. Do you think we will read about other sign shapes? What questions do you have about the shapes we have read about?

Listening Comprehension

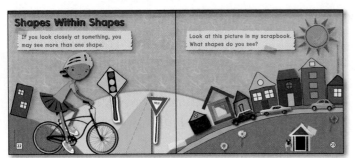

PAGES 22–23

AUTHOR'S PURPOSE

Why do you think the author wrote this informational text? (to show the shapes around us)

pp. 22–23

scrapbook: Explain that a *scrapbook* is a book with blank pages that you can fill up with photos from magazines or newspapers or your own drawings. *Scrapbooks can be a fun way to tell about something you like.*

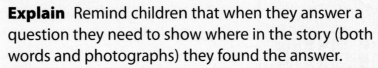

Text Evidence

Explain Remind children that when they answer a question they need to show where in the story (both words and photographs) they found the answer.

Discuss *Why is a triangle a good shape for the roof on a house? How do you know?* (The triangle roof helps when it rains. The rain runs off the sides of the triangle. The words on page 19 tell me this.)

Guided Retelling

Tell children that now they will use the **Retelling Cards** to retell the story.

→ Display Retelling Card 1. Based on children's needs, use either the Guided or ELL retelling prompts. The ELL prompts contain support for English language learners based on level of language acquisition. Repeat with the rest of the cards, using the prompts as a guide.

→ Discuss the selection. Flip through the pages with children and have them name the shapes of the objects.

→ Have partners make the shapes from the text with their hands or arms.

Model Fluency

Reread pages 6 and 7 of *Shapes All Around* and point out the exclamation points at the ends of the sentences. Remind children that exclamation points show strong feelings or excitement. We can use our voice to express how an author is feeling when we read aloud. Reread the page with proper expression. Have children echo the lines.

Retelling Cards

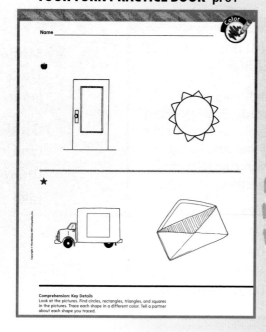

YOUR TURN PRACTICE BOOK p. 61

→ # Word Work

Quick Review

Build Fluency: Sound-Spellings: Show the following **Word-Building Cards:** *a, m, p, s, t.* Have children chorally say each sound. Repeat and vary the pace.

MINILESSON 5 Mins

Phonemic Awareness

Puppet

Phoneme Blending

OBJECTIVES

CCSS Demonstrate basic knowledge of one-to-one letter-sound correspondences by producing the primary or many of the most frequent sounds for each consonant. **RF.K.3a**

CCSS Read common high-frequency words by sight. **RF.K.3c**

Blend phonemes to make a word

❶ **Model** Use the puppet to demonstrate how to blend phonemes to make words. *The puppet is going to say sounds in a word: /t/ /a/ p/. It can blend those sounds to make a word: /taaap/ tap. When the puppet blends the sounds together, it makes the word* tap. *Listen as the puppet blends more sounds to make words.* Model phoneme blending with the following:

/t/ /i/ /n/ tin   /t/ /u/ /g/ tug   /t/ /o/ /p/ top

❷ **Guided Practice/Practice** *Listen to the puppet say the sounds in a different word: /t/ /i/ /p/. Let's blend the sounds and say the words with the puppet: /t/ /i/ /p/, /tiiip/ tip.* Tell children to listen as the puppet says the sounds in words. Tell them to repeat the sounds, and then blend them to say the word.

/t/ /a/ /g/ tag   /t/ /a/ /k/ tack   /t/ /e/ /l/ tell

MINILESSON 5 Mins

Phonics

Tt

turtle

Sound-Spelling Card

Review /t/t

❶ **Model** Display the *turtle* **Sound-Spelling Card.** *This is the letter* t. *The letter* t *stands for the sound /t/ as in the word* turtle. *What is the letter?* (t) *What sound does the letter* t *stand for?* (/t/)

❷ **Guided Practice/Practice** Have children listen as you say some words. Ask them to write the letter *t* on their **Response Boards** if the word begins with /t/. Do the first two words with children.

take   man   toss   ten   sock   tool   tile   tell

Go Digital

Phonemic Awareness

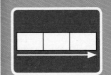

c a t

Phonics

| the | is |
| you | do |

High-Frequency Word Routine

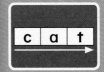

A A
a a

Handwriting

ELL

ENGLISH LANGUAGE LEARNERS

High-Frequency Words: Build Meaning Reinforce the meaning of the word *like* by asking the following questions.

• Do you *like* to run?

• Do you *like* to read?

• Do you *like* to eat snacks?

• Do you *like* to laugh?

Point to the letter *t*. *This is the letter* t. *The letter* t *stands for /t/. Say /t/. This is the letter* a. *The letter* a *stands for /a/. Say /aaa/. This is the letter* p. *The letter* p *stands for /p/. Say /p/. Listen as I blend the sounds: /taaap/. Blend the sounds with me to read the word.*

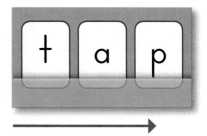

2 **Guided Practice/Practice** Use Word-Building Cards or write the word *tap*. Point to the letter *t* and have children say the sound. Point to the letter *a* and have children say the sound. Point to the letter *p* and have children say the sound. Then moving your hand from left to right under the word, have children blend and read the word, *tap*.

High-Frequency Words

5 Mins *MINILESSON*

like

1 **Guided Practice** Display the **High-Frequency Word Card** *like*. Use the **Read/Spell/Write** routine to teach the word. Ask children to close their eyes, picture the word in their minds, and then write it the way they see it. Have children self-correct by checking the High-Frequency Word Card.

like

High-Frequency Word Card

2 **Practice** Add the high-frequency word *like* to the word bank.

→ Have partners create a sentence using the word.

→ Have children count the number of letters in the word and then write the word again.

Cumulative Review Review words: *I, can, the, we, see, a.*

→ Repeat the **Read/Spell/Write** routine. Then, mix the words and have children chorally say each one.

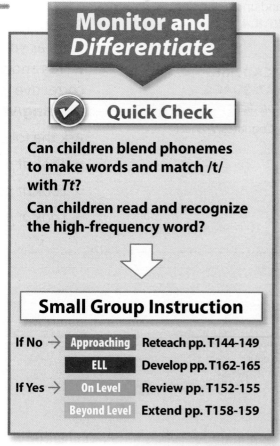

Monitor and *Differentiate*

✓ **Quick Check**

Can children blend phonemes to make words and match /t/ with *Tt*?

Can children read and recognize the high-frequency word?

Small Group Instruction

If No → **Approaching** Reteach pp. T144-149

ELL Develop pp. T162-165

If Yes → **On Level** Review pp. T152-155

Beyond Level Extend pp. T158-159

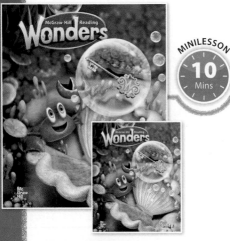

**Reading/Writing
Workshop Big Book
and Reading/Writing
Workshop**

OBJECTIVES

CCSS Read common high-frequency words by sight. **RF.K.3c**

CCSS Read emergent-reader texts with purpose and understanding. **RF.K.4**

ACADEMIC LANGUAGE

• *predict*

• Cognates: *predecir*

MINILESSON 10 Mins

Read "We Like Tam!"

Model Skills and Strategies

Model Book Handling Demonstrate book handling. *This is how I hold a book. This is the front cover. I make sure that the book is not upside down so that I can see the words.*

Model Concepts About Print Point to the first sentence of the story on page 27. Read the sentence and track the print with your finger. Explain what a sentence is. *This is a sentence. It is made up of a group of words.* Point to and read a word from the sentence. *When we read, we begin on the left, like this. When I finish reading, I turn the page.* Then display pages 28 and 29. Point to each page and say: *First we read the left page. Then we read the right page.* Demonstrate how to turn the pages of the book.

Predict Read the title together. Encourage children to describe the picture. Invite them to predict what the story will be about.

Read Have children chorally read the story with you. Point to each word as you read it together. Help children sound out the decodable words and say the sight words. If children have difficulty, provide corrective feedback, and guide them page by page using the student **Reading/Writing Workshop**.

Ask the following:

→ *Look at page 27. What is Tam doing?* (She is looking at Pam.)

→ *Look at page 28. What is Sam holding?* (a toy with a bell for Tam)

→ *Look at page 30. What object is Tam tapping?* (a bell)

Go Digital

"We Like Tam!"

"We Like Tam!"

READING/WRITING WORKSHOP, pp. 26–31

Rereading

Have small groups use the **Reading/Writing Workshop** to reread "We Like Tam!" Then review the skills and strategies using the *Phonics* and *Words to Know* pages that come before the selection.

→ Have children ask themselves questions as they read. Have them point to details in the pictures to help them find the answers. Remind them that they can also find the answers in the words.

→ Have children use page 25 to review the high-frequency word *like*.

→ Have children use page 24 to review that the letter *t* can stand for the sound /t/. Guide them to blend the sounds to read the words.

→ # Language Arts

MINILESSON
10 Mins

Interactive Writing

Writing Trait: Ideas

Review Tell children that writers can observe the world and write about what they see. *I can write about what I see. I will use an action word in my writing. I look around. I see something with a rectangle shape. Can you guess what I see? Yes! I see the board.* Write and say: *I see a rectangle. I see the board.*

Make a Shape Poster

Discuss Display the four-column chart from Day 1. Guide children as they say each shape name. Trace the shape around each item as you name it chorally.

Model/Apply Grammar Tell children that you will work together to write about shapes. Model finding an item that has one of the four shapes. *I see a rectangle. Can you guess what I see? I see a table.* Trace the shape of the item as you name the shape.

Write the following sentence and frame: *I see a rectangle. I see a _____.*

Read the sentences together, tracing the print. Point out that *see* is an action word. Model how to choose a word to complete the second sentence. *What do you see that is a rectangle?* (window, table, book) Write the sentence, such as *I see a window.* Add the word to the chart.

Write Continue with another shape. Provide the sentence and frame: *I see a triangle. I see a _____.*

Guide children to complete the sentence frame with an object in the classroom that has a triangle. Write the word in the sentence and add it to the chart. Share the pen with children and have them write the letters they know.

OBJECTIVES

 Use a combination of drawing, dictating, and writing to compose information/explanatory texts in which they name what they are writing about and supply some information about the topic. **W.K.2**

 Use frequently occurring nouns and verbs. **L.K.1b**

ACADEMIC LANGUAGE

• *observe, rectangle, circle, square, triangle, action word, verb*

• Cognates: *observar, rectángulo, círculo, triángulo, verbo*

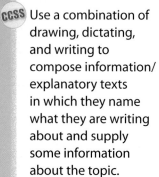

Go Digital

Writing

I see a fish.

Grammar

MINILESSON
5 Mins

Grammar

Verbs

1 **Review** Remind children that a verb is an action word that tells what someone or something does. Write and read aloud: *I paint a picture.*

What is the action word in the sentence? (paint) Underline the word *paint*.

→ Write the following groups of words:

> *a rectangle*
> *I see*

Read the groups of words aloud and have children chorally repeat. Ask children which group of words has an action word.

2 **Guided Practice** Write and read the words *pick, fold,* and *roll.* Tell children that you will write about things you do using these words. *I pick a flower. What word tells about an action?* (pick)

Point to the other words. *Which action word tells what I can do to a ball?* (roll) *Yes, I can roll a ball. What do you do with clothes after they are cleaned?* (You fold them.)

3 **Practice** Have children work in small groups. Provide each group with action words, such as *look, hear,* and *play.* Have groups brainstorm a sentence for each action. Have groups read their sentences aloud.

Talk About It

Have partners work together to orally generate sentences with verbs. Encourage children to create sentences with something they hear, such as *I hear dogs.*

ENGLISH LANGUAGE LEARNERS

Use Visuals Display **Photo Cards** for *ball, cherry, game,* and *ladder.* Say the name of each object. *What can you do with these things?* Have children draw pictures of things they can do for one of the objects. Guide children in writing a label of the action for their drawings. Model the pronunciation for children. Have children repeat chorally after you.

Daily Wrap Up

- Discuss the Essential Question and encourage children to use the oral vocabulary words. *What shapes do we see around us in the classroom?*

- Prompt children to review and discuss the skills they used today. How do those skills help them?

Materials

Reading/Writing Workshop Big Book
UNIT 2

Visual Vocabulary Cards
world
decoration
games

Response Board

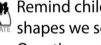

Word-Building Cards

Interactive Read-Aloud Cards

Photo Cards
bat
boat
boot
doll
feet
goat
hat

jet
light
nut
plate
soap
teeth
tie
tiger
top
toys
turkey
turtle

High-Frequency Word Cards
a
can
I
like
see
the
we

Think Aloud Clouds

"My Two-Ton Turtle"

(→) Build the Concept

MINILESSON
10 Mins

Oral Language

ESSENTIAL QUESTION

Remind children that this week they are talking and learning about shapes we see all around us. Guide children to discuss the Essential Question using information from the **Big Book** and the weekly rhyme.

Remind children about the circle shape of the sun in "The Big Round Sun." Say the poem and have children join in.

Oral Vocabulary

Review last week's oral vocabulary words, as well as *materials* and *nature* from Day 1. Then use the **Define/Example/Ask** routine to introduce *world, decoration,* and *games.*

Oral Vocabulary Routine

Define: The **world** is the planet Earth.

Example: There are many countries in the world.

Ask: What is the weather like in our part of the world?

Define: A **decoration** is something added to give color or shape to an object.

Example: I put a yellow, pink, and blue decoration on my cake because those are my favorite colors.

Ask: If you could choose any decoration for a party, what would it be?

Define: **Games** are fun activities with rules that people play.

Example: One of my favorite games is soccer.

Ask: What is one of your favorite games to play outside?

Visual Vocabulary Cards

Vocab
Define
Examp
Ask:

Go Digital

Visual Glossary

Kites in Flight

Think Aloud Cloud

Listening Comprehension

MINILESSON 10 Mins

Read the Interactive Read Aloud

Genre: Informational Text

Tell children you will be reading an informational text. Remind them that *informational text* tells true information about a subject. Display the **Interactive Read-Aloud Cards**.

Read the title. Point out that kites come in many interesting shapes.

Interactive Read-Aloud Cards

Strategy: Ask and Answer Questions

Remind children that good readers ask themselves questions as they read informational texts if there are things they do not understand. Guide children in recalling that they can use the **Think Aloud Cloud** as they ask and answer questions by remembering what they have read, by reading again, or by reading more.

Think Aloud I read that you can see kites all over the world. On this card there is a picture of people flying kites in Washington State, in the United States. I wonder where else in the world they fly kites. Will they look like the kites in the first photo? I will keep reading to try to find the answer to my question.

Read the text. Pause to model asking and answering questions.

Make Connections

COLLABORATE

Guide partners to connect "Kites in Flight" with *Shapes All Around*. *What is something that both of these selections told about?* (shapes, kites) Have children identify objects from both stories that share the same shape. Then ask them to tell about something that they only learned about from one of the selections.

ELL

ENGLISH LANGUAGE LEARNERS

Reinforce Meaning As you read "Kites in Flight," make meaning clear by pointing to specific characters, places, or objects in the photographs, demonstrating word meanings, paraphrasing text, and asking children questions. For example, on Card 2, point to a kite shaped like a square. Say: *This shape is called a square.* Repeat with other shapes.

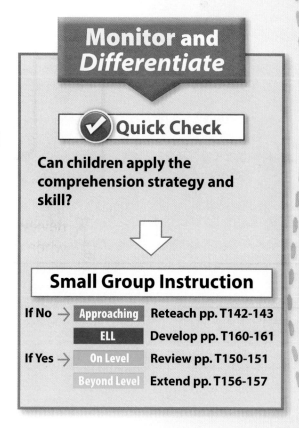

Monitor and *Differentiate*

✓ **Quick Check**

Can children apply the comprehension strategy and skill?

⬇

Small Group Instruction

If No →	**Approaching**	Reteach pp. T142-143
	ELL	Develop pp. T160-161
If Yes →	**On Level**	Review pp. T150-151
	Beyond Level	Extend pp. T156-157

→ # Word Work

Quick Review

Build Fluency: Sound-Spellings: Show the following **Word-Building Cards:** *a, m, p, s, t*. Have children chorally say each sound. Repeat and vary the pace.

MINILESSON
5 Mins

Phonemic Awareness

Photo Card

Phoneme Isolation

OBJECTIVES

CCSS Isolate and pronounce the initial, medial vowel, and final sounds in three-phoneme words. **RF.K.2d**

CCSS Demonstrate basic knowledge of one-to-one letter-sound correspondences by producing the primary or many of the most frequent sounds for each consonant. **RF.K.3a**

❶ **Model** Display the *Turtle* **Photo Card** and say the word. Turtle *has the /t/ sound at the beginning: /t/, /t/,* turtle. *Say the sound with me: /t/.* Tell children that now they will listen for the /t/ sound at the end of words. Display the *Bat* Photo Card. Have children say the word *bat* with you. Bat *has the /t/ sound at the end. Listen: /b/ /a/ /t/,* bat. Emphasize final /t/. *Let's say /t/ because we hear /t/ at the end of* bat: /t/.

❷ **Guided Practice/Practice** Say each of the following words and have children repeat. Have them say /t/ if they hear the sound at the end of the word. Guide children with the first word.

not   hut   mop   fit   cat   sit   cup   mat   lick

Then show Photo Cards for *light, bat, doll, jet, plate, soap, nut*. Have children say the name of each picture with you. Ask them to tell whether or not they hear /t/ at the end of the word.

Photo Cards

♪ Review initial /t/. Play "My Two-Ton Turtle." Have children clap when they hear initial /t/. Demonstrate as you sing with them.

Go Digital

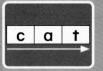

Phonemic Awareness

c a t

Phonics

Handwriting

Phonics

Word-Building Card

Review /t/*t*

① Model Display **Word-Building Card** *t. This is the letter* t. *The letter* t *stands for /t/, the sound you hear at the end of* mat. *Say the sound with me: /t/. I will write the letter* t *because* mat *has the /t/ sound at the end.*

② Guided Practice/Practice Tell children that you will say some words that have /t/ at the end and some words that do not. Have children say /t/ and write the letter *t* on their **Response Boards** when they hear /t/ at the end of a word. Guide practice with the first word.

hat   sip   bat   kit   not   sell   pet

Blend Words with *t* and *m, s, a, p*

① Model Display Word-Building Cards *m, a, t.* Say: *This is the letter* m. *It stands for /m/. This is the letter* a. *It stands for /a/. This is the letter* t. *It stands for /t/. Let's blend the three sounds together: /mmmaaat/. The word is* mat. Continue with *pat, sat, tap.*

② Guided Practice/Practice Write the following words and sentences. Have children read each word, blending the sounds. Guide practice with the first word.

at   Pat   sat   mat

Write these sentences and prompt children to read the connected text, sounding out the decodable words: *I see Pat. I see the mat.*

Corrective Feedback

Blending: Sound Error Model the sound that children missed, then have them repeat. For example, for the word *mat,* say: *My turn.* Tap under the letter *t* and ask: *What's the sound?* Return to the beginning of the word. *Let's start over.* Blend the word with children again.

YOUR TURN PRACTICE BOOK p. 62

→ # Word Work

OBJECTIVES

CCSS Read common high-frequency words by sight. **RF.K.3c**

Sort picture names of objects by initial and final /t/t

ACADEMIC LANGUAGE

sort

MINILESSON 5 Mins

Phonics

Photo Cards

Picture Sort

1 Model Remind children that the letter *t* stands for /t/. Place **Word-Building Card** *t* at the top of a pocket chart. Hold up the **Photo Card** for *tiger*. Tiger *has /t/ at the beginning of the word. Listen: /t/ /t/ tiger.* Place the Photo Card for *tiger* on the left side of the pocket chart. Repeat with final /t/ using the *Boat* Photo Card and place it on the right side of the pocket chart.

Hold up the *Turkey* Photo Card. *Here is the picture for* turkey. Turkey *has the /t/ sound at the beginning. I will place* turkey *under the* tiger *because both words begin with /t/.* Place the *Turkey* Photo Card under the *Tiger* Photo Card. Repeat for final /t/ using the *Nut* Photo Card.

2 Guided Practice/Practice Display and name each of the following Photo Cards: *toys, top, tie, teeth, goat, hat, boot, feet*. Have children sort the Photo Cards by initial and final /t/t .

Photo Cards

Go Digital

Phonics

High-Frequency Word Cards

High-Frequency Words

like

1 **Guided Practice** Display the **High-Frequency Word Card** *like*. Review the word using the **Read/Spell/Write** routine.

2 **Practice** Point to the High-Frequency Word Card *like* and have children read it. Repeat with previous weeks' words *I, can, the, we, see, a*.

Build Fluency

Word Automaticity Write the following sentences. Read each sentence aloud and then have children chorally read as you track the print with your finger.

I like Pam.
We can see Sam.
I like the mat.
We can see Pat.

Read for Fluency Distribute pages 63–64 of the **Your Turn Practice Book** and help children assemble their Take-Home Books. Chorally read the Take-Home Book with children. Then have children reread the book to review high-frequency words and build fluency.

YOUR TURN PRACTICE BOOK pp. 63–64

Monitor and Differentiate

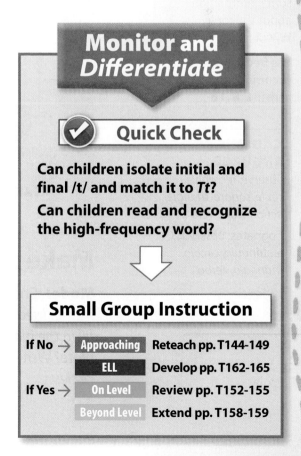

✓ **Quick Check**

Can children isolate initial and final /t/ and match it to *Tt*?

Can children read and recognize the high-frequency word?

Small Group Instruction

If No →	Approaching	Reteach pp. T144-149
	ELL	Develop pp. T162-165
If Yes →	On Level	Review pp. T152-155
	Beyond Level	Extend pp. T158-159

→ # Language Arts

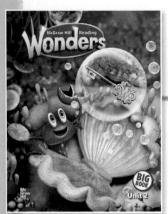

Reading/Writing Workshop Big Book

OBJECTIVES

CCSS Use a combination of drawing, dictating, and writing to compose informative/explanatory texts in which they name what they are writing about and supply some information about the topic. **W.K.2**

CCSS Use frequently occurring nouns and verbs. **L.K.1b**

ACADEMIC LANGUAGE

• *observe, rectangle, circle, square, triangle, action word, verb*

• Cognates: *observar, rectángulo, círculo, triángulo, verbo*

MINILESSON 10 Mins

Independent Writing

Writing Trait: Ideas

1 Practice Tell children that today they will make a shape poster. They will choose a shape and draw pictures of things that have that shape. Then they will label their posters with the shape name and write a sentence.

2 Guided Practice Share the Readers to Writers page in the **Reading/Writing Workshop Big Book**. Read the model sentences aloud.

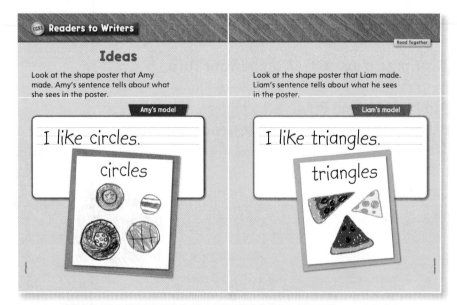

READING/WRITING WORKSHOP BIG BOOK, pp. 38–39

Make a Shape Poster

Model Show the **Photo Card** for *plate*. Write the following sentence frame: *I see a _____.* Point to the blank in the sentence. *We need to fill in the blank to make a complete sentence. What shape do you see in the plate?* Write *circle*. Read the sentence aloud, tracking the print. *I see a circle.*

Go Digital

Present the Lesson

Writing

I see a fish.

Grammar

Prewrite

Brainstorm Have children work with a partner to choose a shape. Ask them to think of objects that have that shape. Display the chart from Day 1 for children to use as a reference.

Draft

Ask children to draw a picture of something that has the shape they chose. Guide children in writing a shape label for their drawing. Help children copy and fill in the sentence frame: *I see a* _____.

Apply Writing Trait As children label their pictures and write their sentences, have them tell you what shape they chose. Ask children why they chose that shape.

Apply Grammar Have children read aloud their sentences. Ask them to identify the action word in their sentence.

Grammar

Verbs

❶ Review Write and read aloud: *throw, eat, bounce, sleep, toss,* and *catch. These are all action words. Some of these words can be used to tell what I can do with a ball.*

Write and read aloud: *I* _____ *the ball.* Ask children to fill in the sentence with an action word from the words on the board. Have children read aloud the sentences chorally.

❷ Guided Practice/Practice Write and read aloud: *I see a* _____. *I point to a* _____. *I will look around the room for an object that has a circle shape. I will point to the object and tell you what it is. I can fill in the sentences by telling what the shape is and what the object is. I see a circle. I point to a clock.* Have children tell you what the action words are in each sentence.

Have children work in pairs. Ask partners to take turns choosing an object in the room with a triangle, square, rectangle, or circle shape. Have partners point to the object and say the above sentence frames with the chosen shape and object.

Talk About It

Have partners work together to orally generate sentences with verbs. Encourage children to create sentences with something they see, such as *I see a box.*

Daily Wrap Up

- Review the Essential Question and encourage children to discuss using the oral vocabulary words *materials* and *nature. What shapes do you see around you? What other things have these shapes?*

- Prompt children to review and discuss the skills they used today. Guide them to give examples of how they used each skill.

Materials

Reading/Writing Workshop Big Book
UNIT 2

Reading/Writing Workshop
UNIT 2

Literature Big Book
Shapes All Around

Visual Vocabulary Cards
like

Word-Building Cards

Puppet

High-Frequency Word Cards
I
like
the

Interactive Read-Aloud Cards

Photo Cards
bike   ladder
cowboy   paint
doctor   phone
fox   top
gorilla   toys
kite

(→) # Extend the Concept

MINILESSON
10 Mins

Oral Language

Go Digital

ESSENTIAL QUESTION

Remind children that this week they have been talking and reading about shapes. Have them recite "The Big Round Sun." *What shape is the sun?* Then ask them to name the shapes in *Shapes All Around.*

Visual Glossary

Phonological Awareness

Onset/Rime Blending

After reciting the poem "The Big Round Sun," point out and say the words *by* and *sky. These words have the same end sounds, but their beginning sounds are different.* Say: /b/ /ī/ and /s/ /kī/. *We can blend other words with the same end sound. Listen to me blend the sounds to make new words:* /l/ /ap/, lap; /t/ /ap/ tap; /s/ /ap/ sap. Have children repeat the words as you blend them. Then have them blend sounds to make words: /t/ /an/ (tan), /m/ /an/ (man), /v/ /an/ (van).

"Kites in Flight"

Review Oral Vocabulary

Reread the Interactive Read Aloud Use the **Define/Example/Ask** routine to review the oral vocabulary words *materials, nature, world, decoration,* and *games.* Then have children listen as you reread "Kites in Flight." Ask the following questions:

→ *How do people in China put a decoration on a silk kite?* (by painting)

→ *In Brazil, children play games with kites that usually have a rectangle with a different shape on top. What is the shape on top?* (triangle)

Category Words

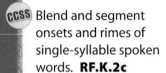

OBJECTIVES

CCSS Use words and phrases acquired through conversations, reading and being read to, and responding to texts. **L.K.6**

CCSS Blend and segment onsets and rimes of single-syllable spoken words. **RF.K.2c**

CCSS Sort common objects into categories (e.g., shapes, foods) to gain a sense of the concepts the categories represent. **L.K.5a**

Develop oral vocabulary

Category Words: Shapes

1 **Explain/Model** Read the following story. Tell children to raise their hands when they hear a shape word.

Julio went to a restaurant with Mom. Mom suggested that they look for different shapes. This is what they found. The plate was a circle. *The table was a* square. *The window was a* rectangle. *The roof was a* triangle. *Julio's hamburger was a* circle. *Mom's sandwich was a* square. *The piece of pie was a* triangle. *Julio didn't know shapes could taste so good!*

Explain to children that shapes can be found all around us. Point out that the door is a rectangle and that the clock is a circle.

2 **Guided Practice** Tell children that they will use classroom objects to sort by shape. Divide the class into four shape groups: *circle, square, rectangle* and *triangle*. Each group will identify objects of that shape within the classroom. Have each group share the objects they found with the class. Guide practice as needed.

LET'S MOVE!

Use the four shape groups that children were assigned. Give the groups directions that include shape words. For example: *Triangles, sit down. Squares, move to the bookcase. Circles, hold hands and form a circle. Rectangles, spin around.*

ENGLISH LANGUAGE LEARNERS

Understand Display Photo Cards that include different shapes, such as *phone, paint,* and *ladder*. Say: *Look for as many shapes as you can in the picture. Tell me what you see.* As children say the shapes, draw them on a piece of paper or on the board. Have children repeat the name of each shape as you draw it.

YOUR TURN PRACTICE BOOK p. 65

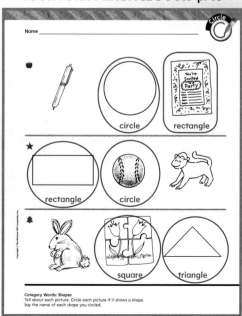

Category Words: Shapes
Tell about each picture. Circle each picture if it shows a shape.
Say the name of each shape you circled.

→ # Listening Comprehension

CLOSE READING

Literature Big Book

OBJECTIVES

CCSS With prompting and support, identify basic similarities in and differences between two texts on the same topic (e.g., in illustrations, descriptions, or procedures). **RI.K.9**

- Understand the characteristics of informational text
- Know and use the text feature bold print to recognize repetition
- Apply the comprehension strategy: Ask and Answer Questions
- Make connections across texts

ACADEMIC LANGUAGE
shape, bold print

MINILESSON
10 Mins

Read "Find the Shapes"

Genre: Informational Text

Display "Find the Shapes" on pages 24–31 of the **Big Book** and read aloud the title. Explain to children that this informational text is about the different shapes of objects.

Set a Purpose for Reading

Read aloud page 24. Tell children to listen as you continue reading to learn about shapes.

Strategy: Ask and Answer Questions

Remind children that good readers ask and answer questions as they read. Have children look at page 24. *We can ask: What shapes do you see? We can answer: circles, squares, triangles, rectangles.*

Text Feature: Bold Print

Explain Point to the bold print on pages 26–29. *The bold print is a question. The same question is repeated for all the riddles.*

Apply Point to the bold print on page 26. *To answer the question, we must read the clues above the question and look at the photographs. Which object answers the bold print question?* (the pillow)

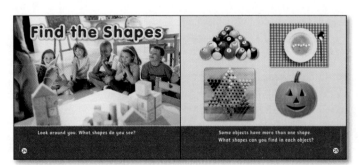

LITERATURE BIG BOOK   **PAGES 24–25**

KEY DETAILS

What shapes do you see in the photograph on page 25? (squares, circles, triangles, rectangles)

Go Digital

"Shapes All Around"

LITERATURE BIG BOOK   PAGES 26–27

KEY DETAILS

Look at the photograph on page 26. How are the pillow and block different? (The pillow is soft and the block is hard.)

LITERATURE BIG BOOK   PAGES 28–29

ASK AND ANSWER QUESTIONS

The riddles on pages 28 and 29 ask the same question: **What am I?** *What is the answer to each riddle?* (a bus; a sailboat)

LITERATURE BIG BOOK   PAGES 30–31

KEY DETAILS

What things in the photograph show shapes at school? (globe, lunch box)

ENGLISH LANGUAGE LEARNERS

Reinforce Meaning As you read aloud the text, make the meaning clear by pointing to details in the photographs. Ask children questions and elicit language.

Retell and Respond

Have children discuss the selection by asking the following questions:

→ *Which object has a circle shape and can bounce on a floor?* (the ball)

→ *What shapes do you see in money?* (circles and rectangles)

Make Connections

Have children recall the selections they have read this week.

→ *How are the selections alike?* (They show objects with different shapes.)

Write About It Write about one of the shapes you read about. Draw a picture of an object with that shape.

 CONNECT TO CONTENT

Sort the Shapes Review with children the objects with square shapes on page 26. (pillow, wood blocks, picture with frame) Have partners describe the properties of each object (size, shape, texture). Explain to children that we can sort objects, using these properties.

STEM

→ # Word Work

MINILESSON
5 Mins

Phonemic Awareness

Puppet

Phoneme Blending

OBJECTIVES

CCSS Distinguish between similarly spelled words by identifying the sounds of letters that differ. **RF.K.3d**

CCSS Read common high-frequency words by sight. **RF.K.3c**

• Blend phonemes to make words

• Blend letter sounds to make words

❶ **Model** *The puppet is going to say the sounds in a word. Listen: /m/ /a/ /t/. It can blend these sounds together: /mmmaaat/,* mat. *Now say the word with the puppet:* mat. *Repeat with* tap.

❷ **Guided Practice/Practice** Have children blend sounds to form words. *The puppet is going to say the sounds in a word. Listen as it says each sound. Repeat the sound, then blend them to say the word.* Guide practice with the first word.

| /s/ /a/ /t/ | /b/ /a/ /t/ | /t/ /o/ /p/ | /d/ /u/ /k/ | /k/ /ī/ /t/ |
| /t/ /i/ /p/ | /l/ /i/ /t/ | /p/ /i/ /t/ | /g/ /e/ /t/ | /h/ /o/ /p/ |

MINILESSON
5 Mins

Phonics

Blend Words with *t* and *m, a, s, p*

❶ **Guided Practice** Display **Word-Building Cards** *s, a, t.* Point to the letter *s.* Say: *This is the letter* s. *Letter* s *stands for /s/. Say /sss/. This is the letter* a. *Letter* a *stands for /a/. Listen as I blend the two sounds together /sssaaa/. Say /sssaaa/. This is the letter* t. *The letter* t *stands for /t/. Listen as I blend the three sounds /sssaaat/,* sat. *Now you say it. Let's change* s *to* m. *Repeat with* mat.

❷ **Practice** Write *mat, sat,* and *map, mat.* Have children blend the words. Say *mat* and *sat* and ask children to tell which sounds are different. (/m/, /s/) Have children look at both words and tell which letters are different. (m, s) Discuss the sounds each letter stands for and how it changes the word. Repeat with *map* and *mat.*

Then write *tap* and *pat.* Have children blend the words. Point out that each word has the same letters. Ask children to tell how the words are different. (The letters are in a different order.) Discuss how the sequence of letters changes the word.

Go Digital

Phonemic Awareness

Phonics

Handwriting

Visual Glossary

| the | is |
| you | do |

High-Frequency Word Routine

Phonics

MINILESSON 5 Mins

Dictation

Review Dictate the following sounds for children to spell. Have them repeat the sound and then write the letter that stands for the sound.

/m/   /a/   /s/   /p/   /t/

Dictate the following words for children to spell: *mat, sat, pat, map.* Model for children how to segment each word to scaffold the spelling.

Say: *When I say the word* mat, *I hear three sounds: /m/ /a/ /t/. I know the letter* m *stands for /m/, the letter* a *stands for /a/, and the letter* t *stands for /t/. I will write the letters* m, a, t *to spell the word* mat.

When children are finished, write the letters and words for them to self-correct.

High-Frequency Words

MINILESSON 5 Mins

Practice Say the word *like* and have children write it. Then display the **Visual Vocabulary Card** *like* and use the Teacher Talk routine on the back.

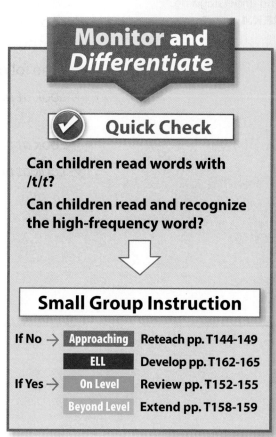

Visual Vocabulary Card

Build Fluency Build sentences in a pocket chart using **High-Frequency Word Cards, Photo Cards**, and teacher-made punctuation cards. Have children chorally read the sentences as you track the print. Then have them identify the word *like.*

> I *like* the top.
> I *like* the kite.
> I *like* the toys.

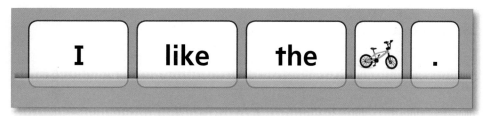

High-Frequency Words Practice

 Have partners create sentences using the word *like.*

Monitor and Differentiate

 **Quick Check**

Can children read words with /t/t?

Can children read and recognize the high-frequency word?

⬇

Small Group Instruction

If No →	Approaching	Reteach pp. T144–149
	ELL	Develop pp. T162–165
If Yes →	On Level	Review pp. T152–155
	Beyond Level	Extend pp. T158–159

→ # Shared Read

Reading/Writing
Workshop Big Book
and Reading/Writing
Workshop

OBJECTIVES

CCSS Read common high-
frequency words by
sight. **RF.K.3c**

CCSS Read emergent-reader
texts with purpose
and understanding.
RF.K.4

MINILESSON
10 Mins

Read "I Like Sam"

Model Skills and Strategies

Model Book Handling Demonstrate book handling. *This is how I
hold a book. This is the front cover. I make sure that the book is not upside
down so that I can see the words. This is how I turn the pages of the book.
When I turn to each page, I stop to read the words on it.*

Model Concepts About Print Read the first sentence of the story
on page 33. Track the print with your finger as you read. *When I read
a sentence, I start on the left side of the page. Remember that a sentence
is made up of words.* Then ask children to point to a word in the
sentence.

Predict Read the title and ask children to describe the illustration.
What do you think this story will be about?

Read Point out each rebus, and discuss what it stands for. Then
have children chorally read the story. Children should sound out the
decodable words and say the sight words. Offer support as needed
using the student **Reading/Writing Workshop**.

Ask the following:

→ *Look at page 33. What is the monkey's name? What is he doing?* (Sam;
he is patting the cap.)

→ *Look at page 34. What is Sam patting?* (a ball)

→ *Look at page 35. What round object is Sam tapping?* (a drum)

Go
Digital

"I Like Sam"

"I Like Sam"

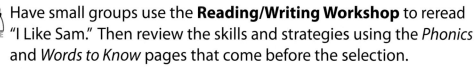

READING/WRITING WORKSHOP, pp. 32–37

Rereading

Have small groups use the **Reading/Writing Workshop** to reread "I Like Sam." Then review the skills and strategies using the *Phonics* and *Words to Know* pages that come before the selection.

→ As children reread each page, encourage them to ask each other questions. Then have them find the answers in the words and illustrations.

→ Have children use page 25 to review the high-frequency word *like*.

→ Have children use page 24 to review that the letter *t* can stand for the sound /t/. Guide children to blend the sounds to read the words.

ELL

ENGLISH LANGUAGE LEARNERS

Reinforce Vocabulary Display the **High-Frequency Word Cards** *I, like, the*. Point to classroom objects and groups of children as you use the high-frequency word in sentences such as the following: *I like the round clock. Do you like the round clock?* (Yes, I like the round clock.) *I like the square rug. Do you like the square rug?* (Yes, I like the square rug.)

→ # Language Arts

 ### MINILESSON
10 Mins

Independent Writing

Writing Trait: Ideas

OBJECTIVES

CCSS With guidance and support from adults, respond to questions and suggestions from peers and add details to strengthen writing as needed. **W.K.5**

CCSS Use frequently occurring nouns and verbs. **L.K.1b**

ACADEMIC LANGUAGE

• *revise, draft, rectangle, circle, square, triangle, action word, verb*

• Cognates: *revisar, rectángulo, círculo, triángulo, verbo*

Revise

Distribute the children's draft shape posters from Day 3.

Apply Writing Trait Ideas Explain that as writers revise, they can add new ideas. Suggest that children look around the room or in picture books for other objects that have the shape on their posters. For example, if the poster is about circles, what other things with circles can they add? Then have children review the poster they prepared on Day 3 and check for the following:

→ Did I choose a shape?

→ Did I draw pictures of things with the shape I chose?

→ Did I label my poster?

→ Does my sentence have an action word?

Apply Grammar Remind children that verbs are action words. *What actions did you use to make your shape poster?* (draw, write) *Why is* draw *a verb?* (The word tells about something I can do; it's an action.)

 Peer Edit Have children work with a partner to do a peer edit. Ask partners to check that each poster is about one shape. Have children check that every object on the poster has the correct shape, and that the label names the shape.

Final Draft

After children have edited their own posters and finished their peer edits, have them prepare the final draft of their posters. Explain that they should space out their pictures and label on the poster so that everything is readable. As children work, conference with them to provide guidance.

Go Digital

Writing

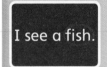

I see a fish.

Grammar

Grammar

MINILESSON 5 Mins

Verbs

❶ Review Have children pantomime actions they do with their hands. Ask them to identify the actions. Write the verbs on the board and read aloud with children.

❷ Guided Practice Have children think of things they do in the morning. *What things do you do in the morning?* (brush teeth, comb hair, eat breakfast) Write children's responses on the board.

Write sentences for their responses: *I brush my teeth. I comb my hair. I eat cereal.*

Ask children to say the action word in each sentence. Read aloud the sentences chorally with children.

❸ Practice Have children work in pairs to think of things they do in the evening.

Write this sentence frame on the board: *I _____.*

Have children work together to complete the sentence frame with something they do at night. Have children draw a picture of what they do. Guide children in writing the action word under their pictures. Ask children to read aloud each sentence they made. Provide support as needed.

Talk About It

Have partners work together to orally generate sentences with verbs. Encourage children to create sentences about something that they do in a park, such as *I play on the swing.*

ELL

ENGLISH LANGUAGE LEARNERS

Picture Cards and Sentences Provide sentences that go with images on **Photo Cards** for *cowboy, doctor, fox, gorilla.* As you read a sentence, hold up a Photo Card as you say the action word, such as *The cowboy rides a horse.*

Daily Wrap Up

- Review the Essential Question and encourage children to discuss using the oral vocabulary words.

- Prompt children to discuss the skills they practiced and learned today. Guide them to share examples of each skill.

→ **Go** Digital

www.connected.mcgraw-hill.com
RESOURCES
Research and Inquiry

→ ## Wrap Up the Week
Integrate Ideas

RESEARCH AND INQUIRY

Shapes All Around Us

OBJECTIVES

CCSS Participate in shared research and writing projects (e.g., explore a number of books by a favorite author and express opinions about them). **W.K.7**

CCSS With guidance and support from adults, recall information from experiences or gather information from provided sources to answer a question. **W.K.8**

ACADEMIC LANGUAGE
resources, research

Make a Chart

Tell children that today they will do a research project to explore the different shapes around them and make a class chart of shapes. Review the steps in the research process below.

STEP 1 Choose a Topic

Divide the class into four groups—circles, rectangles, squares, triangles. Draw the four shapes on the board. Explain that members of each group will work together to identify classroom objects that include their shape.

STEP 2 Find Resources

Talk about locating and using resources. Direct children to review the selections of the week. Prompt them to look around the classroom and observe the shapes of different objects. Have children use the Research Process Checklist online.

STEP 3 Keep Track of Ideas

Allow groups to collect classroom objects that are their chosen shape. Or have them list their ideas by drawing pictures and writing words.

Collaborative Conversations

Take Turns Talking As children engage in partner, small group, and whole class discussions, encourage them to:

→ take turns talking.

→ speak clearly and loudly enough so others can hear.

→ ask others to share their ideas and opinions.

STEM

This is a circle.

STEP 4 Create the Project: Shape Chart

Explain the characteristics of the project:

→ **Chart** The chart will give information about the shapes of objects in the classroom.

→ **Text** Each drawing of an object will have a sentence that tells what shape it is. Provide this sentence frame.

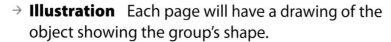

This is a _____ .

→ **Illustration** Each page will have a drawing of the object showing the group's shape.

Explain that each group will create pages for their shape. These pages will be put together on a bulletin board to create a four-column chart.

→ Guide children to write the name of the shape to complete the sentence frame.

→ Have children who can generate more writing do so.

→ Encourage children to include details in their illustration.

ELL ENGLISH LANGUAGE LEARNERS SCAFFOLD

Beginning	Intermediate	Advanced/Advanced High
Actively Engage Have children trace a shape in the air whenever they use a shape name. So, a child might say *The table is a circle* and then draw a circle in the air with his or her finger.	**Know and Use** Challenge children to identify and name multiple objects that show their chosen shape. Have children talk about the objects with sentences such as these: *I see a circle. It is a ____. I see another circle. It is a ____.*	**Describe** Have children extend their ideas outside of the classroom. Direct them to talk about objects that have their chosen shape which they see at home or on the way to school.

Materials

Reading/Writing Workshop Big Book
UNIT 2

Literature Big Book
Shapes All Around

Interactive Read-Aloud Cards

a b c

Word-Building Cards

Visual Vocabulary Cards

like

the

High-Frequency Word Cards

a
can
I
like
see
the
we

Photo Cards

ambulance
ant
ax
box
boy
bus
fan
fire

fish
man
mix
mouse
peach
pear
pen
pie
pizza
pumpkin
saw
seal
soap
teeth
tie

tiger
top
toys
turtle

Response Board

 "My Two-Ton Turtle"

→ Integrate Ideas

TEXT CONNECTIONS

Connect to Essential Question

OBJECTIVES

CCSS With prompting and support, identify basic similarities in and differences between two texts on the same topic (e.g., in illustrations, descriptions, or procedures). **RI.K.9**

CCSS Participate in collaborative conversations with diverse partners about *kindergarten topics and texts* with peers and adults in small and larger groups. **SL.K.1**

- Make connections among texts
- Make connections to the world

Text to Text

Remind children that they have read about shapes this week. Briefly review the week's selections. Tell them that now they will connect the texts, or think about how the selections are alike and different. Model comparing *Shapes All Around* with another selection from the week.

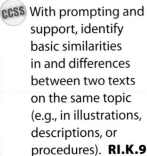

Think Aloud In *Shapes All Around* I saw so many shapes as the girl told us about all the shapes she knows about. In "Kites in Flight," I saw many of those same shapes! During the shape walk, I saw shapes in everyday objects. When I read about kites, I saw how those shapes were all made into kites.

Guide children to connect the various selections they have read this week, including Leveled Readers, and to talk about the shapes they have learned about.

Text to Self

Direct children to look at their clothing and at the things on the table or desk nearby. *What shapes are nearby?* Have children name shapes they see on themselves and on nearby objects.

Text to World

Talk about shapes children see on the way to school. *Do you see big buildings that are rectangles? Do you see buses with wheels that are circles?* Have each child name one thing and tell its shape.

TALK ABOUT READING

OBJECTIVES

 CCSS Confirm understanding of a text read aloud or information presented orally or through other media by asking and answering questions about key details and requesting clarification if something is not understood. **SL.K.2**

Becoming Readers

Talk with children about the genres, strategy, and skill they have learned about this week. Prompt them to discuss how this knowledge helps them to read and understand selections.

→ Remind children that they learned about informational texts. Have children recall some characteristics of informational texts.

→ Discuss with children the strategy of asking and answering questions. *How did stopping to ask and answer questions help you understand something about shapes?*

→ Talk about looking for key details in the text and photos. Remind students that looking at photos can help readers understand the text. *What kinds of photos do you remember from this week's selections? What did you learn by looking at details in the photos?*

RESEARCH AND INQUIRY

OBJECTIVES

 CCSS Participate in shared research and writing projects (e.g., explore a number of books by a favorite author and express opinions about them). **W.K.7**

Wrap Up the Project

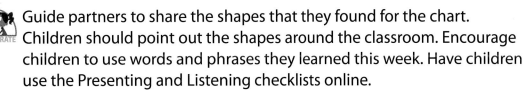 Guide partners to share the shapes that they found for the chart. Children should point out the shapes around the classroom. Encourage children to use words and phrases they learned this week. Have children use the Presenting and Listening checklists online.

→ # Word Work

Quick Review

Build Fluency: Sound-Spellings: Show the following **Word-Building Cards:** *a, m, p, s, t.* Have children chorally say each sound. Repeat and vary the pace.

MINILESSON
5 Mins

Phonemic Awareness

Phoneme Identity

OBJECTIVES

CCSS Spell simple words phonetically, drawing on knowledge of sound-letter relationships. **L.K.2d**

CCSS Read common high-frequency words by sight. **RF.K.3c**

• Identify phonemes that are the same

• Blend sounds to read words with /t/*t*

① Model Display the *Tiger, Tie,* and *Top* **Photo Cards**. *I will say three picture names:* tiger, tie, top. Have children repeat. *Which sound is the same in* tiger, tie, top? *Yes, the first sound, /t/, is the same.*

② Guided Practice/Practice Show children sets of Photo Cards. Name the pictures with children and have them say the sound that is the same. Guide practice with the first set of words.

tie, toys, top	saw, seal, soap	man, mouse, mix
tiger, teeth, turtle	boy, box, bus	pen, peach, pear
ax, ant, ambulance	pizza, pumpkin, pie	fire, fish, fan

MINILESSON
5 Mins

Phonics

Read Words with *t* and *m, a, s, p*

① Guided Practice Remind children that the letter *t* stands for the sound /t/. Display **Word-Building Cards** *t, a, p.* Point to the letter *t*. *The letter* t *stands for /t/. Say /t/. The letter* a *stands for /a/. Say /aaa/. The letter* p *stands for /p/. Say /p/. Let's blend the letters to make the word: /taaap/* tap. *Let's change the* t *to* s. Blend and read *sap* with children.

② Practice Write the words and sentences for children to read:

mat   tap   sat   Tam

We like Pat.
We see a mat.
Pam can tap.
Sam sat at the mat.

Remove words from view before dictation.

♪ Review /t/*t*. Have children write *t* on their **Response Boards**. Play and sing "My Two-Ton Turtle." Have them hold up their Response Boards to show *t* when they hear /t/. Demonstrate as you sing with children.

Go Digital

Phonemic Awareness

c a t

Phonics

Handwriting

| the | is |
| you | do |

High-Frequency Word Cards

Dictation

1 **Review** Dictate the following sounds for children to spell. As you say each sound, have children repeat it and then write the letter on their **Response Boards** that stands for the sound.

/t/   /p/   /s/   /m/   /a/

2 **Dictate** the following words for children to spell. Model for children how to use sound boxes to segment each word to scaffold the spelling. *I will say a word. You will repeat the word, then think about how many sounds are in the word. Use your Sound Boxes to count the sounds. Then write one letter for each sound you hear.*

mat   Pam   at   sat   tap   Sam

Write the letters and words for children to self-correct.

MINILESSON 5 Mins

High-Frequency Words

like

1 **Review** Display **Visual Vocabulary Card** *like*. Have children **Read/Spell/Write** the word. Then choose a Partner Talk Activity.

Visual Vocabulary Cards

Distribute one of the following **High-Frequency Word Cards** to children: *I, can, the, we, see, a, like*. Tell children that you will ask some questions. *If the word on the card answers the question, stand and hold up your word card and say the word.*

Which word rhymes with *man*?
Which word means "you and I"?
Which word begins with /s/?
Which word rhymes with *bike*?
Which words are spelled with only one letter?
Which word is the word *the*?

2 **Build Fluency: Word Automaticity** Display High-Frequency Word Cards *I, can, the, we, see, a* and *like*. Point to each card, at random, and have children read the word as quickly as they can.

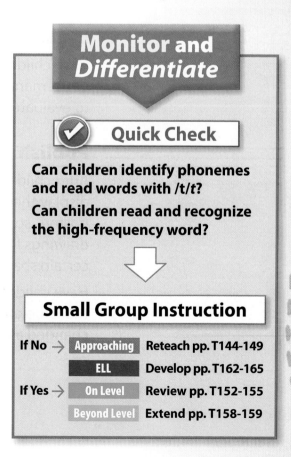

Monitor and *Differentiate*

✓ Quick Check

Can children identify phonemes and read words with /t/t?

Can children read and recognize the high-frequency word?

⬇

Small Group Instruction

If No →	Approaching	Reteach pp. T144-149
	ELL	Develop pp. T162-165
If Yes →	On Level	Review pp. T152-155
	Beyond Level	Extend pp. T158-159

 → # Language Arts

MINILESSON 10 Mins Independent Writing

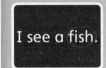
Writing Trait: Ideas

OBJECTIVES

 CCSS Speak audibly and express thoughts, feelings, and ideas clearly. **SL.K.6**

 CCSS Use frequently occurring nouns and verbs. **L.K.1b**

ACADEMIC LANGUAGE

• *present, rectangle, circle, square, triangle, action word, verb*

• Cognates: *rectángulo, círculo, triángulo, verbo*

Prepare

Tell children that they will present their posters from Day 4 to the class. Hold up an example from Day 4 and read it aloud, tracking the print. *I faced you so that you could hear me. I read the words clearly so that everyone could understand me.*

Present

Have children take turns sharing and talking about their posters. Remind children to look toward the class and to read their words clearly so that everyone can hear and understand them. Ask children to point to the things they drew and name each thing. Encourage the rest of the class to listen quietly and to wait until the presenter has finished before they ask any questions.

Evaluate

Have children discuss their own presentations and evaluate their performances, using the presentation rubric. Use the teacher's rubric to evaluate children's writing.

Publish

After children have finished presenting, collect their posters and display them in the classroom. Have children help you sort their posters, so that all posters about one shape are together. Share some drawings from each poster. Discuss how some objects are usually of a certain shape. *What shape is a door?*

Have children add their posters to their Writer's Portfolio. Then have them look back at their previous writing and discuss how they have changed as writers throughout the year.

MINILESSON
5 Mins

Grammar

Verbs

❶ Review Remind children that verbs are action words. Write and read aloud the following sentence: *The girl hops to school.* Ask children to name the action word in the sentence.

❷ Review/Practice Write and read aloud the following sentences: *I walk to school. She rides a bike. He rides in a car. What word tells you about an action in the sentence?* Ask children to name the action in each sentence.

Ask children to think of other ways they can move. Have children tell different kinds of movements. Write their responses on the board. Have children pantomime the movements.

Write the sentence frame: *I can _____.*

Have children write the sentence frame with one way to move.

Have children read aloud their sentences and pantomime the movement.

Guide children in writing the correct action in the sentence.

Wrap Up the Week

- Review blending words with initial and final /t/*t*.
- Remind children that action words tell what someone or something does.
- Use the High-Frequency Word Cards to review the Words to Know.
- Remind children that they can use sentences to give information.

→ Approaching Level

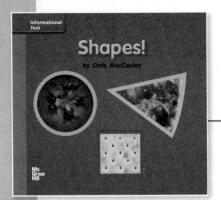

Leveled Reader

OBJECTIVES

 With prompting and support, ask and answer questions about key details in a text. **RI.K.1**

 With prompting and support, describe the relationship between illustrations and the text in which they appear (e.g., what person, place, thing, or idea in the text an illustration depicts). **RI.K.7**

 Read emergent-reader texts with purpose and understanding. **RF.K.4**

Leveled Reader:
Shapes!

Go Digital

Leveled Readers

Before Reading

Preview and Predict

Point to and read each word in the title and in the author's name on the cover. Discuss the picture: *What foods do you see? What shapes can you see?* Preview the photographs and identify the rebus pictures. Ask: *What do you think this text will be about?*

Review Genre: Informational Text

Tell children that this book is an informational text because it gives information; it doesn't tell a made-up story. Explain that informational texts usually have photographs instead of illustrations.

Model Concepts of Print

Point to where you will start reading on page 2. Ask: *Which way do I read? What do I do when I get to the end of this sentence?* Ask children to put their finger on the first word in the sentence.

Review High-Frequency Words

Point out the word *like* on page 2, and read it with children. Ask them to name one thing they like to eat. With children, count the number of times they see the word *like* in the book. (seven)

Essential Question

Set a purpose for reading: *Let's find out what shapes we can see in the foods we eat.* Remind children to use the photographs and the rebuses as they read.

During Reading

Guided Comprehension

As children read *Shapes!* provide guidance by modeling the strategy, the skill, and using photos to confirm unfamiliar words.

Strategy: Ask and Answer Questions

Remind children that as they read they can ask questions about things they don't understand and look for answers in the text and pictures.

Skill: Key Details

Explain to children that the photographs will give details about the foods and their shapes. Point out that the photos and the words work together to give the reader information. After reading, ask: *What details about the story did you learn from the photographs?*

Think Aloud The words and the rebus on page 2 tell me what the narrator likes to eat—tomatoes. The photograph tells me the shape— a circle.

As children read the book, guide them to find details in the pictures that help them identify the foods and their shapes. Have them point to evidence that supports their thinking.

After Reading

Respond to Reading

→ *What is this book about?* (foods and their shapes)

→ *What food is page 4 about?* (pizza) *What shape is the slice of pizza?* (triangle) *How do you know?* (from the words and pictures)

→ *What food is on page 7?* (crackers) *What shape are they?* (square)

Retell

Have children retell the text to a partner. Help them make a personal connection by asking: *What is your favorite shape?*

Model Fluency

Read the text aloud, pausing after each page to have children chorally repeat the words.

Apply

Have children practice reading with partners as you observe and provide assistance as needed.

LITERACY ACTIVITIES

Have children complete the activities on the inside back cover of the reader.

Level Up

IF Children read *Shapes!* **Approaching Level** with fluency and correctly answer the Respond to Reading questions,

THEN Tell children that they will read another story about shapes in our world, only this time, the shapes are in things we play with.

• Have children page through *Play with Shapes!* **On Level** as you identify the things the children in the book play with and their shapes.

• Have children read the story, monitoring their comprehension and providing assistance as necessary.

→ Approaching Level

Phonological Awareness

ONSET AND RIME BLENDING

OBJECTIVES

 Blend and segment onsets and rimes of single-syllable spoken words. **RF.K.2c**

 I Do Tell children that the the word *sun* is made of two parts and that each part has a sound. *The puppet can say the first sound in sun: /s/. The second sound is /un/.* Have the puppet blend the sounds: */s/ /un/, sun.*

 We Do Have the puppet say the sounds in another word: */b/ /ig/, big. Let's say the sounds and then say the word: /b/ /ig/, big.* Repeat with *rain: /r/ /ān/, rain.*

 You Do Ask children to blend the word parts to make a word. Have the puppet say the following: */r/ /ound/ (round); /k/ /ām/ (came).*

Phonemic Awareness

PHONEME ISOLATION

OBJECTIVES

 Isolate and pronounce the initial, medial vowel, and final sounds (phonemes) in three-phoneme words. **RF.K.2d**

 I Do Display the *Turkey* **Photo Card**. *This is a turkey. The first sound I hear in turkey is /t/.* Repeat the picture name, emphasizing the initial /t/ sound. Repeat with the *Bat* Photo Card, emphasizing /t/ in the final position.

 We Do Display and say the name of the *Toys* Photo Card. *Say the picture name with me. Tell me the first sound in* toys. (/t/) Then repeat with the *Feet* Photo Card, emphasizing final /t/.

 You Do Display the *Toe* Photo Card. Have children name it and say the initial sound. Repeat with the *Tiger* (initial position) and the *Goat* (final position) Photo Cards.

You may wish to review Phonological Awareness and Phonemic Awareness with **ELL** using this section.

PHONEME IDENTITY

OBJECTIVES

CCSS Isolate and pronounce the initial, medial vowel, and final sounds (phonemes) in three-phoneme words. **RF.K.2d**

 I Do *Listen as the puppet says three words:* time, tack, tip. *They all begin with the same sound, /t/. Listen again:* time, tack, tip.

 We Do *Let's say some words and sounds with the puppet:* Tell, */t/ /t/ /t/,* tell. Top, */t/ /t/ /t/,* top. Tell *and* top *begin with the same sound, /t/. Repeat with* mat *and* sit. Have children say each word and identify the ending sound.

 You Do Have the puppet say the following words. Ask children to say each word and identify which words begin with the same initial sound.

tin table pan tick tar mud

Have the puppet say the following words. Ask children to say each word and identify which words end with the same sound.

pat ran mat sit can put

PHONEME BLENDING

OBJECTIVES

CCSS Isolate and pronounce the initial, medial vowel, and final sounds (phonemes) in three-phoneme words. **RF.K.2d**

 I Do *The puppet will say the sounds in a word. Listen: /t/ /iii/ /p/. The puppet can blend these sounds together: /tiiip/,* tip. *Repeat with* pat.

 We Do *Now the puppet is going to say the sounds in another word. Say the sounds with the puppet: /t/ /aaa/ /nnn/. Let's blend the sounds together: /taaannn/,* tan. *Repeat with* take *and* mitt.

 You Do Have children blend sounds to form words. Practice together: /t/ /uuu/ /g/, tug. Then have children blend the following sounds to say the words.

/t/ /a/ /b/ tab /k/ /a/ /t/ cat /t/ /o/ /p/ top

/p/ /o/ /t/ pot /t/ /e/ /n/ ten /s/ /i/ /t/ sit

ELL ENGLISH LANGUAGE LEARNERS

For the **ELLs** who need **phonics, decoding,** and **fluency** practice, use scaffolding methods as necessary to ensure children understand the meaning of the words. Refer to the Language Transfer Handbook for phonics elements that may not transfer in students' native languages.

→ # Approaching Level

Phonics

SOUND-SPELLING REVIEW

OBJECTIVES

CCSS Demonstrate basic knowledge of one-to-one letter-sound correspondences by producing the primary sound for each consonant. **RF.K.3a**

 I Do Display **Word-Building Card** *t*. Say the letter name and the sound it stands for: *t, /t/*. Repeat for *a, m, s,* and *p*.

 We Do Display *Ant* **Photo Card** and together say the first letter in the word and the sound that it stands for. Repeat with the *Mule, Six,* and *Pie* Photo Cards.

 You Do Display the *Apple, Moon, Sing,* and *Piano* Photo Cards one at a time. Have children say the first letter in the word and the sound it stands for.

CONNECT *t* TO /t/

OBJECTIVES

CCSS Demonstrate basic knowledge of one-to-one letter-sound correspondences by producing the primary sound for each consonant. **RF.K.3a**

 I Do Display the *Turtle* **Sound-Spelling Card**. *The letter* t *can stand for /t/ at the beginning of* turtle. *What is this letter? (t) What sound does it stand for? (/t/) I will write* t *when I hear /t/ in these words*: pass, tape, teach, move, kit.

 We Do *The word* tall *begins with /t/. Let's write* t. Guide children to write *t* when they hear a word that begins or ends with /t/: *tame, met, miss, tone, test.*

 You Do Say the following words and have children write the letter *t* if a word begins or ends with /t/: *tease, mud, cat, torn, type, song, hat.*

RETEACH

OBJECTIVES

CCSS Demonstrate basic knowledge of one-to-one letter-sound correspondences by producing the primary sound for each consonant. **RF.K.3a**

 I Do Display **Reading/Writing Workshop**, p. 24. *The letter t stands for the /t/ sound you hear at the beginning of* turtle. Say *turtle,* emphasizing the /t/.

 We Do Have children name each picture in the apple row. Repeat the name, emphasizing initial /t/. Repeat for the star row, emphasizing final /t/.

 You Do Guide children in reading the words in the tree row. Then have them read the words in the butterfly row, offering assistance as needed.

BLEND WORDS WITH /t/t

OBJECTIVES

Isolate and pronounce the initial, medial vowel, and final sounds (phonemes) in three-phoneme words. **RF.K.2d**

Display **Word-Building Cards** *a, m, p, s,* and *t.* *This is the letter* t. *It stands for /t/. This is the letter* a. *It stands for /a/. This is the letter* p. *It stands for /p/. Listen as I blend all three sounds: /taaap/, tap. The word is* tap. Repeat for *sat.*

Now let's blend more sounds to make words. Let's make the word mat: */mmmaaat/, mat. Repeat for* Tam *and* map.

Distribute sets of Word-Building Cards with *a, m, p, s,* and *t.* Write: *sat, tap,* and *pat.* Have children form the words and then blend and read the words.

BUILD WORDS WITH /t/t

OBJECTIVES

Demonstrate basic knowledge of one-to-one letter-sound correspondences by producing the primary or many of the most frequent sounds for each consonant. **RF.K.3a**

Display Word-Building Cards *a, t. These are the letters* a *and* t. *They stand for /a/ and /t/. I will blend /a/ and /t/ together: /aaat/, at. The word is* at.

Distribute sets of Word-Building Cards with *a, m, p, s,* and *t.* Show how to make the word *at* and have children do the same. Place the letter *m* in front of *at* and have children do the same. *Let's blend* /mmmaaat/, mat. *Now we have read a new word,* mat.

Have children change the *m* in *mat* to *s* and read the new word, *sat.* Have children change the *s* in *sat* to *p* and read the new word, *pat.* Point out that by changing one letter we make a new word.

BUILD FLUENCY WITH PHONICS

Sound/Spelling Fluency

Display the following Word-Building Cards: *a, m, p, s,* and *t.* Have children chorally say each sound. Repeat and vary the pace.

Fluency in Connected Text

Write the following sentences. *We see Pat. See Pat tap!* Have children read the sentences and identify the words with /t/.

→ # Approaching Level

High-Frequency Words

RETEACH WORDS

OBJECTIVES

 Read common high-frequency words by sight. **RF.K.3c**

 I Do Use the **High-Frequency Word Card** *like* with the **Read/Spell/Write** routine to reteach the high-frequency word *like*.

 We Do Have children turn to p. 25 of **Reading/Writing Workshop** and discuss the first photo. Then read aloud the first sentence. Reread the sentence with children. Then distribute index cards with the word *like* written on them. Have children match their word card with the word *like* in the sentence. Use the same routine for the other sentence on the page.

 You Do Write the sentence frame *We like ____*. Have children copy the sentence frame on their **Response Boards**. Then have partners work together to read and orally complete the frame by talking about foods they like to eat. Reteach previously introduced high-frequency words using the Read/Spell/Write routine.

REREAD FOR FLUENCY

OBJECTIVES

Read common high-frequency words by sight. **RF.K.3c**

 I Do Turn to p. 26, and read aloud the title. *Let's read the title together.* Page through the book. Ask children what they see in each picture. Ask children to find the word *like* on p. 31.

 We Do Then have children open their books and chorally read the story. Have children point to each word as they read. Provide corrective feedback as needed. After reading, ask children to recall the things that Tam taps.

 You Do Have children reread "We Like Tam!" with a partner for fluency.

Repeat for "I Like Sam" on page 32. Have children find the word *like* on p. 37.

Oral Vocabulary

REVIEW WORDS

OBJECTIVES

 Identify real-life connections between words and their uses. **L.K.5c**

Develop oral vocabulary: *materials, nature, world, decoration, games*

 I Do Use the **Define/Example/Ask** routine to review words. Use the following definitions and provide examples:

materials	People use **materials** to make or build things.
nature	Plants and animals in the world around us are part of **nature**.
world	The **world** is the planet Earth.
decoration	A **decoration** is something added to give color or shape to an object.
games	**Games** are fun activities with rules that people play.

We Do Ask questions to build understanding. *What materials could you use to make a card? What is something in nature that smells good? How would you describe the world? What is a decoration you see in the classroom? What kinds of games can you play inside?*

 You Do Have children complete these sentence frames: *The materials I will use to draw a picture are _____. The parts of nature at a zoo are _____. Water is important in our world because _____. A decoration I could use for a birthday party is _____. My favorite game to play on the playground is _____.*

Comprehension

SELF-SELECTED READING

OBJECTIVES

 With prompting and support, ask and answer questions about key details in a text. **RI.K.1**

Apply the strategy and skill to reread the text.

Read Independently

Help children select an informational text with photographs for sustained silent reading. Remind children that they can use photographs to help them understand the text. Tell children to ask and answer questions to help them understand what they read.

Read Purposefully

Before reading, have children point out an interesting photograph. After reading, ask each child to point to the photograph they identified earlier. *How did details in the photograph help you understand the text?*

On Level

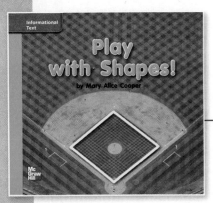

Leveled Reader

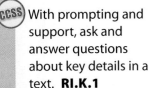

Leveled Reader:
Play with Shapes!

Before Reading

Preview and Predict

Read aloud the title and the author's name. Ask children to name what shapes they see on the cover. Ask them to predict what they might read about in the book. Then walk children through the book. Have them identify each of the things in the book.

Review Genre: Informational Text

Tell children that this book is an informational text because it gives information; it doesn't tell a made-up story. Explain that informational texts usually have photographs instead of illustrations.

Model Concepts of Print

Model left to right progression. Say: *When I read the words on each page, I always start here on the left and move to the right. When we read, we will move our fingers under each word as we read it.*

Review High-Frequency Words

Point out the word *like* on page 2, and read it with children. Have children work with a partner to count the number of times they see the word *like* in the book. (seven)

Essential Question

Set a purpose for reading: *What shapes do the children in the book play with? Let's read the book to find out.* Remind children to use both the photos and the words to answer the question.

During Reading

Guided Comprehension

As children whisper-read, provide guidance by correcting blending and modeling the strategy and skill.

**Go
Digital**

**Leveled
Readers**

Strategy: Ask and Answer Questions

Remind children that as they read they can ask questions about things they don't understand and look for answers in the text and pictures.

Skill: Key Details

Reinforce the importance of using both the photographs and the print to follow what is happening in the story. Remind children that many times, key details can be found in the pictures.

Think Aloud On page 2, I read what the children like to play with. The words don't tell me what shape the blocks are, but the photograph tells me that the blocks are square. Using both the words and the photographs helps me understand what I'm reading.

Guide children to use the photos in the book to identify the types of games and the shape of each game.

After Reading

Respond to Reading

→ *What is this book about?* (things we play with and their shapes)

→ *What do the children play with on page 3?* (a game) *What shape is the game?* (square)

→ *What do the children play with on page 5?* (a ball) *What shape is the ball?* (circle)

Retell

Have children take turns retelling the story. Help them make a personal connection by asking: *What is your favorite thing to play with? What shape is it?*

Model Fluency

Read the text aloud, pausing after each page to have children chorally repeat the words.

Apply

Have children practice reading with partners as you observe and provide assistance as needed.

LITERACY ACTIVITIES

Have children complete the activities on the inside back cover of the reader.

Level Up

Level-up lessons available online.

IF Children read *Play with Shapes!* On Level with fluency and correctly answer the Respond to Reading questions,

THEN Tell children that they will read a story about children who use shapes in their art.

- Have children page through *Use a Shape!* Beyond Level as you help children identify the type of art and help them read words that may be unfamiliar, such as *robot*.

- Have children read the story, monitoring their comprehension and providing assistance as necessary.

→ On Level

Phonemic Awareness

PHONEME ISOLATION

OBJECTIVES

Isolate and pronounce the initial, medial vowel, and final sounds (phonemes) in three-phoneme words. **RF.K.2d**

 Display the *Tiger* **Photo Card**. *This is a* tiger. *The first sound is* /t/. *Say the sound with me.* Repeat with the *Vest* Photo Card and the final sound /t/.

 Say *team* and have children repeat it. *What is the first sound in* team? Say the sound together. Repeat with *tan, pack, set,* and *man* and with the final /t/ in *let* and *cat*.

 Say *tan, tack,* and *tip* and have children tell the initial sound in each word. Then say *pet, not,* and *sit*. Have children tell the final sound in each word.

PHONEME BLENDING

OBJECTIVES

Isolate and pronounce the initial, medial vowel, and final sounds (phonemes) in three-phoneme words. **RF.K.2d**

 Place *Table, Tie, Hat, Top,* and *Bat* Photo Cards facedown. Choose a card but do not show it to children. *These are the sounds in the word:* /h/ /a/ /t/. *Listen as I blend these sounds:* /haaat/, hat. *The word is* hat. Show the picture.

 Choose another picture and say the sounds in the name. Together say the sounds and blend the sounds to say the word. Then show the picture.

 Continue choosing Photo Cards. Say the sounds and have children blend the sounds to say the words.

PHONEME IDENTITY

OBJECTIVES

Isolate and pronounce the initial, medial vowel, and final sounds (phonemes) in three-phoneme words. **RF.K.2d**

 Display *Table, Teeth,* and *Toys* Photo Cards. *Listen as the puppet says the words:* table, teeth, toys. *They all begin with the same sound,* /t/. Repeat.

 Show *Turtle, Tie, Turkey* Photo Cards. Say the words. Have children repeat each word. *Let's tell which sound is at the beginning of:* turtle, tie, turkey. *They begin with the sound* /t/. Repeat with *sit* and *mat* for ending sound /t/.

 Have the puppet say these words: *take, mat, tree, sit, pet, time*. Ask children to say each word and identify which ones begin or end with the sound /t/.

Phonics

REVIEW PHONICS

OBJECTIVES

Demonstrate basic knowledge of one-to-one letter-sound correspondences by producing the primary or many of the most frequent sounds for each consonant. **RF.K.3a**

 I Do

Display **Reading/Writing Workshop**, p. 24. Point to the *Turtle* **Sound-Spelling Card**. *What letter stands for the /t/ sound you hear at the beginning of* turtle? *The letter is* t.

 We Do

Have children say the name of each picture. Then ask them to identify the words that begin with /t/ and the words that end with /t/.

 You Do

Have children read each word. Repeat, asking them to raise their hands if they hear /t/ at the beginning of the word, keeping their hands lowered if they hear /t/ at the end of the word.

PICTURE SORT

OBJECTIVES

Isolate and pronounce the initial, medial vowel, and final sounds (phonemes) in three-phoneme words. **RF.K.2d**

 I Do

Display **Word-Building Cards** *t* and *p* in a pocket chart. Then show the *Mop* **Photo Card**. Say /m/ /o/ /p/, *mop*. Tell children that the sound at the end is /p/. *The letter* p *stands for* /p/. *I will put the* mop *under the letter* p. Show the *Ant* Photo Card. Say /a/ /n/ /t/, ant. Tell children that the sound at the end is /t/. The letter t stands for /t/. *I will put the* ant *under the* t.

 We Do

Show the *Jet* Photo Card and say /j/ /e/ /t/, *jet*. Have children repeat. Then have them tell the sound they hear at the end of *jet*. Ask them if they should place the photo under the *t* or the *p*. (under the t)

 You Do

Continue the activity using the *Bat, Nut, Lamp, Boot, Soup,* and *Up* Photo Cards. Have children say the picture name and the sounds in the name. Then have them place each card under the *t* or *p*.

On Level

Phonics

BLEND WORDS WITH /t/*t*

OBJECTIVES

 Isolate and pronounce the initial, medial vowel, and final sounds (phonemes) in three-phoneme words. **RF.K.2d**

 I Do Write *t, a, p*. *This is the letter* t. *It stands for /t/. Say it with me: /t/. This is the letter* a. *It stands for /a/. Say it with me: /aaa/. This is the letter* p. *It stands for /p/. Say it with me: /p/. I'll blend the sounds together to read the word:* /taaap/, tap.

 We Do Write *at* and *pat*. Guide children to blend the words sound by sound to read each word.

 You Do Write the following words and have children blend the words sound by sound to read each word.

sat   mat   tin   ten

High-Frequency Words

REVIEW WORDS

OBJECTIVES

 Read common high-frequency words by sight. **RF.K.3c**

 I Do Use the **High-Frequency Word Card** *like* with the **Read/Spell/Write** routine to review *like*.

 We Do Have children turn to p. 25 of **Reading/Writing Workshop**. Discuss the photographs and read aloud the sentences. Point to the word *like* and have children read it. Then chorally read the sentences. Have children frame the word *like* in the sentences and read the word.

 You Do Say the word *like*. Ask children to close their eyes, picture the word, and write it as they see it. Have children self-correct.

Reteach previously introduced high-frequency words using the Read/Spell/Write routine.

Fluency Point to the High-Frequency Word Cards *I, can, the, we, see, a, like* in random order. Have children chorally read. Repeat at a faster pace.

REREAD FOR FLUENCY

OBJECTIVES

Read emergent-reader texts with purpose and understanding. **RF.K.4**

 I Do Point to the title "We Like Tam!" on p. 26 of **Reading/Writing Workshop**. Point to the exclamation point. *This end mark shows us that we need to read the title with strong feeling.* Read the title with excitement and have children repeat in the same way. Work with children to read for accuracy and expression. Model reading a page: *When I read, "Tam can see Pam," I read all the way to the end of the sentence before pausing. This makes my reading sound natural, as if I were talking.*

 We Do Reread p. 28. Then have children chorally read the page with you. Continue choral reading the remainder of the pages.

 You Do Have children read "We Like Tam!" Provide time to listen as children read the pages. Comment on their accuracy and expression and provide corrective feedback by modeling proper fluency.

Use the same routine for "I Like Sam" on pp. 32–37.

Comprehension

SELF-SELECTED READING

OBJECTIVES

With prompting and support, ask and answer questions about key details in a text. **RL.K.1**

Apply the strategy and skill to reread the text.

Read Independently

Have children select an informational text with photographs for sustained silent reading. Remind children that photographs can help them understand key details as they read. Explain how the photographs can help them answer questions they ask themselves before, during, and after reading.

Read Purposefully

Before reading, have children choose a photograph that shows an important detail about the text. After reading, guide partners to explain what information they learned from the photograph. Have them share how they used the photograph to ask and answer a question about the text.

→ Beyond Level

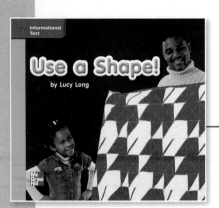

Leveled Reader

OBJECTIVES

CCSS With prompting and support, ask and answer questions about key details in a text. **RI.K.1**

CCSS With prompting and support, describe the relationship between illustrations and the text in which they appear (e.g., what person, place, thing, or idea in the text an illustration depicts). **RI.K.7**

CCSS Read emergent-reader texts with purpose and understanding. **RF.K.4**

Leveled Reader:
Use a Shape!

Go Digital

Leveled Readers

Before Reading

Preview and Predict

Show children the cover of the book. Point to the title and author name as you read them aloud. Ask children to tell you what they see on the cover and to predict what the book might be about. Have children page through the photographs in the book and tell whether the photos confirm or change their predictions.

Review Genre: Informational Text

Remind children that this book is called an informational text because it gives information about making art and does not tell a made-up story. Explain that informational texts usually have photographs instead of illustrations.

Essential Question

Set a purpose for reading: *What shapes do the children use in their art? Let's read the book to find out.* Remind children to use both the photos and the words to answer the question.

During Reading

Guided Comprehension

As children whisper-read the book, model the strategy and skill for them. Tell them that when they come to a word they don't know, they can look at the first letter in the word and the picture to help them.

Strategy: Ask and Answer Questions

Remind children that as they read they can ask questions about things they don't understand and look for answers in the text and photographs.

Skill: Key Details

Remind children that the photographs in the book show what is happening in the text. Explain that the photographs can give details that are not in the text.

Think Aloud On page 2, I read the sentences: *I like to draw houses. I use shapes in my art.* The photograph of the girl drawing shows me what kind of shapes she used to draw her house.

Guide children to use the photographs on pages 4 and 5 to find details about what the children are doing. Ask them what shapes they see. Have children point to evidence in the text or pictures to support their statements.

After Reading

Respond to Reading

→ *What is this book about?* (making different kinds of art)

→ *What kinds of art did you read about in this book?* (drawing houses, cars and trucks; making a quilt and a robot; painting pictures and pots)

→ *What are some shapes you found in the art?* (squares, triangles, circles, rectangles, etc.)

→ *Which art in this book did you like the best? Why?* (Answers will vary.)

Retell

Ask children to retell the text with a partner. Help them make a personal connection by asking: *What kind of art do you like to make? What shapes do you use in your art?*

Gifted and Talented

EVALUATING Have children think of other kinds of art that could be included in a book about shapes. Ask them to think about what shapes they would see in the art.

HAVE children share with partners their idea for another kind of art that uses shapes.

LITERACY ACTIVITIES

Have children complete the activities on the inside back cover of the reader.

Beyond Level

Phonics

REVIEW

OBJECTIVES

 Demonstrate basic knowledge of one-to-one letter-sound correspondences by producing the primary or many of the most frequent sounds for each consonant. **RF.K.3a**

 I Do Display **Reading/Writing Workshop**, p. 24. Point to the *Turtle* **Sound-Spelling Card**. *What is the sound at the beginning of* turtle? (/t/) *What letter can stand for* /t/? *The letter is* t.

 We Do Have children say the name of each picture. Then ask children to share other words they know that begin with /t/.

 You Do Have partners read each word. Ask them to write the words on their **Response Boards**, underlining the letter in each word that stands for /t/.

High-Frequency Words

REVIEW

OBJECTIVES

Read common high-frequency words by sight. **RF.K.3c**

 I Do Create the **High-Frequency Word Cards** for *many* and *people*. Introduce the words using the **Read/Spell/Write** routine.

We Do Display the High-Frequency Word Cards for *a, can, I, like, see, the,* and *we*. Have children help you complete the following sentence frames using the High-Frequency Word Cards: *People like the ___. We can see many ___.*

 You Do Have partners write sentences using the high-frequency words *many* and *people* on their Response Boards. Have them read their sentences.

Fluency Have children turn to pp. 26–31 and 32–37 in Reading/Writing Workshop and reread the stories "We Like Tam!" and "I Like Sam" for fluency.

Innovate Have children create a new page for "We Like Tam!" using the sentence frame *Tam can tap the ___.* For "I Like Sam" have children complete the sentence frame *Sam can pat the ___.* by choosing another object Sam can pat.

Vocabulary

ORAL VOCABULARY: SYNONYMS

OBJECTIVES

With guidance and support from adults, explore word relationships and nuances in word meaning. **L.K.5**

Develop oral vocabulary: Synonyms

Review the meanings of the oral vocabulary words *materials* and *nature*. Explain that a synonym is a word that means almost the same thing as another word. *A synonym for* materials *is* parts. *You put* parts *together to make something.* I used socks and buttons as parts to make my puppet. *A synonym for* nature *is* environment. *The* environment *is made up of the natural world around us.* Plants grow well when they have plenty of water and sunlight in their environment.

Think of a few sentences together using the new words *parts* and *environment*. Say the sentences out loud.

Have partners draw a picture that shows the parts of a toy car and one that shows a flower growing in a sunny, wet environment. Have partners say sentences about their pictures that include the new words.

Extend Have each child choose a different animal. Challenge them to list the materials they need from their environment to build their home. Ask partners to share. Then have partners compare and contrast environments.

Comprehension

SELF-SELECTED READING

OBJECTIVES

With prompting and support, ask and answer questions about key details in a text. **RL.K.1**

Apply the strategy and skill to reread the text.

Read Independently

Have children select an informational text with photographs for sustained silent reading. Remind children that using key details from the photographs can help them ask and answer questions as they read.

Read Purposefully

Before reading, have children choose a photograph that shows an important detail. After reading, invite children to discuss how details from the photograph helped them answer a question during reading.

Independent Study Challenge children to classify objects by having partners find examples of things shaped like squares, triangles, circles, and rectangles in photographs from magazines or child-friendly Internet sites. Ask them to create a simple chart to show the different shapes they found.

English Language Learners

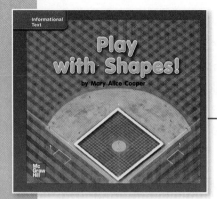

Leveled Reader

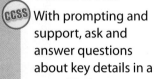

OBJECTIVES

With prompting and support, ask and answer questions about key details in a text. **RI.K.1**

With prompting and support, ask and answer questions about unknown words in a text. **RI.K.4**

Shared Read:
Play with Shapes!

Before Reading

Preview and Predict

Show children the cover of the book and read aloud the title. Ask children to repeat as you point to each word in the title. Discuss the picture on the cover and name the items. Walk children through the book. With each picture, point out and name what the children are playing and then point to the word on the page. Ask children to point to the word and repeat it. For example, for page 2, point to the blocks in the picture and say: *These are blocks.* Then point to the label and the rebus word as you repeat the word. To reinforce the vocabulary, ask children to show you different things in the book: *Show me the blocks. Show me the train.*

Essential Question

Tell children the book is about different games that children like. Set a purpose for reading: *What games do the children like? What shapes can we find in the games? Let's read the book to find out.* Remind children to use both the photos and the words to answer the questions.

During Reading

Interactive Question Response

Pages 2–3 Discuss the photograph on page 2. Ask: *What do we like?* Read aloud the page with the children, pointing to each word in the sentence that answers the question. Point out the outlined shape on the picture of the blocks. Say: *I see a square. The shape is a square.* If children need more support for the language of shapes, draw sketches of a square, rectangle, circle, and triangle on the board and label each sketch. Point to the picture on page 3. Ask: *What do we like?* Then point to the sentence and have children read it with you as they respond to the question.

Go Digital

Leveled Readers

Pages 4–5 Point to the photograph on page 4 and ask children what they see. Point to the train and repeat the word *train*. Ask: *What do we like?* Read aloud the sentence that answers the question, and ask children to read it with you, pointing to each word. Trace the outline of the shape with your finger. Ask: *What shape do you see?* (rectangle) Repeat with page 5.

Pages 6–7 Ask children to tell what shape they see on page 6. Have them trace the outline with their fingers. Have them repeat with you: *The hoop is a circle.* Say: *Let's read the sentence to see what the children like.* Read the sentence aloud with children, pointing to each word in the sentence. Repeat with page 7, having them identify the shape and then read the sentence with you.

Page 8 Point to the tent in the picture. Say: *This is a tent. What can we do in a tent?* Allow responses or tell children: *We can sleep in a tent.* Trace the outline of the shape on the page. Say: *The shape is a triangle.* Point to the sentence and ask children to read it with you.

After Reading

Respond to Reading

→ *What shapes did you read about?* (square, rectangle, circle, triangle)

→ *What is one thing that the children like?* (blocks, game, train, ball, hoop, slide, tent) *Show me how you know.* (Answers will vary.)

→ *Which page do you like best? Why?* (Answers will vary.)

Retell

Say: *Let's look back through the book and retell this story together.* Guide children's retelling by providing labels and sentence patterns.

Model Fluency

Read the sentences one at a time as you track beneath the print, pointing to each word. Have children orally repeat.

Apply

Have children read with partners. Encourage them to point beneath each word as they read to reinforce the basic concept of one-to-one matching of spoken words to print.

LITERACY ACTIVITIES

Have children complete the activities on the inside back cover of the reader.

Level Up

IF Children read *Play with Shapes!* **ELL Level** with fluency and correctly answer the Respond to Reading questions,

THEN Tell children that they will read a more detailed version of the story.

• Have children page through *Play with Shapes!* **On Level** and conduct a picture walk to describe what is happening in each picture.

• Have children read the story, monitoring their comprehension and providing assistance as necessary.

Vocabulary

PRETEACH ORAL VOCABULARY

OBJECTIVES

Speak audibly and express thoughts, feelings, and ideas clearly. **SL.K.6**

LANGUAGE OBJECTIVE

Review vocabulary

 I Do Display images from the **Visual Vocabulary Cards** and follow the routine to preteach the oral vocabulary words.

We Do Display each image again and explain how it illustrates or demonstrates the word. Model using sentences to describe the image.

You Do Display the word card for *materials* again and have children talk to a partner and name the specific materials shown in the picture.

Beginning	Intermediate	Advanced/High
Point to the different materials in the photo and ask: *What might the children make with these materials?*	Have partners talk about the various materials shown in the photo.	Ask children to use *materials* in a sentence.

PRETEACH ELL VOCABULARY

OBJECTIVES

Speak audibly and express thoughts, feelings, and ideas clearly. **SL.K.6**

LANGUAGE OBJECTIVE

Review ELL vocabulary

 I Do Display the images from the **Visual Vocabulary Cards** one at a time to preteach the ELL vocabulary words *geometry* and *fun* and follow the routine. Say each word. Have children repeat it. Define the word in English.

We Do Display each image again and incorporate the word in a short discussion about the image. Model using sentences to describe the image.

You Do Display the image for *fun* and have children say the word. Ask children to name different things they think are *fun* and have them use the sentence starter to express their ideas: *I think _____ is fun.*

Beginning	Intermediate	Advanced/High
Have children draw a picture of a person doing something fun. Ask questions about the drawing to elicit language.	Have partners say sentences with the word *fun*.	Challenge partners to use the word *geometry* in a sentence of their own.

High-Frequency Words

REVIEW WORDS

CCSS

OBJECTIVES
Read common high-frequency words by sight (e.g., *the, of, to, you, she, my, is, are, do, does*). **RF.K.3c**

LANGUAGE OBJECTIVE
Review high-frequency words

 I Do Display the **High-Frequency Word Card** for *like*. Read the word. Use the **Read/Spell/Write** routine to teach the word. Have children write the word on their **Response Boards**.

 We Do Write a sentence frame using the word *like*: *I like* _____. Track print as children read and complete the sentence frame with you. Give children examples of things you like. Model how to complete the sentence frame.

 You Do Ask partners to find the word *like* in the selections.

Beginning	Intermediate	Advanced/High
Help children locate the word *like*. Read the sentence and have children repeat.	Have partners talk about the things they like to do.	Ask children to write the word *like* and use it in a sentence.

REVIEW CATEGORY WORDS

CCSS

OBJECTIVES
Identify real-life connections between words and their use (e.g., note places at school that are colorful). **L.K.5c**

LANGUAGE OBJECTIVE
Use category words

 I Do Display the **Visual Vocabulary Card** for shapes and say each word aloud. Define the word in English; then, if appropriate, in Spanish, identifying any cognates.

 We Do Follow the routine on the card.

 You Do Give more examples of shapes by displaying more drawings or pictures. Have children identify the shapes on their own.

Beginning	Intermediate	Advanced/High
Display a shape and say its name. Have children repeat.	Have partners point out shapes in the classroom. Then have them use the shape word in a sentence.	Have children use the category words in oral sentences.

→ English Language Learners
Writing

SHARED WRITING

OBJECTIVES

CCSS Use a combination of drawing, dictating, and writing to narrate a single event or several loosely linked events, tell about the events in the order in which they occurred, and provide a reaction to what happened. **W.K.3**

LANGUAGE OBJECTIVE

Contribute to a shared writing project

I Do Review the words *circle, square, rectangle,* and *triangle* from the Whole Group Shared Writing project as the names of shapes children have been reading about.

We Do Draw a sketch of each shape. Have children practice naming each shape. With children's help, write a label for each shape.

You Do Have children work with a partner to make a poster about a shape. They should draw the shape and write a label for it on the poster.

Beginning	Intermediate	Advanced/High
Ask children to name each shape before they choose one to make.	Ask children questions about their shape, such as *How many sides does it have?*	Have children describe the shape in their own words.

WRITING TRAIT: IDEAS

OBJECTIVES

CCSS Use a combination of drawing, dictating, and writing to narrate a single event or several loosely linked events, tell about the events in the order in which they occurred, and provide a reaction to what happened. **W.K.3**

LANGUAGE OBJECTIVE

Use ideas in writing

I Do Explain that good writing starts with good ideas. Explain to children that they can get ideas about what to write from the things they read. Reading can give information about what they should write.

We Do Point to the **Big Book** selection for the week. Remind them that the story is about shapes we see around us. Ask: *What did you read about shapes?* Point out ideas from the story that children can use to write about shapes.

You Do Have children write a sentence to tell where they see shapes around them. Provide them with the sentence frame *I see shapes _____.*

Beginning	Intermediate	Advanced/High
Point to and name objects in the Big Book selection. Have children say them, too.	Ask partners to copy and complete the sentence frame.	Ask children to complete the sentence frame. Challenge them to write another sentence.

Grammar

VERBS

OBJECTIVES
Use frequently occurring nouns and verbs. **L.K.1b**

LANGUAGE OBJECTIVE

Identify and use verbs

Language Transfers Handbook

Spanish and English have different uses for *have* and *be*. Spanish speakers may say *I have thirst* or *He has right*. Provide extra support for children when using the words *am, are,* or *is.*

 I Do Review that a verb is an action word. Demonstrate sitting and then say the following sentence: *I sit down.* Say: *The verb in this sentence is* sit. Sit *is a word that shows action.*

 We Do Say the following sentences. Have children help you identify the verb in each. Have them say: *The action word is* _____ .

The dogs run.

The cats jump.

The birds fly.

 You Do Say the following sentence: *Animals* _____ .

Pair children and have them orally complete the sentence by providing details from this week's readings. Circulate, listen in, and take note of each child's language use and proficiency.

Beginning	Intermediate	Advanced/High
Ask: *What do animals do?* Guide them in choosing an action word.	Ask children to complete the sentence frame after taking a picture walk through the week's selections.	Challenge children to list verbs they see in this week's readings.

Use your Quick Check observations and the assessment opportunities identified below to evaluate children's progress in key skill areas.

✔ TESTED SKILLS CCSS	Quick Check Observations	Pencil and Paper Assessment
PHONEMIC AWARENESS/ PHONICS **t** /t/ (initial/final) **RF.K.3a**	Can children isolate /t/ and match it to the letter *Tt*?	Practice Book, pp. 59–60, 62
HIGH-FREQUENCY WORDS *like* **like** **RF.K.3c**	Can children recognize and read the high-frequency word?	Practice Book, pp. 63–64
COMPREHENSION Key Details **RI.K.1, RI.K.7**	As you read *Shapes All Around* with children, can they identify and discuss key details using the photos and the text?	Practice Book, p. 61

Quick Check Rubric

Skills	1	2	3
PHONEMIC AWARENESS/ PHONICS	Does not connect the sound /t/ with the letters *Tt*.	Usually connects the sound /t/ with the letters *Tt*.	Consistently connects the sound /t/ with the letters *Tt*.
HIGH-FREQUENCY WORDS	Does not identify the high-frequency word.	Usually recognizes the high-frequency word with accuracy, but not speed.	Consistently recognizes the high-frequency word with speed and accuracy.
COMPREHENSION	Does not identify key details using the photos and text.	Usually identifies key details using the photos and text.	Consistently identifies key details using the photos and text.

Go Digital! www.connected.mcgraw-hill.com

Using Assessment Results

TESTED SKILLS	If ...	Then ...
PHONEMIC AWARENESS/ PHONICS	**Quick Check Rubric:** Children consistently score 1 or **Pencil and Paper Assessment:** Children get 0–2 items correct	... reteach tested Phonemic Awareness and Phonics skills using Lessons 16–17 and 27–29 in the *Tier 2 Phonemic Awareness Intervention Online PDFs* and Lesson 13 in the *Tier 2 Phonics/Word Study Intervention Online PDFs.*
HIGH-FREQUENCY WORDS	**Quick Check Rubric:** Children consistently score 1	... reteach tested skills by using the High-Frequency Word Cards and asking children to read and spell the word. Point out any irregularities in sound-spellings.
COMPREHENSION	**Quick Check Rubric:** Children consistently score 1 or **Pencil and Paper Assessment:** Children get 0–1 items correct	... reteach tested skill using Lessons 13–15 in the *Tier 2 Comprehension Intervention Online PDFs.*

Response to Intervention

Use the children's assessment results to assist you in identifying children who will benefit from focused intervention.

Use the appropriate sections of the ***Placement and Diagnostic Assessment*** to designate children requiring:

 Tier 2 Intervention Online PDFs

 WonderWorks Intervention Program

→ Phonemic Awareness

→ Phonics

→ Vocabulary

→ Comprehension

→ Fluency

WEEKLY OVERVIEW

Literature Big Book

Listening Comprehension

I Love Bugs!, 4–27
Genre Fiction

"Bugs All Around," 28–32
Genre Informational Text

Interactive Read-Aloud Cards

"From Caterpillar to Butterfly"
Genre Informational Text

Oral Vocabulary

attaches	process
curious	slender
observe	

Minilessons ✔ TESTED SKILLS CCSS

✔ **Comprehension Strategy** .... Ask and Answer Questions, T177

✔ **Comprehension Skill** .... Key Details, T186

☞ **Go** Digital

www.connected.mcgraw-hill.com

Nathan Love

WORLD OF BUGS

Essential Question
What kind of bugs do you know about?

WEEK 3 →

Big Book and Little Book
Reading/Writing Workshop

Shared Reading

I am Pat.

I am at **the** lake.

"Pat," 44–49
Genre Fiction

"Tap! Tap! Tap!" 50–55
Genre Informational Text

High-Frequency Words the, we, see, a, like, T181

Minilessons ✔ TESTED SKILLS CCSS

✔ **Phonics** .... /m/m/, /a/a/, /p/p/, T179

Writing Traits .... Ideas, T182

Grammar .... Verbs, T183

Differentiated Text

Approaching   On Level   Beyond   **ELL**

TEACH AND MANAGE

What You Do

INTRODUCE

Weekly Concept

World of Bugs

**Reading/Writing Workshop
Big Book, 42–43**

TEACH AND APPLY

Listening Comprehension

Big Book
I Love Bugs!
Paired Read "Bugs All Around"
Genre Informational Text

Minilessons
Strategy: Ask and Answer Questions
Skill: Key Details

Shared Reading

Reading/Writing Workshop
"Pat"
"Tap! Tap! Tap!"

Minilessons
Review *m, a, s, p, t,* High–Frequency
Words: *the, we, see, a, like*
Writing, Grammar

Interactive
Whiteboard

Interactive
Whiteboard

Mobile

 Go Digital

What Your Students Do

WEEKLY CONTRACT

PDF Online

PRACTICE AND ONLINE ACTIVITIES

Your Turn Practice Book, pp. 67–76

Leveled Readers

Go Digital

Online
To-Do List

Online
Activities

Mobile

WEEK 3 →

DIFFERENTIATE

Small Group Instruction
Leveled Readers

Mobile

INTEGRATE

Research and Inquiry
Bug Bulletin Board, pp. T216–T217

Text Connections
Compare Bugs, p. T218

Talk About Reading
Using Key Details, p. T219

Online Research

WORKSTATION CARDS

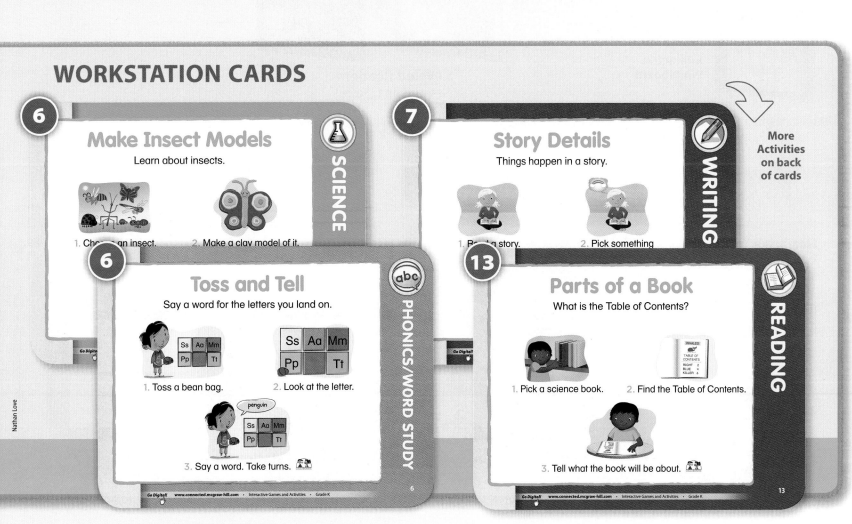

6

Make Insect Models
Learn about insects.

1. Choose an insect.   2. Make a clay model of it.

SCIENCE

6

Toss and Tell
Say a word for the letters you land on.

| Ss | Aa | Mm |
| Pp | | Tt |

1. Toss a bean bag.   2. Look at the letter.

penguin

3. Say a word. Take turns.

PHONICS/WORD STUDY

7

Story Details
Things happen in a story.

1. Read a story.   2. Pick something

WRITING

13

Parts of a Book
What is the Table of Contents?

1. Pick a science book.   2. Find the Table of Contents.

3. Tell what the book will be about.

READING

More Activities on back of cards

Go Digital! www.connected.mcgraw-hill.com • Interactive Games and Activities • Grade K   6

Go Digital! www.connected.mcgraw-hill.com • Interactive Games and Activities • Grade K   13

Nathan Love

DEVELOPING READERS AND WRITERS

Write to Sources and Research

Respond to Reading, T177, T225, T233, T239, T243

Connect to Essential Question, T177, T209

Key Details, 186

Research and Inquiry, T216

Teacher's Edition

Literature Big Book
I Love Bugs!
Paired Read: *"Bugs All Around"*

Interactive Whiteboard

Leveled Readers
Responding to Texts

Writing Process • Independent Writing

Narrative Text
Story Sentences, T204–T205, T214, T222

Conferencing Routines
Peer Conferences, T214

Interactive Whiteboard

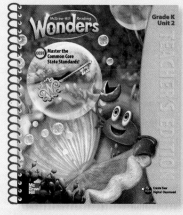

Teacher's Edition

Leveled Workstation Card
Story Details, Card 7

Writing Traits • Shared and Interactive Writing

Writing Trait:
Ideas
Story Sentences, T182, T196

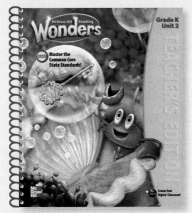

Teacher's Edition

Ideas,
p. 58

Reading/Writing Workshop

**Interactive
Whiteboard**

Leveled Workstation Card
Story Details, Card 7

Grammar and Spelling/Dictation

Grammar
Verbs, T183

Spelling/Dictation
Words with *m, a, s, p, t*, T211,
T221

**Interactive
Whiteboard**

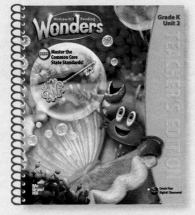

Teacher's Edition

Online Grammar Games

Handwriting

SUGGESTED LESSON PLAN

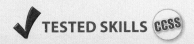 TESTED SKILLS **CCSS**	**DAY 1**	**DAY 2**

READING — Whole Group

Teach and Model

Literature Big Book

Reading/ Writing Workshop

DAY 1

Build Background World of Bugs, T174
Oral Vocabulary Words curious, observe, T174
✓ **Listening Comprehension**
• Genre: Fiction
• Strategy: Ask and Answer Questions, T177
Big Book *I Love Bugs!*
✓ **Word Work**
Phonemic Awareness
• Phoneme Segmentation, T178
Phonics
• Review /m/m, /a/a, /p/p, T179
Handwriting Write Sentences with *Mm, Aa, Ss, Pp, Tt,* T180
High-Frequency Words the, a, see, we, like, T181

Practice *Your Turn* 67

DAY 2

Oral Language World of Bugs, T184
✓ **Category Words** Movement Words, T185
✓ **Listening Comprehension**
• Genre: Fiction
• Strategy: Ask and Answer Questions, T186
• Skill: Key Details
• Guided Retelling
• Model Fluency, T191
Big Book *I Love Bugs!*
✓ **Word Work**
Phonemic Awareness
• Phoneme Segmentation, T192
Phonics
• Review /s/s, /t/t, T192
High-Frequency Words the, a, see, we, like, T193
Shared Reading "Pat," T194–T195

Practice *Your Turn* 68

DIFFERENTIATED INSTRUCTION — Small Group
Choose across the week to meet your student's needs.

Approaching Level

DAY 1
Leveled Reader *We Like Bugs!* T224–T225
Phonological Awareness Count and Pronounce Syllables, T226 **TIER 2**
Phonics Sound-Spelling Review, T228 **TIER 2**
High-Frequency Words Reteach Words, T230 **TIER 2**

DAY 2
Leveled Reader *We Like Bugs!* T224–T225
Phonemic Awareness Phoneme Segmentation, T226 **TIER 2**
Phonics Connect Sounds to Spellings, T228 **TIER 2**
High-Frequency Words Reread for Fluency, T230 **TIER 2**

On Level

DAY 1
Leveled Reader *The Bugs Run,* T232–T233
Phonemic Awareness Phoneme Segmentation, T234

DAY 2
Leveled Reader *The Bugs Run,* T232–T233
Phoneme Awareness Phoneme Blending, T234
Phonics Review Phonics, T235
High-Frequency Words Review Words, T236

Beyond Level

DAY 1
Leveled Reader *I See a Bug!* T238–T239
Phonics Review, T240

DAY 2
Leveled Reader *I See a Bug!* T238–T239
High-Frequency Words Review, T240

English Language Learners

DAY 1
Leveled Reader *The Bugs Run,* T242–T243
Phonological Awareness Count and Pronounce Syllables, T226 **TIER 2**
Phonics Sound-Spelling Review, T228 **TIER 2**
Vocabulary Preteach Oral Vocabulary, T244
Writing Shared Writing, T246

DAY 2
Leveled Reader *The Bugs Run,* T242–T243
Phonemic Awareness Phoneme Segmentation, T226 **TIER 2**
Phonics Connect Sounds to Spellings, T228 **TIER 2**
Vocabulary Preteach ELL Vocabulary, T244

LANGUAGE ARTS — Whole Group

Writing and Grammar

DAY 1
Shared Writing
Writing Trait: Ideas, T182
Write a Story Sentence, T182
Grammar Verbs, T183

DAY 2
Interactive Writing
Writing Trait: Ideas, T196
Write a Story Sentence, T196
Grammar Verbs, T197

Nathan Love

DAY 3	**DAY 4**	**DAY 5** Review and Assess

READING

Oral Language World of Bugs, T198	**Oral Language** World of Bugs, T206	**Integrate Ideas**
Oral Vocabulary attaches, process, slender, T198	✔ **Category Words** Movement Words, T207	• Text Connections, T218
✔ **Listening Comprehension**	✔ **Listening Comprehension**	• Talk About Reading, T219
• Genre: Informational Text	• Genre: Informational Text	• Research and Inquiry, T219
• Strategy: Ask and Answer Questions, T199	• Strategy: Ask and Answer Questions, T208	✔ **Word Work**
• Make Connections, T199	• Text Feature: Captions	**Phonemic Awareness**
Interactive Read Aloud "From Caterpillar to Butterfly," T199	• Make Connections, T209	• Phoneme Segmentation, T220
✔ **Word Work**	**Big Book** Paired Read: "Bugs All Around," T208	**Phonics**
Phonemic Awareness	✔ **Word Work**	• Read Words with *m, a, s, p, t*, T220
• Phoneme Blending, T200	**Phonemic Awareness**	**High-Frequency Words** the, a, see, we, like, T221
Phonics	• Phoneme Blending, T210	
• Review *m, a, s, p, t*, T201	**Phonics**	
High-Frequency Words the, a, see, we, like, T203	• Blend Words with *m, a, s, p, t*, T210	
	High-Frequency Words the, a, see, we, like, T211	
	Shared Reading "Tap! Tap! Tap!" T212–T213	
Practice *Your Turn* 69–72	**Practice** *Your Turn* 73–75	**Practice** *Your Turn* 76

DIFFERENTIATED INSTRUCTION

Leveled Reader *We Like Bugs!* T224–T225	**Leveled Reader** *We Like Bugs!* T224–T225	**Leveled Reader** Literacy Activities, T225
Phonemic Awareness Phoneme Blending, T227	**Phonemic Awareness** Phoneme Segmentation, T227	**Phonemic Awareness** Phoneme Segmentation, T227
Phonics Reteach, T228	**Phonics** Blend Words with *a, m, p, s, t*, T229	**Phonics** Build Words with *a, m, p, s, t*, T229
High-Frequency Words Reteach Words, T230	**Oral Vocabulary** Review Words, T231	Build Fluency with Phonics, T229
		Comprehension Self-Selected Reading, T231

Leveled Reader *The Bugs Run*, T232–T233	**Leveled Reader** *The Bugs Run*, T232–T233	**Leveled Reader** Literacy Activities, T233
Phonemic Awareness Phoneme Blending, T234	**Phonics** Blend Words with *a, m, p, s, t*, T236	**Comprehension** Self-Selected Reading, T237
Phonics Picture Sort, T235	**High-Frequency Words** Reread for Fluency, T237	

Leveled Reader *I See a Bug!* T238–T239	**Leveled Reader** *I See a Bug!* T238–T239	**Leveled Reader** Literacy Activities, T239
Vocabulary Oral Vocabulary: Synonyms, T241	**High-Frequency Words** Innovate, T240	**Comprehension** Self-Selected Reading, T241
Gifted and Talented		*Gifted and Talented*

Leveled Reader *The Bugs Run*, T242–T243	**Leveled Reader** *The Bugs Run*, T242–T243	**Leveled Reader** Literacy Activities, T243
Phonemic Awareness Phoneme Blending, T227	**Phonemic Awareness** Phoneme Segmentation, T227	**Phonemic Awareness** Phoneme Segmentation, T227
Phonics Reteach, T228	**Phonics** Blend Words with *a, m, p, s, t*, T229	**Phonics** Build Words with *a, m, p, s, t*, T229
High-Frequency Words Review Words, T245	**High-Frequency Words** Review Category Words, T245	Build Fluency with Phonics, T229
Writing Writing Trait: Ideas, T246	**Grammar** Verbs, T247	

LANGUAGE ARTS

Independent Writing	**Independent Writing**	**Independent Writing**
Writing Trait: Ideas, T204	Writing Trait: Ideas, T214	Writing a Story Sentence
Write a Story Sentence	Write a Story Sentence	Prepare/Present/Evaluate/Publish, T222
Prewrite/Draft, T205	Revise/Final Draft, T214	**Grammar** Verbs, T223
Grammar Verbs, T205	**Grammar** Verbs, T215	

DIFFERENTIATE TO ACCELERATE

 Scaffold to Access Complex Text

Qualitative / Quantitative
Reader and Task
TEXT COMPLEXITY

IF ➤ the text complexity of a particular section is too difficult for children

THEN ➤ see the references noted in the chart below for scaffolded instruction to help children Access Complex Text.

	Literature Big Book	**Reading/Writing Workshop**	**Leveled Readers**	
		Wonders	We Like / The Bugs / I See a / The Bugs Run	
Quantitative	*I Love Bugs!* **Lexile** 460	*"Pat"* **Lexile** BR	**Approaching Level** **Lexile** BR	**On Level** **Lexile** BR
	"Bugs All Around" **Lexile** 310	"Tap! Tap! Tap!" **Lexile** BR	**Beyond Level** **Lexile** BR	**ELL** **Lexile** BR
Qualitative	**What Makes the Text Complex?** • **Specific Vocabulary** Difficult Adjectives, T186 *See Scaffolded Instruction in Teacher's Edition, T186.*	**What Makes the Text Complex?** **Foundational Skills** • Decoding with *s, t*, T192–T193 • Identifying high-frequency words, T193	**What Makes the Text Complex?** **Foundational Skills** • Decoding with *s, t* • Identifying high-frequency words *the, we, see, a, like* *See Level Up lessons online for Leveled Readers.*	
Reader and Task	The Introduce the Concept lesson on pages T174–T175 will help determine the reader's knowledge and engagement in the weekly concept. See pages T176–T177, T187–T191, T208–T209 and T216–T219 for questions and tasks for this text.	The Introduce the Concept lesson on pages T174–T175 will help determine the reader's knowledge and engagement in the weekly concept. See pages T194–T195, T212–T213 and T216–T219 for questions and tasks for this text.	The Introduce the Concept lesson on pages T174–T175 will help determine the reader's knowledge and engagement in the weekly concept. See pages T224–T225, T232–T233, T238–T239, T242–T243 and T216–T219 for questions and tasks for this text.	

Nathan Love

Monitor and *Differentiate*

IF you need to differentiate instruction

THEN use the Quick Checks to assess children's needs and select the appropriate small group instruction focus.

 **Quick Check**

Comprehension Strategy Ask and Answer Questions, T199

Phonemic Awareness/Phonics Review /m/*m*, /a/*a*, /s/s, /p/p, /t/t, T181, T193, T203, T211, T221

High-Frequency Words *the, we, see, a, like,* T181, T193, T203, T211, T221

If No → **Approaching** **Reteach,** pp. T224–T231

ELL **Develop,** pp. T242–T247

If Yes → **On Level** **Review,** pp. T232–T237

Beyond Level **Extend,** pp. T238–T241

Level Up with Leveled Readers

IF children can read their leveled text fluently and answer comprehension questions

THEN work with the next level up to accelerate children's reading with more complex text.

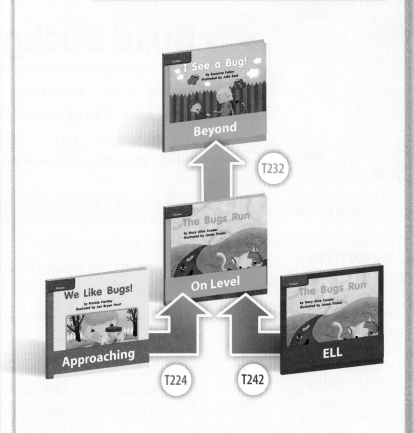

ELL ENGLISH LANGUAGE LEARNERS SCAFFOLD

IF ELL students need additional support **THEN** scaffold instruction using the small group suggestions.

| Reading-Writing Workshop T175 "Bugs, Bugs, Bugs" Integrate Ideas T217 | Leveled Reader T242–T243 *The Bugs Run* | Phonological Awareness Count and Pronounce Syllables, T226 Phoneme Segmentation, T226 Phoneme Blending, T227 Phoneme Segmentation, T227 | Phonics, Review /m/*m*, /a/*a*, /s/s, /p/p, /t/t, T228–T229 | Oral Vocabulary, T244 curious, observe, attaches, process, slender High-Frequency Words, T245 *the, we, see, a, like* | Writing Shared Writing, T246 Writing Trait: Ideas, T246 | Grammar T247 Verbs |

Note: Include ELL Students in all small groups based on their needs.

Materials

Reading/Writing Workshop Big Book
UNIT 2

Literature Big Book
I Love Bugs!

Visual Vocabulary Cards
curious
observe

Photo Cards
ant   insect
boat   ladybug
flute   piano
fly   pizza
guitar
inchworm

High-Frequency Word Cards
a
like
see
the
we

Sound-Spelling Cards
Apple
Map
Piano

Think Aloud Clouds

Response Board

"My Map," "Adam Has an Apple," "Polly and Paul Play the Piano", "Eency Weency Spider"

Reading/Writing Workshop Big Book

OBJECTIVES

CCSS Confirm understanding of information presented orally by asking and answering questions about key details and requesting clarification if something is not understood. **SL.K.2**

CCSS Identify real life connections between words and their use. **L.K.5c**

⊙ Introduce the Concept

MINILESSON
10 Mins
Build Background

ESSENTIAL QUESTION

What kind of bugs do you know about?

Read aloud the Essential Question. *We are going to sing a song about a spider. We can use the word* bugs *when we talk about spiders and insects.*

Eency Weency Spider

Eency, weency spider
went up the water spout.

Down came the rain
and washed the spider out.

Out came the sun
and dried up all the rain,

And the eency, weency spider
went up the spout again.

Sing "Eency Weency Spider" with children. Sing the song again, incorporating the hand play. Ask children to retell the story of the spider, using the hand play. Tell children that this week, they will read to find out about bugs.

Oral Vocabulary Words

Use the **Define/Example/Ask** routine to introduce the oral vocabulary words **curious** and **observe**.

To introduce the theme of "World of Bugs" explain that there are many kinds of bugs. Ask children what bugs they might have observed. What bugs are they curious about? *How can we learn about bugs?*

Go Digital

World of Bugs

Video

Photos

Visual Glossary

Oral Vocabulary Routine

Define: If you are **curious**, you want to learn more about something.

Example: I am curious about space travel, so I will read to learn more about it.

Ask: When have you felt curious? Why?

Define: When you **observe**, you closely watch something or someone.

Example: The coach will observe the baseball players during the game.

Ask: Do you like to observe bugs? Why or why not?

Visual Vocabulary Cards

Talk About It: World of Bugs

Guide children to discuss different kinds of bugs. Ask: *Which bug makes you feel the most curious? What would you like to observe about that bug?* Have children look at page 40 of their **Reading/Writing Workshop** and do the **Talk About It** activity with a partner.

READING/WRITING WORKSHOP BIG BOOK, pp. 42–43

Collaborative Conversations

Provide Details As children engage in partner, small group, and whole group discussions, encourage them to:

→ Give details to express their thoughts, feelings, and ideas clearly.

→ Use details to describe people, places, things, and events.

→ Give details when asking about a thing they don't understand.

→ # Listening Comprehension

Literature Big Book

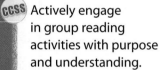

ACADEMIC LANGUAGE
characters, cover

MINILESSON 10 Mins

Read the Literature Big Book

Connect to Concept: World of Bugs

Tell children that you will now read about a boy and all of the bugs that he loves. *What bugs have you seen outside?*

Concepts of Print

Book Handling and Words Display and identify the front and back covers of the **Big Book**. Model how to turn the pages. Explain that the words on the pages are made up of letters. Point to the word *I* on the cover and remind them that the word *I* is always a capital letter.

Genre: Fiction

Model *I Love Bugs!* is a fiction story. Remind children of these characteristics of fiction.

→ The stories are made up: characters are the made up people or animals in the story.

→ Some fiction stories, like this one, have illustrations.

> **Story Words** Preview these words before reading:
>
> **glide:** to move smoothly
> **whiny:** a high-pitched sound
> **frilly:** decorated or pretty

Set a Purpose for Reading

→ Read aloud the title and the author's name. Explain that the author is the person who wrote the book.

→ Point out that for this book, the same person who wrote the words also drew the pictures.

→ Ask children to listen as you read aloud the Big Book to find out how the boy observes bugs and to see what kinds of bugs he loves.

Go Digital

I Love Bugs!

Think Aloud Cloud

Strategy: Ask and Answer Questions

Explain Remind children that good readers ask themselves questions before, during, or after reading to help them better understand the text.

Think Aloud As I look at the cover, I see a boy observing a ladybug with a magnifying glass. I wonder why he is so curious about bugs. What other kinds of bugs will he find? As I read, I will look for the answer. I will ask myself more questions as I read and after I finish reading.

Model As you read, use the **Think Aloud Cloud** to model the strategy.

Think Aloud On pages 4–5, I see that he is using the magnifying glass again. I think he must really like to look at bugs very closely. I wonder if the boy likes to listen to bugs that make sounds, too. I'll keep reading to find my answer.

Respond to Reading

After reading, prompt children to share what they learned about the bugs that the boy described. Discuss which questions they asked while reading and how they answered them. Then have children draw their favorite bug from the story.

Make Connections

Use *I Love Bugs!* to discuss bugs and their characteristics. Revisit the concept behind the Essential Question: *What kind of bugs do you know about?* by paging through the Big Book.

Write About It

Have children write about their favorite bug from the story. Discuss the characteristics of the bugs they choose.

→ # Word Work

MINILESSON
5 Mins

Phonemic Awareness

OBJECTIVES

CCSS Isolate and pronounce the initial, medial vowel, and final sounds in three-phoneme words. **RF.K.2d**

CCSS Demonstrate basic knowledge of one-to-one letter-sound correspondences by producing the primary or many of the most frequent sounds for each consonant. **RF.K.3a**

Phoneme Segmentation

1 Model Use the **Sound Boxes** on the back of the **Response Board** and markers. *Listen as I say a word:* Pam. *Say the word with me:* Pam. *There are three sounds in* Pam. *Say the sounds in* Pam *with me: /p/ /a/ /m/. Let's place a marker in a box for each sound: /p/ /a/ /m/. Demonstrate how to put a marker in each box for each sound. Repeat for tap.*

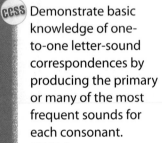

Sound Box

2 Guided Practice/Practice Distribute Response Boards and markers. *Let's listen for the number of sounds in more words. Listen as I say a word:* pat. *Say the word with me:* pat. *Say the sounds and tap with me: /p/ /a/ /t/. Let's place a marker for each sound. How many sounds are in* pat? (3) *Listen as I say a word and its sounds. Say the word and its sounds after me. Put a marker in the Sound Box for each sound you hear.* Then have them say the word.

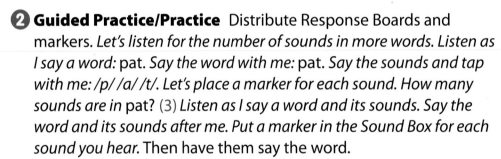

am, /a/ /m/	map, /m/ /a/ /p/	Pam, /P/ /a/ /m/
at, /a/ /t/	sit, /s/ /i/ /t/	sat, /s/ /a/ /t/

ARTICULATION SUPPORT

If children need further support, refer to Articulation Support in Unit 1: page T14 for /m/; page T96 for /a/; page T178 for /s/. Refer to Unit 2: page T14 for /p/; page T96 for /t/.

Go Digital

Phonemic Awareness

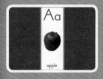

Phonics

Sound-Spelling Card

MINILESSON
10 Mins

Phonics

Review /m/*m*, /a/*a*, /p/*p*

❶ **Model** Display the *Map* **Sound-Spelling Card**. *This is the letter* m. *The letter* m *stands for the sound /m/ as in the word* map. *What is the letter?* (m) *What sound does the letter* m *stand for?* (/m/) Repeat for /a/*a* using the *Apple* and /p/*p* using the *Piano* Sound-Spelling Cards.

❷ **Guided Practice/Practice** Have children listen as you say some words. Ask them to write the letter *m* on their **Response Boards** if the word begins with /m/. Do the first two words with children.

mat	pass	tack	men	pan	mess	mile	pack

Repeat for /a/*a* and /p/*p*.

apple	ant	met	am	pin	at	pick	ax
sat	pack	top	pool	pick	mix	pan	paint

Review /m/*m*. Have children write the letter *m* on their Response Boards. Play "My Map." Have children show their Response Board with the letter *m* when they hear /m/. Repeat with /a/*a*, with "Adam Has an Apple," and /p/*p* with "Polly and Paul Play the Piano."

Corrective Feedback

Sound Error Model the sound /m/ in the initial position, then have children repeat the sound. *My turn.* Mat. */m/.* Mat. */m/. Now it's your turn.* Have children say the word and isolate the initial sound in *map* and write the letter *m*. Repeat for /a/ and /p/.

ELL

ENGLISH LANGUAGE LEARNERS

Phoneme Variations in Language
In some languages, including Hmong, there is no direct transfer for the /p/ sound. Emphasize the /p/ sound and demonstrate correct mouth position.

YOUR TURN PRACTICE BOOK p. 67

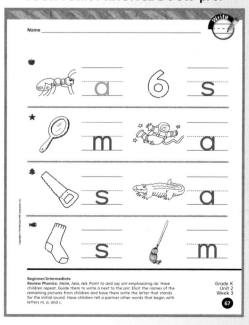

→ Word Work

Handwriting: Write Sentences with *Mm, Aa, Ss, Pp, Tt*

MINILESSON
5 Mins

1 Model Model for children how to write sentences to review and practice writing the letters *m, a, s, p,* and *t.*

→ Write the following sentence. *Pat sat at a mat.* Read the sentence with children and track the print.

→ *I hear the /p/ sound in the word* Pat. *I know that the letter* p *stands for /p/. I will underline the letter* p *because it stands for /p/. Which words have the sound /a/?* (Pat, sat, at, mat) *Which letter stands for /a/?* Underline the letter *a* in *Pat, sat, at,* and *mat.* Continue asking children which word has the sound /p/ and which letter stands for the sound. (Pat; *P*); /t/ (Pat, sat, at, mat; *t*); /m/ (mat; *m*); /s/ (sat; *s*). Underline the letters that stand for the sounds and read the words with children.

2 Guided Practice/Practice

→ Write the following sentence for children to copy: *Sam can tap.* Give them ample time to write the sentence.

→ Chorally read the sentence.

→ Ask children to identify which word has the sound /s/. (Sam) Have them underline the letter that stands for the sound. (*s*) Then have them read the word. Ask children to identify words with the following sounds and to underline the letter that stands for the sound: /a/ (Sam, can tap; *a*); /m/ (Sam; *m*), /t/ (tap; *t*) and /p/ (tap; *p*).

→ Have children check that the words in their sentences are separated by spaces. Remind them that all sentences begin with a capital letter and have end punctuation. Have them correct as needed.

 **Daily Handwriting**

Throughout the week practice writing words and sentences with the letters that have been taught. At the end of the week, have children use **Your Turn Practice Book** page 76 to practice writing words.

MINILESSON
5 Mins

High-Frequency Words

the, a, see, we, like

1 **Model** Write the following sentences:

I *like* bugs! *We see a* small bug. *The* bug tickles me.

Read aloud the sentences. Point to the high-frequency word *like*. Use the **High-Frequency Word Card** *like* and the **Read/Spell/Write** routine to review the word.

→ **Read** Point to the word *like* and say the word. *This is the word* like. *Say it with me:* like. *I like* caterpillars.

→ **Spell** *The word like is spelled l-i-k-e. Spell it with me.*

→ **Write** *Let's write the word in the air as we say each letter: l-i-k-e.*

Repeat the routine for *we, see, a,* and *the*.

2 **Guided Practice/Practice** Build sentences using High-Frequency Word Cards, **Photo Cards**, and teacher-made punctuation cards. Have children point to the high-frequency words *the, a, see, we,* and *like*. Use these sentences.

Also online

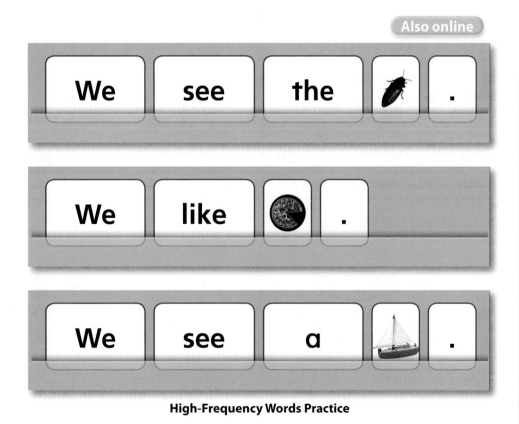

High-Frequency Words Practice

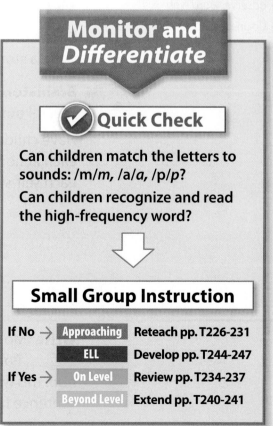

Monitor and Differentiate

✔ **Quick Check**

Can children match the letters to sounds: /m/*m*, /a/*a*, /p/*p*?

Can children recognize and read the high-frequency word?

↓

Small Group Instruction

If No → | Approaching | Reteach pp. T226-231
| ELL | Develop pp. T244-247

If Yes → | On Level | Review pp. T234-237
| Beyond Level | Extend pp. T240-241

→ # Language Arts

MINILESSON
10
Mins

Shared Writing

Writing Trait: Ideas

OBJECTIVES

CCSS Use a combination of drawing, dictating, and writing to narrate a single event or several loosely linked events, tell about the events in the order in which they occurred, and provide a reaction to what happened. **W.K.3**

CCSS Use frequently occurring nouns and verbs. **L.K.1b**

ACADEMIC LANGUAGE
• *observe, word web*
• Cognates: *observar*

❶ **Model** Remind children that we can get ideas from observing our world. We can look at and listen to things to find out more about them. We can get ideas from books, too.

→ Show children the picture of the swarm of bees in the **Big Book**. *What are the bees doing?* (flying) *What sound do the bees make?* (a buzzing sound) *The bees are flying and buzzing. The sentence gives us information about bees.*

❷ **Guided Practice/Practice** Write and read aloud: *The bugs _____.* Show the Big Book page with the grasshopper and worms. Have children describe what the bugs on the page are doing. Record answers on self-stick notes. Read each note aloud as you have children put it on the blank to finish the sentence frame.

Write a Story Sentence

Focus and Plan Tell children that this week they will learn how to write a story sentence about bugs.

 Brainstorm Make a word web, labeling the center circle *Bugs*. Draw several outer circles. Write the title "What Bugs Do" above the web.

Have children name more things that bugs do in *I Love Bugs!* Write each action word on a self-stick note and read the word aloud. Put each self-stick note around the word web.

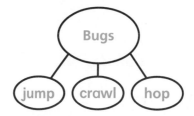

Write Model writing sentences using the word web. Write: *The bugs _____.* Point to the word *jump* on the web and say: *I can use the words from this word web to make a sentence.* Write the word *jump* into the sentence frame. Track the print as you read it aloud.

Go Digital

Writing

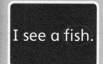
I see a fish.

Grammar

Grammar

Verbs

❶ Model Write and read aloud the words *gather* and *stack*. Then gather some books and stack them. Ask children what you did with the books.

→ Ask a child to pick up an object and place it on a table. Have children tell what actions the child did. (pick up, place)

❷ Guided Practice/Practice Write the sentence frame: *The bug _____*. Display the **Photo Cards** for *ant, fly, inchworm,* and *ladybug*. Ask children how they think each bug moves. *How does an ant move?* (walks, runs, climbs) Write the verb in the sentence frame. Read aloud the sentence and have children chorally repeat.

Model how to make more sentences from the remaining Photo Cards. Have children read the completed sentences along with you. Ask volunteers to circle the verb in each sentence.

Talk About It

Have partners work together to orally generate sentences with verbs. Challenge them to create sentences that tell about things they do after school, such as *I ride my scooter*.

ENGLISH LANGUAGE LEARNERS SCAFFOLD

Beginning

Demonstrate Listening Have children act out verbs with you: *stretch* by stretching your arms, *laugh* by laughing, *listen* by cupping your hand around your ear. Have a volunteer choose and do one of the actions. Ask the other children identify the action. Model correct pronunciation as needed.

Intermediate

Use Visuals Display the Photo Cards for *flute, guitar,* and *piano*. Have children pantomime the actions that musicians do to play each instrument. (flute player: blows) (guitarist: strums) (pianist: presses keys) Guide children in saying the action words. Model correct pronunciation as needed.

Advanced/Advanced High

Practice Have children think about games they like to play. Ask them to think of sentences to tell about the actions they do to play the game, such as *I turn the rope. I jump rope*. Elicit more details to support children's answers.

Daily Wrap Up

- Review the Essential Question and encourage children to discuss it, using the new oral vocabulary words. *What kinds of bugs do you know about?*

- Prompt children to share the skills they learned. How might they use those skills?

Reading/Writing Workshop Big Book
UNIT 2

Literature Big Book
I Love Bugs!

Cards
curious
observe

Response Board

bowl
box
flute
fork
plate
spoon

sun

Sound-Spelling Cards
Sun
Turtle

Word Cards
a
like
see
the
we

→ Build the Concept

MINILESSON 10 Mins Oral Language

OBJECTIVES

CCSS Count, pronounce, blend, and segment syllables in spoken words. **RF.K.2b**

CCSS Use words and phrases acquired through conversations. **L.K.6**

CCSS Use frequently occurring nouns and verbs. **L.K.5d**

Develop oral vocabulary

ACADEMIC LANGUAGE

• *category*

• Cognates: *categoría*

ESSENTIAL QUESTION

What kind of bugs do you know about?

Remind children that this week they are learning what makes bugs alike and different, such as being big, small, noisy, or quiet. They are also learning how bugs move.

Sing with children "Eency Weency Spider." Ask: *What do you know about spiders?*

Phonological Awareness

Count and Pronounce Syllables

Have children listen as you say and clap the word *spider*. Ask: *How many claps did I give* spider? (2) Point out that *spider* has two parts, or syllables. Have children say and clap the title of the song with you. Count the syllables with them; each word has two syllables. Then say and clap *went up the water spout* with children. Have them count the syllables in each word. (1, 1, 1, 2, 1)

Review Oral Vocabulary

Use the **Define/Example/Ask** routine to review the oral vocabulary words **curious** and **observe**. Prompt children to use the words in sentences.

Vocab
Define
Examp
Ask:

Visual Vocabulary Cards

Go Digital

Visual Glossary

Category Words

Category Words: Movement Words

1 Model Use the **Big Book** *I Love Bugs!* to point out movement words: *glide*, page 15; *flutter*, page 17; *fly* and *curl*, page 18; *hop*, page 20; *crawl*, page 21. Explain that these are movement words. They tell how someone or something changes place or position. Point to and discuss the illustrations that represent each movement word. *How do bugs move?* (crawl, creep, jump, fly)

Sing "Eency Weency Spider." Ask children to listen for movement words.

Eency, weency spider went up the water spout.
Down came the rain and washed the spider out.
Out came the sun and dried up all the rain,
And the eency, weency spider went up the spout again.

→ Sing the first line of the song again, substituting the word *crawled* for *went*. Ask children to identify the movement word. (crawled) Then ask them to suggest other movement words. (Possible answers: walked, crept, glided) For each response, sing the song again, substituting the new movement word.

2 Guided Practice/Practice Tell children that some movement words mean almost the same thing, but they are slightly different. Say the following sets of words and ask children to act out the meaning. After children demonstrate the meaning, have them tell how each word is the same and how it is different. Guide practice as needed.

> hop, jump, leap
> gallop, trot, walk
> crawl, slither, creep

LET'S MOVE!

Have children stand in different areas of the classroom. Tell them you will say some words. If the word is a movement word, they should act out the movement.

ENGLISH LANGUAGE LEARNERS

Reinforce Meaning Help children understand that movement words tell how someone or something changes place or position. Review movement words from *I Love Bugs!*, such as *glide*, *flutter*, and *fly*. Demonstrate these words and have children mirror your actions as they repeat the words with you.

→ # Listening Comprehension

 CLOSE READING

Literature Big Book

OBJECTIVES

CCSS Confirm understanding of a text read aloud or information presented orally or through other media by asking and answering questions about key details and requesting clarification if something is not understood. **SL.K.2**

CCSS With prompting and support, retell familiar stories, including key details. **RL.K.2**

- Strategy: Ask and Answer Questions
- Skill: Key Details

15 Mins

Reread Literature Big Book

Genre: Fiction

Display *I Love Bugs!* Remind children that fiction stories are made up. The characters in fiction are made-up, too. Many fiction stories, contain illustrations. *How do you know that* I Love Bugs! *is fiction?* Have children point to evidence in the text and the pictures to show that this is a fiction story.

Strategy: Ask and Answer Questions

Remind children that good readers ask and answer questions before they read and while they read. Say: *As we reread, you can ask more questions and look for the answers later in the story.*

Skill: Key Details

Remind children that they can learn important things that are happening in stories by looking for information in the text and the illustrations. Illustrations sometimes give information that is not in the author's words. Say: *Details in the illustrations can help you answer your questions.* As you read, have children listen for evidence in the text to find details.

Access Complex Text

Specific Vocabulary Children have not been directly exposed to the concept of adjectives yet. Point out the inclusion of several adjectives on each page and explain that these words tell us what kind of bugs the boy is talking about.

→ Turn to page 7. Explain that "jumpy leapy bugs" are bugs that jump and leap.

→ Page through the book, explaining the meaning of some of the more difficult adjectives.

Go Digital

I Love Bugs!

Retelling Cards

LITERATURE BIG BOOK PAGES 4–5

KEY DETAILS

What tool is the boy using to observe the bugs in the illustration? (a magnifying glass)

LITERATURE BIG BOOK PAGES 6–7

KEY DETAILS

The text tells us that the boy loves "jumpy leapy bugs." Look at the illustrations. Which bug is jumping? (grasshopper) If some children are unfamiliar with grasshoppers, have a volunteer hop to show how grasshoppers move.

LITERATURE BIG BOOK PAGES 8–9

ASK AND ANSWER QUESTIONS

Think Aloud I read that the boy loves spiky and spiny bugs. I ask the question: Does the boy like soft bugs, too? I will keep reading to find the answer.

pp. 8–9

spiky, spiny: Point to the sharp claw on the bug on page 9. Hold up a sharpened pencil. Say: *When something is spiky or spiny, it is sharp like the point of this pencil.*

Listening Comprehension

LITERATURE BIG BOOK   PAGES 10–11

ASK AND ANSWER QUESTIONS

Think Aloud Before, I asked if the boy liked soft bugs. I find my answer on these pages. He loves fuzzy and furry bugs. They are soft! I will keep asking and answering questions as I read.

pp. 10–11

whirry: Tell children that *whirry* is a sound some bugs make when they are spinning or flapping their wings very fast. Ask students to make sounds that could be called "whirry."

LITERATURE BIG BOOK   PAGES 12–13

KEY DETAILS

The boy says he loves bugs with bright wings and bugs with stripes. Look at the illustrations. Which bugs have bright wings? (butterflies) *Which bugs have stripes?* (bees and some butterflies)

pp. 12–13

stripes: explain what stripes are by pointing to the boy's shirt in the illustration. Show another example of something striped in the classroom.

LITERATURE BIG BOOK   PAGES 14–15

KEY DETAILS

Which bugs do you think are the "whiny-buzzy" bugs? (the flies) *Which bugs do you think are the "the glide-across-the-ground bugs"?* (the centipedes, the long bug with lots of legs)

pp. 14–15

glide: Tell children that *glide* means the way something moves. Move your hand in smooth waves to show this motion. Ask children to mimic your gesture as they say the word.

LITERATURE BIG BOOK PAGES 16–17

ASK AND ANSWER QUESTIONS

Do you think there are any bugs that the boy doesn't love? How could we find out the answer to this question? (Continue reading.)

LITERATURE BIG BOOK PAGES 18–19

PHONICS

Remind children that they have learned about words that begin or end with the /p/ and /t/ sounds. Reread the sentence on page 18 and have them identify the words with initial or final /p/ and initial and final /t/. (light, up, tight)

pp. 18–19

curl-up: Demonstrate curling up in a ball on the floor. Say: *I am all curled up!* Have children mimic.

LITERATURE BIG BOOK PAGES 20–21

PHONICS

Reread the sentences on the pages, and have children identify the word with the final /p/ sound. (hop)

Listening Comprehension

CLOSE READING
ELL

LITERATURE BIG BOOK PAGES 22–23

HIGH-FREQUENCY WORDS

Have children identify and read the high-frequency word *the* on page 22.

pp. 22–23

eight-legged: Tell children that "eight-legged" is another way of saying that something has eight legs. Have children repeat the phrase. Ask: *What kind of bug has eight legs?* (spider)

LITERATURE BIG BOOK PAGES 24–25

KEY DETAILS

Point out the bug on page 25. Ask: *What is this spider hanging from? How do you know?* (The ceiling. The words say "The hang-from-the-ceiling bugs...")

LITERATURE BIG BOOK PAGES 26–27

AUTHOR'S PURPOSE

Why do you think the author wrote this story? (Possible answer: Maybe she loves bugs like the boy in the story.)

pp. 26–27

send-me-squealing: Tell children that *send-me-squealing* means "to make me afraid." Make a squealing sound and have children mimic you. Then have them repeat the phrase.

Text Evidence

Explain Remind children that when they answer a question, they need to show where in the story (both words and illustrations) they found the answer.

Discuss *How do you know that the boy loves bugs that fly near lights?* (Page 18 says, "I love fly-around-the-light bugs." The illustrations show bugs near a light.)

Guided Retelling

Tell children that now they will use the **Retelling Cards** to retell the story.

→ Display Retelling Card 1. Based on children's needs, use either the Modeled, Guided or ELL retelling prompts. The ELL prompts contain support for English language learners based on levels of language acquisition. Repeat with the rest of the cards, using the prompts as a guide.

→ Discuss the story. Flip through the pages with children and have them raise their hands when they see a bug they have seen in real life. Then have children discuss where they saw these bugs.

→ Have children share one new thing they learned about bugs from the text.

Model Fluency

Reread pages 4–5 of *I Love Bugs!* in a monotone voice. Point out that reading with feeling and expression can help you enjoy a story more. *The boy in the story says that he loves bugs. I will read the words with a lot of feeling in my voice to show how much he loves bugs.* Read the page again, this time with feeling and appropriate intonation. Have children echo read and mimic your tone.

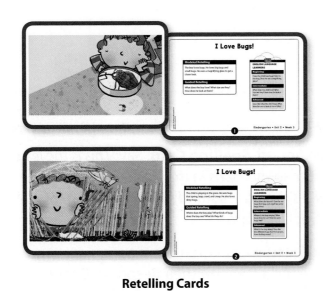

Retelling Cards

YOUR TURN PRACTICE BOOK p. 68

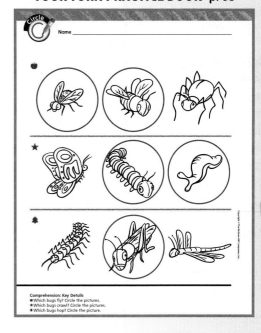

→ # Word Work

Quick Review

Build Fluency: Sound-Spellings: Show the following **Word-Building Cards:** *a, s, t.* Have children chorally say each sound. Repeat and vary the pace.

MINILESSON 5 Mins

Phonemic Awareness

OBJECTIVES

CCSS Isolate and pronounce the initial, medial vowel, and final sounds in three-phoneme words. **RF.K.2b**

CCSS Demonstrate basic knowledge of one-to-one letter-sound correspondences. **RF.K.3a**

CCSS Read common high-frequency words by sight. **RF.K.3c**

Phoneme Segmentation

❶ **Model** Use the **Sound Boxes** on the back of the **Response Boards** and markers. *Listen as I say a word:* sat. *Say the word with me. There are three sounds in* sat. *Say the sounds with me: /s/ /a/ /t/. Let's place a marker in a box for each sound: /s/ /a/ /t/.* Demonstrate for children.

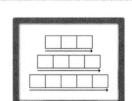

Sound Box

❷ **Guided Practice/Practice** Distribute Response Boards and markers. *Listen as I say a word:* tap. *Say the word with me:* tap. *Say the sounds in* tap *with me: /t/ /a/ /p/. Let's place a marker for each sound. How many sounds are in* tap? (3) *Listen as I say a word and its sounds. Say the word and its sounds after me. Put a marker in the Sound Box for each sound you hear.* Have them say the word.

at, /a/ /t/   sat, /s/ /a/ /t/   pat, /p/ /a/ /t/

MINILESSON 5 Mins

Phonics

ENGLISH LANGUAGE LEARNERS

High-Frequency Words: Reinforce Meaning Display the High-Frequency Word Cards *the, we, see, a, like.* Use the words in simple sentences such as *I see the flag.* As you say each sentence, point to the words and use gestures to convey meaning. Have children repeat the sentences.

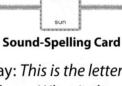

Sound-Spelling Card

Review /s/s, /t/t

❶ **Model** Display the *Sun* **Sound-Spelling Card.** Say: *This is the letter* s. *The letter* s *stands for the sound /s/ as in the word* sun. *What is the letter?* (s) *What sound does the letter* s *stand for?* (/s/) Repeat for /t/t with the *Turtle* Sound-Spelling Card.

❷ **Guided Practice/Practice** Have children listen as you say some words. Ask them to write the letter *s* on their Response Boards if the word begins with /s/. Do the first two words with children.

sat   pass   Sam   bug   sun   soup   sock   pill

Repeat for /t/t.

top   sock   tie   toe   pig   Tom   sun   toss

Go Digital

Phonemic Awareness

Phonics

Handwriting

| the | is |
| you | do |

High-Frequency Word Routine

Blend Words with /a/*a*, /s/*s*, /t/*t*

❶ **Model** Place **Word-Building Cards** *a, t* in a pocket chart. Point to the letter *a. This is the letter* a. *The letter* a *stands for /a/. Say /a/. This is the letter* t. *The letter* t *stands for /t/. Say /t/. Listen as I blend the sounds together: /aaat/. Blend the sounds with me to read the word.*

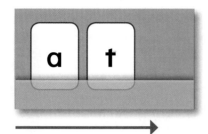

❷ **Guided Practice/Practice** Use Word-Building Cards or write *s a t.* Point to the letter *s* and have children say the sound. Point to the letter *a* and have children say the sound. Point to the letter *t* and have children say the sound. Then move your hand from left to right under the word, as children blend and read the word *sat.*

MINILESSON
5 Mins

High-Frequency Words

the, a, see, we, like

❶ **Guided Practice** Display the **High-Frequency Word Card** *the.* Use the **Read/Spell/Write** routine to review the word. Ask children to close their eyes, picture the word in their minds, and then write it the way they see it. Have children self-correct by checking the High-Frequency Word Card. Repeat with *we, see, a, like.*

COLLABORATE

❷ **Practice** Do the following to review the words in the word bank.

→ Have partners create a sentence using each word.

→ For each word, have children count the amount of letters, look at the letters in the word, and then write the word again.

Cumulative Review Review previously taught words: *I, can.*

→ Repeat the **Read/Spell/Write** routine. Then mix the words and have children chorally say each one.

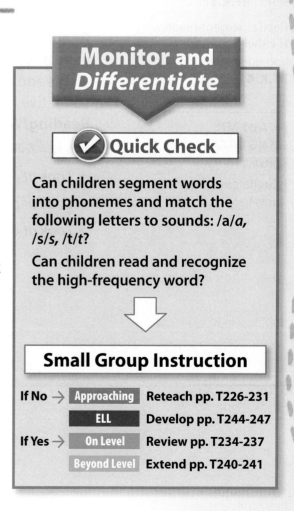

Monitor and Differentiate

✓ **Quick Check**

Can children segment words into phonemes and match the following letters to sounds: /a/*a*, /s/*s*, /t/*t*?

Can children read and recognize the high-frequency word?

Small Group Instruction

If No →	Approaching	Reteach pp. T226–231
	ELL	Develop pp. T244–247
If Yes →	On Level	Review pp. T234–237
	Beyond Level	Extend pp. T240–241

→ # Shared Read

Reading/Writing Workshop Big Book and Reading/Writing Workshop

MINILESSON

10 Mins

Read "Pat"

Model Skills and Strategies

Model Book Handling Demonstrate book handling. *This is the front cover of the book.* Then display the back cover. *This is the back cover of the book.* Model turning the pages of the book.

Model Concepts About Print Turn to page 45 and point to the sentence. *This is a sentence. We know that sentences are made up of words.* Read the sentence, pointing to each word as you read it. Then point to the word *am. This is a word in the sentence. Words are made up of letters. What letters do you see?* (*a, m*) *Let's read the word: am.*

Predict Turn to page 44 and read the title together. Invite children to look closely at the illustration and predict what they think the story will be about.

Read Have children chorally read the story with you. Point to each word as you read it together. Help children sound out decodable words and say the sight words. If children have difficulty, provide corrective feedback and guide them page by page using the student **Reading/Writing Workshop**.

Ask the following:

→ *Look at page 46. What is Pat leaning on?* (a rock)

→ *Look at page 47. What does Pat see?* (a bug)

→ *Look at page 48. Why do you think Pat is tapping the leaf?* (Possible answer: Pat might be trying to get the bug to fly, so he can eat it.)

Reading/Writing Workshop Big Book and Reading/Writing Workshop

OBJECTIVES

CCSS Read common high-frequency words by sight. **RF.K.3c**

CCSS Read emergent-reader texts with purpose and understanding. **RF.K.4**

ACADEMIC LANGUAGE

• *predict*

• Cognates: *predecir*

Go Digital 🖑

"Pat"

"Pat"

READING/WRITING WORKSHOP, pp. 44–49

Rereading

Have small groups use the **Reading/Writing Workshop** to reread "Pat". Then review the skills and strategies using the *Phonics* and *Words to Know* pages that come before the selection.

→ Have children ask themselves questions as they read. Remind them that they can find the answers in the words and the illustrations. If necessary, model how to ask and answer a question.

→ Have children use page 43 to review the high-frequency words *the, we, see, a,* and *like*.

→ Have children use page 42 to review the letters *m, a, s, p,* and *t* and their corresponding sounds. Guide them to blend the sounds to read the words.

→ # Language Arts

Go Digital

Writing

I see a fish.

Grammar

MINILESSON
10 Mins
Interactive Writing

Writing Trait: Ideas

Review Display the cover of *I Love Bugs! What is the boy doing?* (He is observing a bug.) Remind children that when we closely observe things, we learn new things. We can also get new ideas about things from books. *We have been getting ideas about what bugs do from* I Love Bugs! *What are some new things you learned about bugs?* (They move in different ways. They look different.)

Write a Story Sentence

Discuss Display the word web from Day 1. Read aloud each verb. *What do these words tell you about bugs?* (the way bugs move) Talk about other things that bugs do.

Model/Apply Grammar Tell children that you will work together to write a story sentence about a bug. Display the sentence frame from Day 1: *The bug* _____. Remind children that you will use a verb, or action word, to complete the sentence.

Ask children to think of a way a bug moves or acts to complete the sentence, such as *hops*. Write *hops* on a self-stick note and use it to complete the sentence frame. Track the print as you read the sentence aloud.

Write Have children help you create another sentence about other ways bugs move or act, such as *The bug digs*. Share the pen with children and have them write the letters they know. Track the print as you read aloud the sentence: *The bug digs*. Have children chorally read aloud the sentence with you.

OBJECTIVES

CCSS Use a combination of drawing, dictating, and writing to narrate a single event or several loosely linked events, tell about the events in the order in which they occurred, and provide a reaction to what happened. **W.K.3**

CCSS Use frequently occurring nouns and verbs. **L.K.1b**

ACADEMIC LANGUAGE
• *word web, verb*
• Cognates: *verbo*

Grammar

MINILESSON
5 Mins

Verbs

1 Review Demonstrate actions, using your hands and have children tell what action you are doing.

→ Wave your hand as if saying goodbye. *What action word describes what I am doing with my hand?* (wave)

→ Shake your hand as if giving a handshake. *What action word describes what I am doing with my hand?* (shake)

→ Raise your hand. *What action word describes what I am doing with my hand?* (raise)

Write and read the action words aloud. Have children chorally repeat.

2 Guided Practice Have children think of other ways they use their hands to do things. Write the sentence: *I hold a book.* Hold up a book while you read aloud the sentence. Have children tell the action word in the sentence.

3 Practice Have children work with partners. Ask them to draw pictures of something they can do with their hands. Guide children in writing an action word for their picture. Allow time for children to share their drawings.

Talk About It

Have partners work together to orally generate sentences with verbs. Ask them to describe the actions they do with their feet. Have them use the sentence frame, such as *I walk with my feet.*

ENGLISH LANGUAGE LEARNERS

Use Visuals Display the **Photo Cards** for *bowl, box, flute, fork, plate, spoon.* Have children choose the things they use to eat with. Write and read aloud the sentence frame: *I eat with a _____.* Guide children in filling in the sentence with the correct object. *What is the action word in the sentence?* Read aloud the complete sentences.

Daily Wrap Up

● Discuss the Essential Question and encourage children to use the oral vocabulary words. *What bugs are you curious about? What do you observe about those bugs?*

● Prompt children to review and discuss the skills they used today. How do those skills help them?

Materials

Reading/Writing Workshop Big Book
UNIT 2

Visual Vocabulary Cards
process
slender
attaches

Response Board

 a b c
Word-Building Cards

Puppet

Interactive Read-Aloud Cards

Photo Cards
mix   saw
mop   seal
mouse   sock
piano   tiger
pie   top
pig   toys

Sound-Spelling Cards
map   turtle
sun   apple
piano

High-Frequency Word Cards
a
like
see
the
we

"Eeency Weency Spider"
"My Two-Ton Turtle"

 → # Build the Concept

 MINILESSON **10 Mins** ## Oral Language

OBJECTIVES

CCSS Actively engage in group reading activities with purpose and understanding. **RI.K.10**

CCSS Identify real-life connections between words and their use. **L.K.5c**

Develop oral vocabulary

ACADEMIC LANGUAGE

• *informational text*
• Cognates: *texto informativo*

ESSENTIAL QUESTION

Remind children that this week they are talking and learning about bugs. Guide children to discuss the Essential Question using information from the **Big Book** and the weekly song.

Remind children about the bug in "Eency Weency Spider." Sing the song and have children join in.

Oral Vocabulary

Review last week's oral vocabulary words, as well as *curious* and *observe* from Day 1. Then use the **Define/Example/Ask** routine to introduce *process, slender,* and *attaches.*

> ### Oral Vocabulary Routine
>
> **Define:** When something goes through a **process**, it changes as it follows a set of steps.
>
> **Example:** We started the process of making a cake.
>
> **Ask:** What is a process you know about from nature?
>
> **Define: Slender** means slim and narrow.
>
> **Example:** The slender pieces of wheat wave in the wind.
>
> **Ask:** What is an object you see in the classroom that is slender?
>
> **Define:** When something **attaches** itself to something else, the two things join together.
>
> **Example:** My mom attaches the leash to our dog's collar.
>
> **Ask:** What is a material that attaches a swing to a tree branch?

Vocab...
Define...
Examp...
Ask:

Visual Vocabulary Cards

Go Digital

Visual Glossary

"From Caterpillar to Butterfly"

I wonder...
Think Aloud Cloud

→ Listening Comprehension

MINILESSON 10 Mins

Read the Interactive Read Aloud

Genre: Informational Text

Tell children you will be reading an informational text. Remind them that *informational text* explains or gives true information about a subject. Display the **Interactive Read-Aloud Cards**.

Read the title. Explain that a caterpillar goes through steps to become a butterfly.

Interactive Read-Aloud Cards

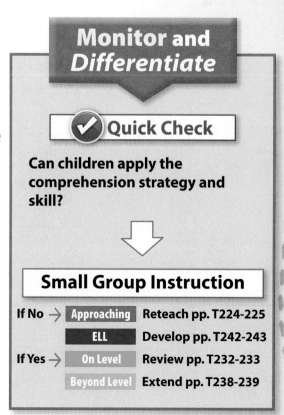

ENGLISH LANGUAGE LEARNERS

Reinforce Meaning As you read "From Caterpillar to Butterfly," make meaning clear by pointing to specific characters, places, or objects in the photographs, demonstrating word meanings, paraphrasing text, and asking children questions. For example, on Card 4, point to the chrysalis. Say: *This is a chrysalis.* Repeat with *butterfly*.

Strategy: Ask and Answer Questions

Guide children in recalling that good readers ask themselves questions as they read informational texts. Tell them this helps them understand the information they are reading. Remind children that they can use the **Think Aloud Cloud** as they ask and answer questions by remembering what they have read, by reading again, or by reading more.

Think Aloud Near the end of the story, I read that the butterfly is tired and weak when it pushes through the chrysalis, and its wings are wet. How will it be able to fly with wet wings? I don't understand. I'll read on to see if I can answer my question. As I read on, I am able to answer my question. The wings dry in the sun, and then the butterfly flies away to look for food.

Read "From Caterpillar to Butterfly." Pause to model asking and answering questions throughout reading.

Make Connections

COLLABORATE

Guide partners to connect "From Caterpillar to Butterfly" with *I Love Bugs!* Discuss the ways both selections tell about bugs. Remind children that *I Love Bugs!* is fiction, and "From Caterpillar to Butterfly" is informational text.

Monitor and *Differentiate*

✓ **Quick Check**

Can children apply the comprehension strategy and skill?

⬇

Small Group Instruction

If No →	**Approaching**	Reteach pp. T224–225
	ELL	Develop pp. T242–243
If Yes →	**On Level**	Review pp. T232–233
	Beyond Level	Extend pp. T238–239

→ # Word Work

MINILESSON 5 Mins

Phonemic Awareness

Puppet

Phoneme Blending

OBJECTIVES

CCSS Isolate and pronounce the initial, medial vowel, and final sounds in three-phoneme words. **RF.K.2d**

Blend sounds to make words

❶ **Model** *The **puppet** is going to say the sounds in a word. Listen: /m/ /a/ /t/. It can blend these sounds together: /mmmaaat/,* mat. *Now say the word with the puppet:* mat. Repeat with *Sam.*

❷ **Guided Practice/Practice** Have children blend sounds to form words. *The puppet is going to say the sounds in a word. Listen as it says each sound. Repeat the sounds then blend them to say the word.* Guide practice with the first word.

/s/ /a/ /t/	/m/ /a/ /p/	/p/ /a/ /t/	/a/ /m/	/t/ /a/ /p/
/b/ /i/ /g/	/k/ /a/ /t/	/h/ /i/ /z/	/p/ /a/ /n/	/f/ /a/ /n/

For additional support, review /m/, /a/, /s/, /p/, and /t/. Play and sing, "My Map," "Adam Has an Apple," "See the Sun Rise," "Polly and Paul Play the Piano," and "My Two-Ton Turtle." Have children clap when they hear /m/, /a/, /s/, /p/, or /t/.

Go Digital

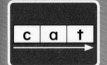

Phonemic Awareness

Phonics

Handwriting

Phonics

10 Mins

| Mm | Ss | Pp | Tt |
| map | sun | piano | turtle |

Sound-Spelling Cards

Review *m, a, s, p, t*

❶ **Model** Display the *Map* **Sound-Spelling Card**. Review initial and final /m/*m* using the words *map* and *am*. Repeat the routine for /s/*s*, /p/*p*, /t/*t* using the *Sun, Piano,* and *Turtle* Sound-Spelling Cards. Display the *Apple* Sound-Spelling Card. Review initial and medial *a* /a/ using the words *am* and *tap*.

❷ **Guided Practice/Practice** Have children practice connecting the letter and sound. Point to the Sound-Spelling Card and the letter *m. What is this letter?* (m) *What sound does it stand for?* (/m/) Repeat the routine for /a/*a*, /s/*s*, /p/*p*, /t/*t*.

♪ Review /s/*s*. Have children write the letter *s* on their **Response Boards**. Play "See the Sun Rise." Have children show their Response Board with the letter *s* when they hear /s/. Repeat with /t/*t*, with "My Two-Ton Turtle."

Blend Words with Short *a* and *m, s, p, t*

❶ **Model** Display **Word-Building Cards** *m, a, t*. Say: *This is the letter* m. *It stands for* /m/. *This is* a. *It stands for* /a/. *This is* t. *It stands for* /t/. *Let's blend the three sounds together:* /mmmaaat/. *The word is* mat.

❷ **Guided Practice/Practice** Use Word-Building Cards or write the following words. Have children read each word, blending the sounds. Guide practice with the first word.

at   Pat   sat   mat   map   tap

Write these sentences. Prompt children to read the text, sounding out the decodable words: *Pat can tap. We sat at the mat.*

Corrective Feedback

Sound Error Model the sound that children missed, then have them repeat. For example, for the word *mat*, say: *My turn.* Tap under the letter *t* and ask: *What's the sound?* Return to the beginning of the word. *Let's start over.* Blend the word with children again.

YOUR TURN PRACTICE BOOK pp. 69–70

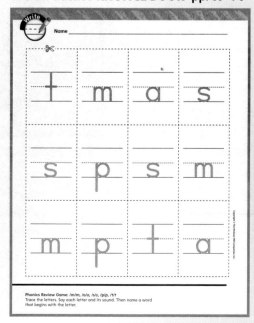

→ # Word Work

Photo Cards

Go Digital

MINILESSON
5 Mins

Phonics

Picture Sort

OBJECTIVES

CCSS Read common high-frequency words by sight. **RF.K.3c**

Sort picture names of objects by initial sound

ACADEMIC LANGUAGE
sort

① **Model** Remind children that the letter *m* can stand for /m/. Place the **Word-Building Card** *m* in one column in a pocket chart. *What is the letter?* (m) *What sound does it stand for?* (/m/) Continue the same routine for the letters *s, p,* and *t.*

Hold up the *Mix* **Photo Card**. *Here is the picture for* mix. Mix *has the /m/ sound at the beginning. I will place* mix *under the letter* m *because the letter* m *stands for /m/.* Use the same routine for *sock, piano,* and *tiger.*

② **Guided Practice/Practice** Display and name each of the following Photo Cards: *mouse, seal, pig, pie, top, saw, toys, mop.* Have children sort the Photo Cards by initial sound. Have them tell the initial sound and under which letter the Photo Card should be placed.

You may also wish to review initial and medial a /a/. Use the following Photo Cards: *ambulance, ant, apple, astronaut, ax, bat, fan, hat, map, yak.*

Phonics

the | is
you | do

High-Frequency Word Routine

Photo Cards

High-Frequency Words

the, a, see, we, like

❶ **Guided Practice** Display **High-Frequency Word Cards** *the, a, see, we,* and *like*. Review the words using the **Read/Spell/Write** routine.

❷ **Practice** Point to the High-Frequency Word Card *the* and have children read it. Repeat with the words *we, see, a, like*.

Build Fluency

Word Automaticity Have children read aloud the following sentences. Repeat several times.

> I like Sam.
> We see Pam tap.
> I like the mat.
> I see a map.

Read for Fluency Distribute pages 71–72 of the **Your Turn Practice Book** and help children assemble their Take-Home Books. Chorally read the Take-Home Book with children. Then have children reread the book to review high-frequency words and build fluency.

YOUR TURN PRACTICE BOOK pp. 71–72

Monitor and Differentiate

✓ Quick Check

Can children blend phonemes to make words and sort words with /m/m, /a/a, /s/s, /t/t, /p/p?

Can children read and recognize the high-frequency word?

⬇

Small Group Instruction

If No →	Approaching	Reteach pp. T226-231
	ELL	Develop pp. T244-247
If Yes →	On Level	Review pp. T234-237
	Beyond Level	Extend pp. T240-241

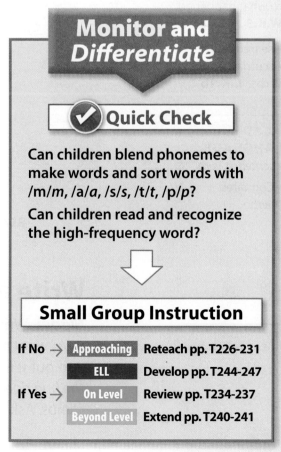

→ # Language Arts

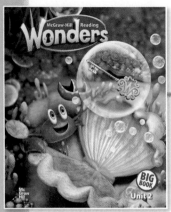

Reading/Writing Workshop Big Book

OBJECTIVES

CCSS Use a combination of drawing, dictating, and writing to narrate a single event or several loosely linked events, tell about the events in the order in which they occurred, and provide a reaction to what happened. **W.K.3**

CCSS Use frequently occurring nouns and verbs. **L.K.1b**

ACADEMIC LANGUAGE

• *sentence, verb*
• Cognates: *verbo*

MINILESSON 10 Mins

Independent Writing

Writing Trait: Ideas

1 Model Tell children that today they will write a story sentence about a bug. Show the **Big Book** page 25, with the spider. Point to the hanging spider. Write and read aloud: *The spider hangs from a ceiling.* Explain that *hangs* is an action word. Write *hang* on a self-stick note and add it to the word web from Day 1.

2 Guided Practice Share the Readers to Writers page in the **Reading/Writing Workshop Big Book**. Read the model sentence aloud. Guide children in substituting an action word, such as, *The bug crawls on the leaf,* or *The bug eats the leaf.*

READING/WRITING WORKSHOP BIG BOOK, p. 58

Write a Story Sentence

Model Write and read aloud: *The bug _____.* Point to the blank and say: *I want to write a story about a bug.* Write *climbs* on a self-stick note and put it in the sentence frame. *This sentence tells a story about what the bug does.* Read the sentence aloud, tracking the print: *The bug climbs.* Ask children how they feel about bugs that climb.

Go Digital

Present the Lesson

Writing

I see a fish.

Grammar

Prewrite

Brainstorm Tell children that before they can begin writing a story sentence, they must choose a bug to draw. Display the Big Book and **Photo Cards** *fly, inchworm, insect, ladybug,* and *moth* to help children with ideas. Have children work with a partner to choose bugs and talk about what the bugs can do.

Draft

Ask children to draw pictures of the bugs they chose. Guide children in writing this sentence frame: *The bug* _____ . Help them choose an action word that tells what the bug does in their pictures. Help children write story sentences about their bugs using action words.

Apply Writing Trait As children write their sentences, have them tell you what their bugs are doing in their stories.

Apply Grammar Tell children to point to and tell you the action word. Remind children that action words are called "verbs."

MINILESSON

5 Mins

Grammar

Action Words (Verbs)

❶ Review Remind children that action words tell what someone or something is doing.

→ Write and read aloud the following sentences: *She gives me a book. I read the book.*

Ask children to identify the action words in each sentence.

❷ Guided Practice/Practice Have children think of the actions they do in school.

Have children work in pairs. Ask them to discuss things they do in school. Write: *I* _____ . Guide children in writing the action word to complete the sentence.

Talk About It

Have partners work together to orally generate sentences with verbs. Have children use the same action word in different sentences, such as *I draw a cat. I draw a dog.*

Daily Wrap Up

- Review the Essential Question and encourage children to discuss it, using the oral vocabulary words *curious* and *observe*. *What would you like to observe about bugs? How can you learn more about bugs?*

- Prompt children to review and discuss the skills they used today. Guide them to give examples of how they used each skill.

Materials

Reading/Writing Workshop Big Book
UNIT 2

Literature Big Book
I Love Bugs!

Visual Vocabulary Cards
a
see
we
like

Puppet

Word-Building Cards

Interactive Read-Aloud Cards

High-Frequency Word Cards
a
like
see
the
we

Photo Cards
baby   kite
bike   koala
bird   rope
dinosaur
football
horse
inchworm
jump

(→) # Extend the Concept

MINILESSON
10 Mins

Oral Language

OBJECTIVES

CCSS Count, pronounce, blend, and segment syllables in spoken words. **RF.K.2b**

CCSS Use words and phrases acquired through conversations, reading and being read to, and responding to texts. **L.K.6**

Develop oral vocabulary

ESSENTIAL QUESTION

Remind children that this week they have been talking and reading about kinds of bugs. Have them recite "Eency Weency Spider." *What does the spider in the song do? Is it like the spider in* I Love Bugs!?

Phonological Awareness

Count and Pronounce Syllables

Point to the word *water*. Say: *We can break the word* water *into parts: /wô/ /tər/. We can count the parts, or syllables, in this word. The word* water *has two parts.* Clap each part as you say the word: /wô/ /tər/. *Let's say and count the parts of another word. Listen:* butterfly. *How many parts does* butterfly *have?* (three) Invite volunteers to clap the parts of the words *picture* and *two*. Repeat with *spout* and *window*.

Review Oral Vocabulary

Reread the Interactive Read Aloud Use the **Define/Example/Ask** routine to review the oral vocabulary words *curious, observe, process, slender,* and *attaches*. Then have children listen as you reread "From Caterpillar to Butterfly." Ask the following questions:

→ *What is the first step in the process of a caterpillar becoming a butterfly?* (egg)

→ *A caterpillar forms a hard case after it attaches itself to a plant. What is the name of this hard case?* (chrysalis)

Go Digital

Visual Glossary

"From Caterpillar to Butterfly"

Category Words

Category Words: Movement Words

① **Explain/Model** Draw a simple outline of a body. Work with children to label the body parts: *face; arms; hands; legs; feet.* Explain that we use movement words to describe how each body part can move. *Your face can smile. Let me see you smile. Your hands can scratch. What do scratching hands look like? Your feet can kick. What can a foot kick?* Ask children to demonstrate these movements. Then work with children to name other movement words for each body part, such as: face: *frown, chew, wink, yawn*; arms and hands: *swing, clap, throw, wave*; legs and feet: *walk, run, stomp, jump.*

② **Guided Practice** Remind children that some words can mean almost the same thing. Have children act out the following word pairs in order to distinguish shades of meaning. After children demonstrate, have them tell how the words are similar and how they are different. Guide practice as needed.

> grin, smile
> march, walk
> chew, crunch
> whisper, mumble
> throw, toss
> growl, roar
> flutter, fly

LET'S MOVE!

Have children stand up. Display Photo Cards for people, animals, and things that can move. Have children act out how each person, animal, or thing might move. Ask children to name the movement word that describes the movement.

ENGLISH LANGUAGE LEARNERS

Demonstrate Understanding
Display the Photo Cards from the lesson and pair English Language Learners with fluent speakers. Have partners make up sentences using the Photo Card and a movement word.

YOUR TURN PRACTICE BOOK p. 73

Name _____

swimming	jumping	mitten
pickle	flying	climbing
running	apple	walking

Category Words: Movement Words
Tell about each picture. Put a marker on each picture if it shows movement.

→ # Listening Comprehension

CLOSE READING

Literature Big Book

OBJECTIVES

CCSS With prompting and support, ask and answer questions about key details in a text. **RI.K.1**

- Understand the characteristics of informational text
- Use the text feature captions to gather information
- Apply the comprehension strategy: Ask and Answer Questions
- Make connections across texts

ACADEMIC LANGUAGE
caption

MINILESSON **10** Mins

Read "Bugs All Around"

Genre: Informational Text

Display "Bugs All Around" on pages 28–32 of the **Big Book** and read aloud the title. Remind children that informational text tells about real people, places, and/or things.

Set a Purpose for Reading

Read aloud page 28. Tell children to listen as you continue reading to learn about bugs.

Strategy: Ask and Answer Questions

Remind children that good readers ask and answer questions as they read. Have children look at page 28. *We can ask: How are some bugs alike? We can answer: Some bugs have six legs.*

Text Feature: Captions

Explain Point out the first caption on page 28. *Captions give more information about what is shown in a photograph. This caption tells me this bug is a ladybug.*

Apply Turn to page 29. Point to the caption. *What does this caption tell us about the ants?* (They work hard.)

Go Digital

I Love Bugs!

LITERATURE BIG BOOK   PAGES 28–29

HIGH-FREQUENCY WORDS

Have children identify and read the high-frequency words *like* and *a* on page 29. Repeat the routine with the words *we* and *see* on page 30.

LITERATURE BIG BOOK   PAGES 30–31

KEY DETAILS

Look at the photograph on page 31. What does the photograph show you? (how a grasshopper moves)

LITERATURE BIG BOOK   PAGE 32

ASK AND ANSWER QUESTIONS

What is something that bugs do not like? (to be touched)

Retell and Respond

Have children discuss the selection by asking the following questions:

→ *How are a ladybug and an ant alike?* (They both have six legs.)

→ *How is a butterfly different than a grasshopper?* (A butterfly can fly and a grasshopper cannot fly.)

Make Connections

Have children recall the selections they have read this week.

→ The selections this week have been about bugs. *Which kind of bug was the boy's favorite?* (spider)

Write About It Write about what a caterpillar turns into in the end. Draw a picture.

ENGLISH LANGUAGE LEARNERS

Reinforce Meaning As you read aloud the text, make the meaning clear by pointing to details in the photographs and captions. Ask children questions and elicit language.

CONNECT TO CONTENT

Looking at Bugs Review the way some bugs are alike (some have six legs). Have partners draw pictures to show how two bugs are different.

STEM

→ # Word Work

Quick Review
Build Fluency: Sound-Spellings: Show the following **Word-Building Cards:** *a, m, p, s, t.* Have children chorally say each sound. Repeat and vary the pace.

MINILESSON
5 Mins

Phonemic Awareness

Puppet

OBJECTIVES

CCSS Distinguish between similarly spelled words by identifying the sounds of letters that differ. **RF.K.3d**

CCSS Read common high-frequency words by sight. **RF.K.3c**

• Blend phonemes to form words

• Blend letter sounds to form words

Phoneme Blending

❶ **Model** *The puppet is going to say the sounds in a word. Listen: /t/ /a/ /p/. The puppet can blend these sounds together: /taaap/,* tap. *Now say the word with the puppet:* tap. *Repeat with* sat.

❷ **Guided Practice/Practice** Have children blend sounds to form words. *The puppet is going to say the sounds in a word. Listen as it says each sound. Repeat the sound, then blend them to say the word.* Guide practice with the first word.

/m/ /a/ /p/	/p/ /a/ /t/	/a/ /t/	/m/ /a/ /t/	/p/ /a/ /m/
/p/ /i/ /g/	/h/ /o/ /t/	/n/ /ō/	/s/ /i/ /k/	/h/ /e/ /n/

MINILESSON
5 Mins

Phonics

Blend Words with *m, a, s, p, t*

❶ **Guided Practice** Display **Word-Building Cards** *p, a, t.* Point to the letter *p.* Say: *This is the letter* p. *The letter* p *stands for /p/. Say /p/. This is the letter* a. *The letter* a *stands for /a/. Listen as I blend the two sounds together: /paaa/. Say /paaa/. This is the letter* t. *The letter* t *stands for /t/. Listen as I blend the three sounds: /paaat/,* pat. *Now you say it. Let's change* p *to* s. *Use the same routine to blend* sat.

❷ **Practice** Write *at, sat, mat, map, tap.* Have children blend the letters to read the words. Point out the words *at* and *sat.* Ask children which letters are the same. (*a, t*) Ask them how the words are different. (*Sat* has the letter *s.*) Point out that by adding the letter *s,* we can make a new word. Continue comparing words, noticing how the sounds and letters are the same and how they are different. Point out that words with the same ending sounds and letters, such as *at, sat, mat* or *map* and *tap* also rhyme.

Go Digital

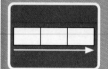
Phonemic Awareness

Phonics

Handwriting

Visual Glossary

High-Frequency Word Routine

Dictation

Review Dictate the following sounds for children to spell. Have them repeat the sound and then write the letter that stands for the sound.

/m/   /a/   /s/   /p/   /t/

Dictate the following words for children to spell: *tap, Pam, sat, map.* Model for children how to segment each word to scaffold the spelling.

Say: *When I say the word* tap, *I hear three sounds: /t/ /a/ /p/. I know the letter* t *stands for /t/, the letter* a *stands for /a/, and the letter* p *stands for /p/. I will write the letters* t, a, p *to spell the word* tap.

When children are finished, write the letters and words for them to self-correct.

High-Frequency Words

Practice Say the words *the, a, see, we,* and *like* and have children write them. Then display the **Visual Vocabulary Cards** for each word. Follow the Teacher Talk routine on the back.

Build Fluency Build sentences in a pocket chart using **High-Frequency Word Cards**, **Photo Cards**, and teacher-made punctuation cards. Have children chorally read the sentences as you track the print. Then have them identify the words *the, a, see, we, like.*

> *We like the* moon.
>
> *We see a* star.
>
> I *see a* mouse.

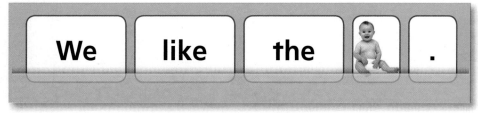

High-Frequency Words Practice

Have partners create sentences using the words *the, a, see, we, like.*

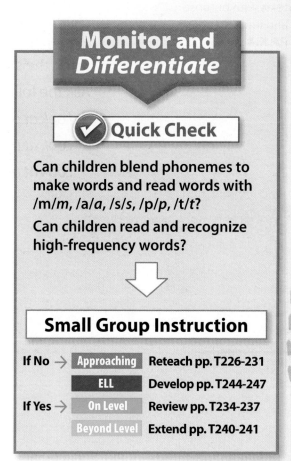

Monitor and *Differentiate*

✓ **Quick Check**

Can children blend phonemes to make words and read words with /m/m, /a/a, /s/s, /p/p, /t/t?

Can children read and recognize high-frequency words?

⬇

Small Group Instruction

If No →	**Approaching**	Reteach pp. T226–231
	ELL	Develop pp. T244–247
If Yes →	**On Level**	Review pp. T234–237
	Beyond Level	Extend pp. T240–241

→ # Shared Read

Go Digital

"Tap! Tap! Tap!"

Reading/Writing Workshop Big Book and Reading/Writing Workshop

---

OBJECTIVES

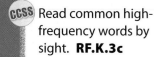 Read common high-frequency words by sight. **RF.K.3c**

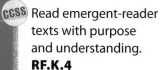 Read emergent-reader texts with purpose and understanding. **RF.K.4**

MINILESSON 10 Mins

Read "Tap! Tap! Tap!"

Model Skills and Strategies

Model Book Handling Point to the front cover of the book. *This is the front cover of the book.* Then display the back cover of the book. *This is the back cover of the book.* Model turning the pages of the book.

Model Concepts About Print Open the book, point to the title of the story, and read it. Tap *is a word that is made up of three letters:* t, a, *and* p. Have volunteers take turns pointing to the first letter and last letter in the word and saying the names of each letter. Then ask children to tell how many times they see the word *Tap.*

Predict Read the title and ask children to repeat it. Encourage them to describe the photograph on the title page. *What do you think the selection will be about?*

Read Point out each rebus, and discuss what it stands for. Then have children chorally read the selection. Children should sound out the decodable words and say the sight words. Offer support as needed using the student **Reading/Writing Workshop**.

Ask the following:

→ *Look at page 51. Where is the family?* (They are at a lake.)

→ *Look at page 54. What does the boy see?* (a ladybug)

→ *Look at page 55. What is the father pointing to?* (The father is pointing to a bird called a woodpecker.)

"Tap! Tap! Tap!"

READING/WRITING WORKSHOP, pp. 50–55

Rereading

Have small groups use the **Reading/Writing Workshop** to reread "Tap! Tap! Tap!" Then review the skills and strategies using the *Phonics* and *Words to Know* pages that come before the selection.

→ Encourage children to ask themselves questions and find the answers in the words. Remind them that they can also find answers by looking closely at the photographs.

→ Have children use page 43 to review the high-frequency words *the, we, see, a,* and *like.*

→ Have children use page 42 to review the letters *m, a, s, p,* and *t,* and their corresponding sounds. Guide them to blend the sounds to read the words.

ELL

ENGLISH LANGUAGE LEARNERS

Reinforce Vocabulary Display the **High-Frequency Word Cards** *the, we, see, a,* and *like.* Point to classroom objects as you use the high-frequency word in sentences such as the following: *I like the book on bugs. Do you like the book on bugs?* (Yes, we like the book on bugs.) *I see a calendar. Can you see a calendar?* (Yes, we can see a calendar.)

 **Language Arts**

Independent Writing

Go Digital

OBJECTIVES

CCSS With guidance and support from adults, respond to questions and suggestions from peers and add details to strengthen writing as needed. **W.K.5**

CCSS Use frequently occurring nouns and verbs **L.K.1b**

ACADEMIC LANGUAGE

- *revise, action word, draft*
- Cognates: *revisar*

Writing Trait: Ideas

Revise

Distribute children's drawings and story sentences from Day 3.

Apply Writing Trait Ideas Explain that as writers revise, they can add more ideas to their sentences. Write and read aloud: *The bug digs.* Have children look at the word web about bugs. Tell children that they can choose other action words from it to add to their sentences. Write *and* on a self-stick note and add it after *digs.* Ask children to choose another word from the word web, such as *crawls.* Have children add the *crawls* self-stick note to the sentence. Help children add more to their story sentences in the same way. Then have children read the sentences they wrote and check for the following:

→ What is the action word?

→ What information is in the sentence?

→ Does my sentence tell what a bug does?

Apply Grammar Tell children that verbs give information as well as action to a story. Read aloud the sentence: *The ant pulls a long leaf. What action is the ant doing? Yes, the ant is pulling a leaf that is probably bigger than it.*

 Peer Edit Have children work with a partner to do a peer edit. Ask partners to check that the sentences use an action word that makes sense for the bug in the drawing. Partners should read the sentences aloud to see if there is another verb that they would like better. Provide time for children to make revisions to their sentences.

Final Draft

After children have edited their own papers and finished their peer edits, have them write their final draft. Explain that they should leave spaces between words so that readers can read their writing. As children work, conference with them to provide guidance.

Writing

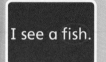
I see a fish.

Grammar

Grammar
MINILESSON
5 Mins

Verbs

❶ Review Remind children that an action word is a verb. A verb tells what someone or something does. Write this sentence on the board: *The painter climbs the ladder.* Track the print as you read it aloud. *What does the painter do?* (climb) Underline the action word *climb* and tell children that *climb* is a verb.

❷ Guided Practice Write these sentences on the board:

→ *We go to the park.*

→ *She jumps rope.*

Track and read aloud the first sentence. Ask children to identify the action word. Circle the verb. Have children read aloud the sentence with you. Repeat with the other sentence.

❸ Practice Have children work in pairs and draw something they do in a park. Write the sentence frame: *In the park I _____.* Have children copy the sentence frame at the bottom of their drawings. Guide them in completing the sentence with an action word that is described in the drawing.

Talk About It

Have partners work together to orally generate sentences with verbs. Challenge them to create sentences with more than one verb, using the conjunction *and.* For example: *I sit and read.*

ELL

ENGLISH LANGUAGE LEARNERS

Picture Cards and Sentences
Provide sentences that go with images on **Photo Cards** for *bike, football, jump rope,* and *kite.* For example: *I ride a bike in the park.* As you say a sentence aloud, hold up a Photo Card as you say the action, such as *bike.* Ask children to tell what they do with a bike.

Daily Wrap Up

- Review the Essential Question and encourage children to discuss it, using the oral vocabulary words.

- Prompt children to discuss the skills they practiced and learned today. Guide them to share examples of each skill.

Go Digital

www.connected.mcgraw-hill.com
RESOURCES
Research and Inquiry

→ ## Wrap Up the Week
Integrate Ideas

RESEARCH AND INQUIRY

World of Bugs

OBJECTIVES

 Participate in shared research and writing projects (e.g., explore a number of books by a favorite author and express opinions about them). **W.K.7**

 With guidance and support from adults, recall information from experiences or gather information from provided sources to answer a question. **W.K.8**

ACADEMIC LANGUAGE
bookmark (v.)

Bug Bulletin Board

Explain that today children will do a research project with a partner to show different bugs in their environments. Review the steps in the research process below.

STEP 1 Choose a Topic

Help children choose a bug for their display by naming the bugs in the main selection of the Literature Big Book. Prompt children to state a fact or two about each bug.

STEP 2 Find Resources

Talk about identifying and locating resources. Direct children to use the selections from the week. Guide children in finding information from other books in the library and from the Internet. Have children use the Research Process Checklist online.

STEP 3 Keep Track of Information

Encourage children to note the information they find by drawing pictures or writing words. Suggest that children print a page from the Internet or flag a page in a book that they want to use as a resource.

Collaborative Conversations

Listen Carefully As children engage in partner, small group, and whole class discussions, encourage them to:

→ look at the person who is speaking.

→ listen to the words that the person is saying.

→ respect others by not interrupting them.

→ repeat classmates' ideas to check understanding.

STEM

STEP 4 **Create the Project:
Bug Bulletin Board**

Explain the characteristics of the project:

→ **Information** The bug bulletin board will give information about bugs.

→ **Label** Each drawing will have a label with the name of the bug. Provide this sentence frame.

This is a _____.

→ **Illustration** The drawing of the bug will have details about the bug's environment.

Explain that the bulletin board will show each bug in its environment. It will include areas for flying bugs, crawling bugs, and bugs that live below the surface of the ground. Have partners sort through their information to decide how to show the bug in their drawing.

→ Encourage children who can generate more writing to do so.

→ Help children place their labeled bugs on the board.

 **ENGLISH LANGUAGE LEARNERS
SCAFFOLD**

Beginning	Intermediate	Advanced/Advanced High
Use Sentence Frames Pair children with more fluent speakers. Provide sentence frames to help children talk about their bugs. For example: *This bug _____. It uses its _____.*	**Demonstrate Understanding** Encourage children to tell as much about their bugs as they can. Prompt them with questions such as these: *What body parts does this bug have? How does it use its body parts?* Have children point to parts of their illustrations as they answer.	**Expand** Encourage the use of longer sentences by providing this sentence frame: *This bug uses its _____ to _____.* As children talk about their bugs, elicit fuller responses by asking additional questions. Restate students' responses in complete sentences, if necessary.

Materials

Reading/Writing Workshop Big Book
UNIT 2

Literature Big Book
I Love Bugs!

Interactive Read-Aloud Cards

Word-Building Cards

Visual Vocabulary Cards

a
like
see
the
we

the

High-Frequency Word Cards

a
like
see
the
we

Photo Cards
bat
table

Response Board

"See the Sun Rise"

→ Integrate Ideas

TEXT CONNECTIONS

Connect to Essential Question

OBJECTIVES

 With prompting and support, compare and contrast the adventures and experiences of characters in familiar stories. **RL.K.9**

 Participate in collaborative conversations with diverse partners about *kindergarten topics and texts* with peers and adults in small and larger groups. **SL.K.1**

- Make connections among texts
- Make connections to the world

Text to Text

Remind children that they have been reading selections about bugs all week. Tell them that now they will connect the texts, or think about how the selections are alike and different. Model comparing *I Love Bugs!* with another selection from the week.

 Think Aloud *I Love Bugs!* and "The Bugs Run" both told about bugs. *I Love Bugs!* told about lots of different kinds of bugs that the boy loves. "The Bugs Run" told about the different bugs that the kitten chases. At the end of the story, the bugs chase the kitten!

Guide children to compare the selections from the week, including the Leveled Readers, and to recall information about the bugs they learned about.

Text to Self

Have children recall when they have encountered bugs. *Was the experience good or bad? How did the bug move?*

Text to World

Tell children that insects help to keep the earth clean and that many birds and animals eat bugs. *Why is it important that we have lots of different kinds of animals, including bugs?*

TALK ABOUT READING

OBJECTIVES

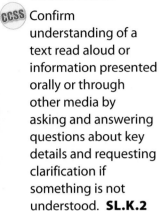 Confirm understanding of a text read aloud or information presented orally or through other media by asking and answering questions about key details and requesting clarification if something is not understood. **SL.K.2**

Becoming Readers

Talk with children about the genres, strategy, and skill they have learned about this week. Prompt them to discuss how this knowledge helps them to read and understand selections.

→ Remind children that they learned about fiction. Have children recall some characteristics of fiction.

→ Discuss with children the strategy of asking and answering questions. *As we read selections this week, how did stopping to ask and answer questions help you understand something about bugs?*

→ Talk about how children learned to look for key details in the words and illustrations to help them understand the text. *In* I Love Bugs!, *what kind of information did you learn by looking closely at illustrations?*

RESEARCH AND INQUIRY

OBJECTIVES

 Participate in shared research and writing projects (e.g., explore a number of books by a favorite author and express opinions about them). **W.K.7**

Wrap Up the Project

Guide partners to share information about their bugs and to point out details in their illustrations on the bulletin board. Encourage children to use words and phrases they learned this week. Have children use the Presenting and Listening checklists online.

the following **Word-Building Cards:** *a, m, p, s, t.* Have children chorally say each sound. Repeat and vary the pace.

Phonemic Awareness

OBJECTIVES

CCSS Spell simple words phonetically, drawing on knowledge of sound-letter relationships. **L.K.2d**

CCSS Read common high-frequency words by sight. **RF.K.3c**

- Segment words into phonemes
- Blend sounds to read words

Phoneme Segmentation

❶ **Model** Use the Sound Boxes on the back of the **Response Boards** and markers. *Listen as I say a word:* sat. *Say the word with me:* sat. *There are three sounds in* sat. *Say the sounds in* sat *with me: /s/ /a/ /t/. Let's place a marker in a box for each sound: /s/ /a/ /t/.* Repeat for *Sam.* Demonstrate for children.

❷ **Guided Practice/Practice** Distribute Response Boards and markers. *Listen as I say a word and its sounds. Say the word and its sounds after me. Put a marker in the Sound Box for each sound you hear.* Have children tell the number of sounds in the word. Guide children with the first word.

mat, /m/ /a/ /t/	am, /a/ /m/	pat, /p/ /a/ /t/
Tam, /t/ /a/ /m/	map, /m/ /a/ /p/	Pam, /p/ /a/ /m/

Phonics

Read Words with *m, a, s, p, t*

❶ **Guided Practice** Display **Word-Building Cards** *p, a, t.* Point to the letter *p. The letter p stands for the sound /p/. Say /p/. The letter* a *stands for /a/. Say /a/. The letter* t *stands for /t/. Say /t/. Let's blend the sounds: /paaat/* pat. *Now let's change the* p *to* s. Blend and read the word *sat* with children.

❷ **Practice** Write the words and sentences for children to read:

mat   tap   sat   map   Pam

We see the map.   We like Pam.
Sam can tap.   Pat sat at the mat.

Remove words from view before dictation.

♪ Play and sing the letter songs to review sound-spellings. Have children show the letter on their Response Boards that matches the sound when they hear the sound. Demonstrate as you sing.

Go Digital

Phonemic Awareness

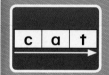

Phonics

Handwriting

High-Frequency Word Routine

Dictation

❶ **Review** Dictate the following sounds for children to spell. As you say each sound, have children repeat it and then write the letter on their **Response Boards** that stands for the sound.

/t/   /p/   /s/   /m/   /a/

❷ **Dictate** the following words for children to spell. Model for children how to use sound boxes to segment each word to scaffold the spelling. *I will say a word. You will repeat the word, then think about how many sounds are in the word. Use your sound boxes to count the sounds. Then write one letter for each sound you hear.*

mat   Pam   at   sat   tap   Sam

Then write the letters and words for children to self-correct.

High-Frequency Words

MINILESSON 5 Mins

the, a, see, we, like

❶ **Review** Display **Visual Vocabulary Cards** *the, a, see, we, like*. Have children **Read/Spell/Write** the words. Then choose a Partner Talk activity.

Distribute one of the following **High-Frequency Word Cards** to children: *the, we, see, a, like*. Tell children that you will say some sentences. *When you hear the word that is on your card, stand and hold up your word card.*

The bug is on me!
I picked up *a* caterpillar.
We can hear crickets.
Max will *see* fireflies at night.
Do you *like* to catch fireflies?

❷ **Build Fluency: Word Automaticity** Display the High-Frequency Word Cards *I, can, the, we, see, a* and *like*. Point to each card, at random, and have children read the word as quickly as they can.

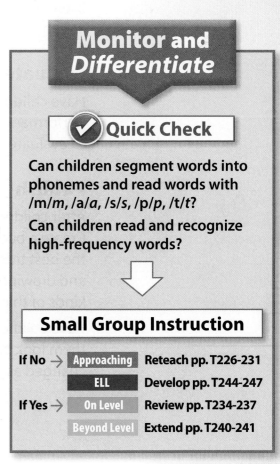

Monitor and *Differentiate*

✓ **Quick Check**

Can children segment words into phonemes and read words with /m/*m*, /a/*a*, /s/*s*, /p/*p*, /t/*t*?

Can children read and recognize high-frequency words?

Small Group Instruction

If No →	Approaching	Reteach pp. T226–231
	ELL	Develop pp. T244–247
If Yes →	On Level	Review pp. T234–237
	Beyond Level	Extend pp. T240–241

→ # Language Arts

MINILESSON
10 Mins

Independent Writing

Writing a Story Sentence

Prepare

Tell children that they will present their finished story sentences to the class. Hold up an example from Day 4 and read it aloud, tracking the print. *I read my sentence loudly enough so that everyone could hear me. I read my sentence with expression so it would sound more interesting to listen to.*

Present

Have children take turns standing up and reading their sentences aloud. Remind children to use the appropriate volume so everyone can hear and to read their sentences with expression so the audience will be more interested in listening. Encourage the rest of the class to listen quietly and to wait until the presenter has finished before they ask any questions.

Evaluate

Have children discuss their own presentations and evaluate their performances, using the presentation rubric. Use the teacher's rubric to evaluate children's writing.

Publish

After children have finished presenting, collect their story sentences. Create a book about bugs. Have children share ideas for titles. Vote on the best title for the collection of bug stories. Share some sentences and drawings from the book. Discuss how some bugs do the same kinds of things. Discuss how bugs are different.

Have children add their writing to their Writer's Portfolio. Then have them look back at their previous writing and discuss how they have changed as writers throughout the year.

OBJECTIVES

 Speak audibly and express thoughts, feelings, and ideas clearly. **SL.K.6**

 Use frequently occurring nouns and verbs. **L.K.1b**

ACADEMIC LANGUAGE
- *present, publish*
- Cognates: *presente*

Writing

I see a fish.

Grammar

Grammar

Verbs

1 **Review** Remind children that a verb tells what someone or something does. Have children either *skip, jump,* or *hop* in place.

→ Write the sentences: *The children skip. The children jump. The children hop.* Read aloud the sentences with children. Ask children to name the verbs in each sentence.

2 **Review/Practice** Show the **Photo Card** for *bat.* Act out swinging a bat. Ask children what action you acted out. Write and read aloud the sentence: *I swing a bat.* Have a volunteer circle the verb.

Have children work in pairs. Show the Photo Card for *table.* Write and read aloud the sentence frame: *I _____ on a table.* Ask children to act out things they do on a table, such as *I eat on a table.* Have children give an action word for the sentence. Guide children in writing their sentences.

As needed, circulate to help children express their thoughts and to offer corrective feedback.

Wrap Up the Week

- Review blending words with initial and final /m/*m,* initial and medial /a/*a,* initial /s/*s,* initial and final /p/*p,* and initial and final /t/*t.*

- Remind children that verbs are action words that tell what someone or something does.

- Use the High-Frequency Word Cards to review the Words to Know.

- Remind children that they can use sentences to tell a story about their ideas.

→ Approaching Level

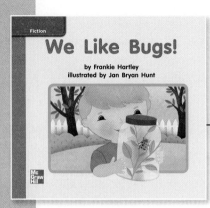

Leveled Reader

OBJECTIVES

 With prompting and support, ask and answer questions about key details in a text. **RL.K.1**

 Demonstrate understanding of the organization and basic features of print. **RF.K.1**

 Read emergent-reader texts with purpose and understanding. **RF.K.4**

Leveled Reader:
We Like Bugs!

Leveled Readers

Before Reading

Preview and Predict

Read aloud the title and the names of the author and illustrator. Ask children to describe what they see on the cover. Ask them what they think the book will be about. Page through the book, reviewing the illustrations and identifying the rebus pictures. Have children confirm or change their predictions as they look at the illustrations.

Review Genre: Fiction

Explain that fiction stories are about characters and events that are not real. Ask: *How can you tell this book is fiction?* (The book has illustrations showing made-up characters, and not real people.)

Model Concepts of Print

Demonstrate the basic features of books as children follow along with their books. *This is the cover of the book. It tells me the name of the story and the author and illustrator. Let's turn to page 2. The story starts here on the left. I will read the sentence from left to right.*

Review High-Frequency Words

Point out the word *the* on page 2 and read it with children. Have them look through the book and find the word on pages 3–8.

Essential Question

Set a purpose for reading. *What kind of bugs do you know about? Let's see if the bugs in the story are bugs we know about.*

During Reading

Guided Comprehension

As children read *We Like Bugs!,* monitor and provide guidance by modeling how to use the strategy and skill.

Strategy: Ask and Answer Questions

Remind children that as they read they can ask questions about things they don't understand and look for answers in the text and pictures.

Skill: Key Details

Remind children that often the words in a story don't include all the details. Readers can learn more about the story by looking for details in the illustrations. After you read each page, ask: *What details did you find in the illustration? How do those details add to the story?*

Think Aloud The words on page 4 don't tell me who is holding the ant, but I can see in the illustration that a girl is holding a jar with the ant inside. The jar has a lid on it and there are holes in the lid so the ant can breathe. I learned all these details by looking at the picture.

Guide children to look for key details in the illustrations that the words do not provide.

After Reading

Respond to Reading

→ *Where does the story take place?* (outside) *How do you know this?* (from details in picture such as the green grass) *What do the children have in the jars?* (bugs)

→ *What happens at the end of the story?* (The children release the bugs.)

→ *What do you know about the bugs in this story?* (Answers will vary.)

Retell

Have children take turns retelling the story. Help them make a personal connection by asking: *What kind of bugs do you like? Why?*

Model Fluency

Reread the story aloud, pausing after each page to have children chorally repeat.

Apply

Have children practice reading aloud with partners.

LITERACY ACTIVITIES

Have children complete the activities on the inside back cover of the reader.

Level Up

Level-up lessons available online.

IF Children read *We Like Bugs!* **Approaching Level** with fluency and correctly answer the Respond to Reading questions,

THEN Tell children that they will read another story about bugs.

• Have children page through *The Bugs Run* **On Level** as you introduce the game (chase) and the characters (a kitten and various bugs). Preview the illustration on page 8.

• Have children read the story, monitoring their comprehension and providing assistance as necessary.

Phonological Awareness

COUNT AND PRONOUNCE SYLLABLES

OBJECTIVES

 Count, pronounce, blend, and segment syllables in spoken words. **RF.K.2b**

 I Do After singing "Eency Weency Spider, with children, tell children that words have parts. Have them listen as you say and clap the syllables in the word *spider*: spi-der. *How many times did I clap for* spider? (two) *That's right, two claps.* Point out that this means that *spider* has two parts, or syllables.

 We Do Have children say the words in the title of the song with you. Then have them say, clap, and count the syllables in each word.

 You Do Say and clap *eency,* (2) *rain,* (1) *water,* (2) *spout* (1) with children. Have them count the syllables in each word.

Phonemic Awareness

PHONEME SEGMENTATION

OBJECTIVES

 Demonstrate basic knowledge of one-to-one letter-sound correspondences by producing the primary or many of the most frequent sound for each consonant. **RF.K.3a**

I Do Use the **Sound Boxes** and markers. *Listen as I say a word:* pat. *There are three sounds in* pat: /p/ /a/ /t/. *I'll place a marker in the box for each sound.* Point to each sound box and have children say the sound with you. Repeat for *tap.*

 We Do Distribute Sound Boxes and markers. *Listen as I say a word:* sat. *Say the sounds with me:* /s/ /a/ /t/. *Now place a marker in a box for each sound.* Repeat for the word *Pam.*

 You Do Say the word *map.* Have children repeat the word, then segment into sounds. Have them place a marker in a box for each sound and tell the number of sounds. Continue with the words *at, sap,* and *am.*

You may wish to review Phonological Awareness and Phonemic Awareness with **ELL** using this section.

PHONEME BLENDING

OBJECTIVES

CCSS Isolate and pronounce the initial, medial vowel, and final sounds (phonemes) in three-phoneme words. **RF.K.2d**

 The puppet will say the sounds in a word, then blend those sounds to say a word: /s/ /a/ /t/, /sssaaat/, sat. *Say the sounds with me:* /s/ /a/ /t/. *Now blend the sounds and say the word with me:* /sssaaat/, sat. Continue the routine with *man*.

 Listen to the puppet say the sounds in another word: /m/ /a/ /p/. *Let's blend the sounds and say the word:* /mmmaaap/ map. Continue the routine with *tap* and *Sam*.

 Tell children to listen as the puppet says the sounds in these words: *tap, Sam, pat, sit, Tim.* For each word, have children repeat the sounds, then blend them to say the word.

PHONEME SEGMENTATION

OBJECTIVES

CCSS Demonstrate basic knowledge of one-to-one letter-sound correspondences by producing the primary or many of the most frequent sound for each consonant. **RF.K.3a**

 Use the **Sound Boxes** and markers. *Listen as I say a word:* map. *There are three sounds in* map: /m/ /a/ /p/. *I'll place a marker for each sound.* Point to the sounds in turn and have children say them with you. Repeat for *sat*.

 Distribute Sound Boxes and markers. *Listen:* tap, /t/ /a/ /p/. *Say the word and sounds with me:* tap, /t/ /a/ /p/. *Place a marker for each sound.* Repeat for the word *fit*.

 Say the word *am*. Have children repeat the word, then say its sounds. Have them place a marker for each sound. Continue with the words *mat, tap, mad, pet, fin,* and *at*.

ELL ENGLISH LANGUAGE LEARNERS

For the **ELLs** who need **phonics, decoding,** and **fluency** practice, use scaffolding methods as necessary to ensure children understand the meaning of the words. Refer to the Language Transfer Handbook for phonics elements that may not transfer in students' native languages.

Phonics

SOUND-SPELLING REVIEW

OBJECTIVES

CCSS Demonstrate basic knowledge of one-to-one letter-sound correspondences by producing the primary sound for each consonant. **RF.K.3a**

I Do Display **Word-Building Card** *a*. Say the letter name and the sound it stands for. For example: Letter *a*, /a/. Repeat for *m, p, s,* and *t*.

We Do Display and name the *Astronaut* **Photo Card** and together say the initial sound and the letter that it stands for. Repeat with the *Tiger, Pumpkin, Saw,* and *Mule* Photo Cards.

You Do Display and name the Photo Cards one at a time. For each card, have children say the first sound in the word and the letter that it stands for.

CONNECT SOUNDS TO SPELLINGS

OBJECTIVES

CCSS Demonstrate basic knowledge of one-to-one letter-sound correspondences by producing the primary sound for each consonant. **RF.K.3a**

I Do Display the *Apple* **Sound-Spelling Card**. *The sound at the beginning of* apple *is /a/. The letter* a *stands for /a/. Which letter stands for /a/?* (a) Repeat for /m/*m*, /p/*p*, /s/*s*, and /t/*t*.

We Do Actor *begins with /*a/. *Let's write* a *on our* **Response Boards**. Say *mice, silk, talk, page.* Guide children to write the letter that stands for the initial sound.

You Do Say the following words and have children write the letter that stands for the initial sound in the word: *sing, tent, pay, add, mix.*

RETEACH

OBJECTIVES

CCSS Demonstrate basic knowledge of one-to-one letter-sound correspondences by producing the primary sound for each consonant. **RF.K.3a**

I Do To review letter sounds, display **Reading/Writing Workshop**, p. 42. Point to each picture in the apple and star rows and say the picture name.

We Do Have children name each picture in the apple and star rows. Repeat and emphasize initial sounds.

You Do Guide children in reading the tree and fish rows of decodable words, offering assistance as needed.

BLEND WORDS WITH /a/*a*, /m/*m*, /p/*p*, /s/*s*, /t/*t*

OBJECTIVES

(CCSS) Isolate and pronounce the initial, medial vowel, and final sounds (phonemes) in three-phoneme words. **RF.K.2d**

 Display **Word-Building Card** *mat. This is the letter* m. *It stands for* /m/. *This is the letter* a. *It stands for* /a/. *This is the letter* t. *It stands for* /t/. *Listen as I blend all three sounds:* /mmmaaat/, mat. *The word is* mat. *Repeat for* Pam.

 Now let's blend more sounds to make words. Make the word *Tam. Let's blend* /t/ /a/ /m/: /taaammm/, Tam. Have children blend to read the word. Repeat with the word *tap. Let's blend* /t/ /a/ /p/: /taaap/, tap.

 Distribute sets of Word-Building Cards with *a, m, p, s, t.* Write: *map, sap, pat.* Have children form the words and then blend and read the words.

BUILD WORDS WITH SHORT /a/*a*, /m/*m*, /p/*p*, /s/*s*, /t/*t*

OBJECTIVES

(CCSS) Demonstrate basic knowledge of one-to-one letter-sound correspondences by producing the primary or many of the most frequent sound for each consonant. **RF.K.3a**

 Display **Word-Building Cards** *a* and *m. These are the letters* a *and* m. *They stand for* /a/ *and* /m/. *I will blend* /a/ *and* /m/ *together* /aaammm/. *The word is* am.

 Distribute sets of Word-Building Cards with *a, m, p, s, t.* Show how to make the word *at* and have children do the same. Place the letter *s* in front of it and have children do the same. Let's blend /sss/ /aaa/ /t/: /sssaat/, sat. Now we have read a new word, *sat.*

 Have children change the *s* in *sat* to *p* and read the new word, *pat.* Have children change the *p* in *pat* to *m* and read the new word, *mat.* Point out that by changing one letter we make a new word.

BUILD FLUENCY WITH PHONICS

Sound/Spelling Fluency

Display the following Word-Building Cards: *a, m, p, s,* and *t.* Have children chorally say each sound. Repeat and vary the pace.

Fluency in Connected Text

Write the following sentences. *Pat can see Sam. I like to tap.* Have children read the sentences and identify the words with /a/, /m/, /p/, /s/, and /t/.

→ Approaching Level

High-Frequency Words

RETEACH WORDS

 TIER 2

OBJECTIVES

 Read common high-frequency words by sight. **RF.K.3c**

 I Do
Use the **High-Frequency Words Cards** with the **Read/Spell/Write** routine to reteach the high-frequency words *the, we, see, a,* and *like.*

We Do
Have children turn to p. 43 of **Reading/Writing Workshop**. Read the sentence in the tree row and have children point to the words *we, see* and *a*. Repeat with the fish row and the words *like* and *the*.

 You Do
Have children read the words in the apple and star rows. Say the word *the*. Have children close their eyes, picture the word, and write it as they see it. Have children self-correct. Repeat with *we, see, a, like*.

REREAD FOR FLUENCY

TIER 2

OBJECTIVES

 Read common high-frequency words by sight. **RF.K.3c**

 I Do
Turn to p. 44, and read aloud the title. *Let's read the title together.* Page through the book. Ask children what they see in each picture. Ask children to find the word *the* on pp. 46 and 48, the words *a* and *see* on p. 47, and the word *like* on p. 49.

 We Do
Then have children open their books and chorally read the story. Have children point to each word as they read. Provide corrective feedback as needed. After reading, ask children to recall what Pat can see on a leaf.

 You Do
Have children reread "Pat" with a partner for fluency.

Repeat for "Tap! Tap! Tap!" on p. 50. Have children find the following words: *the* on p. 51; *see* on p. 52; *a* on p. 53; *like* on p. 54; *We* on p. 55.

Oral Vocabulary

REVIEW WORDS

OBJECTIVES

 Identify real-life connections between words and their use. **L.K.5c**

Develop oral vocabulary: *curious, observe, process, slender, attaches*

 I Do

Use the **Define/Example/Ask** routine to review words. Use the following definitions and provide examples:

curious   If you are **curious**, you want to learn more about a topic or thing.

observe   When you **observe**, you closely watch something or someone.

process   When something goes through a **process**, it changes as it follows a set of steps.

slender   **Slender** means slim and narrow.

attaches   When something **attaches** itself to something else, the two things join together.

 We Do

Ask questions to build understanding. *How can you learn more when you are curious about something? What can you observe in the night sky? What is your process for getting ready for school? What is something in the classroom that is slender? When a leash attaches to a dog's collar, what will probably happen next?*

You Do

Have children complete these sentence frames: *I am curious about _____. Zookeepers observe animals because _____. A step in the process to make a sandwich is _____. I use the word* slender *to describe grass because _____. She attaches the papers together using _____.*

SELF-SELECTED READING

OBJECTIVES

 With prompting and support, ask and answer questions about key details in a text. **RL.K.1**

Apply the strategy and skill to reread the text.

Read Independently

Help children select a story to read for sustained silent reading. Remind children that they can use the illustrations to help them understand key details in the story. Tell children to ask and answer questions about the illustrations as they read.

Read Purposefully

Before reading, have children point out an interesting illustration. After reading, ask children to point to the illustration they identified earlier. Have them share how they used the illustration to answer a question they asked during reading. What is a key detail in the illustration that helped them better understand the story?

→ On Level

Leveled Reader

OBJECTIVES

 With prompting and support, ask and answer questions about key details in a text. **RL.K.1**

With prompting and support, identify characters, settings, and major events in a story. **RL.K.3**

Demonstrate understanding of the organization and basic features of print. Understand that words are separated by spaces in print. **RF.K.1c**

Read emergent-reader texts with purpose and understanding. **RF.K.4**

Leveled Reader:
The Bugs Run

Go Digital

Leveled Readers

Before Reading

Preview and Predict

Read the title and the name of the author and illustrator. Have children identify the animals on the cover. Preview the illustrations in the book and identify the rebus pictures. Explain that the animals are the characters in the story. Ask: *What do you think the book is about?* (a kitten playing chase with bugs)

Review Genre: Fiction

Remind children that fiction stories are made up stories that have characters and events that are not real. Ask: *How do you know this story is fiction?* (The bugs and the kitten are playing chase, like children do.) Have children point to evidence in the illustrations to support their answers.

Model Concepts of Print

Point to each word on page 2. Say: *I read each word. Each word is made up of letters. I can see that each word is separated by a space.* Have children point to the words and spaces between them on page 3.

Review High-Frequency Words

Point out the word *see* on page 2, and read it with children. Have them look through the book and find the word on pages 3 and 4.

Essential Question

Set a purpose for reading: *What kind of bugs do you know about? Let's read to see if we know about any of the bugs in this story.*

During Reading

Guided Comprehension

As children whisper-read, monitor their reading and provide support by correcting blending and modeling the strategy and skill.

Strategy: Ask and Answer Questions

Remind children that as they read they can ask questions about things they don't understand and look for answers in the text and pictures.

Skill: Key Details

Remind children that the illustrations show what is happening in the story and that they often add to the information in the text.

Think Aloud On page 3, the words tell me about a spider that is running. The picture tells me why the spider runs—because a kitten is chasing it. The words on page 3 don't tell me what happened to the ant on page 2, but the picture does. It tells me that the ant is now safe on a leaf.

Have children use the pictures on pages 5, 6, and 7 to find details about what happens to each bug after it is chased by the kitten. Have children point to evidence in the book to support their statements.

After Reading

Respond to Reading

→ *What are the bugs doing on each page?* (running) *Why?* (They are being chased by the kitten.)

→ *Do the bugs like being chased?* (yes) *Why do you think so?* (The pictures show that they are having fun.)

→ *What happens at the end of the story?* (All the bugs chase the kitten.)

Retell

Have children take turns retelling the story. Help them make personal connections by asking: *What is fun about playing chase with a friend?*

Model Fluency

Read the sentences aloud with fluency and expression. Point out that reading with expression makes the story more fun and interesting.

Apply

Invite children to practice reading aloud with partners. Encourage them to vary the tone of their voices as they read.

LITERACY ACTIVITIES

Have children complete the activities on the inside back cover of the reader.

Level Up

IF Children read *The Bugs Run* `On Level` with fluency and correctly answer the Respond to Reading questions,

THEN Tell children that they will read another story about bugs.

• Have children page through *I See a Bug!* `Beyond Level` as you introduce the characters and preview the story.

• Have children read the story, monitoring their comprehension and providing assistance as necessary.

PHONEME SEGMENTATION

OBJECTIVES

 Demonstrate basic knowledge of one-to-one letter-sound correspondences by producing the primary or many of the most frequent sounds for each consonant. **RF.K.3a**

 I Do Use **Sound Boxes** and markers. *Listen as I say a word:* sap. *Say the word with me:* sap. *There are three sounds in* sap: /s/ /a/ /p/. *I'll place a marker for each sound:* /s/ /a/ /p/. Point to the sounds in turn and have children say them with you. Repeat for *can*.

 We Do Distribute Sound Boxes and markers. Say the word *mat. Say* it *with me. Listen:* /m/ /a/ /t/. *Say the sounds with me:* /m/ /a/ /t/. *Now place a marker in a box for each sound.* Repeat for the word *Pam*.

 You Do Say the word *Sam*. Have children repeat the word, then say its sounds. Have them tell the number of sounds in the word, then place a marker in a sound box for each sound. Continue with *am, pat, tap,* and *map*.

PHONEME BLENDING

OBJECTIVES

Isolate and pronounce the initial, medial vowel, and final sounds (phonemes) in three-phoneme words. **RF.K.2d**

 I Do Place the *Six, Pen, Pig, Map, Bus, Ax, Ant* and *Toe* **Photo Cards** facedown. Choose a card. Do not show it to children. Say the sounds in the word. *These are the sounds in the word:* /m/ /a/ /p/. *I will blend the sounds:* /mmmaaap/, *map. The word is* map. Show the picture.

 We Do Choose another picture and say the sounds in the word. Together say the sounds and blend the sounds to say the word. Then show the picture.

 You Do Continue choosing Photo Cards. Say the sounds and have children blend the sounds to say the word. Show the picture.

Phonics

REVIEW PHONICS

OBJECTIVES

 Demonstrate basic knowledge of one-to-one letter-sound correspondences by producing the primary or many of the most frequent sounds for each consonant. **RF.K.3a**

I Do To review letter sounds, display **Reading/Writing Workshop**, p. 42. Point to each picture in the apple and star rows and say the picture name.

We Do Have children say the name of each picture. Then ask them to identify the words that begin with /m/, /a/, /t/, or /p/ and the words that end with /p/ or /t/.

You Do Have children read the words in the tree and fish rows. Have them reread the words and raise their hands if they hear /s/ at the beginning of a word. Repeat, having them raise their hands if they hear /p/ at the end of the word. Have them continue, raising their hands for initial and final /t/ and initial and medial /a/.

PICTURE SORT

OBJECTIVES

 Isolate and pronounce the initial, medial vowel, and final sounds (phonemes) in three-phoneme words. **RF.K.2d**

I Do Display **Word-Building Cards** *t* and *s* in a pocket chart. Then show the *Top* **Photo Card** and say the name. Tell children that the sound at the beginning of *top* is /t/. *The letter* t *stands for* /t/. *I will put the* top *Photo Card under the letter* t. Show the *Six* Photo Card. Say /s/ /i/ /ks/, *six*. Tell children that the sound at the beginning is /s/. *The letter* s *stands for* /s/. *I will put the* Six *Photo Card under the* s. Repeat by blending and sorting words beginning with /a/ and /m/, and /p/ and /s/.

We Do Show the *Sun* Photo Card and say *sun*, /s/ /u/ /n/. Have children repeat. Then have them tell the sound they hear at the beginning of *sun*. Ask them if they should place the photo under the *t* or the *s*. *(s)* Repeat with the other review letters.

You Do Continue the activity using the *Toe, Soup, Tie,* and *Sock* Photo Cards. Have children say the picture name and the sounds in the name. Then have them place the card under the *t* or *s*. Repeat with Photo Cards for the other letters.

Phonics

OBJECTIVES

 Isolate and pronounce the initial, medial vowel, and final sounds (phonemes) in three-phoneme words. **RF.K.2d**

 I Do Use **Word-Building Cards** or write *s, a, t. This is the letter* s. *It stands for /sss/. Say it with me: /sss/. This is the letter* a. *It stands for /a/. Say it with me: /aaa/. This is the letter* t. *It stands for /t/. Say it with me: /t/. I'll blend the sounds together to read the word*: /sssaaat/, sat.

 We Do Write *am* and *Sam*. Guide children to blend the words sound by sound to read each word.

 You Do Write the following words and have children blend the words sound by sound to read each word.

sap   mat   pat   map   tap

High-Frequency Words

OBJECTIVES

 Read common high-frequency words by sight. **RF.K.3c**

 I Do Use the **High-Frequency Word Cards** to review the words *I, can, the, we, see, a,* and *like* using the **Read/Spell/Write** routine.

 We Do Have children turn to p. 43 of **Reading/Writing Workshop**. Read the sentence in the tree row and have children point to the words *we, see* and *a*. Repeat with the fish row with the words *like* and *the*.

 You Do Have children read the words in the apple and star rows. Say the word *the*. Have children close their eyes, picture the word, and write it as they see it. Have children self-correct. Repeat for *we, see, a, like*.

Fluency Point to the High-Frequency Word Cards *I, can, like, we, a, see,* and *the* in random order. Have children chorally read. Repeat at a faster pace.

REREAD FOR FLUENCY

OBJECTIVES

Read emergent-reader texts with purpose and understanding. **RF.K.4**

 I Do Turn to and read "Pat" in **Reading/Writing Workshop**, pp. 44–49. *We can make our reading sound more interesting by raising and lowering our voices to show feeling, or expression.* Work with children to read for accuracy and expression. Model reading a page: *When I read, "I like the bug," I read all the way to the end of the sentence before pausing. This makes my reading sound natural, as if I were talking.*

 We Do Reread p. 47. Then have children chorally read the page with you. Continue choral reading the remainder of the pages.

 You Do Have children read "Pat." Provide time to listen as children read the pages. Comment on their accuracy and expression and provide corrective feedback by modeling proper fluency.

Use the same routine for "Tap! Tap! Tap!" on pp. 50–55.

Comprehension

SELF-SELECTED READING

OBJECTIVES

With prompting and support, ask and answer questions about key details in a text. **RL.K.1**

Apply the strategy and skill to reread the text.

Read Independently

Have children select a story to read for sustained silent reading. Remind them to use the illustrations to help them understand key details in a story. Explain that the illustrations can help them ask and answer questions as they read.

Read Purposefully

Before reading, have children choose an illustration that shows an important detail in the story. After reading, invite children to explain how the illustration helped them answer a question they asked before, during, or after reading.

→ Beyond Level

Leveled Reader

OBJECTIVES

CCSS With prompting and support, retell familiar stories, including key details. **RL.K.2**

CCSS With prompting and support, identify characters, settings, and major events in a story. **RL.K.3**

CCSS With prompting and support, name the author and illustrator of a story and define the role of each in telling the story. **RL.K.6**

CCSS Read emergent-reader texts with purpose and understanding. **RF.K.4**

Leveled Reader:
I See a Bug!

Leveled Readers

Before Reading

Preview and Predict

Ask children to point to and read the title. Then read the names of the author and illustrator. Ask children to tell what the author does and what the illustrator does. Point to the illustration on the cover. Ask: *What do you think the book will be about?* Have children page through the book and look at the illustrations. Did they confirm their predictions?

Review Genre: Fiction

Remind children that fiction stories are about made-up characters and events. Say: *The characters in this story are not real. They are created by the author. The things that happen in the story did not really happen.*

Essential Question

Remind children of the Essential Question: *What kind of bugs do you know about?* Have children set a purpose for reading by saying: *Let's read to find out if you will find bugs that you know about.*

During Reading

Guided Comprehension

Have children whisper-read *I See a Bug!* Remind them that when they come to an unfamiliar word, they can look at the other words in the sentence, or use picture clues. Model how to use the strategy and skill.

Strategy: Ask and Answer Questions

Remind children that as they read, they can ask and answer questions to help them follow what is happening in the text.

Skill: Key Details

Remind children that as they read, they should look at the illustrations. The illustrations show what is happening in the story and they often give readers information that isn't in the text.

Think Aloud On page 2, I read that the boy is scared of the bug. The picture shows me that the bug is a caterpillar. On page 3, the girl tells the boy that the bug will turn into a butterfly. The picture shows me how a caterpillar turns into a butterfly.

Guide children to use the text and pictures on pages 4 and 5 to ask and answer questions about what the boy sees and what the girl says about the bee. Have children point to evidence in the text and the pictures to support their statements.

After Reading

Respond to Reading

→ *Who are the characters in this story?* (two children: a girl and a boy) *Where does the story take place?* (in a backyard)

→ *What happens at the end of the story?* (The boy decides that he likes bugs, too.)

→ *Which bugs in this story are bugs that you know about?* (Answers will vary.)

Retell

Have children act out the story with a partner, each taking the part of the boy or the girl. Help them make a personal connection by asking: *What bugs do you like? Why?*

Gifted and Talented

EVALUATING Have children recall the different bugs in the story. Ask: *Which are bugs you know about? What do you know about them? Where have you seen these bugs?* Challenge children to think of other bugs they might find in a backyard setting.

HAVE children make a chart of bugs they know about. Have them include the name of each bug, a short description, and a picture they've drawn.

LITERACY ACTIVITIES

Have children complete the activities on the inside back cover of the reader.

Beyond Level

Phonics

OBJECTIVES

Demonstrate basic knowledge of one-to-one letter-sound correspondences by producing the primary or many of the most frequent sounds for each consonant. **RF.K.3a**

 To review letter sounds, display **Reading/Writing Workshop**, p. 42. Point to each picture in the apple and star rows and say the picture name.

 Have children say the name of each picture. Then point to and name the *tomato* picture. Ask children to say the beginning sound, /t/, then share other words they know that begin with the same sound. Repeat for *pencil* and *moon*.

 Have partners read each decodable word. Ask them to write the words on their **Response Boards**, underlining the letter in each word that stands for the sounds /s/, /a/, /p/, /t/, or /m/.

High-Frequency Words

OBJECTIVES

Read common high-frequency words by sight. **RF.K.3c**

 Create the **High-Frequency Word Cards** for *make* and *happy*. Introduce the words using the **Read/Spell/Write** routine.

 Display the High-Frequency Word Cards for *I, can, a, like, see, the,* and *we.* Have children help you complete the following sentence frames using the High-Frequency Word Cards: *We can make a _____. I like the happy _____.*

 Have partners write sentences using the High-Frequency Words *make* and *happy* on their **Response Boards**. Have them read their sentences.

Fluency Have children turn to pp. 44–49 and 50–55 in **Reading/Writing Workshop** and reread the stories "Pat" and "Tap! Tap! Tap!" for fluency.

Innovate Have children create a new page for "Pat" using the sentence frame *I am at the _____.* For "Tap! Tap! Tap!" have children complete: *I can see a _____.* by choosing something else the boy might see outside his window.

Vocabulary

ORAL VOCABULARY: SYNONYMS

OBJECTIVES

 With guidance and support from adults, explore word relationships and nuances in word meaning. **L.K.5**

Develop oral vocabulary: Synonyms

 Review the meanings of the oral vocabulary words *curious* and *observe*. Explain that a synonym is a word that means almost the same thing as another word. *A synonym for* curious *is* interested. *When you are* interested *in something, you want to learn more about it*. We were interested in the big bug. *A synonym for* observe *is* watch. *When you* observe *something, you watch it*. I like to watch baseball games.

 Say a few sentences together using the new words *interested* and *watch*.

 Have partners say two or three sentences about a new movie or TV show. Tell them to include the words *interested* and *watch* in the sentences. Ask partners to share their sentences with the class.

 Extend Challenge children to use the words to interview a partner about what they know about bugs. Then ask children to share two facts they learned about their partner and bugs.

Comprehension

SELF-SELECTED READING

OBJECTIVES

 With prompting and support, ask and answer questions about key details in a text. **RL.K.1**

Apply the strategy and skill to reread the text.

Read Independently

Have children select a story to read for sustained silent reading. Remind them that asking and answering questions before, during, and after reading can help them understand important story details, and that the illustrations can often help them answer their questions.

Read Purposefully

Before reading, ask children to choose an illustration that shows an important detail. After reading, invite children to display the illustration and explain how details in the illustration helped them answer a question they had while reading.

 Independent Study Have children look at photographs from the week's readings. Challenge partners to write a sentence about what they think will happen next in each photograph.

English Language Learners

Leveled Reader

OBJECTIVES

 With prompting and support, ask and answer questions about key details in a text. **RL.K.1**

 With prompting and support, identify characters, settings, and major events in a story. **RL.K.3**

 Read emergent-reader texts with purpose and understanding. **RF.K.4**

Shared Read:
The Bugs Run

Leveled Readers

Before Reading

Preview and Predict

Read the title as you point to each word. Make sure children understand the English word *bug*. Point to the cover and say: *I see a kitten and some bugs.* Point to and name each bug. Then do a picture walk and identify the rebus pictures and labels for *ant, spider, beetle, ladybug, bee, caterpillar,* and *kitten.* Use simple language to describe each picture. Immediately follow up with questions, such as *What kind of bug is this? What are [the kitten and the bug] doing?*

Essential Question

Set a purpose for reading: *What kind of bugs do you know about? Let's read to see if they are in this book.* Encourage children to seek clarification when they come to a word that doesn't make sense to them. Model asking for clarification: *I don't know what this kind of bug is. Can you tell me?*

During Reading

Interactive Question Response

Pages 2–3 Point to page 2. Reinforce the language pattern. For example, say: *I see an ant. Who runs in this picture? Yes, the ant runs. The kitten runs too. Let's read the sentence that tells us what the ant is doing. Read the words with me: See the ant run.* Then point to the illustration on page 3. Ask: *Who runs on this page? Yes, the spider runs. Let's read the sentence together.* Point out that the ant from page 2 is on a leaf.

Pages 4–5 Point to page 4. Ask: *Where is the spider?* Point to the label in the illustration on page 4 and read the word. *Who runs on this page? Yes, the beetle runs. Let's read the sentence to find out who we see run.* Point to the text on page 5. *Let's read to find out who we see run.* (the ladybug)

Pages 6–7 Point to the illustration on page 6. *Where is the ladybug now?* (on a flower) *Who can we see run?* (the bee) *Let's find the text that tells us that. Read the sentence.* Point to the illustration and label on page 7. *I see a caterpillar. What does it do?* (It runs.) *Let's read the text that tells us what the caterpillar does.*

Page 8 *Who do we see run?* (the kitten) *Let's read the sentence together: See the kitten run. Who else do we see?* (the ant, the spider, the beetle, the ladybug, the bee, and the caterpillar) *What are all the bugs doing?* (chasing the kitten) *Talk with a partner about the bugs you know in this story.*

After Reading

Respond to Reading

→ *What bug do you see run first?* (the ant) *What bug do you see run next?* (the spider)

→ *Who runs after the bugs?* (the kitten)

→ *What does the kitten do at the end of the story?* (runs) *Why?* (The bugs are chasing the kitten.)

Retell

Say: *Let's retell the book by using our hands. As you say the words with me, make your fingers run like a bug. See the ant run. See the spider run. See the beetle run. See the ladybug run. See the bee run. See the caterpillar run.* (Use both hands for the kitten.) *See the kitten run.*

Model Fluency

Read the sentences one at a time as you track the print. Have children chorally repeat.

Apply

Have children form groups of three. Have them take turns reading while the other two act out the story.

Level Up

Level-up lessons available online.

IF Children read *The Bugs Run* ELL Level with fluency and correctly answer the Respond to Reading questions,

THEN Tell children that they will read another story about bugs.

• Have children page through *The Bugs Run* On Level and conduct a picture walk to describe each picture and introduce the language pattern in the story.

• Have children read the story, monitoring their comprehension and providing assistance as necessary.

LITERACY ACTIVITIES

Have children complete the activities on the inside back cover of the reader.

Vocabulary

OBJECTIVES

 CCSS Speak audibly and express thoughts, feelings, and ideas clearly. **SL.K.6**

LANGUAGE OBJECTIVE

Preview vocabulary

 I Do Display images from the **Visual Vocabulary Cards** one at a time to preteach the oral vocabulary words *curious* and *observe*.

We Do Display each image again and explain how it illustrates the word. Model using sentences to describe the image.

You Do Display the words again and have partners talk about how the picture demonstrates the word.

Beginning	Intermediate	Advanced/High
Ask children to chorally repeat each word as you hold up each card.	Use each word in a simple sentence. Ask children to repeat after you.	Ask children to use both words in sentences.

OBJECTIVES

 CCSS Speak audibly and express thoughts, feelings, and ideas clearly. **SL.K.6**

LANGUAGE OBJECTIVE

Preview ELL vocabulary

 I Do Display the **Visual Vocabulary Cards** one at a time to preteach the ELL vocabulary words *chase* and *insect* and follow the routine. Say each word and have children repeat it. Define the word in English.

 We Do Display each image again and incorporate the word in a short discussion about the image. Model using sentences to describe the image.

 You Do Display the card for *chase* and have children say the word. Provide children opportunities to use the word in a sentence by providing this sentence starter: *I can chase* _____.

Beginning	Intermediate	Advanced/High
Have children draw a picture of themselves chasing a person or animal. Ask questions about the drawing to elicit language.	Ask partners to talk about people or animals they might chase.	Ask children to use the words in an oral sentence. Provide guidance if necessary.

High-Frequency Words

REVIEW WORDS

OBJECTIVES

CCSS Read common high-frequency words by sight (e.g., *the, of, to, you, she, my, is, are, do, does*). **RF.K.3c**

LANGUAGE OBJECTIVE

Review high-frequency words

 I Do Display the **High-Frequency Word Cards** for the words from the last five weeks: *the, we, see, a,* and *like*. Read the words. Use the **Read/Spell/Write** routine. Have children write the words on their **Response Boards**.

 We Do Write a sentence frame for each of the high-frequency words. Work with children to read each sentence and complete it with an object from the classroom. *This is the _____. We have _____. I see a _____. Here is a _____. I like _____.*

 You Do Display one card at a time as children chorally read them. Mix and repeat. Note words children need to review.

Beginning	Intermediate	Advanced/High
Ask children to say each word aloud, providing help with pronunciation as needed.	Provide partners with the following sentence frames: *We see a _____. We like the _____.*	Ask children to write three words and use them in oral sentences.

REVIEW CATEGORY WORDS

OBJECTIVES

CCSS Identify real-life connections between words and their use (e.g., note places at school that are *colorful*). **L.K.5c**

LANGUAGE OBJECTIVE

Use category words

 I Do Write and say movement words such as *crawl, walk, jump,* and *fly.* Define the word in English and then, if appropriate, in Spanish, identify any cognates.

 We Do Ask children to repeat the words. Demonstrate the movements and have children demonstrate them as well.

 You Do Display visuals of animals or people moving. Ask children to name the type of movement they see in the picture.

Beginning	Intermediate	Advanced/High
Help children pronounce each word correctly as they repeat it chorally after you.	Have partners talk about the different ways they can move.	Challenge partners to tell a short story using three movement words.

SHARED WRITING

OBJECTIVES

 CCSS Use a combination of drawing, dictating, and writing to narrate a single event or several loosely linked events, tell about the events in the order in which they occurred, and provide a reaction to what happened. **W.K.3**

LANGUAGE OBJECTIVE

Contribute to a shared writing project

 I Do Review the words *jump, crawl,* and *hop* from the Whole Group Shared Writing project as possible ideas for ways that bugs move. Model writing a sentence using a verb: *Ants crawl.*

 We Do Ask children to choose an idea from the word web in the Whole Group activity. Have children help you write a shared sentence: *Grasshoppers jump.*

 You Do Have children write a simple sentence by combining the word *bugs* and a verb they choose from the web to make a sentence, such as *Bugs jump.* Have children write the sentence and read it aloud.

Beginning	Intermediate	Advanced/High
Help children write and say the sentence correctly.	Provide children with a more detailed sentence: *Bugs _____ and _____.*	Challenge children to write a sentence about a bug and how it moves.

WRITING TRAIT: IDEAS

OBJECTIVES

 CCSS Use a combination of drawing, dictating, and writing to narrate a single event or several loosely linked events, tell about the events in the order in which they occurred, and provide a reaction to what happened. **W.K.3**

LANGUAGE OBJECTIVE

Use ideas in writing

 I Do Explain to children that writers need information and ideas before they can write. Tell them that they can get information and ideas from the books they read and the things they see in real life.

 We Do Point to the **Big Book** selection *I Love Bugs!* Remind children that the story tells about different kinds of bugs. Ask: *What can we learn about bugs?* Point out ideas from the story that help give children ideas about bugs.

 You Do Have children write a sentence to show what they know about bugs. Provide them with the sentence frame: *Bugs _____.*

Beginning	Intermediate	Advanced/High
Help children complete the sentence frame with words that show actions, such as *crawl, fly,* or *jump.* Have them act out their sentences.	Ask children to discuss the Big Book pictures before they complete the sentence frame.	Have children write a sentence about a specific bug they see in the Big Book selection.

Grammar

VERBS

OBJECTIVES

Use frequently occurring nouns and verbs. **L.K.1b**

LANGUAGE OBJECTIVE

Identify and use verbs

Language Transfers Handbook

In Hmong, verbs can be used consecutively without conjunctions or punctuation. Children may say *I took a book went studied at the library.* Provide extra feedback to children to clarify sentences with words such as *to* and *and*.

 I Do Review that a verb is an action word. Say the following sentence: *The girl laughs.* Repeat the sentence. Say: *The verb in this sentence is* laughs. Laughs *is a word that describes an action.*

 We Do Say the following sentences. Have children help you and identify the verb in each. Have them say: *The action word is* _____.

Spiders spin webs.

A ladybug crawls.

The bee buzzes.

 You Do Say the following sentence: *Bugs can* _____.

Pair children and have them orally complete the sentence frame by providing details from this week's readings. Circulate, listen in, and take note of each child's language use and proficiency.

Beginning	Intermediate	Advanced/High
Guide children to use illustrations from this week's readings to say verbs to complete the sentence frame.	Have partners use the selections talk about the different things bugs can do.	Ask children to complete the sentence frame with little or no help, and then read the sentence aloud.

Weekly Assessment

Use your Quick Check observations and the assessment opportunities identified below to evaluate children's progress in key skill areas.

✓ TESTED SKILLS CCSS	Quick Check Observations	Pencil and Paper Assessment
PHONICS Review **RF.K.3a** **s**	Can children match the letters to the sounds: /m/ *m*, /a/ *a*, /s/ *s*, /p/ *p*, /t/ *t*?	Practice Book, p. 67
HIGH-FREQUENCY WORDS *the, a, see, we, like* **RF.K.3c** **see**	Can children recognize and read the high-frequency words?	Practice Book, pp. 71–72
COMPREHENSION Key Details **RL.K.1, RL.K.7**	As you read *I Love Bugs!* with children, can they identify and discuss key details using the illustrations and the text?	Practice Book, p. 68

Quick Check Rubric

Skills	1	2	3
PHONICS	Does not connect the sounds /m/, /a/, /s/, /p/, /t/ with the letters *Mm, Aa, Ss, Pp, Tt.*	Usually connects the sounds /m/, /a/, /s/, /p/, /t/ with the letters *Mm, Aa, Ss, Pp, Tt.*	Consistently connects the sounds /m/, /a/, /s/, /p/, /t/ with the letters *Mm, Aa, Ss, Pp, Tt.*
HIGH-FREQUENCY WORDS	Does not identify the high-frequency words.	Usually recognizes the high-frequency words with accuracy, but not speed.	Consistently recognizes the high-frequency words with speed and accuracy.
COMPREHENSION	Does not identify key details using the illustrations and text.	Usually identifies key details using the illustrations and text.	Consistently identifies key details using the illustrations and text.

Go Digital! www.connected.mcgraw-hill.com

Using Assessment Results

TESTED SKILLS	If ...	Then ...
PHONICS	**Quick Check Rubric:** Children consistently score 1 or **Pencil and Paper Assessment:** Children get 0–2 items correct	... reteach tested Phonics skills using Lessons 6–7, 9, and 12–13 in the *Tier 2 Phonics/Word Study Intervention Online PDFs.*
HIGH-FREQUENCY WORDS	**Quick Check Rubric:** Children consistently score 1	... reteach tested skills by using the High-Frequency Word Cards and asking children to read and spell the word. Point out any irregularities in sound-spellings.
COMPREHENSION	**Quick Check Rubric:** Children consistently score 1 or **Pencil and Paper Assessment:** Children get 0–1 items correct	... reteach tested skill using Lessons 10–12 in the *Tier 2 Comprehension Intervention Online PDFs.*

Response to Intervention

Use the children's assessment results to assist you in identifying children who will benefit from focused intervention.

Use the appropriate sections of the *Placement and Diagnostic Assessment* to designate children requiring:

TIER 2 **Tier 2 Intervention Online PDFs**

TIER 3 **WonderWorks Intervention Program**

→ Phonemic Awareness

→ Phonics

→ Vocabulary

→ Comprehension

→ Fluency

Unit Assessment

✔ COMPREHENSION:	✔ HIGH-FREQUENCY WORDS:	✔ PHONEMIC AWARENESS:	✔ PHONICS:	✔ CATEGORY WORDS:
• Key Details **RL.K.1, RL.K.7** • Key Details **RI.K.1, RI.K.7**	• *a, like, the, see, we* **RF.K.3c**	• Phoneme Isolation **RF.K.2d** • Phoneme Blending **RF.K.2b** • Phoneme Segmentation **RF.K.2b**	• p (initial/ final) **RF.K.3a** • t (initial/ final) **RF.K.3a**	• Shape **L.K.5a** • Movement **L.K.5a**

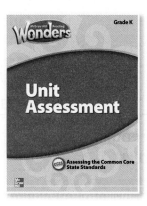

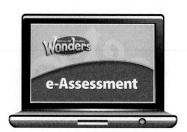

Use Multiple Assessments for Instructional Planning

To create instructional profiles for your children, look for patterns in the results from the following assessment.

Running Records

Use the instructional reading level determined by the Running Record calculations for regrouping decisions.

Using Assessment Results

TESTED SKILLS	If ...	Then ...
COMPREHENSION	Children answer 0–3 items correctly ...	... reteach tested skills using the *Tier 2 Comprehension Intervention Online PDFs*
HIGH-FREQUENCY WORDS	Children answer 0–1 items correctly ...	... reteach tested skills using Section 3 of the *Tier 2 Fluency Intervention Online PDFs*
PHONEMIC AWARENESS	Children answer 0–3 items correctly ...	... reteach tested skills using the *Tier 2 Phonemic Awareness Intervention Online PDFs*
PHONICS	Children answer 0–3 items correctly ...	... reteach tested skills using the *Tier 2 Phonics/Word Study Intervention Online PDFs* and Section 2 of the *Tier 2 Fluency Intervention Online PDFs*
CATEGORY WORDS	Children answer 0–1 items correctly ...	... reteach tested skills using the *Tier 2 Vocabulary Intervention Online PDFs*

Response to Intervention

Use the appropriate sections of the *Placement and Diagnostic Assessment* and children's assessment results to designate children requiring:

 Tier 2 Intervention Online PDFs

 WonderWorks Intervention Program

→ Phonological and Phonemic Awareness

→ Phonics

→ Vocabulary

→ Comprehension

→ Fluency

Program Information

 For Additional Resources

Unit Bibliography

Word Lists

Literature and Informational Text Charts

Web Sites

Resources

www.connected.mcgraw-hill.com

 **SCOPE & SEQUENCE**

	K	1	2	3	4	5	6
READING PROCESS							
Concepts About Print/Print Awareness							
Recognize own name							
Understand directionality (top to bottom; tracking print from left to right; return sweep, page by page)	✔						
Locate printed word on page	✔						
Develop print awareness (concept of letter, word, sentence)	✔						
Identify separate sounds in a spoken sentence	✔						
Understand that written words are represented in written language by a specific sequence of letters	✔						
Distinguish between letters, words, and sentences	✔						
Identify and distinguish paragraphs							
Match print to speech (one-to-one correspondence)	✔						
Name uppercase and lowercase letters	✔						
Understand book handling (holding a book right-side-up, turning its pages)	✔						
Identify parts of a book (front cover, back cover, title page, table of contents); recognize that parts of a book contain information	✔						
Phonological Awareness							
Recognize and understand alliteration							
Segment sentences into correct number of words							
Identify, blend, segment syllables in words		✔					
Recognize and generate rhyming words	✔	✔					
Identify, blend, segment onset and rime	✔	✔					
Phonemic Awareness							
Count phonemes	✔	✔					
Isolate initial, medial, and final sounds	✔	✔					
Blend spoken phonemes to form words	✔	✔					
Segment spoken words into phonemes	✔	✔					
Distinguish between long- and short-vowel sounds	✔	✔					
Manipulate phonemes (addition, deletion, substitution)	✔	✔					
Phonics and Decoding /Word Recognition							
Understand the alphabetic principle	✔	✔					
Sound/letter correspondence	✔	✔	✔	✔			
Blend sounds into words, including VC, CVC, CVCe, CVVC words	✔	✔	✔	✔			
Blend common word families	✔	✔	✔	✔			

KEY	✔ = Assessed Skill
	Tinted panels show skills, strategies, and other teaching opportunities.

	K	1	2	3	4	5	6
Initial consonant blends		✔	✔	✔			
Final consonant blends		✔	✔	✔			
Initial and medial short vowels	✔	✔	✔	✔	✔	✔	✔
Decode one-syllable words in isolation and in context	✔	✔	✔	✔			
Decode multisyllabic words in isolation and in context using common syllabication patterns		✔	✔	✔	✔	✔	✔
Distinguish between similarly spelled words	✔	✔	✔	✔	✔	✔	✔
Monitor accuracy of decoding							
Identify and read common high-frequency words, irregularly spelled words	✔	✔	✔	✔			
Identify and read compound words, contractions		✔	✔	✔	✔	✔	✔
Use knowledge of spelling patterns to identify syllables		✔	✔	✔	✔	✔	✔
Regular and irregular plurals	✔	✔	✔	✔	✔	✔	✔
Long vowels (silent *e*, vowel teams)	✔	✔	✔	✔	✔	✔	
Vowel digraphs (variant vowels)		✔	✔	✔	✔	✔	✔
r-Controlled vowels		✔	✔	✔	✔	✔	✔
Hard/soft consonants		✔	✔	✔	✔	✔	✔
Initial consonant digraphs		✔	✔	✔	✔	✔	
Medial and final consonant digraphs		✔	✔	✔	✔	✔	
Vowel diphthongs		✔	✔	✔	✔	✔	✔
Identify and distinguish letter-sounds (initial, medial, final)	✔	✔	✔				
Silent letters		✔	✔	✔	✔	✔	✔
Schwa words				✔	✔	✔	✔
Inflectional endings		✔	✔	✔	✔	✔	✔
Triple-consonant clusters		✔	✔	✔	✔	✔	
Unfamiliar and complex word families				✔	✔	✔	✔
Structural Analysis/Word Analysis							
Common spelling patterns (word families)		✔	✔	✔	✔	✔	✔
Common syllable patterns		✔	✔	✔	✔	✔	✔
Inflectional endings		✔	✔	✔	✔	✔	✔
Contractions		✔	✔	✔	✔	✔	✔
Compound words		✔	✔	✔	✔	✔	✔
Prefixes and suffixes		✔	✔	✔	✔	✔	✔
Root or base words			✔	✔	✔	✔	✔
Comparatives and superlatives			✔	✔	✔	✔	✔
Greek and Latin roots			✔	✔	✔	✔	✔
Fluency							
Apply letter/sound knowledge to decode phonetically regular words accurately	✔	✔	✔	✔	✔	✔	✔
Recognize high-frequency and familiar words	✔	✔	✔	✔	✔	✔	✔
Read regularly on independent and instructional levels							
Read orally with fluency from familiar texts (choral, echo, partner, Reader's Theater)							
Use appropriate rate, expression, intonation, and phrasing		✔	✔	✔	✔	✔	✔
Read with automaticity (accurately and effortlessly)		✔	✔	✔	✔	✔	✔
Use punctuation cues in reading		✔	✔	✔	✔	✔	✔

	K	1	2	3	4	5	6
Adjust reading rate to purpose, text difficulty, form, and style							
Repeated readings							
Timed readings		✔	✔	✔	✔	✔	✔
Read with purpose and understanding		✔	✔	✔	✔	✔	✔
Read orally with accuracy		✔	✔	✔	✔	✔	✔
Use context to confirm or self-correct word recognition		✔	✔	✔	✔	✔	✔

READING LITERATURE

Comprehension Strategies and Skills

	K	1	2	3	4	5	6
Read literature from a broad range of genres, cultures, and periods		✔	✔	✔	✔	✔	✔
Access complex text		✔	✔	✔	✔	✔	✔
Build background							
Preview and predict							
Establish and adjust purpose for reading							
Evaluate citing evidence from the text							
Ask and answer questions	✔	✔	✔	✔	✔	✔	✔
Inferences and conclusions, citing evidence from the text	✔	✔	✔	✔	✔	✔	✔
Monitor/adjust comprehension including reread, reading rate, paraphrase							
Recount/Retell	✔	✔					
Summarize			✔	✔	✔	✔	✔
Story structure (beginning, middle, end)	✔	✔	✔	✔	✔	✔	✔
Visualize							
Make connections between and across texts		✔	✔	✔	✔	✔	✔
Point of view		✔	✔	✔	✔	✔	✔
Author's purpose							
Cause and effect	✔	✔	✔	✔	✔	✔	✔
Compare and contrast (including character, setting, plot, topics)	✔	✔	✔	✔	✔	✔	✔
Classify and categorize		✔	✔				
Literature vs informational text	✔	✔	✔				
Illustrations, using	✔	✔	✔	✔			
Theme, central message, moral, lesson		✔	✔	✔	✔	✔	✔
Predictions, making/confirming	✔	✔	✔				
Problem and solution (problem/resolution)		✔	✔	✔	✔	✔	✔
Sequence of events	✔	✔	✔	✔	✔	✔	✔

Literary Elements

	K	1	2	3	4	5	6
Character	✔	✔	✔	✔	✔	✔	✔
Plot development/Events	✔	✔	✔	✔	✔	✔	✔
Setting	✔	✔	✔	✔	✔	✔	✔
Stanza				✔	✔	✔	✔
Alliteration						✔	✔
Assonance						✔	✔
Dialogue							
Foreshadowing						✔	✔

KEY	✔ = Assessed Skill Tinted panels show skills, strategies, and other teaching opportunities.

	K	1	2	3	4	5	6
Flashback						✔	✔
Descriptive and figurative language		✔	✔	✔	✔	✔	✔
Imagery					✔	✔	✔
Meter					✔	✔	✔
Onomatopoeia							
Repetition		✔	✔	✔	✔	✔	✔
Rhyme/rhyme schemes		✔	✔	✔	✔	✔	✔
Rhythm		✔	✔				
Sensory language							
Symbolism							

Write About Reading/Literary Response Discussions

	K	1	2	3	4	5	6
Reflect and respond to text citing text evidence		✔	✔	✔	✔	✔	✔
Connect and compare text characters, events, ideas to self, to other texts, to world							
Connect literary texts to other curriculum areas							
Identify cultural and historical elements of text							
Evaluate author's techniques, craft							
Analytical writing							
Interpret text ideas through writing, discussion, media, research							
Book report or review							
Locate, use, explain information from text features		✔	✔	✔	✔	✔	✔
Organize information to show understanding of main idea through charts, mapping							
Cite text evidence	✔	✔	✔	✔	✔	✔	✔
Author's purpose/ Illustrator's purpose							

READING INFORMATIONAL TEXT

Comprehension Strategies and Skills

	K	1	2	3	4	5	6
Read informational text from a broad range of topics and cultures	✔	✔	✔	✔	✔	✔	✔
Access complex text		✔	✔	✔	✔	✔	✔
Build background							
Preview and predict	✔	✔	✔				
Establish and adjust purpose for reading							
Evaluate citing evidence from the text							
Ask and answer questions	✔	✔	✔	✔	✔	✔	✔
Inferences and conclusions, citing evidence from the text	✔	✔	✔	✔	✔	✔	✔
Monitor and adjust comprehension including reread, adjust reading rate, paraphrase							
Recount/Retell	✔	✔					
Summarize				✔	✔	✔	✔
Text structure	✔	✔	✔	✔	✔	✔	✔
Identify text features		✔	✔	✔	✔	✔	✔
Make connections between and across texts	✔	✔	✔	✔	✔	✔	✔
Author's point of view					✔	✔	✔	✔
Author's purpose		✔	✔				

	K	1	2	3	4	5	6
Cause and effect	✔	✔	✔	✔	✔	✔	✔
Compare and contrast	✔	✔	✔	✔	✔	✔	✔
Classify and categorize		✔	✔				
Illustrations and photographs, using	✔	✔	✔	✔			
Instructions/directions (written and oral)		✔	✔	✔	✔	✔	✔
Main idea and key details	✔	✔	✔	✔	✔	✔	✔
Persuasion, reasons and evidence to support points/persuasive techniques						✔	✔
Predictions, making/confirming	✔	✔					
Problem and solution		✔	✔	✔	✔	✔	✔
Sequence, chronological order of events, time order, steps in a process	✔	✔	✔	✔	✔	✔	✔

Writing About Reading/Expository Critique Discussions

	K	1	2	3	4	5	6
Reflect and respond to text citing text evidence		✔	✔	✔	✔	✔	✔
Connect and compare text characters, events, ideas to self, to other texts, to world							
Connect texts to other curriculum areas							
Identify cultural and historical elements of text							
Evaluate author's techniques, craft							
Analytical writing							
Read to understand and perform tasks and activities							
Interpret text ideas through writing, discussion, media, research							
Locate, use, explain information from text features		✔	✔	✔	✔	✔	✔
Organize information to show understanding of main idea through charts, mapping							
Cite text evidence		✔	✔	✔	✔	✔	✔
Author's purpose/Illustrator's purpose							

Text Features

	K	1	2	3	4	5	6
Recognize and identify text and organizational features of nonfiction texts		✔	✔	✔	✔	✔	✔
Captions and labels, headings, subheadings, endnotes, key words, bold print	✔	✔	✔	✔	✔	✔	✔
Graphics, including photographs, illustrations, maps, charts, diagrams, graphs, time lines	✔	✔	✔	✔	✔	✔	✔

Self-Selected Reading/Independent Reading

	K	1	2	3	4	5	6
Use personal criteria to choose own reading including favorite authors, genres, recommendations from others; set up a reading log							
Read a range of literature and informational text for tasks as well as for enjoyment; participate in literature circles							
Produce evidence of reading by retelling, summarizing, or paraphrasing							

Media Literacy

	K	1	2	3	4	5	6
Summarize the message or content from media message, citing text evidence							
Use graphics, illustrations to analyze and interpret information	✔	✔	✔	✔	✔	✔	✔
Identify structural features of popular media and use the features to obtain information, including digital sources				✔	✔	✔	✔
Identify reasons and evidence in visuals and media message							
Analyze media source: recognize effects of media in one's mood and emotion							

KEY	✔ = Assessed Skill Tinted panels show skills, strategies, and other teaching opportunities.

	K	1	2	3	4	5	6
Make informed judgments about print and digital media							
Critique persuasive techniques							

WRITING

Writing Process

	K	1	2	3	4	5	6
Plan/prewrite							
Draft							
Revise							
Edit/proofread							
Publish and present including using technology							
Teacher and peer feedback							

Writing Traits

	K	1	2	3	4	5	6
Conventions		✔	✔	✔	✔	✔	✔
Ideas		✔	✔	✔	✔	✔	✔
Organization		✔	✔	✔	✔	✔	✔
Sentence fluency		✔	✔	✔	✔	✔	✔
Voice		✔	✔	✔	✔	✔	✔
Word choice		✔	✔	✔	✔	✔	✔

Writer's Craft

	K	1	2	3	4	5	6
Good topic, focus on and develop topic, topic sentence			✔	✔	✔	✔	✔
Paragraph(s); sentence structure			✔	✔	✔	✔	✔
Main idea and supporting key details			✔	✔	✔	✔	✔
Unimportant details							
Relevant supporting evidence			✔	✔	✔	✔	✔
Strong opening, strong conclusion			✔	✔	✔	✔	✔
Beginning, middle, end; sequence		✔	✔	✔	✔	✔	✔
Precise words, strong words, vary words			✔	✔	✔	✔	✔
Figurative and sensory language, descriptive details							
Informal/formal language							
Mood/style/tone							
Dialogue				✔	✔	✔	✔
Transition words, transitions to multiple paragraphs				✔	✔	✔	✔
Select focus and organization			✔	✔	✔	✔	✔
Points and counterpoints/Opposing claims and counterarguments							
Use reference materials (online and print dictionary, thesaurus, encyclopedia)							

Writing Applications

	K	1	2	3	4	5	6
Writing about text	✔	✔	✔	✔	✔	✔	✔
Personal and fictional narrative (also biographical and autobiographical)	✔	✔	✔	✔	✔	✔	✔
Variety of expressive forms including poetry	✔	✔	✔	✔	✔	✔	✔
Informative/explanatory texts	✔	✔	✔	✔	✔	✔	✔
Description	✔	✔	✔	✔			
Procedural texts		✔	✔	✔	✔	✔	✔
Opinion pieces or arguments	✔	✔	✔	✔	✔	✔	✔

	K	1	2	3	4	5	6
Communications including technical documents		✔	✔	✔	✔	✔	✔
Research report	✔	✔	✔	✔	✔	✔	✔
Responses to literature/reflection				✔	✔	✔	✔
Analytical writing							
Letters		✔	✔	✔	✔	✔	✔
Write daily and over short and extended time frames; set up writer's notebooks							

Penmanship/Handwriting

	K	1	2	3	4	5	6
Write legibly in manuscript using correct formation, directionality, and spacing							
Write legibly in cursive using correct formation, directionality, and spacing							

SPEAKING AND LISTENING

Speaking

	K	1	2	3	4	5	6
Use repetition, rhyme, and rhythm in oral texts							
Participate in classroom activities and discussions							
Collaborative conversation with peers and adults in small and large groups using formal English when appropriate							
Differentiate between formal and informal English							
Follow agreed upon rules for discussion							
Build on others' talk in conversation, adding new ideas							
Come to discussion prepared							
Describe familiar people, places, and things and add drawings as desired							
Paraphrase portions of text read alone or information presented							
Apply comprehension strategies and skills in speaking activities							
Use literal and nonliteral meanings							
Ask and answer questions about text read aloud and about media							
Stay on topic when speaking							
Use language appropriate to situation, purpose, and audience							
Use nonverbal communications such as eye contact, gestures, and props							
Use verbal communication in effective ways and improve expression in conventional language							
Retell a story, presentation, or spoken message by summarizing							
Oral presentations: focus, organizational structure, audience, purpose							
Give and follow directions							
Consider audience when speaking or preparing a presentation							
Recite poems, rhymes, songs							
Use complete, coherent sentences							
Organize presentations							
Deliver presentations (narrative, summaries, research, persuasive); add visuals							
Speak audibly (accuracy, expression, volume, pitch, rate, phrasing, modulation, enunciation)							
Create audio recordings of poems, stories, presentations							

Listening

	K	1	2	3	4	5	6
Identify musical elements in language							
Determine the purpose for listening							

KEY ✔ = Assessed Skill
Tinted panels show skills, strategies, and other teaching opportunities.

	K	1	2	3	4	5	6
Understand, follow, restate, and give oral directions							
Develop oral language and concepts							
Listen openly, responsively, attentively, and critically							
Listen to identify the points a speaker makes							
Listen responsively to oral presentations (determine main idea and key details)							
Ask and answer relevant questions (for clarification to follow-up on ideas)							
Identify reasons and evidence presented by speaker							
Recall and interpret speakers' verbal/nonverbal messages, purposes, perspectives							

LANGUAGE

Vocabulary Acquisition and Use

	K	1	2	3	4	5	6
Develop oral vocabulary and choose words for effect							
Use academic language		✔	✔	✔	✔	✔	✔
Identify persons, places, things, actions		✔	✔	✔			
Classify, sort, and categorize words	✔	✔	✔	✔	✔	✔	✔
Determine or clarify the meaning of unknown words; use word walls		✔	✔	✔	✔	✔	✔
Synonyms, antonyms, and opposites		✔	✔	✔	✔	✔	
Use context clues such as word, sentence, paragraph, definition, example, restatement, description, comparison, cause and effect		✔	✔	✔	✔	✔	✔
Use word identification strategies		✔	✔	✔	✔	✔	✔
Unfamiliar words		✔	✔	✔	✔	✔	✔
Multiple-meaning words		✔	✔	✔	✔	✔	✔
Use print and online dictionary to locate meanings, pronunciation, derivatives, parts of speech		✔	✔	✔	✔	✔	✔
Compound words		✔	✔	✔	✔	✔	✔
Words ending in -er and -est		✔	✔	✔	✔	✔	
Root words (base words)		✔	✔	✔	✔		✔
Prefixes and suffixes		✔	✔	✔	✔	✔	✔
Greek and Latin affixes and roots			✔	✔	✔	✔	✔
Denotation and connotation					✔	✔	✔
Word families		✔	✔	✔	✔	✔	✔
Inflectional endings		✔	✔	✔	✔	✔	✔
Use a print and online thesaurus			✔	✔	✔	✔	✔
Use print and online reference sources for word meaning (dictionary, glossaries)	✔	✔	✔	✔	✔	✔	✔
Homographs				✔	✔	✔	✔
Homophones			✔	✔	✔	✔	✔
Contractions		✔	✔	✔			
Figurative language such as metaphors, similes, personification			✔	✔	✔	✔	✔
Idioms, adages, proverbs, literal and nonliteral language			✔	✔	✔	✔	✔
Analogies							
Listen to, read, discuss familiar and unfamiliar challenging text							
Identify real-life connections between words and their use							
Use acquired words and phrases to convey precise ideas							
Use vocabulary to express spatial and temporal relationships							

	K	1	2	3	4	5	6
Identify shades of meaning in related words	✔	✔	✔	✔	✔	✔	✔
Word origins				✔	✔	✔	✔
Morphology				✔	✔	✔	✔
Knowledge of Language							
Choose words, phrases, and sentences for effect							
Choose punctuation effectively							
Formal and informal language for style and tone including dialects							
Conventions of Standard English/Grammar, Mechanics, and Usage							
Sentence concepts: statements, questions, exclamations, commands		✔	✔	✔	✔	✔	✔
Complete and incomplete sentences; sentence fragments; word order		✔	✔	✔	✔	✔	✔
Compound sentences, complex sentences				✔	✔	✔	✔
Combining sentences		✔	✔	✔	✔	✔	✔
Nouns including common, proper, singular, plural, irregular plurals, possessives, abstract, concrete, collective		✔	✔	✔	✔	✔	✔
Verbs including action, helping, linking, irregular		✔	✔	✔	✔	✔	✔
Verb tenses including past, present, future, perfect, and progressive		✔	✔	✔	✔	✔	✔
Pronouns including possessive, subject and object, pronoun-verb agreement, indefinite, intensive, reciprocal; correct unclear pronouns		✔	✔	✔	✔	✔	✔
Adjectives including articles, demonstrative, proper adjectives that compare		✔	✔	✔	✔	✔	✔
Adverbs including telling how, when, where, comparative, superlative, irregular		✔	✔	✔	✔	✔	✔
Subject, predicate; subject-verb agreement		✔	✔	✔	✔	✔	✔
Contractions		✔	✔	✔	✔	✔	✔
Conjunctions				✔	✔	✔	✔
Commas			✔	✔	✔	✔	✔
Colons, semicolons, dashes, hyphens						✔	✔
Question words							
Quotation marks			✔	✔	✔	✔	✔
Prepositions and prepositional phrases, appositives		✔	✔	✔	✔	✔	✔
Independent and dependent clauses						✔	✔
Italics/underlining for emphasis and titles							
Negatives, correcting double negatives					✔	✔	✔
Abbreviations			✔	✔	✔	✔	✔
Use correct capitalization in sentences, proper nouns, titles, abbreviations		✔	✔	✔	✔	✔	✔
Use correct punctuation		✔	✔	✔	✔	✔	✔
Antecedents				✔	✔	✔	✔
Homophones and words often confused			✔	✔	✔	✔	✔
Apostrophes				✔	✔	✔	✔
Spelling							
Write irregular, high-frequency words	✔	✔	✔				
ABC order	✔	✔					
Write letters	✔	✔					
Words with short vowels	✔	✔	✔	✔	✔	✔	✔
Words with long vowels	✔	✔	✔	✔	✔	✔	✔

KEY	✔ = Assessed Skill
	Tinted panels show skills, strategies, and other teaching opportunities.

	K	1	2	3	4	5	6
Words with digraphs, blends, consonant clusters, double consonants		✔	✔	✔	✔	✔	✔
Words with vowel digraphs and ambiguous vowels		✔	✔	✔	✔	✔	✔
Words with diphthongs		✔	✔	✔	✔	✔	✔
Words with r-controlled vowels		✔	✔	✔	✔	✔	✔
Use conventional spelling		✔	✔	✔	✔	✔	✔
Schwa words				✔	✔	✔	✔
Words with silent letters			✔	✔	✔	✔	✔
Words with hard and soft letters			✔	✔	✔	✔	✔
Inflectional endings including plural, past tense, drop final e and double consonant when adding -ed and -ing, changing y to i		✔	✔	✔	✔	✔	✔
Compound words		✔	✔	✔	✔	✔	✔
Homonyms/homophones			✔	✔	✔	✔	✔
Prefixes and suffixes		✔	✔	✔	✔	✔	✔
Root and base words (also spell derivatives)				✔	✔	✔	✔
Syllables: patterns, rules, accented, stressed, closed, open				✔	✔	✔	✔
Words with Greek and Latin roots						✔	✔
Words from mythology						✔	✔
Words with spelling patterns, word families		✔	✔	✔	✔	✔	✔

RESEARCH AND INQUIRY

Study Skills

	K	1	2	3	4	5	6
Directions: read, write, give, follow (includes technical directions)			✔	✔	✔	✔	✔
Evaluate directions for sequence and completeness				✔	✔	✔	✔
Use library/media center							
Use parts of a book to locate information							
Interpret information from graphic aids		✔	✔	✔	✔	✔	✔
Use graphic organizers to organize information and comprehend text		✔	✔	✔	✔	✔	✔
Use functional, everyday documents				✔	✔	✔	✔
Apply study strategies: skimming and scanning, note-taking, outlining							

Research Process

	K	1	2	3	4	5	6
Generate and revise topics and questions for research				✔	✔	✔	✔
Narrow focus of research, set research goals				✔	✔	✔	✔
Find and locate information using print and digital resources		✔	✔	✔	✔	✔	✔
Record information systematically (note-taking, outlining, using technology)				✔	✔	✔	✔
Develop a systematic research plan				✔	✔	✔	✔
Evaluate reliability, credibility, usefulness of sources and information						✔	✔
Use primary sources to obtain information					✔	✔	✔
Organize, synthesize, evaluate, and draw conclusions from information							
Cite and list sources of information (record basic bibliographic data)					✔	✔	✔
Demonstrate basic keyboarding skills							
Participate in and present shared research							

Technology

	K	1	2	3	4	5	6
Use computer, Internet, and other technology resources to access information							
Use text and organizational features of electronic resources such as search engines, keywords, e-mail, hyperlinks, URLs, Web pages, databases, graphics							
Use digital tools to present and publish in a variety of media formats							

INDEX

A

D

E

M

N

O

alliteration, **7**:T44

repetition, **7**:T177, **9**:T177

rhyme/rhyme scheme, **6**:T44, **7**:T177, **9**:T177

rhythm, **7**:T177, **9**:T177

writing, **5**:T18, T32, T40, T50, T58

See also **Genre; Songs, rhymes, chants.**

Pre-Decodable Reader, **1**:S14, S24, S38, S48, S62, S72

Predict, **1**:S14, S24, S38, S48, S62, S72, T30, T48, T60, T68, T78, T112, T130, T194, T242, **2**:T60, T68, T78, T112, T142, T150, T156, T160, T224, T232, T238, T242, **3**:T30, T48, T60, T112, T130, T142, T150, T156, T160, T194, T212, T224, T232, T238, T242, **4**:T30, T60, T68, T74, T78, T112, T142, T150, T156, T160, T194, T224, T232, T238, T242, **5**:T60, T68, T74, T78, T112, T142, T150, T156, T160, T194, T224, T232, T238, T242, **6**:T30, T78, T112, T142, T150, T156, T160, T194, T224, T232, T238, T242, **7**:T30, T74, T78, T112, T142, T150, T156, T160, T194, T224, T232, T238, T242, **8**:T60, T68, T112, T142, T150, T156, T160, T194, T224, T232, T238, T242, **9**:T30, T60, T68, T74, T78, T112, T142, T150, T156, T194, T224, T238, T242, **10**:T32, T62, T70, T76, T114, T144, T152, T158, T162, T196, T226, T234, T240, T244

See also **Comprehension strategies: predictions, make, confirm, revise; Setting purposes for reading.**

Prefixes. *See* **Vocabulary strategies.**

Presentation, oral. *See* **Oral presentations.**

Previewing literature. *See* **Predict; Setting purposes for reading.**

Print awareness

book handling, opening, parts, **1**:S14, S24, S31, S38, S55, S62, S72, T12, T30, T48, T60, T94, T112, T130, T142, T176, T194, **2**:T12, T30, T48, T94, T112, T130, T176, T194, T212, **3**:T12, T30, T48, T60, T112, T130, T194, T212, **4**:T30, T48, T112, T130, T194, T212, **5**:T212, **9**:T194

book parts, **1**:T176, **2**:T212, T224, **3**:T48, **4**:T130, **5**:T12, T94

print type, **1**:T106

sentences, **6**:T12, T24, T30, T48, T68, T107, T130, T142, T150, T176, T194, T212, T224, **7**:T30, T48, T60, T130

uppercase and lowercase letters, **4**:T189, T194, T212, T232, **5**:T12, **6**:T224, **8**:T30

word boundaries, **2**:T176, T232, **5**:T94, **7**:T194, T212, **9**:T188, T194, T224, T232, **10**:T114, T178, T196, T214, T226

See also **Concepts of/about print.**

Procedural text. *See* **Genre: reading informational text.**

Punctuation. *See* **Grammar: punctuation of sentences.**

Q

Questions, asking. *See* **Comprehension strategies: ask and answer questions.**

R

Read alouds. *See* **Big Book, read the literature; Big Book, reread the literature; Interactive Read Aloud; Shared read.**

Reading across texts, **1**:S27, S51, S75, T44–T45, T126–T127, T208–T209, **2**:T44–T45, T126–T127, **3**:T44–T45, T126–T127, T208–T209, **4**:T44–T45, T126–T127, T208–T209, **5**:T44–T45, T126–T127, T208–T209, **6**:T44–T45, T126–T127, T208–T209, **7**:T44–T45, T126–T127, T208–T209, **8**:T44–T45, T126–T127, T208–T209, **9**:T44–T45, T126–T127, T208–T209, **10**:T46–T47, T128–T129, T210–T211

See also **Text connections: text to text.**

Reading independently, **1**:T67, T73, T77, T149, T155, T159, T231, T237, T241, **2**:T67, T73, T77, T149, T155, T159, T231, T237, T241, **3**:T67, T73, T77, T149, T155, T159, T231, T237, T241, **4**:T67, T73, T77, T149, T155, T159, T231, T237, T241, **5**:T67, T73, T77, T149, T155, T159, T231, T237, T241, **6**:T67, T73, T77, T149, T155, T159, T231, T237, T241, **7**:T67, T73, T77, T149, T155, T159, T231, T237, T241, **8**:T67, T73, T77, T149, T155, T159, T231, T237, T241, **9**:T67, T73, T77, T149, T155, T159, T231, T237, T241, **10**:T69, T75, T79, T151, T157, T161, T233, T239, T243

Reading purposefully, **1**:T67, T73, T77, T149, T155, T159, T231, T237, T241, **2**:T67, T73, T77, T149, T155, T159, T231, T237, T241, **3**:T67, T73, T77, T149, T155, T159, T231, T237, T241, **4**:T67, T73, T77, T149, T155, T159, T231, T237, T241, **5**:T67, T73, T77, T149, T155, T159, T231, T237, T241, **6**:T67, T73, T77, T149, T155, T159, T231, T237, T241, **7**:T67, T73, T77, T149, T155, T159, T231, T237, T241, **8**:T67, T73, T77, T149, T155, T159, T231, T237, T241, **9**:T67, T73, T77, T149, T155, T159, T231, T237, T241, **10**:T69, T75, T79, T151, T157, T161, T233, T239, T243

Rereading, **1**:S14, S17, S24, S38, S41, S48, S62, S65, S72, T31, T42, T49, T113, T124, T131, T195, T206, T213, **2**:T31, T49, T113, T131, T195, T213, **3**:T31, T49, T113, T131, T195, T213, **4**:T31, T48, T113, T130, T195, T212, **5**:T31, T42, T48, T113, T130, T195, T212, **6**:T31, T48, T113, T130, T195, T212, **7**:T31, T48, T113, T130, T195, T212, **8**:T31, T48, T113, T124, T131, T195, T212, **9**:T31, T48, T113, T130, T195, T206, T212, **10**:T33, T44, T50, T115, T126, T132, T197, T208, T214

See also **Big Book, reread the literature; Comprehension strategies: reread.**

Research and inquiry, **1**:T52–T55, T134–T137, T216–T219, **2**:T52–T55, T134–T137, T216–T219, **3**:T52–T55, T134–T137, T216–T219, **4**:T52–T55, T134–T137, T216–T219, **5**:T52–T55, T134–T137, T216–T219, **6**:T52–T55, T134–T137, T216–T219, **7**:T52–T55, T134–T137, T216–T219, **8**:T52–T55, T134–T137, T216–T219, **9**:T52–T55, T134–T137, T216–T219, **10**:T54–T55, T136–T139, T218–T221

Research process, **1**:T52–T53, T134–T135, T216–T217, **2**:T52–T53, T134–T135, T216–T217, **3**:T52–T53, T134–T135, T216–T217, **4**:T52–T53, T134–T135, T216–T217, **5**:T52–T53, T134–T135, T216–T217, **6**:T52–T53, T134–T135, T216–T217, T248–T249, **7**:T52–T55, T134–T135, T216–T217, T249, **8**:T52–T53, T134–T135, T216–T217, T249, **9**:T52–T53, T134–T135, T216–T217, **10**:T54–T55, T136–T137, T218–T219

Respond to reading

informational text, **1**:S31, S55, S60, T45, T127, T160–T161, T177, T225, T233, T239, T243, **2**:T13, T45, T61,

S

U

Uppercase/lowercase letters

letter recognition, **1**:S8, S13, S18, S23, S28, S32, S37, S42, S47, S52, S56, S61, S66, S71, S76

penmanship, **1**:T16, T98, T180, **2**:T16, T98, **3**:T16, T98, T180, **4**:T16, T98, **5**:T16, T98, **6**:T16, T98, **7**:T16, T98, **8**:T16, T98, **9**:T16

V

Visualize. *See* **Comprehension strategies**.

Visual Vocabulary Cards, **1**:T11, T20, T34, T80, T81, T93, T102, T116, T162, T184, T198, T244, **2**:T20, T34, T47, T80, T93, T102, T116, T129, T163, T175, T198, **3**:T11, T34, T124, T162, T184, T198, **4**:T11, T20, T34, T80, T93, T102, T116, T175, T184, T198, **5**:T11, T20, T34, T80, T93, T102, T116, T175, T184, T198, **6**:T11, T20, T34, T75, T93, T102, T116, T124, T162, T175, T184, T198, **7**:T11, T20, T34, T93, T102, T116, T124, T162, T175, T184, T198, T206, **8**:T20, T34, T47, T80, T102, T116, T124, T129, T163, T175, T184, T198, **9**:T20, T34, T80, T81, T93, T102, T116, T162, T175, T198, T244, **10**:T11, T20, T36, T49, T82, T95, T104, T164, T177, T186, T200, T246

Vocabulary acquisition

category words

action words, **3**:T21, T43, T81

animal homes, **7**:T185, T207, T245

animal parts, **7**:T21, T43, T81

baby animals, **10**:T187, T209, T247

colors, **2**:T21, T43, T81

days of the week, **1**:S59, S69

family words, **1**:T103, T125, T163

farm animals, **9**:T103, T125, T163

feeling words, **1**:T21, T43, T81

food words, **4**:T103, T125, T163, **5**:T185, T207, T245, **9**:T185, T207, T245

household furniture, **9**:T21, T43, T81

job words, **4**:T21, T43, T81

movement words, **2**:T185, T207, T245

names, **1**:S11, S21

numbers, **1**:S35, S45

opposites, **8**:T185, T207, T245, **10**:T105, T127, T165

ordinal numbers, **8**:T103, T125, T163

pets, **7**:T103, T125, T163

position words, **4**:T185, T207, T245

question words, **6**:T185, T207, T245, **10**:T21, T45, T83

seasons, **6**:T21, T43, T81

sensory words, **1**:T185, T207, T245

sequence words, **3**:T185, T207, T245

shape words, **2**:T103, T125, T163

size words, **5**:T21, T43, T81

sound words, **3**:T103, T125, T163

tree parts, **5**:T103, T125, T163

vehicles, **8**:T21, T43, T81

weather words, **6**:T103, T125, T163

cognates, **1**:T81, T163, T245, **2**:T81, T163, T245, **3**:T81, T163, T245, **4**:T81, T163, T245, **5**:T81, T163, T245, **6**:T81, T163, T245, **7**:T81, T163, T245, **8**:T81, T163, T245, **9**:T81, T163, T245, **10**:T83, T165, T247

computer-related, **6**:T248, **7**:T248, **8**:T248, **9**:T248, **10**:T248

domain-specific, **1**:T103, T125, T163, **4**:T21, T43, T81, T103, T125, T163, **5**:T103, T125, T163, T185, T207, T245, **6**:T21, T43, T81, T103, T125, T163, **7**:T21, T43, T81, T103, T125, T163, T185, T207, T245, **8**:T21, T43, T81, **9**:T21, T43, T81, T103, T125, T163, T185, T207, T245, **10**:T187, T209, T247

function words and phrases. *See* **English Language Learners: high-frequency words, vocabulary.**

general academic, **1**:S14, S62, S69, T38, T52, T134, T176, T216, **2**:T52, T122, T126, T132, T134, T140

oral vocabulary, **1**:S16, S20, S26, S40, S44, S50, S64, S68, S74, T10–T11, T20, T34, T42, T67, T77, T80, T92–T93, T102, T116, T124, T149, T159, T162, T174–T175, T184, T198, T206, T231, T241, T244, **2**:T10–T11, T20, T34, T42, T67, T77, T80, T92–T93, T102, T116, T124, T149, T159, T162, T174–T175, T184, T198, T206, T231, T241, T244, **3**:T10–T11, T20, T34, T42, T67, T77, T80, T92–T93, T102, T116, T124, T149, T159, T162, T174–T175, T184, T198, T206, T231, T241, T244, **4**:T10–T11, T20, T34, T42, T77, T80, T92–T93, T102, T116, T124, T149, T159, T162, T174–T175, T184, T198, T206, T231, T241, T244, **5**:T10–T11, T20, T34, T42, T77, T80, T92–T93, T102, T116, T124, T149, T159, T162, T174–T175, T184, T198, T206, T231, T241, T244, **6**:T10–T11, T20, T34, T42, T67, T77, T80, T92–T93, T102, T116, T124, T149, T159, T162, T174–T175, T184, T198, T206, T231, T241, T244, **7**:T10–T11, T20, T34, T42–T43, T67, T77, T80, T92–T93, T102, T116, T124, T149, T159, T162, T174–T175, T184, T198, T206, T231, T241, T244, **8**:T10–T11, T20–T21, T34, T42, T67, T77, T80, T92–T93, T102, T116, T124, T149, T159, T162, T174–T175, T184, T198, T206, T231, T241, T244, **9**:T10–T11, T20, T34, T42, T67, T77, T80, T92–T93, T102, T116, T124, T149, T159, T162, T174–T175, T184, T198, T206, T231, T241, T244, **10**:T10–T11, T20, T36, T44, T69, T79, T82, T94–T95, T104, T118, T126, T151, T161, T164, T176–T177, T186, T200, T208, T233, T243, T246

selection words, **2**:T12, T94, **4**:T12, T176, **7**:T12, **9**:T176, **10**:T178

story words, **1**:T12, T94, T176, **2**:T176, **3**:T12, T94, T176, **4**:T94, **5**:T12, T94, T176, **6**:T12, T94, T176, **7**:T94, T176, **8**:T12, T94, T176, **9**:T12, **10**:T12, T96

word walls, **1**:S33. *See also* **High-frequency words.**

word webs, **1**:S16, S20, S26, S40, S44, S64, S68, T182, **2**:T182, **6**:T100, **7**:T18, **8**:T18, **10**:T136

See also **Academic language; High-frequency words; Oral language.**

Vocabulary strategies

ask and answer questions, **10**:T97

compound words, **7**:T21, T43

context clues, sentence clues, **5**:T207, **6**:T21, T43, **8**:T43, **9**:T185, T207, **10**:T21, T45

figurative language, **6**:T103, T125, **7**:T185, T207

inflectional endings, **5**:T103, T125

plurals, **5**:T21, T43

shades of meaning, **6**:T103, T125, **7**:T185, T207

W

Common Core State Standards Correlations

English Language Arts

College and Career Readiness Anchor Standards for READING

The K–5 standards on the following pages define what students should understand and be able to do by the end of each grade. They correspond to the College and Career Readiness (CCR) anchor standards below by number. The CCR and grade-specific standards are necessary complements—the former providing broad standards, the latter providing additional specificity—that together define the skills and understandings that all students must demonstrate.

Key Ideas and Details

1. Read closely to determine what the text says explicitly and to make logical inferences from it; cite specific textual evidence when writing or speaking to support conclusions drawn from the text.

2. Determine central ideas or themes of a text and analyze their development; summarize the key supporting details and ideas.

3. Analyze how and why individuals, events, and ideas develop and interact over the course of a text.

Craft and Structure

4. Interpret words and phrases as they are used in a text, including determining technical, connotative, and figurative meanings, and analyze how specific word choices shape meaning or tone.

5. Analyze the structure of texts, including how specific sentences, paragraphs, and larger portions of the text (e.g., a section, chapter, scene, or stanza) relate to each other and the whole.

6. Assess how point of view or purpose shapes the content and style of a text.

Integration of Knowledge and Ideas

7. Integrate and evaluate content presented in diverse media and formats, including visually and quantitatively, as well as in words.

8. Delineate and evaluate the argument and specific claims in a text, including the validity of the reasoning as well as the relevance and sufficiency of the evidence.

9. Analyze how two or more texts address similar themes or topics in order to build knowledge or to compare the approaches the authors take.

Range of Reading and Level of Text Complexity

10. Read and comprehend complex literary and informational texts independently and proficiently.

CCSS Common Core State Standards
English Language Arts

Grade K

Each standard is coded in the following manner:

Strand	Grade Level	Standard
RL	K	1

Reading Standards for Literature

Key Ideas and Details		McGraw-Hill Reading Wonders
RL.K.1	With prompting and support, ask and answer questions about key details in a text.	**READING WRITING WORKSHOP BIG BOOK:** Unit 1, Week 3: 44-49 **LEVELED READERS:** Unit 1, Week 2: *Hop!* (A), *We Hop!* (O), *We Can Move!* (B) **Unit 2, Week 3:** *We Like Bugs!* (A), *The Bugs Run* (O), *I See a Bug!* (B) **Unit 3, Week 1:** *We Run* (A), *Go, Nat!* (O) **Unit 3, Week 2:** *A Noisy Night* (B) **Unit 4, Week 2:** *My Neighbors* (A), *Neighborhood Party* (O), *Parade Day* (B) **Unit 5, Week 1:** *My Garden* (A), *My Garden Grows* (O) **Unit 6, Week 2:** *The Rain* (A), *Weather Is Fun* (O), *Kate and Tuck* (B) **Unit 7, Week 3:** *We Want Water* (A), *A New Home* (O), *Bird's New Home* (B) **Unit 8, Week 3:** *Going Up* (A), *In the Clouds* (O), *How Sun and Moon Found Home* (B) **Unit 9, Week 1:** *Let Me Help You* (A), *How Can Jane Help?* (O), *I Used to Help Too* (B) **Unit 10, Week 1:** *Animal Band* (A), *We Want Honey* (O), *A Good Idea* (B) **YOUR TURN PRACTICE BOOK:** 29, 37, 45, 234 **READING WORKSTATION ACTIVITY CARDS:** 1, 2 **TEACHER'S EDITION:** Unit 1: T23, T106, T189 Unit 2: T177, T186-191 Unit 3: T25, T104-109 Unit 4: T35, T104-108, T142-143, T150-151, T186-191, T224-225, T232-233, T238-239 Unit 5: T61, T69, T238-239 Unit 6: T23-26, T61, T69, T75, T105-108, T143, T151, T186-191 Unit 7: T45, T107 Unit 8: T61, T69, T75, T105-108, T186-191 Unit 9: T22-26, T61, T69, T75, T104-109 Unit 10: T106-110, T145, T153, T159 **LITERATURE BIG BOOKS:** Unit 1, Week 1: *What About Bear?* Unit 2 Week 3: *I Love Bugs!* Unit 3, Week 1: *How Do Dinosaurs Go to School?* Unit 4, Week 2: *What Can You Do With a Paleta?* Unit 6, Week 1: *Mama, Is It Summer Yet?* Unit 6, Week 2: *Rain* Unit 7, Week 2: *The Birthday Pet* Unit 7, Week 3: *Bear Snores On* Unit 8, Week 1: *When Daddy's Truck Picks Me Up* Unit 9, Week 2: *Hen Hears Gossip* Unit 10, Week 2: *All Kinds of Families* **INTERACTIVE READ-ALOUD CARDS:** SS: "The Ugly Duckling", "Tikki Tikki Tembo" Unit 1, Week 1: "The Lion and the Mouse" Unit 1, Week 2: "The Tortoise and the Hare" Unit 2, Week 1: "Timimoto" Unit 4, Week 1: "Little Juan and the Cooking Pot" Unit 4, Week 3: "A Bundle of Sticks"
RL.K.2	With prompting and support, retell familiar stories, including key details.	**LEVELED READERS:** Unit 1, Week 2: *Hop!* (A), *We Hop!* (O, ELL), *We Can Move!* (B) **Unit 2, Week 3:** *I See a Bug!* (B) **Unit 3, Week 1:** *We Run* (A), *Go, Nat!* (O, ELL), *The Birdhouse* (B) **Unit 3, Week 2:** *City Sounds* (A), *Farm Sounds* (O, ELL), *A Noisy Night* (B) **Unit 4, Week 3:** *We Clean!* (A), *Can You Fix It?* (O, ELL), *Helping Mom* (B) **Unit 5, Week 1:** *The Mystery Seeds* (B) **Unit 6, Week 1:** *It Is Hot!* (A), *Little Bear* (O, ELL), *Ant and Grasshopper* (B) **Unit 6, Week 2:** *The Rain* (A), *Weather Is Fun* (O, ELL), *Kate and Tuck* (B) **Unit 8, Week 1:** *I Go Places* (A), *Run, Quinn!* (O, ELL), *Going to Gran's House* (B) **Unit 10, Week 2:** *My Box* (A), *Let's Make a Band* (O, ELL), *Going Camping* (B) **READING WORKSTATION ACTIVITY CARDS:** 5 **YOUR TURN PRACTICE BOOK:** 157, 167 **TEACHER'S EDITION:** Unit 1: T27, T109, T191 Unit 2: T75, T109, T143, T151, T157, T161, T186-191 Unit 3: T27, T109, T191 Unit 4: T109, T143, T151, T157, T225, T233, T239 Unit 5: T61, T69, T75, T79, T109, T143, T151, T157, T191, T225, T233, T239 Unit 6: T27, T61, T109, T191, T225 Unit 7: T109, T143, T144, T151, T157, T158, T191, T225, T233, T239 Unit 8: T61, T69, T75, T143, T151, T157, T191, T225, T233, T239 Unit 9: T27, T61, T69, T75, T79, T109, T143, T151, T159, T225, T233, T239 Unit 10: T29, T63, T71, T77, T81, T111, T145, T153, T157, T191, T227, T235, T241 **LITERATURE BIG BOOKS:** Unit 1, Week 1: *What About Bear?* Unit 1, Week 2: *Pouch!* Unit 3, Week 1: *How Do Dinosaurs Go to School?* Unit 3, Week 2: *Clang! Clang! Beep! Beep! Listen to the City* Unit 6, Week 1: *Mama, Is It Summer Yet?* Unit 7, Week 2: *The Birthday Pet*

Reading Standards for Literature

Key Ideas and Details		McGraw-Hill Reading Wonders
RL.K.3	With prompting and support, identify characters, settings, and major events in a story.	**LEVELED READERS:** Unit 1, Week 2: *Hop!* (A), *We Hop!* (O), *We Can Move!* (B) **Unit 2, Week 3:** *The Bugs Run* (O) **Unit 3, Week 2:** *A Noisy Night* (B) **Unit 3, Week 3:** *We Can Go* (A), *Going by Cab* (O), *Cal's Busy Week* (B) **Unit 4, Week 2:** *My Neighbors* (A), *Neighborhood Party* (O) **Unit 5, Week 1:** *My Garden* (A), *My Garden Grows* (O), *The Mystery Seeds* (B) **Unit 7, Week 2:** *My Cats* (A), *Their Pets* (O), *Will's Pet* (B) **Unit 8, Week 1:** *I Go Places* (A), *Run, Quinn!* (O), *Going to Gran's House* (B) **Unit 9, Week 2:** *Mike Helps Out* (A), *Clive and His Friend* (O), *Farmer White's Best Friend* **YOUR TURN PRACTICE BOOK:** 129, 217, 234 **READING WORKSTATION ACTIVITY CARDS:** 3, 4, 6, 7, 10, 11 **TEACHER'S EDITION: Unit 1:** T75, T108 **Unit 3:** T156-157, T186-191, T224-225 **Unit 4:** T104-109, T142-143, T150-151 **Unit 5:** T22-27, T60-61, T68-69, T74-75 **Unit 7:** T104-109, T142-143, T150-151, T156-157, T186-191, T224-225, T232-233, T238-239 **Unit 8:** T22-27, T60-61, T68-69, T75, T186-191 **Unit 9:** T22-29, T60-61, T68-69, T74-75, T104-109, T117, T142-143, T150-151, T156-157 **Unit 10:** T22-29, T62-63, T70-71, T76-77 **LITERATURE BIG BOOKS: Unit 3, Week 3:** *Please Take Me for a Walk* **Unit 4, Week 2:** *What Can You Do with a Paleta?* **Unit 7, Week 3:** *Bear Snores On* **Unit 8, Week 3:** *Bringing Down the Moon* **Unit 9, Week 1:** *Peter's Chair* **Unit 9, Week 2:** *Hen Hears Gossip* **Unit 10, Week 1:** *What's the Big Idea, Molly?* **INTERACTIVE READ-ALOUD CARDS: SS:** "The Ugly Duckling", "Tikki Tikki Tembo" **Unit 1, Week 1:** "The Lion and the Mouse" **Unit 1, Week 2:** "The Tortoise and the Hare" **Unit 3, Week 1:** "The Boy Who Cried Wolf" **Unit 4, Week 1:** "Little Juan and the Cooking Pot" **Unit 7, Week 3:** "Anansi: An African Tale" **Unit 9, Week 2:** "The Little Red Hen"

Craft and Structure		McGraw-Hill Reading Wonders
RL.K.4	Ask and answer questions about unknown words in a text.	**READING/WRITING WORKSHOP BIG BOOK: Unit 1, Week 2:** 32-37 **Unit 2, Week 1:** 8-13 **LEVELED READERS: Unit 4, Week 3:** *We Clean!* (A), *Can You Fix It?* (O, ELL), *Helping Mom* (B) **TEACHER'S EDITION: Unit 1:** T74 **Unit 4:** T127, T225, T238 **Unit 6:** T23, T189 **Unit 7:** T45 **Unit 9:** T45 **Unit 10:** T47
RL.K.5	Recognize common types of texts (e.g., storybooks, poems).	**LEVELED READERS: Unit 6, Week 1:** *Ant and Grasshopper* (B) **TEACHER'S EDITION: Unit 1:** T25, T208, T218 **Unit 4:** T126-127 **Unit 5:** T44-45, T54-55 **Unit 6:** T44, T74-75, T186 **Unit 7:** T44-45 **Unit 9:** T44-45, T126 **Unit 10:** T46 **LITERATURE BIG BOOK: Unit 1, Week 3:** *I Smell Springtime* **Unit 5, Week 1:** *Tommy* **Unit 6, Week 1:** *Covers* **Unit 7, Week 1:** *Kitty Caught a Caterpillar* **INTERACTIVE READ-ALOUD CARDS: SS:** "The Ugly Duckling", "Tikki Tikki Tembo" **Unit 1, Week 1:** "The Lion and the Mouse" **Unit 1, Week 2:** "The Tortoise and the Hare" **Unit 2, Week 1:** "Timimoto" **Unit 3, Week 1:** "The Boy Who Cried Wolf" **Unit 4, Week 3:** "A Bundle of Sticks" **Unit 5, Week 2:** "The Pine Tree" **Unit 6, Week 2:** "The Frog and the Locust" **Unit 6, Week 3:** "Rainbow Crow" **Unit 7, Week 3:** "Anansi: An African Tale" **Unit 8, Week 1:** "The King of the Winds" **Unit 9, Week 2:** "The Little Red Hen" **Unit 9, Week 3:** "Spider Woman Teaches the Navajo" **Unit 10, Week 1:** "The Elves and the Shoemakers"
RL.K.6	With prompting and support, name the author and illustrator of a story and define the role of each in telling the story.	**LEVELED READERS: Unit 2, Week 3:** *I See a Bug!* (B) **Unit 4, Week 2:** *Parade Day* (B), *Helping Mom* (B) **Unit 10, Week 1:** *A Good Idea* (B) **TEACHER'S EDITION: Unit 1:** T68, T94, T142 **Unit 2:** T176, T238-239 **Unit 3:** T12, T94, T176 **Unit 4:** T94, T156, T238 **Unit 5:** T12 **Unit 6:** T12, T94, T176 **Unit 7:** T94, T176 **Unit 8:** T12, T176 **Unit 9:** T12, T94-95 **Unit 10:** T12, T76, T96 **LITERATURE BIG BOOKS: Unit 1, Week 1:** *What About Bear?* **Unit 1, Week 2:** *Pouch!* **Unit 2, Week 3:** *I Love Bugs!* **Unit 3, Week 1:** *How Do Dinosaurs Go to School?* **Unit 5, Week 1:** *My Garden* **Unit 6, Week 2:** *Rain* **Unit 7, Week 2:** *The Birthday Pet* **Unit 8, Week 1:** *When Daddy's Truck Picks Me Up* **Unit 9, Week 2:** *Hen Hears Gossip* **Unit 10, Week 1:** *What's the Big Idea, Molly?* **READING WORKSTATION ACTIVITY CARDS:** 6

Reading Standards for Literature

Integration of Knowledge and Ideas		McGraw-Hill Reading Wonders
RL.K.7	With prompting and support, describe the relationship between illustrations and the story in which they appear (e.g., what moment in a story an illustration depicts).	**LEVELED READERS:** Unit 5, Week 1: *My Garden Grows* (O, ELL) **Unit 5, Week 3:** *Farm Fresh Finn* (B) **Unit 6, Week 1:** *It Is Hot!* **Unit 7, Week 3:** *Bird's New Home* (B) **READING WORKSTATION ACTIVITY CARDS:** 1, 4, 11 **TEACHER'S EDITION:** Unit 1: T25, T60-61, T108 Unit 3: T24, T60-T61, T68-T69 Unit 5: T22-27, T68-69, T238-239 Unit 6: T25, T60-61, T105, T188 Unit 7: T238-239 Unit 8: T25 Unit 10: T46-47 **LITERATURE BIG BOOKS:** Unit 1, Week 1: *What About Bear?* Unit 2, Week 3: *I Love Bugs!* Unit 3, Week 1: *How Do Dinosaurs Go to School?* Unit 3, Week 2: *Clang! Clang! Beep! Beep! Listen to the City* Unit 5, Week 1: *My Garden* Unit 6, Week 3: *Waiting Out the Storm* Unit 8, Week 1: *When Daddy's Truck Picks Me Up* Unit 9, Week 1: *The Clean Up!* Unit 10, Week 1: *The Variety Show* Unit 10, Week 2: *All Kinds of Families!* **INTERACTIVE READ-ALOUD CARDS:** Unit 5, Week 2: "The Pine Tree" Unit 6, Week 2: "The Frog and the Locust" Unit 6, Week 3: "Rainbow Crow"
RL.K.8	(Not applicable to literature.)	
RL.K.9	With prompting and support, compare and contrast the adventures and experiences of characters in familiar stories.	**LEVELED READERS:** Unit 3, Week 1: *Go, Nat!* (O, ELL) **READING WORKSTATION ACTIVITY CARD:** 15 **TEACHER'S EDITION:** Unit 1: S27, S51, S75, T35, T117, T136 Unit 2: T218-219 Unit 3: T35, T136, T218-219 Unit 4: T136-137 Unit 6: T54, T117, T136, T199, T218 Unit 7: T136-137, T199, T218 Unit 8: T35, T54, T218 Unit 9: T54, T117, T136 Unit 10: T37, T56, T138 **LITERATURE BIG BOOKS:** Unit 1, Week 1: *What About Bear?* Unit 1, Week 2: *Pouch!, Baby Animals on the Move* **INTERACTIVE READ-ALOUD CARDS:** Unit 1, Week 1: "The Lion and the Mouse" Unit 1, Week 2: "The Tortoise and the Hare" Unit 2, Week 1: "Timimoto" Unit 7, Week 3: "Anansi: An African Tale" Unit 8, Week 1: "The King of the Winds" Unit 10, Week 1: "The Elves and the Shoemakers"
Range of Reading and Level of Text Complexity		McGraw-Hill Reading Wonders
RL.K.10	Actively engage in group reading activities with purpose and understanding.	**READING/WRITING WORKSHOP BIG BOOKS:** SS: 36-41 Unit 1: 34-39, 46-51 Unit 2: 10-15, 28-33, 34-39 Unit 3: 10-15, 28-33, 46-51 Unit 4: 24-31, 38-45 Unit 5: 10-17, 38-45 Unit 6: 24-31, 38-45 Unit 7: 24-31, 38-45 Unit 8: 10-17, 24-31 Unit 9: 10-17, 24-31 Unit 10: 10-17, 24-31 **LEVELED READERS:** Unit 5, Week 1: *My Garden Grows* (ELL) Unit 7, Week 2: *Their Pets* (ELL) Unit 7, Week 3: *A New Home* (ELL) **TEACHER'S EDITION:** Unit 1: S12, S14, S17, S22, S24, S31, S36, S38, S41, S46, S48, S55, S62, S65, S70, S72, T22-27, T126-127 Unit 2: T30-31, T112-113, T130-131 Unit 3: T34-35, T94-95, T212-213 Unit 4: T112-113, T126-127, T130-131, T194-195, T199 Unit 5: T12-13, T48-49, T78-79, T117, T194-195 Unit 6: T12-13, T22-26, T94-95, T104-108, T117, T130-131, T176-177, T186-190, T194-195, T199 Unit 7: T112-113, T130-131, T160-161, T176-177, T194-195, T199, T212-213, T242-243 Unit 8: T12-13, T30-31, T34-35, T48-49, T112-113, T176-177, T212-213 Unit 9: T12-13, T30-31, T48-49, T94-95, T112-113, T117, T199, T212-213 Unit 10: T12-13, T32-33, T50-51, T96-97, T132-133 **INTERACTIVE READ-ALOUD CARDS:** SS: "The Ugly Duckling", "Tikki Tikki Tembo" Unit 1, Week 1: "The Lion and the Mouse" Unit 1, Week 2: "The Tortoise and the Hare" Unit 3, Week 2: "The Turtle and the Flute" Unit 4, Week 1: "Little Juan and the Cooking Pot" Unit 4, Week 3: "A Bundle of Sticks" Unit 5, Week 2: "The Pine Tree" Unit 6, Week 2: "The Frog and the Locust" Unit 6, Week 3: "Rainbow Crow" Unit 7, Week 3: "Anansi: An African Tale" Unit 8, Week 1: "The King of the Winds" Unit 9, Week 2: "The Little Red Hen" Unit 9, Week 3: "Spider Woman Teaches the Navajo" Unit 10, Week 1: "The Elves and the Shoemakers"

Reading Standards for Informational Text

Key Ideas and Details		McGraw-Hill Reading Wonders
RI.K.1	With prompting and support, ask and answer questions about key details in a text.	**READING/WRITING WORKSHOP BIG BOOKS:** Unit 2: 14-19 **LEVELED READERS:** Unit 1, Week 3: *The Beach* (A), *At School* (O), *See It Grow!* (B) **Unit 2, Week 1:** *We Need Tools* (A), *A Trip* (O), *What Can You See?* (B) **Unit 2, Week 2:** *Shapes!* (A), *Play with Shapes!* (O), *Use a Shape!* (B) **Unit 4, Week 1:** *You Cook* (A), *On the Job* (O), *The Neighborhood* (B) **Unit 8, Week 2:** *See This!* (A), *Places to See* (O), *My Trip to Yellowstone* (B) **Unit 9, Week 3:** *Look Where It Is From* (A), *What's for Breakfast?* (O), *Nature at the Craft Fair* (B) **Unit 10, Week 3:** *Help Clean Up* (A), *Let's Save Earth* (O), *Babysitters for Seals* (B) **YOUR TURN PRACTICE BOOK:** 53, 147 **READING WORKSTATION ACTIVITY CARDS:** 1 **TEACHER'S EDITION: Unit 1:** T126-127, T186-191, T225, **Unit 2:** T22-27, T44-45, T107 **Unit 4:** T22-27, T44-45, T61, T69, T75, T186-191, T208-209 **Unit 5:** T104-109, T151, T157, T186-191, T209 **Unit 6:** T23-26, T105-108, T187-188 **Unit 7:** T23, T25 **Unit 8:** T104-109, T126-127, T142-143, T151, T157, T209 **Unit 9:** T35, T127, T186-191 **Unit 10:** T188-193, T227, T241 **LITERATURE BIG BOOKS: Unit 1, Week 2:** *Baby Animals on the Move* **Unit 1, Week 3:** *Senses at the Seashore* **Unit 2, Week 1:** *The Handiest Things in the World, Discover with Tools* **Unit 4, Week 1:** *Whose Shoes?"A Shoe for Every Job"* **Unit 4, Week 3:** *Roadwork* **Unit 5, Week 2:** *A Grand Old Tree* **Unit 5, Week 3:** *An Orange in January* **Unit 7, Week 1:** *ZooBorns!* **Unit 9, Week 3:** *Bread Comes to Life* **Unit 10, Week 3:** *Panda Kindergarten* **INTERACTIVE READ-ALOUD CARDS: SS:** "Kindergarteners Can!" **Unit 1, Week 3:** "A Feast of the Senses" **Unit 2, Week 3:** "From Caterpillar to Butterfly" **Unit 4, Week 2:** "Cultural Festivals" **Unit 9, Week 1:** "Helping Out at Home" **Unit 10, Week 2:** "The Perfect Color"
RI.K.2	With prompting and support, identify the main topic and retell key details of a text.	**LEVELED READERS: Unit 1, Week 3:** *The Beach* (A), *At School* (O, ELL), *See It Grow!* (B) **Unit 2, Week 1:** *We Need Tools* (A), *A Trip* (O, ELL), *What Can You See?* (B) **Unit 5, Week 2:** *The Tree* (A), *Many Trees* (O, ELL), *Our Apple Tree* (B) **Unit 5, Week 3:** *The Farmers' Market* (A), *Let's Make a Salad!* (O, ELL) **Unit 9, Week 3:** *Look Where It Is From* (A) **READING WORKSTATION ACTIVITY CARDS:** 5 **TEACHER'S EDITION: Unit 4:** T191 **Unit 5:** T104-109, T126-127, T142-143, T150-151, T156-157, T186-T190, T208-209, T224-225 **Unit 8:** T104-109, T127, T160-161, T248-249 **Unit 9:** T127, T186-191, T224-225, T232-233, T248-249 **Unit 10:** T188-193, T211, T226-227, T240-241, T250-251 **LITERATURE BIG BOOKS: Unit 1, Week 3:** *Senses on the Seashore* **Unit 5, Week 2:** *A Grand Old Tree,* "From a Seed to a Tree" **Unit 5, Week 3:** *An Orange in January* **Unit 8, Week 2:** *Ana Goes to Washington, D.C.* **Unit 9, Week 3:** *Bread Comes to Life* **Unit 10, Week 3:** *Panda Kindergarten* **INTERACTIVE READ-ALOUD CARDS: Unit 1, Week 3:** "A Feast of the Senses" **Unit 2, Week 3:** "From Caterpillar to Butterfly" **Unit 4, Week 2:** "Cultural Festivals" **Unit 9, Week 1:** "Helping Out at Home" **Unit 10, Week 2:** "The Perfect Color"
RI.K.3	With prompting and support, describe the connection between two individuals, events, ideas, or pieces of information in a text.	**LEVELED READERS: Unit 7:** *Two Cubs* (A), *Animal Bodies* (O, ELL), *Two Kinds of Bears* (B); **Unit 9:** *Look Where It is From* (A), *What's for Breakfast?* (O, ELL) **READING WORKSTATION ACTIVITY CARDS:** 8, 9 **TEACHER'S EDITION: Unit 6:** T24, T25, T106 **Unit 7:** T22-26, T60-61, T68-69, T74-75, T208-209 **Unit 8:** T44-45, T95 **LITERATURE BIG BOOKS: Unit 2, Week 2:** *Shapes All Around* **Unit 7, Week 1:** *ZooBorns!* **Unit 7, Week 3:** "Animal Homes" **Unit 8, Week 1:** *Getting from Here to There* **Unit 8, Week 2:** *Ana Goes to Washington, D.C.* **Unit 9, Week 3:** *Bread Comes to Life* **INTERACTIVE READ-ALOUD CARDS: Unit 2, Week 3:** "From Caterpillar to Butterfly" **Unit 6, Week 1:** "A Tour of the Seasons" **Unit 8, Week 2:** "The Best of the West" **Unit 9, Week 1:** "Helping Out at Home" **Unit 10, Week 3:** "Protect the Environment"
Craft and Structure		McGraw-Hill Reading Wonders
RI.K.4	With prompting and support, ask and answer questions about unknown words in a text.	**LEVELED READERS: Unit 1, Week 3:** *At School* (O, ELL), *See It Grow!* (B) **Unit 2, Week 1:** *A Trip* (O, ELL) **Unit 4, Week 1:** *You Cook* (A), *On the Job* (O, ELL) **Unit 5, Week 2:** *The Tree* (A) **Unit 5, Week 3:** *The Farmers' Market* (A) **Unit 7, Week 1:** *Animal Bodies* (O, ELL) **Unit 9, Week 3:** *Nature at the Craft Fair* (B) **Unit 10, Week 3:** *Let's Save Earth* (O, ELL), *Babysitters for Seals* (B) **TEACHER'S EDITION: Unit 4:** T127 **Unit 5:** T107 **Unit 7:** T209 **Unit 8:** T127, T209 **Unit 10:** T234
RI.K.5	Identify the front cover, back cover, and title page of a book.	**READING/WRITING WORKSHOP: Unit 1:** 8-13, 26-31, 44-49 **Unit 2:** 8-13, 26-31, 44-49 **Unit 3:** 8-13, 26-31, 44-49 **Unit 4:** 8-15, 22-29, 36-43 **LEVELED READERS: Unit 10, Week 3:** *Help Clean Up* (A) **TEACHER'S EDITION: Unit 1:** T30-31, T176 **Unit 4:** T12 **Unit 5:** T94, T176, T232 **Unit 7:** T12, T60, T68, T74, T94 **Unit 8:** T87, T94 **Unit 9:** T176 **Unit 10:** T178, T226 **LITERATURE BIG BOOKS: Unit 1, Week 3:** *Senses at the Seashore* **Unit 2, Week 1:** *The Handiest Things in the World* **Unit 4, Week 1:** *Whose Shoes? A Shoe for Every Job*

Reading Standards for Informational Text

Craft and Structure		McGraw-Hill Reading Wonders
RI.K.6	Name the author and illustrator of a text and define the role of each in presenting the ideas or information in a text.	**LEVELED READERS:** Unit 5, Week 3: *Let's Make a Salad!* (O, ELL), **Unit 7, Week 1:** *Two Cubs* (A), *Animal Bodies* (O, ELL), *Two Kinds of Bears* (B) **READING WORKSTATION ACTIVITY CARDS:** 12 **TEACHER'S EDITION:** Unit 1: T176 Unit 2: T12 Unit 4: T12 Unit 5: T94, T176, T232 Unit 6: T12, T94, T176 Unit 7: T12, T60, T68, T74, T94 Unit 8: T94 Unit 9: T176 Unit 10: T178 **LITERATURE BIG BOOKS:** Unit 1, Week 3: *Senses at the Seashore* Unit 2, Week 1: *The Handiest Things in the World* Unit 2, Week 2: *Shapes All Around* Unit 8, Week 2: *Ana Goes to Washington, D.C.* Unit 9, Week 3: *Bread Comes to Life*

Integration of Knowledge and Ideas		McGraw-Hill Reading Wonders
RI.K.7	With prompting and support, describe the relationship between illustrations and the text in which they appear (e.g., what person, place, thing, or idea in the text an illustration depicts).	**READING/WRITING WORKSHOP BIG BOOK:** Unit 2, Week 1: 14-19 **LEVELED READERS:** Unit 1, Week 3: *The Beach* (A) Unit 2, Week 1: *We Need Tools* (A) Unit 2, Week 2: *Shapes!* (A), *Play with Shapes!* (O, ELL), *Use a Shape!* (B) Unit 9, Week 3: *What's for Breakfast?* (O, ELL) **READING WORKSTATION ACTIVITY CARDS:** 1 **TEACHER'S EDITION:** Unit 1: T126-T127, T186-191, T224-225 Unit 2: T24, T60-61, T124-T127, 143 Unit 3: T45, 127, T208-209 Unit 4: T22-27 Unit 6: T126-127, T209 Unit 9: T208-209, T232-233 Unit 10: T190, T244-245 **LITERATURE BIG BOOKS:** Unit 1, Week 3: *Senses at the Seashore*, pp. 4-34 Unit 2, Week 1: *The Handiest Things in the World* Unit 2, Week 2: *Shapes All Around* Unit 3, Week 2: *Sounds Are Everywhere* Unit 3, Week 3: *A Neighborhood* Unit 4, Week 1: *Whose Shoes? A Shoe for Every Job* Unit 6, Week 2: *Cloud Watch* Unit 9, Week 3: *Nature's Artists* **INTERACTIVE READ-ALOUD CARDS:** Unit 3, Week 3: "Field Trips" Unit 6, Week 1: "A Tour of the Seasons" Unit 9, Week 1: "Helping Out at Home"
RI.K.8	With prompting and support, identify the reasons an author gives to support points in a text.	**READING WORKSTATION ACTIVITY CARDS:** 12 **TEACHER'S EDITION:** Unit 2: T26, T108 Unit 4: T26, T190 Unit 5: T108, T190 Unit 8: T108 Unit 9: T190 Unit 10: T210-211 **LITERATURE BIG BOOKS:** Unit 1, Week 3: *Senses at the Seashore* Unit 2, Week 1: *The Handiest Things in the World* Unit 2, Week 2: *Shapes All Around* Unit 4, Week 1: *Whose Shoes? A Shoe for Every Job* Unit 4, Week 3: *Roadwork* Unit 5, Week 2: *A Grand Old Tree* Unit 5, Week 3: *An Orange in January* Unit 8, Week 2: *Ana Goes to Washington, D.C.* Unit 9, Week 3: *Bread Comes to Life* Unit 10, Week 3: *Save Big Blue!*
RI.K.9	With prompting and support, identify basic similarities in and differences between two texts on the same topic (e.g., in illustrations, descriptions, or procedures).	**READING/WRITING WORKSHOP BIG BOOK:** Unit 1, Week 3: *A Feast of the Senses* **READING WORKSTATION ACTIVITY CARDS:** 16 **TEACHERS EDITION:** Unit 1: T199 Unit 2: T54-55, T117, T126-127 Unit 4: T116-117, T218-219 Unit 5: T136-137, T198-199, T208-209, T218-219 Unit 7: T35, T54, T117 Unit 8: T136 Unit 9: T218 Unit 10: T128-129, T201, T220 **LITERATURE BIG BOOKS:** Unit 1, Week 3: *Senses at the Seashore* Unit 2, Week 1: *The Handiest Things in the World* Unit 2, Week 2: *Shapes All Around*, "Find the Shapes" Unit 5, Week 3: *An Orange in January*, "Farmers' Market" Unit 10, Week 2: *Good For You* **INTERACTIVE READ-ALOUD CARDS:** Unit 1, Week 3: "A Feast of the Senses" Unit 2, Week 2: "Kites in Flight" Unit 5, Week 3: "Farms Around the World" Unit 7, Week 1: "Baby Farm Animals" Unit 7, Week 2: "The Family Pet" Unit 10, Week 3: "Protect the Environment!"

Range of Reading and Level of Text Complexity		McGraw-Hill Reading Wonders
RI.K.10	Actively engage in group reading activities with purpose and understanding.	**READING/WRITING WORKSHOP BIG BOOKS:** Start Smart: 18-23, 53-58 Unit 1: 10-15, 28-33, 52-57 Unit 2: 16-21, 52-57 Unit 3: 34-39, 52-57 Unit 4: 10-17 Unit 5: 24-31 Unit 6: 10-17 Unit 7: 10-17 Unit 8: 38-45 Unit 9: 38-45 Unit 10: 38-45 **LEVELED READERS:** Unit 5, Week 2: *Many Trees* (ELL) **TEACHER'S EDITION:** Unit 1: S60, T112-113, T126-127, T199 Unit 2: T22-27, T44-45, T74-75, T186-191 Unit 3: T126-127, T198-199, T212-213 Unit 4: T12-13, T30-31, T116-117, T176-177 Unit 5: T34-35, T92-95, T160-161, T174-177, T198-199 Unit 6: T35, T126-127, T208-209 Unit 7: T12-13, T22-27, T30-31, T34-35, T48-49, T116-117 Unit 8: T94-95, T116-117 Unit 9: T34-35, T176-177, T194-195, T208-209 Unit 10: T118-119, T178-179, T201 **INTERACTIVE READ-ALOUD CARDS:** SS: "Kindergarteners Can!" Unit 1, Week 3: "A Feast of the Senses" Unit 2, Week 3: "From Caterpillar to Butterfly" Unit 3, Week 3: "Field Trips" Unit 4, Week 2: "Cultural Festivals" Unit 5, Week 1: "Growing Plants" Unit 5, Week 3: "Farms Around the World" Unit 6, Week 1: "A Tour of the Seasons" Unit 7, Week 1: "Baby Farm Animals" Unit 7, Week 2: "The Family Pet" Unit 8, Week 2: "The Best of the West" Unit 8, Week 3: "A View from the Moon" Unit 9, Week 1: "Helping Out at Home" Unit 10, Week 2: "The Perfect Color" Unit 10, Week 3: "Protect the Environment"

Reading Standards for Foundational Skills

These standards are directed toward fostering students' understanding and working knowledge of concepts of print, the alphabetic principle, and other basic conventions of the English writing system. These foundational skills are not an end in and of themselves; rather, they are necessary and important components of an effective, comprehensive reading program designed to develop proficient readers with the capacity to comprehend texts across a range of types and disciplines. Instruction should be differentiated: good readers will need much less practice with these concepts than struggling readers will. The point is to teach students what they need to learn and not what they already know—to discern when particular children or activities warrant more or less attention.
Note: In Kidergarten, children are expected to demonstrate increasing awareness and competence in the areas that follow.

Print Concepts		McGraw-Hill Reading Wonders
RF.K.1	Demonstrate understanding of the organization and basic features of print.	**TEACHER'S EDITION:** Unit 1: S10, S18, S23, S28, S29, S32, S37, S39, S42, S43, S47, S52, S53, S56, S61, S62, S63, S66, S71, S77, T12, T15, T16, T60, T97, T98, T180, T189, T192 Unit 2: T12, T15, T30, T97, T112, T179, T180, T212, T224 Unit 3: T15, T26, T94, T97, T106, T112, T130, T142, T176, T179, T211, T232 Unit 4: T12, T15, T23, T30, T47, T48, T60, T68, T94, T97, T105, T108, T112, T129, T130, T142, T150, T179, T187, T194, T211, T212, T224 Unit 5: T12, T15, T30, T47, T48, T60, T68, T94, T97, T112, T129, T130, T142, T150, T176, T179, T211, T212, T224, T232 Unit 6: T12, T15, T29, T37, T47, T97, T129, T179, T211 Unit 7: T15, T16, T47, T94, T97, T98, T129, T150, T176, T179, T180, T211, T212, T232 Unit 8: T12, T15, T47, T48, T68, T94, T97, T129, T142, T179 Unit 9: T12, T15, T25, T47, T60, T94, T97, T129, T142, T176, T179, T211 Unit 10: T12, T15, T49, T62, T96, T97, T13, T144, T178, T179, T213
RF.K.1a	Follow words from left to right, top to bottom, and page by page.	**READING/WRITING WORKSHOP:** Start Smart: 4-5, 22-23, 40-41 **LITERATURE BIG BOOK:** Start Smart, Week 3: *ABC Big Book* Unit 4, Week 2: *What Can You Do With a Paleta?* **TEACHER'S EDITION:** Unit 1: S10, S62, T12, T60, T189 Unit 2: T30, T112, T224 Unit 3: T26, T94, T176 Unit 4: T12, T23, T30, T48, T60, T68, T94, T105, T108, T112, T130, T142, T150, T187, T194, T212, T224 Unit 5: T68, T94, T112, T130, T142, T150, T176, T212, T224, T232 Unit 6: T12 Unit 7: T94, T150 Unit 8: T12, T68, T94, T142 Unit 9: T12, T25, T60, T94, T142 Unit 10: T12, T62, T96, T144, T178
RF.K.1b	Recognize that spoken words are represented in written language by specific sequences of letters.	**TEACHER'S EDITION:** Unit 1: S39, S63 Unit 2: T212 Unit 3: T47-129, T211 Unit 4: T47, T129, T211 Unit 5: T47, T129, T211 Unit 6: T29, T37, T47, T129, T211 Unit 7: T47, T129, T176, T211, T212 Unit 8: T47, T48, T129, T211 Unit 9: T47, T129, T176, T211 Unit 10: T49, T131, T213
RF.K.1c	Understand that words are separated by spaces in print.	**TEACHER'S EDITION:** Unit 1: S29, S39, S43, S53, S63, S77 Unit 2: T12, T180 Unit 3: T94, T106, T112, T130, T142, T232 Unit 5: T12, T30, T48, T60, T94 Unit 7: T232
RF.K.1d	Recognize and name all upper- and lowercase letters of the alphabet.	**YOUR TURN PRACTICE BOOK:** 3, 7, 8, 11, 15, 16, 20, 24, 34, 42, 50, 58, 66, 84, 92, 100, 108, 116, 134, 142, 143-144, 162, 172, 192, 202, 212, 222, 232 **TEACHER'S EDITION:** Unit 1: S23, S18, S23, S28, S32, S37, S42, S47, S52, S56, S61, S66, S71, T15, T16, T97, T98, T180, T192 Unit 2: T15, T97, T179 Unit 3: T15, T97, T179 Unit 4: T15, T97, T179 Unit 5: T15, T97, T179 Unit 6: T15, T97, T179 Unit 7: T15, T16, T97, T98, T179, T180 Unit 8: T15, T97, T179 Unit 9: T15, T97, T179 Unit 10: T15, T97, T179
Phonological Awareness		McGraw-Hill Reading Wonders
RF.K.2	Demonstrate understanding of spoken words, syllables, and sounds (phonemes).	**TEACHER'S EDITION:** Unit 1: S13, S18, S23, S42, S47, S52, S56, S61, S66, S71, T14, T36, T102, T118, T124, T184, T206 Unit 2: T14, T20, T42, T70, T96, T102, T124, T144, T178, T184, T206, T210, T226 Unit 3: T20, T36, T42, T62, T96, T102, T118, T124, T144, T184, T206, T226 Unit 4: T20, T28, T42, T56, T62, T70, T102, T118, T128, T138, T145, T152, T184, T192, T200, T206, T210, T220, T226 Unit 5: T14, T20, T28, T36, T42, T62, T63, T72, T102, T110, T118, T124, T138, T144, T145, T152, T184, T192, T206, T210, T226, T227, T234 Unit 6: T20, T28, T36, T42, T46, T56, T62, T63, T70, T102, T124, T138, T144, T152, T154, T184, T192, T206, T210, T220, T227, T234 Unit 7: T20, T28, T36, T42, T46, T62, T102, T110, T118, T124, T128, T138, T144, T145, T178, T184, T206, T210, T220, T226, T234 Unit 8: T20, T28, T42, T46, T56, T62, T63, T102, T110, T118, T124, T128, T138, T144, T145, T152, T184, T200, T206, T226, T227, T234 Unit 9: T14, T20, T42, T62, T102, T124, T144, T184, T206, T210, T220, T226, T227, T234 Unit 10: T20, T44, T48, T58, T64, T72, T104, T126, T130, T140, T146, T147, T154, T212, T222, T229, T236
RF.K.2a	Recognize and produce rhyming words.	**LITERATURE BIG BOOKS:** Start Smart, Weeks 1-3: *Big Book of Rhymes* **TEACHER'S EDITION:** Unit 1: S23, S42, S47, S52, T102, T124 Unit 2: T210 Unit 3: T20, T42, T62 Unit 4: T184, T206, T226 Unit 5: T184, T206, T226 Unit 6: T102, T124, T144 Unit 7: T102, T124, T144 Unit 8: T102, T124, T144 Unit 9: T102, T124, T144
RF.K.2b	Count, pronounce, blend, and segment syllables in spoken words.	**LITERATURE BIG BOOK:** Smart Start, Week 3: *Big Book of Rhymes* **TEACHER'S EDITION:** Unit 1: S56, S61, S66, S71 Unit 2: T184, T206, T226 Unit 3: T184, T206, T226 Unit 5: T20, T42, T62 Unit 9: T20, T42, T62, T184, T206, T226 Unit 10: T20, T44, T64

Reading Standards for Foundational Skills

Phonological Awareness		McGraw-Hill Reading Wonders
RF.K.2c	Blend and segment onsets and rimes of single-syllable spoken words.	**YOUR TURN PRACTICE BOOK:** 88, 96, 104, 112, 124, 130, 138, 148, 158, 168, 182, 183, 188, 198, 208, 228, 242, 243, 248, 256, 264, 272, 280, 293 **TEACHER'S EDITION: Unit 1:** T184, T206 **Unit 2:** T102, T124, T144 **Unit 3:** T102, T124, T144 **Unit 4:** T20, T42, T62 **Unit 5:** T102, T124, T144 **Unit 6:** T20, T42, T62 **Unit 7:** T20, T42, T62, T184, T206, T226 **Unit 8:** T20, T42, T62, T184, T206, T226 **Unit 10:** T104, T126, T146
RF.K.2d	Isolate and pronounce the initial, medial vowel, and final sounds (phonemes) in in three-phoneme (consonant-vowel-consonant, or CVC) words. (This does not include CVCs ending with /l/, /r/, or /x/.)	**YOUR TURN PRACTICE BOOK:** 80, 193 **TEACHER'S EDITION: Unit 1:** T14, T36, T118 **Unit 2:** T14, T70, T96, T178 **Unit 3:** T36, T96, T118 **Unit 4:** T28, T70, T110, T118, T128, T138, T145, T152, T192, T200, T210, T220 **Unit 5:** T14, T28, T36, T63, T72, T110, T118, T138, T145, T152, T192 **Unit 6:** T28, T36, T46, T56, T62, T63, T70, T138, T152, T154, T184, T192, T206 **Unit 7:** T28, T36, T110, T118, T178 **Unit 8:** T28, T46, T56, T63, T110, T118, T145, T152
RF.K.2e	Add or substitute individual sounds (phonemes) in simple, one-syllable words to make new words.	**TEACHER'S EDITION: Unit 5:** T210, T220, T227, T234 **Unit 6:** T210, T220, T227, T234 **Unit 7:** T128, T138, T145, T152, T210, T220, T227, T234 **Unit 8:** T128, T138, T145, T152, T200, T227, T234 **Unit 9:** T210, T220, T227, T234 **Unit 10:** T48, T58, T72, T130, T140, T147, T154, T212, T222, T229, T236
Phonics and Word Recognition		McGraw-Hill Reading Wonders
RF.K.3	Know and apply grade-level phonics and word analysis skills in decoding words.	**TEACHER'S EDITION: Unit 1:** S19, S43, S67, T28, T29, T97, T105, T121, T179, T181, T210, T211, T220, T245 **Unit 2:** T15, T39, T46, T97, T128-129, T179, T203, T221 **Unit 3:** T15, T38, T39, T46, T56, T97, T110, T111, T128, T179, T181, T210 **Unit 4:** T15, T17, T28-29, T30-31, T37 , T39, T46, T47, T48-49, T57, T66, T73, T76, T81, T97, T99, T110, T111, T112-113, T121, T128, T129, T130-131, T139, T148, T155, T158, T163, T179, T181, T193, T194-195, T203, T210, T211, T212-213, T221, T230, T237, T240, T245 **Unit 5:** T14, T17, T28, T29, T30-31, T36, T39, T47, T48-49, T56, T57, T66, T73, T76, T81, T99, T110-111, T112-113, T118, T119, T121, T128, T129, T130-131, T138, T139, T146, T148, T153, T155, T158, T163, T181, T192, T193, T194-195, T200, T203, T210, T211, T212-213, T220, T221, T228, T230, T237, T240, T245 **Unit 6:** T15, T17, T29, T30-31, T39, T46, T47, T48-49, T57, T66, T73, T81, T97, T99, T111, T112-113, T121, T128, T129, T130-131, T139, T148, T155, T158, T163, T178, T179, T181, T193, T194-195, T201, T203, T210, T212-213, T221, T230, T237, T240, T245 **Unit 7:** T15, T17, T28-29, T30-31, T37, T46, T47, T48-49, T56, T57, T64, T65, T66, T73, T76, T81, T96, T97, T99, T110, T112-113, T119, T121, T128, T129, T130-131, T139, T146, T148, T155, T158, T163, T178, T179, T181, T192, T193, T194-195, T201, T203, T210, T211, T212-213, T220, T221, T230, T237, T240, T245 **Unit 8:** T15, T17, T29, T30-31, T39, T46, T47, T48-49, T57, T66, T73, T76, T81, T97, T99, T111, T112-113, T121, T128, T129, T130-131, T139, T148, T155, T158, T163, T179, T181, T193, T194-195, T201, T203, T210, T211, T212-213, T220, T221, T230, T237, T240, T245 **Unit 9:** T15, T17, T29, T30-31, T37, T39, T46, T47, T48-49, T56, T57, T64, T65, T66, T71, 72, T73, T76, T81, T97, T99, T110-111, T112-113, T119, T120, T121, T128, T129, T130-131, T138, T139, T146, T147, T148, T153, T154, T155, T158, T163, T179, T181, T192-193, T194-195, T201, T202, T203, T210, T211, T212-213, T220, T221, T228, T229, T230, T235, T236, T237, T240, T245 **Unit 10:** T15, T17, T30-31, T32-33, T39, T40, T41, T48, T49, T50-51, T58, T59, T66, T67, T68, T74, T75, T83, T97, T99, T101, T110, T112-113, T114-115, T121, T123, T130, T131, T140, T141, T148, T149, T150, T156, T157, T160, T165, T179, T181, T182, T183, T191, T194-195, T196-197, T203, T204, T205, T212-213, T222, T223, T230, T231, T232, T238, T239, T242, T247
RF.K.3a	Demonstrate basic knowledge of one-to-one letter-sound correspondences by producing the primary or many of the most frequent sounds for each consonant.	**PHONICS/WORD STUDY WORKSTATION ACTIVITY CARDS:** 1, 2, 3, 4, 5, 6, 7, 8, 9, 10, 11, 12, 13, 14, 15, 16, 17, 18, 19, 20, 21, 22, 23, 24 **TEACHER'S EDITION: Unit 1:** T28, T179, T210, T220 **Unit 2:** T15, T97, T179 **Unit 3:** T97, T110, T179 **Unit 4:** T97, T110, T179 **Unit 5:** T14, T28, T36, T56, T118, T138, T192, T200, T220, T228 **Unit 6:** T15, T97, T179 **Unit 7:** T56, T96, T97, T110, T146, T178, T179, T192, T220 **Unit 8:** T15, T97, T179 **Unit 10:** T97, T110, T179

Reading Standards for Foundational Skills

Phonics and Word Recognition		McGraw-Hill Reading Wonders
RF.K.3b	Associate the long and short sounds with the common spellings (graphemes) for the five major vowels.	**YOUR TURN PRACTICE BOOK:** 36, 62, 101-102, 135-136, 138, 246, 248, 254, 256, 262, 264, 270, 278 **PHONICS/WORD STUDY WORKSTATION ACTIVITY CARDS:** 2, 7, 10, 14, 19, 25, 26, 27, 28, 29, 30 **TEACHER'S EDITION:** Unit 1: T97, T105 Unit 2: T46, T128–T129, T221 Unit 3: T15, T38, T56 Unit 4: T15, T28-29, T37 Unit 5: T110-111, T119, T146, T153 Unit 6: T193, T201, T211 Unit 7: T15, T28-29, T37, T46, T64, T65, T119, T201 Unit 8: T201, T220 Unit 9: T15, T29, T37, T56, T64, T65, T71, 72, T76, T97, T110-111, T119, T120, T138, T146, T147, T153, T154, T179, T192-193, T201, T202, T220, T228, T229, T235, T236 Unit 10: T15, T30-31, T39, T40, T58, T66, T67, T74, T99, T112-113, T121, T140, T148, T149, T156, T181, T182, T191, T194-195, T203, T204, T222, T230, T231, T238

Phonological Awareness		McGraw-Hill Reading Wonders
RF.K.3c	Read common high-frequency words by sight (e.g., *the, of, to, you, she, my, is, are, do, does*).	**READING/WRITING WORKSHOP:** Start Smart: 9, 16-22, 27 Unit 1: 7-13, 14-19, 25-31 Unit 2: 7-13, 14-19, 25-31 Unit 3: 7-13, 25-31, 32-37 Unit 4: 7-15, 21-29, 35-43 Unit 5: 7-15, 21-29, 35-43 Unit 6: 7-15, 21-29, 35-43 Unit 7: 7-15, 21-29, 35-43 Unit 8: 7-15, 21-29, 35-43 Unit 9: 7-15, 21-29, 35-43 Unit 10: 7-15, 21-29, 35-43 **YOUR TURN PRACTICE BOOK:** 4, 9-10, 12, 17-18, 21, 25-26], 31-32, 39-40, 47-48, 55-56, 63-64, 71-72, 89-90, 97-98, 105-106, 113-114, 121-122, 131-132, 139-140, 149-150, 159-160, 169-170, 179-180, 189-190, 199-200, 209-210, 219-220, 229-230, 239-240, 249-250, 257-258, 265-266, 273-274, 281-282, 291-292 **TEACHER'S EDITION:** Unit 1: S19, S43, S67, T29, T121, T181, T211, T245 Unit 2: T39, T129, T203 Unit 3: T39, T111, T181 Unit 4: T17, T29, T30-31, T39, T47, T48-49, T57, T66, T73, T76, T81, T99, T111, T112-113, T121, T129, T130-131, T139, T148, T155, T158, T163, T181, T193, T194-195, T203, T211, T212-213, T221, T230, T237, T240, T245 Unit 5: T17, T29, T30-31, T39, T47, T48-49, T57, T66, T73, T76, T81, T99, T111, T112-113, T121, T129, T130-131, T139, T148, T155, T158, T163, T181, T193, T194-195, T203, T211, T212-213, T221, T230, T237, T240, T245 Unit 6: T17, T29, T30-31, T39, T47, T48-49, T57, T66, T73, T81, T99, T111, T112-113, T121, T129, T130-131, T139, T148, T155, T158, T163, T181, T193, T194-195, T203, T211, T212-213, T221, T230, T237, T240, T245 Unit 7: T17, T29, T30-31, T39, T47, T48-49, T57, T66, T73, T76, T81, T99, T111, T112-113, T121, T129, T130-131, T139, T148, T155, T158, T163, T181, T193, T194-195, T203, T211, T212-213, T221, T230, T237, T240, T245 Unit 8: T17, T29, T30-31, T39, T47, T48-49, T57, T66, T73, T76, T81, T99, T111, T112-113, T121, T129, T130-131, T139, T148, T155, T158, T163, T181, T193, T194-195, T203, T211, T212-213, T221, T230, T237, T240, T245 Unit 9: T17, T29, T30-31, T39, T47, T48-49, T57, T66, T73, T76, T81, T99, T111, T112-113, T121, T129, T130-131, T139, T148, T155, T158, T163, T181, T193, T194-195, T203, T211, T212-213, T221, T230, T237, T240, T245 Unit 10: T17, T31, T32-33, T41, T49, T50-51, T59, T68, T75, T78, T83, T101, T113, T114-115, T123, T131, T141, T150, T157, T160, T165, T183, T195, T196-197, T205, T212-213, T223, T232, T239, T242, T247
RF.K.3d	Distinguish between similarly spelled words by identifying the sounds of the letters that differ.	**TEACHER'S EDITION:** Unit 2: T46, T128 Unit 3: T46, T128, T210 Unit 4: T46, T128, T210 Unit 5: T128, T210 Unit 6: T46, T128, T210 Unit 7: T46, T128, T210 Unit 8: T46, T128, T210 Unit 9: T46, T128, T210 Unit 10: T48, T130, T212

Reading Standards for Foundational Skills

Fluency		McGraw-Hill Reading Wonders
RF.K.4	Read emergent-reader texts with purpose and understanding.	**READING/WRITING WORKSHOP:** Unit 1: 32-37, 44-49, 50-55 Unit 2: 32-37, 44-49, 50-55 Unit 3: 8-13, 32-37, 50-55 Unit 4: 8-15, 22-29, 36-43 Unit 5: 8-15, 22-29, 36-43 Unit 6: 8-15, 22-29, 36-43 Unit 7: 8-15, 22-29, 36-43 Unit 8: 8-15, 22-29, 36-43 Unit 9: 8-15, 22-29, 36-43 Unit 10: 8-15, 22-29, 36-43

LEVELED READERS: Unit 1, Week 1: *Soup!* (A), *Mouse and Monkey* (O, ELL), *Come and Play!* (B) Unit 1 Week 2: *Hop!* (A), *We Hop!* (O, ELL) *We Can Move!* (B) Unit 1, Week 3: *The Beach* (A), *At School* (O, ELL), *See It Grow!* (B) Unit 2, Week 1: *We Need Tools* (A), *A Trip* (O, ELL), *What Can You See?* (B) Unit 2, Week 2: *Shapes!* (A), *Play with Shapes!* (O, ELL), *Use a Shape!* (B) Unit 2, Week 3: *We Like Bugs!* (A), *The Bugs Run* (O, ELL), *I See a Bug!* (B) Unit 3, Week 1: *We Run* (A), *Go, Nat!* (O, ELL), *The Birdhouse* (B) Unit 3, Week 2: *City Sounds* (A), *Farm Sounds* (O, ELL), *A Noisy Night* (B) Unit 3, Week 3: *We Can Go* (A), *Going by Cab* (O, ELL), *Cal's Busy Week* (B) Unit 4, Week 1: *You Cook* (A), *On the Job* (O, ELL), *The Neighborhood* (B) Unit 4, Week 2: *My Neighbors* (A), *Neighborhood Party* (O, ELL), *Parade Day* (B) Unit 4, Week 3: *We Clean!* (A) *Can You Fix It?* (O, ELL), *Helping Mom* (B) Unit 5, Week 1: *My Garden* (A), *My Garden Grows* (O, ELL), *The Mystery Seeds* (B) Unit 5, Week 2: *The Tree* (A), *Many Trees* (O, ELL), *Our Apple Tree* (B) Unit 5, Week 3: *The Farmer* (A), *Let's Make a Salad!* (O, ELL), *Farm Fresh Finn* (B) Unit 6, Week 1: *It Is Hot!* (A), *Little Bear* (O, ELL), *Ant and Grasshopper* (B) Unit 6, Week 2: *The Rain* (A), *Weather Is Fun* (O, ELL), *Kate and Tuck* (B) Unit 6 Week 3: *Bad Weather* (A), *Getting Ready* (O, ELL), *The Storm* (B) Unit 7, Week 1: *Two Cubs* (A), *Animal Bodies* (O, ELL), *Two Kinds of Bears* (B) Unit 7, Week 2: *My Cats* (A), *Their Pets* (O, ELL), *Will's Pet* (B) Unit 7, Week 3: *We Want Water* (A) *A New Home* (O, ELL), *Bird's New Home* (B) Unit 8, Week 1: *I Go Places* (A), *Run, Quinn!* (O, ELL), *Going to Gran's House* (B) Unit 8, Week 2: *See This!* (A), *Places to See* (O, ELL), *My Trip to Yellowstone* (B) Unit 8, Week 3: *Going Up* (A), *In the Clouds* (O, ELL), *How Sun and Moon Found Home* (B) Unit 9, Week 1: *Let Me Help You* (A), *How Can Jane Help?* (O, ELL), *I Used to Help, Too* (B) Unit 9, Week 2: *Mike Helps Out* (A), *Clive and His Friend* (O, ELL), *Farmer White's Best Friend* (B) Unit 9, Week 3: *Look Where It Is From* (A), *What's for Breakfast?* (O, ELL), *Nature at the Craft Fair* (B) Unit 10, Week 1: *Animal Band* (A), *We Want Honey* (O, ELL), *A Good Idea* (B) Unit 10, Week 2: *My Box* (A), *Let's Make a Band* (O, ELL), *Going Camping* (B) Unit 10, Week 3: *Help Clean Up* (A), *Let's Save Earth* (O, ELL), *Babysitters for Seals* (B)

TEACHER'S EDITION: Unit 1: S14, S48, T48-49, T112-113, T150-151, T232-233 Unit 2: T48-49, T130-131, T224-225 Unit 3: T60-61, T130-131, T212-213 Unit 4: T30-31, T48-49, T60-61, T65, T68-69, T72, T74-75, T78-79, T112-113, T130-131, T142-143, T147, T150-151, T156-157, T160-161, T194-195, T212-213, T224-225, T229, T232-233, T236, T238-239, T242-243 Unit 5: T30-31, T48-49, T60-61, T65, T68-69, T72, T74-75, T78-79, T112-113, T130-131, T142-143, T147, T150-151, T156-157, T160-161, T194-195, T212-213, T224-225, T229, T232-233, T236, T238-239, T242-243 Unit 6: T30-31, T48-49, T60-61, T65, T68-69, T72, T74-75, T78-79, T112-113, T130-131, T142-143, T147, T150-151, T194-195, T212-213, T224-225, T229, T232-233, T236 Unit 7: T30-31, T48-49, T60-61, T65, T68-69, T72, T74-75, T78-79, T112-113, T130-131, T142-143, T147, T150-151, T156-157, T160-161, T194-195, T212-213, T224-225, T229, T232-233, T236, T238-239, T242-243 Unit 8: T30-31, T48-49, T60-61, T65, T68-69, T72, T74-75, T78-79, T112-113, T130-131, T10-131, T142-143, T147, T150-151, T156-157, T160-161, T194-195, T212-213, T224-225, T229, T232-233, T236, T238-239, T242-243 Unit 9: T30-31, T48-49, T60-61, T65, T68-69, T72, T74-75, T78-79, T112-113, T130-131, T142-143, T147, T150-151, T156-157, T160-161, T194-195, T212-213, T224-225, T229, T232-233, T236, T238-239, T242-243 Unit 10: T32-33, T50-51, T62-63, T67, T70-71, T74, T76-77, T80-81, T114-115, T132-133, T144-145, T149, T152-153, T156, T158-159, T162-163, T196-197, T214-215, T226-227, T231, T234-235, T238, T240-241, T244-245

College and Career Readiness Anchor Standards for WRITING

The K–5 standards on the following pages define what students should understand and be able to do by the end of each grade. They correspond to the College and Career Readiness (CCR) anchor standards below by number. The CCR and grade-specific standards are necessary complements—the former providing broad standards, the latter providing additional specificity—that together define the skills and understandings that all students must demonstrate.

Text Types and Purposes

1. Write arguments to support claims in an analysis of substantive topics or texts, using valid reasoning and relevant and sufficient evidence.

2. Write informative/explanatory texts to examine and convey complex ideas and information clearly and accurately through the effective selection, organization, and analysis of content.

3. Write narratives to develop real or imagined experiences or events using effective technique, well-chosen details, and well-structured event sequences.

Production and Distribution of Writing

4. Produce clear and coherent writing in which the development, organization, and style are appropriate to task, purpose, and audience.

5. Develop and strengthen writing as needed by planning, revising, editing, rewriting, or trying a new approach.

6. Use technology, including the Internet, to produce and publish writing and to interact and collaborate with others.

Research to Build and Present Knowledge

7. Conduct short as well as more sustained research projects based on focused questions, demonstrating understanding of the subject under investigation.

8. Gather relevant information from multiple print and digital sources, assess the credibility and accuracy of each source, and integrate the information while avoiding plagiarism.

9. Draw evidence from literary or informational texts to support analysis, reflection, and research.

Range of Writing

10. Write routinely over extended time frames (time for research, reflection, and revision) and shorter time frames (a single sitting or a day or two) for a range of tasks, purposes, and audiences.

English Language Arts

Grade K

Writing Standards

Text Types and Purposes		*McGraw-Hill Reading Wonders*
W.K.1	Use a combination of drawing, dictating, and writing to compose opinion pieces in which they tell a reader the topic or the name of the book they are writing about and state an opinion or preference about the topic or book (e.g., My favorite book is…).	**READING/WRITING WORKSHOP: Unit 1:** 38-39 **Unit 3:** 58 **Unit 5:** 32-33 **Unit 6:** 18-19 **Unit 9:** 18-19 **Unit 10:** 46-47 **TEACHER'S EDITION: Unit 1:** T87, T100, T114, T122 **Unit 3:** T196, T204, T214 **Unit 5:** T100, T114, T122-123, T132, T144 **Unit 6:** T32, T40, T41 **Unit 9:** T5, T18, T32, T40-41, T50 **Unit 10:** T17, T184, T198, T206, T216 **WRITING WORKSTATION ACTIVITY CARDS:** 5, 20
W.K.2	Use a combination of drawing, dictating, and writing to compose informative/explanatory texts in which they name what they are writing about and supply some information about the topic.	**READING/WRITING WORKSHOP: Unit 2:** 20-21 **Unit 4:** 44 **Unit 5:** 44-45 **Unit 6:** 44 **Unit 7:** 16-17, 44 **Unit 8:** 30-31 **Unit 9:** 44 **TEACHER'S EDITION: Unit 1:** S15, S33, S53, S67, S77, T182, T196, T204 **Unit 2:** T100, T122, T164 **Unit 3:** T18, T32, T40 **Unit 4:** T18, T32, T40, T114, T122, T196, T204 **Unit 5:** T182, T196, T204 **Unit 6:** T52-53, T135 **Unit 7:** T18, T32, T40, T100, T114, T122 **Unit 8:** T53, T100, T114, T122, T135 **Unit 9:** T182, T196, T204, T214 **Unit 10:** T18, T34, T42-43, T52 **WRITING WORKSTATION ACTIVITY CARDS:** 18, 23
W.K.3	Use a combination of drawing, dictating and writing to narrate a single event or several loosely linked events, tell about the events in the order in which they occurred, and provide a reaction to what happened.	**READING/WRITING WORKSHOP: Unit 3:** 38-39, 56 **Unit 5:** 44 **Unit 6:** 30 **Unit 8:** 16, 46-47 **Unit 9:** 30 **Unit 10:** 16 **TEACHER'S EDITION: Unit 2:** T196, T204, T246 **Unit 3:** T114, T122, T164 **Unit 5:** T32, T40, T82, T164, T246 **Unit 6:** T114, T123, T164, T246 **Unit 8:** T32, T40, T82, T196, T204 **Unit 9:** T82, T100, T114, T122-123, T132 **Unit 10:** T18, T34, T42, T43, T52, T84, T116, T166, T248 **WRITING WORKSTATION ACTIVITY CARDS:** 1, 4, 5, 7, 15

Writing Standards

Production and Distribution of Writing		McGraw-Hill Reading Wonders
W.K.4	(Begins in grade 3.)	
W.K.5	With guidance and support from adults, respond to questions and suggestions from peers and add details to strengthen writing as needed.	**TEACHER'S EDITION: Unit 1:** T32, T40 (Go Digital: Writing), T50, T58 (Go Digital: Writing), T122 (Go Digital: Writing), T132, T140 (Go Digital: Writing), T204 (Go Digital: Writing), T214, T222 (Go Digital: Writing) **Unit 2:** T40 (Go Digital: Writing), T50, T58 (Go Digital: Writing), T122 (Go Digital: Writing), T132, T140 (Go Digital: Writing), T204 (Go Digital: Writing), T214, T222 (Go Digital: Writing) **Unit 3:** T40 (Go Digital: Writing), T50, T58 (Go Digital: Writing), T122 (Go Digital: Writing), T132, T140 (Go Digital: Writing), T204 (Go Digital: Writing), T222 (Go Digital: Writing) **Unit 4:** T40 (Go Digital: Writing), T50, T58 (Go Digital: Writing), T122 (Go Digital: Writing), T132, T140 (Go Digital: Writing), T204 (Go Digital: Writing), T214, T222 (Go Digital: Writing) **Unit 5:** T40 (Go Digital: Writing), T50, T58 (Go Digital: Writing), T122 (Go Digital: Writing), T132, T140 (Go Digital: Writing), T204 (Go Digital: Writing), T214, T222 (Go Digital: Writing) **Unit 6:** T40 (Go Digital: Writing), T50, T58 (Go Digital: Writing), T122 (Go Digital: Writing), T132, T140 (Go Digital: Writing), T204 (Go Digital: Writing), T214, T222 (Go Digital: Writing) **Unit 7:** T40 (Go Digital: Writing), T58 (Go Digital: Writing), T122 (Go Digital: Writing), T140 (Go Digital: Writing), T164, T204 (Go Digital: Writing), T222 (Go Digital: Writing) T246 **Unit 8:** T40 (Go Digital: Writing), T50, T58 (Go Digital: Writing), T122 (Go Digital: Writing), T132, T140 (Go Digital: Writing), T164, T204 (Go Digital: Writing), T214, T222 (Go Digital: Writing), T246 **Unit 9:** T40 (Go Digital: Writing), T50, T58 (Go Digital: Writing), T122 (Go Digital: Writing), T132, T140 (Go Digital: Writing), T204 (Go Digital: Writing), T214, T222 (Go Digital: Writing) **Unit 10:** T42 (Go Digital: Writing), T52, T60 (Go Digital: Writing), T124 (Go Digital: Writing), T134, T142 (Go Digital: Writing), T166, T206 (Go Digital: Writing), T224 (Go Digital: Writing), T248 **WRITING WORKSTATION ACTIVITY CARDS:** 10, 11, 12, 13, 14, 16
W.K.6	With guidance and support from adults, explore a variety of digital tools to produce and publish writing, including in collaboration with peers.	**TEACHER'S EDITION: Unit 1:** T134 **Unit 2:** T216 **Unit 6:** T248-249 **Unit 7:** T52, T134, T216, T248-249 **Unit 8:** T52, T134, T216, T248-249 **Unit 9:** T216, T248-249 **Unit 10:** T218, T250-251 **ConnectED Digital Resources:** My Binder (My Work)
Research to Build and Present Knowledge		*McGraw-Hill Reading Wonders*
W.K.7	Participate in shared research and writing projects (e.g., explore a number of books by a favorite author and express opinions about them).	**TEACHER'S EDITION: Unit 1:** T52, T134, T216 **Unit 2:** T52, T134, T216 **Unit 3:** T52, T134, T216 **Unit 4:** T52, T134, T216 **Unit 5:** T52, T100, T114, T122-123 **Unit 6:** T52, T134, T216 **Unit 7:** T52, T134, T216, T248-249 **Unit 8:** T52, T134, T216 **Unit 9:** T52, T134, T216 **Unit 10:** T54, T136, T218 **WRITING WORKSTATION ACTIVITY CARDS:** 20, 23 **ConnectED Digital Resources:** Collaborate (Projects)
W.K.8	With guidance and support from adults, recall information from experiences or gather information from provided sources to answer a question.	**READING/WRITING WORKSHOP: Unit 7:** 44 **TEACHER'S EDITION: Unit 1:** T32, T40, T100 **Unit 2:** T52, T134, T216 **Unit 3:** T100, T214 **Unit 4:** T18, T52, T100, T134, T182, T216 **Unit 5:** T18, T52, T134, T216 **Unit 6:** T52, T100, T134, T216 **Unit 7:** T50, T52, T132, T134, T196, T204, T214, T216 **Unit 8:** T52, T134, T216 **Unit 9:** T52, T134, T216 **Unit 10:** T54, T102, T136, T218
W.K.9	(Begins in grade 4.)	
Range of Writing		*McGraw-Hill Reading Wonders*
W.K.10	(Begins in grade 3.)	

College and Career Readiness Anchor Standards for SPEAKING AND LISTENING

The K–5 standards on the following pages define what students should understand and be able to do by the end of each grade. They correspond to the College and Career Readiness (CCR) anchor standards below by number. The CCR and grade-specific standards are necessary complements—the former providing broad standards, the latter providing additional specificity—that together define the skills and understandings that all students must demonstrate.

Comprehension and Collaboration
1. Prepare for and participate effectively in a range of conversations and collaborations with diverse partners, building on others' ideas and expressing their own clearly and persuasively.
2. Integrate and evaluate information presented in diverse media and formats, including visually, quantitatively, and orally.
3. Evaluate a speaker's point of view, reasoning, and use of evidence and rhetoric.

Presentation of Knowledge and Ideas
4. Present information, findings, and supporting evidence such that listeners can follow the line of reasoning and the organization, development, and style are appropriate to task, purpose, and audience.
5. Make strategic use of digital media and visual displays of data to express information and enhance understanding of presentations.
6. Adapt speech to a variety of contexts and communicative tasks, demonstrating command of formal English when indicated or appropriate.

Common Core State Standards
English Language Arts
Grade K

Speaking and Listening Standards

Comprehension and Collaboration		McGraw-Hill Reading Wonders
SL.K.1	Participate in collaborative conversations with diverse partners about kindergarten topics and texts with peers and adults in small and larger groups.	**TEACHER'S EDITION:** Unit 1: S10-11, S44, S58, T11, T54-55, T117, T134, T136-137, T216 **Unit 2:** T34, T51, T52, T134, T222 **Unit 3:** T20, T33, T45, T175, T216 **Unit 4:** T11, T20, T52, T54, T58, T93, T134, T136, T140, T175, T216, T218 **Unit 5:** T11, T20, T52, T93, T120, T136, T174, T175, T216, T222 **Unit 6:** T11, T52, T54, T93, T136, T140, T216, T218 **Unit 7:** T10-11, T52, T54, T55, T93, T134, T136, T137, T175, T218, T219 **Unit 8:** T11, T54, T58, T80, T92, T93, T134, T136, T140, T175, T218, T222 **Unit 9:** T10-11, T52, T54, T93, T136, T140, T175, T218, T222 **Unit 10:** T11, T20, T56, T60, T95, T104, T136, T138, T142, T177, T186, T220, T224
SL.K.1a	Follow agreed-upon rules for discussions (e.g., listening to others and taking turns speaking about the topics and texts under discussion).	**READING/WRITING WORKSHOP:** Unit 1: 6-7, 24-25 **Unit 2:** 24-25 **Unit 3:** 6-7, 24-25, 42-43 **Unit 4:** 6-7, 20-21, 34-35 **Unit 5:** 6-7, 20-21, 34-35 **Unit 6:** 6-7, 20-21, 36-43 **Unit 7:** 6-7, 20-21, 34-35 **Unit 8:** 6-7, 20-21 **Unit 9:** 6-7, 8-15, 20-21, 34-35 **Unit 10:** 6-7, 20-21 **YOUR TURN PRACTICE BOOK:** 31-32, 45, 68, 70-71, 81-82, 93 **READING WORKSTATION ACTIVITY CARDS:** 1, 6, 18, 19 **WRITING WORKSTATION ACTIVITY CARDS:** 1, 11, 13, 21+D89 **TEACHER'S EDITION:** Unit 1: T11, T134, T216 **Unit 2:** T52, T134, T222 **Unit 3:** T175, T216 **Unit 4:** T11, T52, T58, T93, T134, T140, T216 **Unit 5:** T11, T52, T93, T175, T216 **Unit 6:** T11, T52, T93, T140, T216 **Unit 7:** T11, T52, T55, T93, T134, T137, T219 **Unit 8:** T11, T58, T93, T134, T140, T222 **Unit 9:** T11, T52, T93, T140, T175, T222 **Unit 10:** T11, T60, T95, T142, T224
SL.K.1b	Continue a conversation through multiple exchanges.	**READING/WRITING WORKSHOP:** Unit 1: SS4-SS5, SS22-SS23, SS40-SS41, 6-7, 24-25, 42-43 **Unit 2:** 6-7, 8, 14-19, 24, 25, 42-43, 46, 47, 48, 51, 54, 55, 58 **Unit 3:** 6-7, 14-19, 24-35, 42-43 **Unit 4:** 6-7, 20-21, 34-35 **Unit 5:** 6-7, 20-21, 34-35 **Unit 6:** 8-15 **Unit 7:** 6-7, 8-15, 20-21, 22-29, 34-35, 36-43 **Unit 8:** 6-7, 8-15, 20-21, 22-29, 34-35, 36-43 **Unit 9:** 6-7, 8-15, 20-21, 22-29, 34-35 **Unit 10:** 6-7, 8-15, 20-21, 22-29, 34-35, 36-43 **YOUR TURN PRACTICE BOOK:** 29, 45, 53, 61, 68 **READING WORKSTATION ACTIVITY CARDS:** 1, 6, 17, 18 **WRITING WORKSTATION ACTIVITY CARDS:** 1, 9, 11 **PHONICS/WORD STUDY WORKSTATION ACTIVITY CARDS:** W11, W12, R2, R3 **SCIENCE/SOCIAL STUDIES WORKSTATION ACTIVITY CARDS:** W4, W26, R10 **LITERATURE BIG BOOKS:** Smart Start: *Animals in the Park* **Unit 2, Week 1:** *The Handiest Things in the World* **Unit 2, Week 2:** *Shapes All Around* **Unit 3, Week 2:** *Clang! Clang! Beep! Beep! Listen to the City* **Unit 4, Week 1:** *Whose Shoes? A Shoe for Every Job* **Unit 4, Week 2:** *What Can You Do with a Paleta?* **Unit 4, Week 3:** *Roadwork* **Unit 5, Week 3:** *An Orange in January* **Unit 6, Week 1:** *Mama, Is It Summer Yet?* **Unit 6, Week 2:** *Rain* **Unit 7, Week 1:** *ZooBorns!* **Unit 7, Week 2:** *The Birthday Pet* **Unit 8, Week 1:** *When Daddy's Truck Picks Me Up* **Unit 8, Week 2:** *Ana Goes to Washington, D.C.* **Unit 9, Week 3:** *Bread Comes to Life* **Unit 10, Week 3:** *Panda Kindergarten* **TEACHER'S EDITION:** Unit 1: S10-S11, S21, S26-S27, S34-S35, S44-S45, S54, S58-S59, S64, S68-S69, S74-S75, T11, T34, T35, T52, T53, T54-55, T81, T84, T93, T101, T117, T123, T133, T134, T135, T136-137, T162, T175, T183, T197, T199, T215, T216, T217, T218 **Unit 2:** T11, T19, T33, T41, T51, T52, T64, T93, T134, T136, T137, T175, T204, T215, T216, T217, T218 **Unit 3:** T11, T19, T54-55, T58, T93, T117, T134, T135, T136-137, T175, T216, T217, T218 **Unit 4:** T11, T54, T93, T134, T136, T175, T216, T218 **Unit 5:** T11, T52, T54, T93, T136, T175, T216, T218 **Unit 6:** T11, T52, T54, T136, T218 **Unit 7:** T10-11, T52, T54, T93, T134, T136, T175, T218 **Unit 8:** T11, T54, T58, T80, T92, T93, T136, T140, T175, T218, T222 **Unit 9:** T10-11, T54, T93, T136, T140, T175, T218 **Unit 10:** T11, T56, T95, T136, T138, T177, T220 **INTERACTIVE READ-ALOUD CARDS:** Smart Start, Week 1: "The Ugly Duckling" **Smart Start, Week 2:** "Tikki Tikki Tembo" **Smart Start, Week 3:** "Kindergarteners Can!" **Unit 1, Week 1:** "The Lion and the Mouse" **Unit 1, Week 2:** "The Tortoise and the Hare" **Unit 1, Week 3:** "A Feast of the Senses" **Unit 2, Week 1:** "Timimoto" **Unit 2, Week 2:** "Kites in Flight" **Unit 2, Week 3:** "From Caterpillar to Butterfly" **Unit 3, Week 1:** "The Boy Who Cried Wolf" **Unit 3, Week 2:** "The Turtle and the Flute" **Unit 3, Week 3:** "Field Trips" **Unit 4, Week 1:** "Little Juan and the Cooking Pot" **Unit 4, Week 2:** "Cultural Festivals" **Unit 4, Week 3:** "The Bundle of Sticks" **Unit 5, Week 1:** "Growing Plants" **Unit 5, Week 2:** "The Pine Tree" **Unit 5, Week 3:** "Farmers Around the World" **Unit 6, Week 1:** "A Tour of the Seasons" **Unit 6, Week 1:** "The Frog and the Locust" **Unit 6, Week 3:** "Rainbow Crow" **Unit 7, Week 1:** "Baby Farm Animals" **Unit 7, Week 2:** "The Family Pet" **Unit 7, Week 3:** "Anansi, An African Tale" **Unit 8, Week 1:** "The King of the Winds" **Unit 8, Week 2:** "The Best of the West" **Unit 8, Week 3:** "A View From the Moon" **Unit 9, Week 1:** "Helping Out at Home" **Unit 9, Week 2:** "The Little Red Hen" **Unit 9, Week 3:** "Spider Woman Teaches the Navajo" **Unit 10, Week 1:** "The Elves and the Shoemakers" **Unit 10, Week 1:** "Good for You!" **Unit 10, Week 1:** "Help Save Big Blue!"

Speaking and Listening Standards

Comprehension and Collaboration		McGraw-Hill Reading Wonders
SL.K.2	Confirm understanding of a text read aloud or information presented orally or through other media by asking and answering questions about key details and requesting clarification if something is not understood.	**READING/WRITING WORKSHOP:** Unit 1: 6-7, 26-31, 33, 35, 37, 42-43, 45, 47, 49, 51, 53, 55 **Unit 2:** 6-7, 8, 9, 10, 13, 14-19, 24-25, 27, 28, 30, 33, 34, 35, 46, 47, 48, 51, 54, 55, 58 **Unit 3:** 6-7, 9, 12, 13, 16, 17, 19, 33, 34, 37, 42-43, 46, 47, 49, 51, 53, 55 **Unit 4:** 6-7, 9-15, 20-21, 23-25, 28-29, 34-43 **Unit 5:** 8-15, 23-28 **Unit 6:** 8-15, 22-29 **Unit 7:** 8-15, 18-19, 20-21, 22-29, 34-35, 36-43 **Unit 8:** 6-7, 8-15, 20-21, 22-29, 34-35, 36-43 **Unit 9:** 6-7, 8-15, 20-21, 22-29, 34-35, 36-43 **Unit 10:** 6-7, 8-15, 20-21, 22-29, 34-35, 36-43 **LEVELED READERS: Unit 1, Week 3:** *The Beach* (A), *See It Grow!* (O, ELL), *At School* (B) **Unit 2, Week 1:** *We Need Tools* (A), *A Trip* (O, ELL), *What Can You See?* (B) **Unit 3, Week 1:** *We Run* (A), *Go, Nat!* (O, ELL), *The Birdhouse* (B) **Unit 4, Week 2:** *My Neighbors* (A), *Neighborhood Party* (O, ELL), *Parade Day* (B) **Unit 5, Week 1:** *My Garden* (A), *My Garden Grows* (O, ELL), *The Mystery Seeds* (B) **Unit 5, Week 3:** *The Farmer* (A), *Let's Make a Salad!* (O, ELL), *Farm Fresh Finn* (B) **Unit 6, Week 1:** *It Is Hot!* (A), *Little Bear* (O, ELL), *Ant and Grasshopper* (B) **Unit 7, Week 2:** *My Cats* (A), *Their Pets* (O, ELL), *Will's Pet* (B) **Unit 7, Week 3:** *We Want Water* (A), *A New Home* (O, ELL), *Bird's New Home* (B) **Unit 8, Week 2:** *See This!* (A), *Places to See* (O, ELL), *My Trip to Yellowstone* (B) **Unit 8, Week 3:** *Going Up* (A), *In the Clouds* (O, ELL) *How Sun and Moon Found Home* (B) **Unit 9, Week 2:** *Mike Helps Out* (A), *Clive and His Friend* (O, ELL), *Farmer White's Best Friend* (B) **Unit 9, Week 3:** *Look Where It Is From* (A), *What's for Breakfast?* (O, ELL), *Nature at the Craft Fair* (B) **Unit 10, Week 2:** *My Box* (A), *Let's Make a Band* (O, ELL), *Going Camping* (B) **Unit 10, Week 3:** *Help Clean Up* (A), *Let's Save Earth* (O, ELL) *Babysitters for Seals* (B) **YOUR TURN PRACTICE BOOK:** 29-30, 35-38, 45-46, 53, 59-61, 68, 79-80, 85-86, 93-94, 99, 101-103, 107, 109-111, 115, 118, 123, 127-128, 129, 137, 141, 143-144, 147, 153-154, 164-165, 174, 187, 207, 217, 221, 227, 231, 234 **READING WORKSTATION ACTIVITY CARDS:** 7, 8, 16, 20 **WRITING WORKSTATION ACTIVITY CARDS:** 4, 6, 9 **TEACHER'S EDITION: Unit 1:** T11, T22-26, T186-191 **Unit 2:** T35, T186-191, T244 **Unit 3:** T104-108, T137, T175 **Unit 4:** T11, T55, T92, T137, T175, T219, T244 **Unit 5:** T11, T52, T93, T175, T186 **Unit 6:** T11, T20, T26, T93, T175 **Unit 7:** T11, T52, T55, T93, T137, T175, T219, T242 **Unit 8:** T11, T55, T78, T92-93 **Unit 9:** T11, T52, T55, T80, T93, T137, T162, T175, T219, T242 **Unit 10:** T11, T57, T80, T95, T139, T221, T244 **LITERATURE BIG BOOKS: Unit 1, Week 1:** *What About Bear?* **Unit 1, Week 2:** *Pouch!* **Unit 1, Week 3:** *Senses at the Seashore* **Unit 2, Week 1:** *The Handiest Things in the World* **Unit 2, Week 2:** *Shapes All Around* **Unit 3, Week 1:** *How Do Dinosaurs Go to School?* **Unit 3, Week 2:** *Clang! Clang! Beep! Beep! Listen to the City* **Unit 3, Week 3:** *Please Take Me for a Walk* **Unit 4, Week 1:** *Whose Shoes? A Shoe for Every Job* **Unit 4, Week 2:** *What Can You Do with a Paleta?* **Unit 4, Week 3:** *Roadwork* **Unit 5, Week 1:** *My Garden* **Unit 5, Week 2:** *A Grand Old Tree* **Unit 6, Week 3:** *Waiting Out the Storm* **Unit 7, Week 3:** *Bear Snores On* **Unit 8, Week 3:** *Bringing Down the Moon* **Unit 9, Week 1:** *Peter's Chair* **Unit 9, Week 2:** *Hen Hears Gossip* **Unit 10, Week 1:** *What's the Big Idea, Molly?* **Unit 10, Week 2:** *All Kinds of Families* **INTERACTIVE READ-ALOUD CARDS: Smart Start, Week 1:** "The Ugly Duckling" **Smart Start, Week 2:** "Tikki Tikki Tembo" **Smart Start, Week 3:** "Kindergarteners Can!" **Unit 1, Week 1:** "The Lion and the Mouse" **Unit 1, Week 2:** "The Tortoise and the Hare" **Unit 1, Week 3:** "A Feast of the Senses" **Unit 2, Week 1:** "Timimoto" **Unit 2, Week 2:** "Kites in Flight" **Unit 2, Week 3:** "From Caterpillar to Butterfly" **Unit 4, Week 1:** "Little Juan and the Cooking Pot" **Unit 4, Week 2:** "Cultural Festivals" **Unit 4, Week 3:** "The Bundle of Sticks" **Unit 5, Week 1:** "Growing Plants" **Unit 5, Week 2:** "The Pine Tree" **Unit 6, Week 1:** "A Tour of the Seasons" **Unit 6, Week 2:** "The Frog and the Locust" **Unit 6, Week 3:** "Rainbow Crow" **Unit 8, Week 1:** "The King of the Winds" **Unit 8, Week 2:** "The Best of the West" **Unit 8, Week 3:** "A View From the Moon" **Unit 9, Week 1:** "Helping Out at Home" **Unit 9, Week 2:** "The Little Red Hen" **Unit 9, Week 3:** "Spider Woman Teaches the Navajo" **Unit 10, Week 1:** "Help Save Big Blue!"

Speaking and Listening Standards

Comprehension and Collaboration		McGraw-Hill Reading Wonders
SL.K.3	Ask and answer questions in order to seek help, get information, or clarify something that is not understood.	**READING/WRITING WORKSHOP:** Unit 1: 6-7, 26-31, 33, 36, 37, 42-43, 45, 47, 49, 51, 53, 55 **Unit 2:** 6, 7, 14-19 **Unit 3:** 8-13, 14-19, 42-43 **Unit 4:** 6-7, 9, 11, 14, 20-29, 34-43 **Unit 5:** 6-7, 9, 11, 14, 20-29, 34-43 **Unit 6:** 6-7, 9, 11, 14, 20-29, 34-43 **Unit 7:** 6-7, 20-21 **Unit 8:** 6-7, 20-21 **Unit 9:** 6-7, 20-21 **Unit 10:** 6-7 **LEVELED READERS: Unit 2, Week 1:** *We Need Tools* (A), *What Can You See?* (O, ELL), *A Trip* (B) **Unit 4, Week 1:** *You Cook* (A), *On the Job* (O, ELL), *The Neighborhood* (B) **Unit 4, Week 3:** *We Clean!* (A), *Can You Fix It?* (O, ELL), *Helping Mom* (B) **Unit 5, Week 1:** *My Garden* (A), *My Garden Grows* (O, ELL), *The Mystery Seeds* (B) **Unit 5, Week 3:** *The Farmer* (A), *Let's Make a Salad!* (O, ELL), *Farm Fresh Finn* (B) **Unit 6, Week 1:** *It Is Hot!* (A), *Little Bear* (O, ELL), *Ant and Grasshopper* (B) **Unit 6, Week 3:** *Bad Weather* (A), *Getting Ready* (O, ELL), *The Storm* (B) **Unit 7, Week 1:** *Two Cubs* (A), *Animal Bodies* (O, ELL), *Two Kinds of Bears* (B) **Unit 8, Week 2:** *See This!* (A), *Places to See* (O, ELL), *My Trip to Yellowstone* (B) **Unit 9, Week 1:** *Let Me Help You* (A) *How Can Jane Help?* (O, ELL), *I Used to Help Too* (B) **Unit 10, Week 1:** *Animal Band* (A), *We Want Honey* (O, ELL), *A Good Idea* (B) **Unit 10, Week 3:** *Help Clean Up* (A), *Let's Save Earth* (O, ELL) *Babysitters for Seals* (B) **READING WORKSTATION ACTIVITY CARDS:** 7, 16, 20 **WRITING WORKSTATION ACTIVITY CARDS:** 4, 6, 9 **TEACHER'S EDITION: Unit 1:** T13, T216, T233 **Unit 2:** T95, T131, T137 **Unit 3:** T31, T49 **Unit 4:** T11, T55, T93, T137, T216, T219 **Unit 5:** T11, T52, T134, T216 **Unit 6:** T11, T93 **Unit 7:** T52, T93, T134, T182, T196, T205 **Unit 8:** T11, T93, T175 **Unit 9:** T13, T22, T52, T55 **Unit 10:** T11, T95, T97 **LITERATURE BIG BOOKS: Unit 1, Week 1:** *What About Bear?* **Unit 1, Week 2:** *Pouch!* **Unit 1, Week 3:** *Senses at the Seashore* **Unit 2, Week 1:** *The Handiest Things in the World* **Unit 2, Week 2:** *Shapes All Around* **Unit 3, Week 1:** *How Do Dinosaurs Go to School?* **Unit 3, Week 2:** *Clang! Clang! Beep! Beep! Listen to the City* **Unit 3, Week 3:** *Please Take Me for a Walk* **Unit 4, Week 1:** *Whose Shoes? A Shoe for Every Job* **Unit 4, Week 2:** *What Can You Do with a Paleta?* **Unit 4, Week 3:** *Roadwork* **Unit 9, Week 1:** *Peter's Chair* **Unit 9, Week 2:** *Hen Hears Gossip* **Unit 10, Week 2:** *All Kinds of Families!* **Unit 10, Week 3:** *Panda Kindergarten* **INTERACTIVE READ-ALOUD CARDS: Unit 1, Week 1:** "The Lion and the Mouse" **Unit 1, Week 2:** "The Tortoise and the Hare" **Unit 1, Week 3:** "A Feast of the Senses" **Unit 2, Week 1:** "Timimoto" **Unit 2, Week 2:** "Kites in Flight" **Unit 2, Week 3:** "From Caterpillar to Butterfly" **Unit 3, Week 1:** "The Boy Who Cried Wolf" **Unit 3, Week 2:** "The Turtle and the Flute" **Unit 4, Week 1:** "Little Juan and the Cooking Pot" **Unit 4, Week 2:** "Cultural Festivals" **Unit 9, Week 2:** "The Little Red Hen"

Presentation of Knowledge and Ideas		McGraw-Hill Reading Wonders
SL.K.4	Describe familiar people, places, things, and events and, with prompting and support, provide additional detail.	**READING/WRITING WORKSHOP BIG BOOK: Unit 1:** 6-7, 42-43 **Unit 2:** 6-7, 24-25, 42-43 **Unit 3:** 6-7, 24-25, 42-43 **Unit 4:** 6-7, 20-21, 34-35 **Unit 5:** 6-7, 20-21, 34-35 **Unit 6:** 6-7, 20-21, 34-35 **Unit 7:** 6-7, 20-21, 34-35 **Unit 8:** 6-7, 20-21, 34-35 **Unit 9:** 6-7, 20-21, 34-35 **Unit 10:** 6-7, 20-21, 34-35 **YOUR TURN PRACTICE BOOK:** 27-28, 35-38, 51-52, 61, 67, 68, 83, 85-86, 93-94, 103, 107, 109-110, 115, 117, 118, 141, 157, 167, 174, 193, 221, 231 **READING WORKSTATION ACTIVITY CARDS:** 10, 12, 14, 16 **WRITING WORKSTATION ACTIVITY CARDS:** 1, 2, 8, 16, 19, 22 **TEACHER'S EDITION: Unit 1:** S58, S74-75, T19, T33, T134, T183, T197, T205 **Unit 2:** T175, T182 **Unit 3:** T11, T93, T175, T177 **Unit 4:** T10-11, T18-19, T92, T114-115, T132-133, T135, T175, T182-183, T197, T214-215 **Unit 5:** T54, T136, T175, T218 **Unit 6:** T11, T13, T52, T54, T136, T175, T218 **Unit 7:** T54, T136, T163, T175, T218 **Unit 8:** T54, T175, T216 **Unit 9:** T11, T93, T136, T175, T183 **Unit 10:** T102, T116, T136, T177 **LITERATURE BIG BOOKS: Smart Start:** *Animals in the Park* **Unit 1, Week 1:** *What About Bear?* **Unit 1, Week 2:** *Pouch!* **Unit 1, Week 3:** *Senses at the Seashore* **Unit 2, Week 3:** *I Love Bugs!* **Unit 4, Week 1:** *Whose Shoes? A Shoe for Every Job* **Unit 4, Week 2:** *What Can You Do with a Paleta?* **Unit 4, Week 3:** *Roadwork* **Unit 5, Week 1:** *My Garden* **Unit 5, Week 2:** *A Grand Old Tree* **Unit 5, Week 3:** *An Orange in January* **Unit 6, Week 1:** *Mama, Is It Summer Yet?* **Unit 6, Week 2:** *Rain* **Unit 7, Week 1:** *ZooBorns!* **Unit 7, Week 2:** *The Family Pet* **Unit 7, Week 3:** *Bear Snores On* **Unit 8, Week 1:** *When Daddy's Truck Picks Me Up* **Unit 8, Week 2:** *Ana Goes to Washington, D.C.* **Unit 9, Week 1:** *Peter's Chair* **Unit 9, Week 2:** *Hen Hears Gossip* **Unit 9, Week 3:** *Bread Comes to Life* **Unit 10, Week 1:** *What's the Big Idea, Molly?* **Unit 10, Week 2:** *All Kinds of Families!* **INTERACTIVE READ-ALOUD CARDS: Smart Start, Week 2:** "Tikki Tikki Tembo" **Smart Start, Week 3:** "Kindergarteners Can!" **Unit 1, Week 1:** "The Lion and the Mouse" **Unit 1, Week 2:** "The Tortoise and the Hare" **Unit 1, Week 3:** "A Feast of the Senses" **Unit 2, Week 1:** "Timimoto" **Unit 2, Week 2:** "Kites in Flight" **Unit 2, Week 3:** "From Caterpillar to Butterfly" **Unit 3, Week 1:** "The Boy Who Cried Wolf" **Unit 3, Week 2:** "The Turtle and the Flute" **Unit 4, Week 3:** "The Bundle of Sticks" **Unit 5, Week 3:** "Farms Around the World" **Unit 6, Week 3:** "Rainbow Crow" **Unit 7, Week 3:** "Anansi: An African Tale" **Unit 8, Week 3:** "A View From the Moon" **Unit 9, Week 3:** "Spider Woman Teaches the Navajo" **Unit 10, Week 1:** "The Elves and the Shoemakers" **Unit 10, Week 1:** "Good for You!"

Speaking and Listening Standards

Presentation of Knowledge and Ideas		*McGraw-Hill Reading Wonders*
SL.K.5	Add drawings or other visual displays to descriptions as desired to provide additional detail.	**YOUR TURN PRACTICE BOOK:** 27-28, 30-32, 35-38, 43-46, 51-53, 59-60, 61, 62, 67-70, 77-80, 83, 85-86, 88, 93-94, 99, 101-102, 103-104, 107, 109-112, 115, 117-118, 123, 127-128, 129, 130, 133, 135-136, 137, 138, 141, 143-144, 147, 148, 151, 153-154, 157, 158, 164-165, 167, 168, 174, 187, 193, 207, 217, 221, 227, 231, 234 **READINGWORK STATION ACTIVITY CARDS:** 1, 6, 12, 15, 16, 20 **WRITING WORKSTATION ACTIVITY CARDS:** 1, 2, 4, 9, 17, 20, 23 **TEACHER'S EDITION: Unit 1:** T32, T41, T123, T214 **Unit 2:** T40-41, T123, T132 **Unit 3:** T41, T134, T217 **Unit 4:** T32, T41, T52, T123, T134, T205 **Unit 5:** T53, T134, T217 **Unit 6:** T53, T122-123, T135, T140, T163, T197, T205, T222 **Unit 7:** T33, T41, T114, T123 **Unit 8:** T53, T132, T134, T216 **Unit 9:** T41, T53, T123, T205, T214, T241 **Unit 10:** T43, T137, T216
SL.K.6	Speak audibly and express thoughts, feelings, and ideas clearly.	**READING/WRITING WORKSHOP: Unit 1:** 6-7, 8-13, 14-19, 24-25, 26-31, 42-43 **Unit 2:** 6-7, 8, 9, 10, 13, 14-19, 24-25, 33, 34, 35, 42-43, 46, 47, 48, 51, 54, 55, 58 **Unit 3:** 6-7, 13, 26, 27, 30, 31, 42-43, 44-49 **Unit 4:** 6-8, 22-29, 34-35 **Unit 5:** 6-7 **Unit 6:** 6-7 8-15, 22-29 **Unit 7:** 6-7 **Unit 8:** 20-21, 34-35 **LEVELED READERS: Unit 1, Week 2:** *Hop!* (A), *We Hop!* (O, ELL), *We Can Move!* (B) **Unit 2, Week 3:** *We Like Bugs!* (A), *The Bugs Run* (O, ELL), *I See a Bug* (B) **Unit 3, Week 1:** *We Run* (A), *Go, Nat!* (O, ELL), *The Birdhouse* (B) **Unit 5, Week 3:** *The Farmer* (A), *Let's Make a Salad!* (O, ELL), *Farm Fresh Finn* (B) **Unit 6, Week 1:** *It Is Hot!* (A), *Little Bear* (O, ELL), *Ant and Grasshopper* (B) **Unit 6, Week 2:** *The Rain* (A), *Weather Is Fun* (O, ELL), *Kate and Tuck* (B) **YOUR TURN PRACTICE BOOK:** 29, 37, 39-40, 43-44, 45, 47-48, 53, 61, 68, 71-72, 81-82, 83, 89-90, 97-98, 103, 105-106, 107, 113-114, 115, 121-122, 129, 131-132, 137, 141, 147, 149-150, 151, 187, 221, 227, 231 **READING WORKSTATION ACTIVITY CARDS:** 1, 3, 12, 17 **WRITING WORKSTATION ACTIVITY CARDS:** 1, 2, 6, 20, 25 **TEACHER'S EDITION: Unit 1:** T134, T175, T222 **Unit 2:** T58, T175, T222 **Unit 3:** T58, T140, T222 **Unit 4:** T58, T140, T175, T222 **Unit 5:** T11, T58, T140, T222 **Unit 6:** T11, T58, T140, T175, T222 **Unit 7:** T52, T58, T140, T175, T222 **Unit 8:** T11, T58, T93, T40, T175, T222 **Unit 9:** T11, T52, T58, T140, T222, T245 **Unit 10:** T11, T95, T142, T177, T224 **LITERATURE BIG BOOKS: Unit 1, Week 1:** *What About Bear?* **Unit 1, Week 2:** *Pouch!* **Unit 1, Week 3:** *Senses at the Seashore* **Unit 2, Week 1:** *The Handiest Things in the World* **Unit 2, Week 2:** *Shapes All Around* **Unit 2, Week 3:** *I Love Bugs!* **Unit 3, Week 2:** *A Grand Old Tree* **Unit 3, Week 3:** *An Orange in January* **Unit 5, Week 1:** *My Garden* **Unit 6, Week 1:** *Mama, Is It Summer Yet?* **Unit 8, Week 2:** *Ana Goes to Washington, D.C.* **INTERACTIVE READ-ALOUD CARDS: Unit 1, Week 1:** "The Lion and the Mouse" **Unit 1, Week 2:** "The Tortoise and the Hare" **Unit 1, Week 3:** "A Feast of the Senses" **Unit 2, Week 1:** "Timimoto" **Unit 2, Week 2:** "Kites in Flight" **Unit 2, Week 3:** "From Caterpillar to Butterfly" **Unit 3, Week 1:** "The Boy Who Cried Wolf" **Unit 3, Week 2:** "The Turtle and the Flute" **Unit 3, Week 3:** "Field Trips" **Unit 4, Week 1:** "Little Juan and the Cooking Pot" **Unit 4, Week 2:** "Cultural Festivals" **Unit 4, Week 3:** "The Bundle of Sticks" **Unit 5, Week 1:** "Growing Plants" **Unit 7, Week 2:** "The Family Pet"

College and Career Readiness Anchor Standards for **LANGUAGE**

The K–5 standards on the following pages define what students should understand and be able to do by the end of each grade. They correspond to the College and Career Readiness (CCR) anchor standards below by number. The CCR and grade-specific standards are necessary complements—the former providing broad standards, the latter providing additional specificity—that together define the skills and understandings that all students must demonstrate.

Conventions of Standard English

1. Demonstrate command of the conventions of standard English grammar and usage when writing or speaking.

2. Demonstrate command of the conventions of standard English capitalization, punctuation, and spelling when writing.

Knowledge of Language

3. Apply knowledge of language to understand how language functions in different contexts, to make effective choices for meaning or style, and to comprehend more fully when reading or listening.

Vocabulary Acquisition and Use

4. Determine or clarify the meaning of unknown and multiple-meaning words and phrases by using context clues, analyzing meaningful word parts, and consulting general and specialized reference materials, as appropriate.

5. Demonstrate understanding of figurative language, word relationships, and nuances in word meanings.

6. Acquire and use accurately a range of general academic and domain-specific words and phrases sufficient for reading, writing, speaking, and listening at the college and career readiness level; demonstrate independence in gathering vocabulary knowledge when encountering an unknown term important to comprehension or expression.

CCSS Common Core State Standards
English Language Arts
Grade K

Language Standards

Conventions of Standard English		McGraw-Hill Reading Wonders
L.K.1	Demonstrate command of the conventions of standard English grammar and usage when writing or speaking.	**TEACHER'S EDITION: Unit 1:** T16, T19, T32-33, T41, T36, T98, T101, T114-115, T122-123, T125, T133, T141, T165, T180, T183, T197, T205, T214-215, T223, T247 **Unit 2:** T16, T18-19, T32-33, T40-41, T50-51, T59, T83, T98, T101, T115, T123, T133, T141, T165, T180, T183, T185, T197, T205, T215, T223 **Unit 3:** T16, T98, T180, T183, T197, T215 **Unit 4:** T16, T18-19, T32-33, T40-41, T47, T51, T59, T98, T101, T114-115, T122-123, T129, T133, T139, T141, T180, T182-183, T196-197, T204-205, T211, T215, T221, T223 **Unit 5:** T16, T21, T43, T83, T98, T103, T180, T196, T247 **Unit 6:** T16, T19, T33, T41, T44, T47, T51, T53, T59, T83, T98, T101, T114, T115, T123, T129, T133, T141, T180, T183, T185, T197, T205, T207, T211, T215, T223, T247 **Unit 7:** T16, T19, T33, T41, T47, T51, T83, T98, T114-115, T123, T129, T133, T139, T141, T165, T180, T182, T183, T196, T197, T204-205, T211, T215, T223, T247 **Unit 8:** T16, T19, T21, T33, T41, T47, T50-51, T83, T98, T101, T115, T123, T129, T133, T141, T180, T182-183, T196-197, T205, T211, T215, T223 **Unit 9:** T16, T19, T21, T32-33, T41, T47, T51, T59, T83, T98, T101, T103, T114-115, T123, T133, T141, T165, T129, T180, T183, T185, T197, T205, T211, T215, T223, T247 **Unit 10:** T16, T21, T34, T42, T49, T85, T100, T131, T182, T187, T198, T213, T249
L.K.1a	Print many upper- and lowercase letters.	**TEACHER'S EDITION: Unit 1:** T16, T98, T180 **Unit 2:** T16, T98, T180 **Unit 3:** T16, T98, T180 **Unit 4:** T16, T47, T98, T129, T139, T180, T211, T221 **Unit 5:** T16, T98, T180 **Unit 6:** T16, T47, T98, T129, T180, T211 **Unit 7:** T16, T47, T98, T129, T139, T180, T211 **Unit 8:** T16, T47, T98, T129, T180, T211 **Unit 9:** T16, T47, T98, T129, T180, T211 **Unit 10:** T16, T49, T100, T131, T182, T213 **YOUR TURN PRACTICE BOOK:** 34, 42, 50, 58, 66, 76, 84, 92, 100, 108, 116, 126, 134, 142, 152, 162, 172, 184, 192, 202, 212, 222, 232, 244, 252, 260, 268, 276, 284
L.K.1b	Use frequently occurring nouns and verbs.	**TEACHER'S EDITION: Unit 1:** T19, T32-33, T41, T36, T101, T114-115, T122-123, T125, T133, T141, T165, T183, T197, T205, T214-215, T223, T247 **Unit 2:** T18-19, T32-33, T40-41, T50-51, T59, T83, T101, T115, T123, T133, T141, T165, T183, T185, T197, T205, T215, T223 **Unit 5:** T103 **Unit 6:** T19, T33, T44, T51, T53, T83, T114, T223, T247 **Unit 7:** T19, T33, T41, T51, T83, T114-115, T123, T133, T141, T165, T183, T197, T205, T215, T223, T247 **Unit 8:** T10, T18, T114, T115 **Unit 9:** T21, T103, T185 **Unit 10:** T187 **YOUR TURN PRACTICE BOOK:** 23, 41, 65, 73, 83, 107, 115, 141, 151, 161, 191, 201, 211, 221, 241, 251, 259, 267, 295
L.K.1c	Form regular plural nouns orally by adding /s/ or /es/ (e.g., *dog, dogs; wish, wishes*).	**TEACHER'S EDITION: Unit 5:** T21, T43 **Unit 6:** T33, T41, T51, T59, T101, T115, T123, T133, T141, T183, T197, T205, T215
L.K.1d	Understand and use question words (interrogatives) (e.g., *who, what, where, when, why, how*).	**TEACHER'S EDITION: Unit 3:** T183, T197, T215 **Unit 6:** T185, T207 **Unit 7:** T182, T196, T204-205 **Unit 9:** T103, T125 **Unit 10:** T21
L.K.1e	Use the most frequently occurring prepositions (e.g., *to, from, in, out, on, off, for, of, by, with*).	**TEACHER'S EDITION: Unit 3:** T29, T47 **Unit 5:** T193, T211 **Unit 7:** T29, T47 **Unit 8:** T19, T33, T41, T50-51, T83, T101, T115, T123, T133, T141, T183, T197, T205, T223
L.K.1f	Produce and expand complete sentences in shared language activities.	**TEACHER'S EDITION: Unit 4:** T18-19, T32-33, T40-41, T51, T59, T101, T114-115, T122-123, T133, T141, T182-183, T196-197, T204-205, T215, T223 **Unit 5:** T83, T196, T247 **Unit 8:** T182-183, T196-197, T215, T223; **Unit 9:** T19, T32-33, T41, T51, T59, T83, T101, T114-115, T123, T133, T141, T165, T183, T197, T205, T215, T223, T247 **Unit 10:** T34, T42, T85, T198, T249

Language Standards

Conventions of Standard English		McGraw-Hill Reading Wonders
L.K.2	Demonstrate command of the conventions of standard English capitalization, punctuation, and spelling when writing.	**TEACHER'S EDITION: Unit 1:** T16, T72, T129, T211, T221 **Unit 2:** T47, T57, T129, T139, T211, T221 **Unit 3:** T19, T47, T50-51, T53, T57, T59, T83, T101, T115, T120, T123, T132-133, T139, T141, T183, T196-197, T205, T211, T214-215, T221, T223, T247 **Unit 4:** T16, T47, T57, T98, T129, T139, T211, T221 **Unit 5:** T16, T47, T57, T98, T101, T115, T123, T139, T180, T211, T221 **Unit 6:** T12, T16, T47, T57, T98, T129, T139, T176, T211, T221 **Unit 7:** T16, T47, T57, T98, T129, T139, T180, T211, T214, T221 **Unit 8:** T16, T32, T47, T98, T101, T114, T129, T132, T164, T211, T221 **Unit 9:** T47, T129, T211 **Unit 10:** T49, T53, T103, T116, T131, T213, T216
L.K.2a	Capitalize the first word in a sentence and the pronoun *I*.	**TEACHER'S EDITION: Unit 3:** T19, T50-51, T53, T59, T83, T115, T123, T132-133, T197, T223 **Unit 5:** T101, T115, T123 **Unit 8:** T32, T101, T114, T132 **Unit 10:** T53, T103, T116, T216
L.K.2b	Recognize and name end punctuation.	**TEACHER'S EDITION: Unit 3:** T101, T115, T123, T132-133, T141, T183, T196-197, T205, T214-215, T223, T247 **Unit 6:** T12, T176 **Unit 7:** T214 **Unit 8:** T32, T101, T114, T132, T164
L.K.2c	Write a letter or letters for most consonant and short-vowel sounds (phonemes).	**TEACHER'S EDITION: Unit 1:** T16, T72, T129, T211 **Unit 2:** T47, T129, T211 **Unit 3:** T47, T120, T211 **Unit 4:** T16, T47, T98, T129, T139, T211, T221 **Unit 5:** T16, T47, T98, T180, T211 **Unit 6:** T16, T47, T98, T129, T211 **Unit 7:** T16, T47, T57, T98, T129, T139, T180, T211 **Unit 8:** T16, T47, T98, T129, T211 **Unit 9:** T47, T129, T211 **Unit 10:** T49, T131, T213 **YOUR TURN PRACTICE BOOK:** 34, 42, 50, 58, 51-52, 62, 66, 76, 84, 85, 86, 88, 92, 100, 104, 108, 116, 126, 130, 134, 138, 142, 148, 158, 162, 164-165, 168, 172, 192, 202, 212, 222, 232 **PHONICS AND WORD STUDY WORKSTATION ACTIVITY CARDS:** 1, 2, 3, 4, 5, 6, 7, 8, 9, 10, 11, 12, 13, 14, 15, 16, 17, 18, 19, 20, 21, 22, 23, 24
L.K.2d	Spell simple words phonetically, drawing on knowledge of sound-letter relationships.	**TEACHER'S EDITION: Unit 1:** T221 **Unit 2:** T57, T139, T221 **Unit 3:** T57, T139, T221 **Unit 4:** T47, T57, T129, T139, T211, T221 **Unit 5:** T57, T139, T221 **Unit 6:** T57, T139, T221 **Unit 7:** T47, T57, T129, T139, T211, T221 **Unit 8:** T47, T129, T139, T211, T221 **YOUR TURN PRACTICE BOOK:** 30, 38, 46, 54, 62, 74, 75, 80, 88, 96, 104, 112, 124, 125, 130, 138, 148, 158, 168, 182, 183, 188, 198, 208, 228, 242, 243, 256, 264, 272, 280, 293, 294
Knowledge of Language		**McGraw-Hill Reading Wonders**
L.K.3	(Begins in grade 2.)	
Vocabulary Acquisition and Use		**McGraw-Hill Reading Wonders**
L.K.4	Determine or clarify the meaning of unknown and multiple-meaning words and phrases based on *kindergarten reading and content*.	**TEACHER'S EDITION: Unit 4:** T127 **Unit 5:** T45, T46, T108, T187 **Unit 6:** T21, T23, T33, T41 **Unit 7:** T24, T45, T189, T209 **Unit 9:** T21, T24, T25, T43, T185, T189, T207 **Unit 10:** T25, T187, T209
L.K.4a	Identify new meanings for familiar words and apply them accurately (e.g., knowing *duck* is a bird and learning the verb to *duck*).	**TEACHER'S EDITION: Unit 5:** T108, T185, T187 T207 **Unit 6:** T21, T189 **Unit 7:** T24, T45, T189 **Unit 8:** T21 **Unit 9:** T25, T45, T185, T207 **Unit 10:** T25, T47
L.K.4b	Use the most frequently occurring inflections and affixes (e.g., *-ed*, *-s*, *re-*, *un-*, *pre-*, *-ful*, *-less*) as a clue to the meaning of an unknown word.	**TEACHER'S EDITION: Unit 5:** T45, T46, T187 **Unit 6:** T23, T33, T41 **Unit 9:** T21, T24, T43, T189 **Unit 10:** T187, T209

Language Standards

Vocabulary Acquisition and Use		McGraw-Hill Reading Wonders
L.K.5	With guidance and support from adults, explore word relationships and nuances in word meanings.	**TEACHER'S EDITION: Unit 1:** T10-11, T34, T43 **Unit 2:** T10, T43, T103, T116, T125, T135, T175, T185, T207, T245 **Unit 3:** T10, T116, T175 **Unit 4:** T10-11, T12-13, T21, T34, T43, T44-45, T54, T67, T80, T81, T83, T92-93, T94-95, T103, T116, T125, T126-127, T133, T136, T141, T149, T165, T174-175, T176-177, T183, T185, T188, T198, T207, T208-209, T218, T231, T245, T247 **Unit 5:** T10-11, T12-13, T21, T34, T43, T54, T67, T80, T81, T92-93, T94-95, T116, T149, T174-175, T185, T195, T207, T218, T245 **Unit 6:** T10-11, T20, T34, T35, T42, T43, T44, T67, T81, T92-93, T103, T108, T116, T125, T126-127, T136, T149, T163, T174-175, T176-177, T185, T198, T208-209, T218, T231, T245 **Unit 7:** T10-11, T12-13, T21, T25, T34, T43, T54, T67, T81, T92-93, T94-95, T103, T116, T126-127, T136, T149, T163, T174-175, T185, T190, T207, T208-209, T218, T231, T245 **Unit 8:** T10-11, T12-13, T21, T23, T34, T43, T44-45, T54, T67, T81, T92-93, T94-95, T103, T116, T125, T126-127, T136, T149, T163, T174-175, T185, T198, T207, T208-209, T218, T231, T245 **Unit 9:** T10-11, T12-13, T34, T44-45, T54, T67, T81, T92-93, T103, T116, T126-127, T136, T149, T163, T174-175, T176-177, T185, T198, T207, T208-209, T218, T231, T245 **Unit 10:** T10-11, T25, T36, T46-47, T56, T69, T83, T94-95, T96-97, T105, T106-111, T118, T127, T128-129, T136-137, T138, T151, T165, T176-177, T178-179, T187, T189, T190, T200, T209, T210-211, T220, T233, T247
L.K.5a	Sort common objects into categories (e.g., shapes, foods) to gain a sense of the concepts the categories represent.	**TEACHER'S EDITION: Unit 2:** T43, T103, T125, T135 **Unit 4:** T103, T183 **Unit 5:** T21, T185, T207 **Unit 6:** T43 **Unit 8:** T43 **Unit 10:** T127, T129, T136-137
L.K.5b	Demonstrate understanding of frequently occurring verbs and adjectives by relating them to their opposites (antonyms).	**YOUR TURN PRACTICE BOOK:** 241, 283 **TEACHER'S EDITION: Unit 6:** T44 **Unit 7:** T25 **Unit 8:** T23, T185, T207 **Unit 9:** T189 **Unit 10:** T25, T105, T127, T189, T190
L.K.5c	Identify real-life connections between words and their use (e.g., note places at school that are colorful).	**READING/WRITING WORKSHOP: Unit 1:** Smart Start: 4-5, 22-23, 40-41; 6-7, 24-25, 42-43 **Unit 2:** 6-7, 24-25, 42-43 **Unit 3:** 6-7, 24-25, 42-43 **Unit 4:** 6-7, 20-21, 34-35 **Unit 5:** 6-7, 20-21, 34-35 **Unit 6:** 6-7, 20-21, 34-35 **Unit 7:** 6-7, 20-21, 34-35 **Unit 8:** 6-7, 20-21, 34-35 **Unit 9:** 6-7, 20-21, 34-35 **Unit 10:** 6-7, 20-21, 34-35 **YOUR TURN PRACTICE BOOK:** 23, 33, 41, 49, 57, 65, 73, 83, 107, 115, 133, 141, 151, 161, 171, 191, 201, 211, 221, 241, 251, 259, 267, 275, 283, 295 **TEACHER'S EDITION: Unit 1:** T10-11, T34, T43 **Unit 2:** T10, T116, T175 **Unit 3:** T10, T116, T175 **Unit 4:** T10-11, T12-13, T21, T34, T43, T44-45, T54, T67, T80, T81, T83, T92-93, T94-95, T103, T116, T125, T126-127, T133, T136, T141, T149, T165, T174-175, T176-177, T183, T185, T198, T207, T208-209, T218, T231, T245, T247 **Unit 5:** T10-11, T12-13, T21, T34, T43, T54, T67, T80, T81, T92-93, T94-95, T116, T149, T174-175, T185, T198, T218, T245 **Unit 6:** T10-11, T20, T34, T35, T42, T67, T81, T92-93, T103, T116, T125, T126-127, T136, T149, T163, T174-175, T176-177, T185, T198, T208-209, T218, T231, T245 **Unit 7:** T10-11, T12-13, T21, T25, T34, T43, T54, T67, T81, T92-93, T94-95, T103, T116, T126-127, T136, T149, T163, T174-175, T185, T207, T208-209, T218, T231, T245 **Unit 8:** T10-11, T34, T81, T92-93, T102, T116, T124, T136, T149, T163, T174-175, T185, T198, T207, T208-209, T218, T231, T245 **Unit 9:** T10-11, T12-13, T20, T34, T42-43, T54, T67, T92-93, T103, T116-117, T124-125, T136, T149, T174-175, T176-177, T185, T198, T206-207, T218, T231 **Unit 10:** T10-11, T25, T36, T46-47, T56, T69, T83, T94-95, T96-97, T106-111, T118, T128-129, T138, T151, T165, T176-177, T178-179, T187, T190, T200, T209, T210-211, T220, T233, T247 **INTERACTIVE READ-ALOUD CARDS: SS:** "The Ugly Duckling", "Kindergarteners Can!", "Tikki Tikki Tembo" **Unit 1, Week 1:** "The Lion and the Mouse" **Unit 1, Week 2:** "The Tortoise and the Hare" **Unit 2, Week 3:** "From Caterpillar to Butterfly" **Unit 3, Week 2:** "The Turtle and the Flute" **Unit 4, Week 1:** "Little Juan and the Cooking Pot" **Unit 4, Week 2:** "Cultural Festivals" **Unit 4, Week 3:** "A Bundle of Sticks" **Unit 6, Week 3:** "Rainbow Crow" **Unit 7, Week 3:** "Anansi: An African Tale" **Unit 9, Week 2:** "The Little Red Hen" **Unit 9, Week 3:** "Spider Woman Teaches the Navajo" **Unit 10, Week 1:** "The Elves and the Shoemakers" **ConnectED Digital Resources:** Visual Glossary

L.K.5d	Distinguish shades of meaning among verbs describing the same general action (e.g., *walk, march, strut, prance*) by acting out the meanings.	**TEACHER'S EDITION:** Unit 2: T185, T207, T245 Unit 4: T188 Unit 6: T35, T108 Unit 7: T185, T190, T207
L.K.6	Use words and phrases acquired through conversations, reading and being read to, and responding to texts.	**READING/WRITING WORKSHOP:** Smart Start: 4-5, 22-23, 40-41 Unit 1: 6-7, 24-25, 42-43 Unit 2: 6-7, 24-25, 42-43 Unit 3: 6-7, 24-25, 42-43 Unit 4: 6-7, 20-21, 34-35 Unit 5: 6-7, 20-21, 34-35 Unit 6: 6-7, 20-21, 34-35 Unit 7: 6-7, 20-21, 34-35 Unit 8: 6-7, 20-21, 34-35 Unit 9: 6-7, 20-21, 34-35 Unit 10: 6-7, 20-21, 34-35 **TEACHER'S EDITION:** Unit 1: S26, S34, S44 Unit 2: T20-21, T93, T198 Unit 3: T20, T93, T198 Unit 4: T10-11, T12-13, T20-21, T22-27, T34, T42-43, T44-45, T54-55, T67, T80, T81, T92-93, T94-95, T176-177, T184-185, T186-191, T198, T205, T206-207, T208-209, T215, T218-219, T223, T218-219, T231, T244, T245 Unit 5: T10-11, T12-13, T20-21, T22-27, T34, T42-43, T44-45, T54-55 , T117, T162-163, T174-175, T176-177, T184-185, T186-191, T198, T199, T206-207, T208-209, T218-219, T231, T244-245 Unit 6: T10-11, T20-21, T34-35, T42-43, T44-45, T54-55, T67, T80, T81, T92-93, T94-95, T102-103, T104-109, T116, T124-125, T126-127, T136-137, T149, T231, T244 Unit 7: T10-11, T12-13, T20-21, T22-27, T34-35, T42-43, T44-45, T54-55, T67, T80, T81, T92-93, T94-95, T102-103, T104-109, T116, T124-125, T126-127, T136-137, T149, T231, T244, T245 Unit 8: T10-11, T12-13, T20-21, T22-27, T34-35, T42-43, T44-45, T54-55, T67, T80, T81, T92-93, T94-95, T102-103, T104-109, T116, T124-125, T126-127, T136-137, T149, T231, T244, T245 Unit 9: T10-11, T12-13, T20-21, T22-27, T34-35, T42-43, T44-45, T54-55, T162, T163, T174-175, T176-177, T184-185, T186-191, T198, T199, T206-207, T208-209, T218-219, T231, T244, T245 Unit 10: T10-11, T12-13, T20-21, T22-29, T36, T44-45, T46-47, T56-57, T69, T82, T83, T94-95, T96-97, T104-105, T106-111, T118, T126-127, T128-129, T138-139, T151, T179, T233, T246, T247 **LITERATURE BIG BOOKS:** Unit 1, Week 2: *Pouch!* Unit 2, Week 2: *Shapes All Around* Unit 2, Week 3: *I Love Bugs!* Unit 3, Week 1: *How Do Dinosaurs Go to School?* Unit 4, Week 1: *Whose Shoes? A Shoe for Every Job* Unit 4, Week 2: *What Can You Do with a Paleta?* Unit 5, Week 2: *A Grand Old Tree* Unit 5, Week 3: *An Orange in January* Unit 6, Week 1: *Mama, Is It Summer Yet?* Unit 7, Week 1: *ZooBorns!* Unit 7, Week 2: *The Birthday Pet* Unit 8, Week 2: *Ana Goes to Washington, D.C.* Unit 8, Week 3: *Bringing Down the Moon* Unit 9, Week 3: *Bread Comes to Life* Unit 10, Week 1: *What's the Big Idea, Molly?* Unit 10, Week 2: *All Kinds of Families!* **INTERACTIVE READ-ALOUD CARDS:** SS: "The Ugly Duckling", "Kindergarteners Can!", "Tikki Tikki Tembo" Unit 1, Week 1: "The Lion and the Mouse" Unit 1, Week 2: "The Tortoise and the Hare" Unit 2, Week 3: "From Caterpillar to Butterfly" Unit 3, Week 2: "The Turtle and the Flute" Unit 4, Week 1: "Little Juan and the Cooking Pot" Unit 4, Week 2: "Cultural Festivals" Unit 4, Week 3: "A Bundle of Sticks" Unit 6, Week 3: "Rainbow Crow" Unit 7, Week 3: "Anansi: An African Tale" Unit 9, Week 2: "The Little Red Hen" Unit 9, Week 3: "Spider Woman Teaches the Navajo" Unit 10, Week 1: "The Elves and the Shoemakers"